Praise for *Shadows & Light*

This book is a magic piece of candy, transporting the reader back to earlier days of celluloid villains and heroes, where hindsight is twenty/twenty and artistic license will get you into any room in town. Gary's creative walk through Hollywood brings back wonderful memories of a by-gone era and recollections I thought I'd forgotten. Collectively, the personalities that people this book deserve to be remembered as the free thinking, pioneering individuals they were. I am proud to have been a small part of the Process.

  —Chuck Bail, iconic actor/director/stuntman, Stuntman's Hall of Fame

They say if you were in the art of cinema during the 60s, 70s and 80s, you would never remember it. Gary Kent puts the lie to that statement in that he not only remembers, he has committed it to magnificent prose in a book that honors an exciting, turbulent time in the art of movie making magic.

  —Paul Lewis, producer/production manager (*Easy Rider, Colors*)

Gary Kent has either an extraordinary memory or an extraordinary imagination. His experiences on my movies in the 1960s explore a parallel universe of which I was unaware, but, because of his detailed recreation, I accept as accurate and true. It's a fascinating trip, and a riveting read.

  —Monte Hellman, director/producer (*Ride The Whirlwind, The Shooting, Two Lane Blacktop, Reservoir Dogs*)

With the acting chops to appear in films, enough backbone to make a living as a stuntman, and the determination to learn every job on a film set, Gary Kent carved out a forty plus year career in the movie biz. He was right there in the thick of things when the new breed of movie mavericks embarrassed the old Hollywood system by blindsiding it with creativeness and originality the likes of which has not been seen since. *Shadows & Light* takes the reader on Kent's journey as one of the unsung heroes of independent cinema. He threw himself heart and soul into every project he was associated with, and has lived to tell the tales. This is the story of the journey one hardworking family man took with the rest of the cinematic outlaws during a revolutionary time in Hollywood movie making. It may never be repeated. Due to the body of work they left behind, it can never be marginalized and will never be forgotten.

  —Ken Kish, producer and owner, Cinema Wasteland Movie Exposition

Tripping from the psychedelic 60s to the filmmaker-centric new century, Gary Kent weaves an expertly written and all-true story of the world of movies, with all of the action, actresses, drink, drugs, sex, and creative genius!

—Don Coscarelli, producer/director (*Bubba Ho-Tep, Phantasm*)

Gary Kent gives us an all access backstage pass to the days when filmmaking was poetry, when guys like Jack Nicholson and Warren Oates were working out of offices the size of closets, and craft service was a bologna sandwich. Kent's memories are intimate and evocative, sliding through your consciousness like a fine wine, leaving the taste of a touching time when movies were really movies—a time in our culture that is missed now more than ever.

—Esai Morales, award-winning actor (*La Bamba, NYPD Blue*), Screen Actor's Guild Board of Directors, co-founder of National Hispanic Foundation for The Arts.

Stuntman Gary Kent may have had his fair share of knocks upside the head, but fortunately, his memories are crystal clear. In Shadows and Light, he shares those funny, rough-and-tumble, inspirational memories with vivid clarity.

—Melissa Delaney, editor in chief, *Austin Monthly*

Gary Kent chronicles the subtle birth and growth of a dazzling cinematic style, born from the evolving mindset of its audience. It's a world I know and Gary got it right! He turns the trick without breaking a sweat, easy reading, like breathing fresh air, yet loaded with brilliant metaphors and insights that make this book meaningful. Very stylish work.

—Richard Rush, director (*The Stunt Man, Color of Night*)

What a surprise it must be for anyone who has seen Gary Kent in countless movies menacing the girl, getting punched out by the hero, falling off horses, jumping through plate glass windows, to find that this rugged stuntman and all-around tough guy has a heart as pure and open as any child's. And what a delight for those of us who know his work and his times to discover that he also has a memory as prehensile as any bear-trap. Gary's odyssey takes him into the world of A-list Hollywood, Poverty Row impresarios, mad geniuses, doomed starlets and, maybe most compellingly, among the stuntmen, bit players, horse wranglers, and grips who labor behind the scenes but are no less fascinating than the baby faces who get the big close-ups. What a canvas! What a life! What a book!

—Lars Nilsen, Alamo Drafthouse

Shadows & Light

Shadows & Light

Journeys With Outlaws in Revolutionary Hollywood

by Gary Kent

Dalton Publishing

AUSTIN, TEXAS

Dalton Publishing
P.O. Box 242
Austin, Texas 78767
www.daltonpublishing.com

Edited by Ric Williams
Assisted Editing and Fact Checking by Neil Kahn

Cover Design by Gabrielle Faust with Jason Hranicky
Interior Design and Typesetting by Deltina Hay and Jason Hranicky

ISBN-13: 978-0-9817443-7-7

Library of Congress Cataloging-in-Publication Data

Kent, Gary, 1933-
  Shadows & light : journeys with outlaws in revolutionary Hollywood / by Gary
Kent.
    p. cm.
  ISBN 978-0-9817443-7-7
  1. Kent, Gary, 1933- 2. Motion picture producers and directors--United States-
-Biography. 3. Actors--United States--Biography. 4. Stunt performers--United
States--Biography. I. Title. II. Title: Shadows and light.
  PN1998.3.K3955A3 2009
  791.4302'8092--dc22
  [B]
                              2009011191

Acknowledgements

It is impossible to give thanks to the legions of beings, human and animal, who have influenced the writing of this book. They know who they are and they surely know how eternally grateful I am for their support and considerations. There are some few, however, who deserve special mention, and I will do so here. These friends, peers, and fellow voyagers on my eclectic journey, through their dogged loyalty and unrelenting encouragement, have inspired me beyond measure. It is largely due to their continued efforts on my behalf that I have brought the "sailor home from the sea, and the hunter home from the hill" (Robert Louis Stevenson, "Requiem"). Here then, in no particular order, are the names of these remarkable people: Darwin McTighe, Rex Cumming, Barbara Robin, Michael McFarland, Don Jones, Don Coscarelli, John Parker, Michael Hall, Richard Rush, Claude Rush, Robert Bayless, Ken Kish, Lars Nilsen, Anne Heller, Bob Ivy, Chuck Bail, Susan Bail, Linda Tomlan, Eric Vickers, Dale Reynolds, Melody Sutter, Gabrielle Faust, Jan Grape, Brian Albright, Larry Fultz, Paul Lewis, Brian Allen, Walter Boxer, Brad Buekberg, Tom Weaver, Eric Caiden, Esai Morales, and lastly, my beloved Tomi, Precious the cat, and Frosty.

I wish to thank my publisher, Deltina Hay, without whose faith this book would be a mere stack of papers, and thanks also to her tireless assistant publisher, Neil Kahn. Lastly, a very special thanks to Ric Williams, a magnificently gifted and tenacious editor, who prodded, poked and pleaded with me until *Shadows & Light: Journeys With Outlaws In Revolutionary Hollywood*, was breathed into existence.

Table of Contents

To
Tomi Barrett Kent,
the light of my universe,
and
Greg, Colleen, Andy, Chris, Alex, Michael
Timothy, Nicolette, Hannah, and Ethan,
the sunshine

Chapter One

Gary Kent, earning his chops the hard way, Ride in the Whirlwind, *1965.*
Photo courtesy of the author.

Riding The Whirlwind

Remember, remember always that all of us, and you and I especially, are descended from immigrants and revolutionists.
—Franklin D. Roosevelt, *New York Times*, 1928

The driver of the Volkswagen was inches away from a violent death. He leaned forward, straining to see through the dust caked windshield; he had the automobile pushed to the max, skirting the rim of a desolate box canyon forty miles west of Kanab, Utah. On his left a slab of gray earth rose hood-high, then leveled into miles of flat Utah badlands. On his right, just beyond the lip of the canyon, the landscape fell away, tumbling fifteen hundred feet into a narrow strip of jagged rocks.

Jack Nicholson jammed the accelerator to the floor. The back end of the vehicle skidded toward the precipice. WHUMP! The left front tire dropped into a pothole the size of a bucket, slamming the quarter-panel into the road-bank. The engine sputtered and died.

Jack sat for a moment, pondering. "Damn, if it weren't for the alkali, I woulda' seen that hole for sure."

Up ahead, an impoverished Rambler wagon was experiencing the same navigational problems. The wagon's driver, Paul Lewis (*Easy Rider*), could barely make out the road. A cloud of gray dust hid the distance between solid ground and cliff's edge. Paul knew the weakness of the wagon, no guts, an automatic with worn rubber; still, he punched it, trying to catch up with the cause of all that turbulence.

Thirty yards in front of the Rambler was a Mack 4x4, its huge tires biting into the terrain, spitting out chunks of alkali and caliche. I was inside the cab, doing my best to keep anyone from passing me.

Nicholson, Lewis, and I were in Utah making a couple of movies and this evening we had peeled out of the location site and were racing each other back to company headquarters at Kanab, a tiny village perched on the rim of Zion National Canyon. For the next two months it would be home for cast and crew. All twenty of us.

Please Pass the Panama Red

The year was 1965. The Vietnam War was raging. President Lyndon Johnson promised the nation he would do everything in his power to keep South Vietnam free from communism. On the West Coast, hippies and pot were starting to appear openly in L.A.'s Griffith Park, while in Watts, the worst race riot in twenty years went down, killing thirty-four.

In San Francisco, flower children were dancing to The Jefferson Airplane and grooving on the free food supplied by The Diggers at The Golden Gate. Their compadres, the Vietniks, marched past the Presidio shouting slogans and earnestly waving anti-war banners.

New York City elected John Lindsay as mayor, the first Republican to run The Big Apple since Fiorello La Guardia. Mariner 4 was sending 8x10 glossies back from Mars, and a couple of Frenchmen picked up the Nobel Prize for proving that viruses hijack cells.

Things were starting to change all over the free world, just not in Kanab. There, except for the short skirts of the waitresses at Ruby's Cafe and the occasional 18-wheeler rumbling through town, it might as well have been 1910.

That suited our purposes just fine. We needed the lonely texture of the landscape to cloak our motives. We were doing two personal, introspective Westerns. Jack Nicholson was the star and co-producer of both films. Paul Lewis was production manager. And me? I was the stuntman.

> *Beneath all the phony tinsel is the real tinsel.*
> —Oscar Levant, describing Hollywood

It had started back in Hollywood, where Jack and his partner, Monte Hellman (*Two-Lane Blacktop*), were anxious to make their own movies. In the early 60s, if you passionately wanted to make a film independent of the major studios and you had no money, no bankable stars, and a non-formula screenplay, there was only one person you could go to—Roger Corman.

Roger Corman is suave, connected, approachable to fledgling movie talent, and tight as a wet boot. Hellman and Nicholson had worked for Corman on several of his low budget projects, notably *The Little Shop of Horrors* and *The Terror*. They designed the two Westerns to specifically appeal to him: small casts, location shooting, mostly exteriors, non-union crew. Roger signed on as executive producer and they had the money to make their films—$60,000.

Monte would direct. Jack would star along with a cast consisting of friends and working acquaintances. The ensemble included Warren Oates (from TV's *Stoney Burke*), Millie Perkins (*The Diary of Anne Frank*), Will Hutchins (*Sugarfoot*), Harry Dean Stanton (*Cool Hand Luke*), and Cameron Mitchell (*The High Chaparral*). Next they needed someone to handle the logistics, someone to hire crew, secure locations, permits and lodgings, someone to manage the unmanageable. Corman recommended Paul Lewis.

Lewis had been manager of The Actor's Playhouse in New York and production and company manager of the highly successful off-Broadway production of the musical *Simply Heavenly*. In Hollywood, Paul had been company manager of Genet's *The Blacks* at the Ivar Theatre.

Impressed with Paul's background, Jack and Monte hired him to manage their movies. In many ways, Lewis turned out to be as thrifty as Corman. When the three of them went location scouting for the two Utah films, Paul would check into a motel and rent a room for himself, while Jack and Monte hid on the floor of his old Rambler wagon. After he got the key, Paul would sneak the other two into the room. They would toss coins to see who got to sleep on the bed.

Paul hired a friend of mine, Art Names (*The Black Klansman*), to work on the sound crew for both films. Shortly thereafter, I entered the scene.

> *Until I experience something to the contrary, I just flow with coincidence or, to put it in professional terminology, "What the fuck?"*
>
> —Paul Krasner, as quoted in *Deep Self* by John Lilly

It was nine a.m. and raining, which is not always a happy event in Los Angeles. The rain heightens the sludge and piles garbage in the open gutters. It pulls hillsides out from underneath houses, collapses cliffs, and tosses pools of dark ooze onto the highways. If a rain lasts for more than two days in L.A., people get real moody. It had been raining steadily for four days.

We were having coffee, Art and I, at Denny's on Sunset Boulevard near LaBrea. Art talked and I watched the hookers walking their walk on the south side of the boulevard. Faux fur and stiletto heels in a downpour. Once, at the same restaurant, I saw a man immolate himself on the sidewalk across the street. He sat down on the curb, doused himself with gasoline, then, before anyone knew what was happening, he struck a match.

"Desperate measures," I thought, then heard Art saying something about two movies that were going to film in Utah. "They're looking for a good stuntman," he continued. "You interested?" He handed me Paul's office number.

I went to a wall phone near the men's room and called. "Hello, Paul, my name is Kent and I'm a stuntman." He asked me to come by for a talk.

I had time to reflect on the way to the interview, driving west on the Strip, past Chateau Marmont, through the La Cienega intersection, past the kid with the long hair picking up cigarette butts outside The Whiskey. I had lied. I was not a stuntman. I was an actor, out of work, like thousands of other actors. Oh, I *had* been working some amateur rodeos down in Compton with my pal, John "Bud" Cardos (*Kingdom of the Spiders*). Nothing to brag about, ribbon roping and some saddle bronc stuff. Drinking mescal, mostly—chasing that worm and getting our asses thrown off horses not meant to be rode.

> *Secret for a Happy Life: Find somethin' ya' love doin'.*
> *Then do it 'til it kills ya'.*
> —Willy G., homeless Texas alcoholic

I pulled into a parking lot behind a stucco building on the southwest corner of Sunset and Doheny. Paul was sharing an office with a dark, serious looking actor named Johnny Seven (*The Apartment*). Seven offered me a chair. Through the office windows, I could see the rain-soaked traffic on the boulevard below. A long row of brake lights blinked continuously, like strange, outdoor ornaments.

Paul entered the room. He was around thirty-five, medium build, sporting an East Coast attitude and a mustache that would do a pirate proud. We howdied and shook. I liked him immediately.

I don't think Paul had ever hired a stuntman. He asked me a couple of questions that didn't make sense. I fired off some colorful answers. The next thing I knew, I was on my way out the door, with his approval and directions to the producer's office for a final interview.

Thirty minutes later I was in Beverly Hills, inside a weathered brick two-story, looking for Jack Nicholson. His office was at the top of the stairwell, very narrow and ringed with shelves, reams of paper, and stacks of envelopes. I do not remember a desk. It could easily have been an office supply room.

There was nothing momentous or portentous about the occasion, nothing to suggest that this guy Nicholson was about to become a major motion picture star and remain so for decades (except for the killer smile and dead serious demeanor about his work). I told him Paul Lewis has recommended me for the stunt job.

"The problem, as I see it," Jack explained, fingering his script, "is we've got to have a horse get sick, begin stumbling, fall down, lay down, and die. Do you know how to do that?"

"No problem," I lied. "Paul said something about a couple of saddle falls and a tumble off a stagecoach?"

My plan was to get his mind off the stumbling horse. Fall off things I knew how to do. A horse that gradually took sick and died was another story. That animal, I figured, was going to have to be one hell of an actor.

Jack went briefly over the story lines. In the first film, *The Shooting*, a decent cowhand, Warren Oates, is hired to hunt down and shoot his own brother for the accidental killing of a child. As Will Hutchins' character, Coley Boyard, tells it, "He got to drinkin' and he rode over a little person!"

In *Ride in the Whirlwind*, a screenplay Jack had written himself, three likable trail hands, Cameron Mitchell, Tom Filer, and Nicholson, are mistaken for stagecoach robbers and are chased by a posse through the Utah wilderness. Two are killed, one escapes.

The birth and death of *real* Westerners wrap my life, head to toe, like a long, colorful cape. Bronc busters, drovers, cavalrymen and cattlemen, ranchers, rounders, and scoundrels, we share the same skin. Their dusty blood flows along my bones, keeping me warm and my feet against the earth. For me, most of the Westerns from Hollywood weren't honest and their plots were thin as bus station chili. I would just as soon bite a bug as sit through their bullshit.

In that little Beverly Hills office that somber morning, Jack was telling me stories that delighted my heart: no John Wayne, no Gary Cooper, no singing cowboys in shiny shirts. No good guys. No bad guys. Just people caught up in situations above and beyond their normal lives. This was dangerous territory.

Roger Corman was known for exploitation films, monsters and werewolves and teenage girls losing their virginity in the back seat of a Chevy—films like *Attack of the Giant Leeches* and *T-Bird Gang*. Now this cocky young actor from Jersey was going to make a couple of Westerns for grownups? How were they going to get it marketed? Who would bother to go see it? I knew one thing for sure, I would! My enthusiasm carried the day. Jack hired me.

Durin' daylight, she's hotter'n a pot a neckbones!

—Death Valley Scottie, describing the Mojave Desert

I rode to location with Art Names in his red Triumph convertible. We took the Grapevine to Barstow, then hooked a right through Calico, the ghost town, and a spot in the road called Yermo. Warren Oates also drove from L.A. and he praised the man who ran the one filling station in Yermo. "He was a happy man," Warren grinned. "The only truly happy man I've ever met in my life and he's runnin' a gas station in Yermo, California!"

Warren never said why the man was so happy. Remembering Yermo as Art and I saw it, it surely had to do with the fact there was no hurry or worry in Yermo. No television, no radio, just a whole sky full of sky, a sunset the color of fire, and a quiet so sweet you could taste it on your tongue.

We crossed the Great Mojave at night; still, the temperature was pegging ninety-nine at the witching hour. Art had the top down and the desert and the dark jumped right into the car with us. Simon and Garfunkel were on the radio: "Don't talk of love, well, I've heard the word before, it's sleeping in my memory." Overhead, a trillion otherworldly lights blinked earthward. Things were as warm and cozy as the inside of a mitten.

I could see Art clearly, about five-foot-nothing and a half, sturdy, with thick eyeglasses and the requisite mustache of the times. He was tougher than a stewed skunk, all one hundred and forty pounds of him. He was a World War II vet, 82nd Airborne, reputedly the meanest fighting outfit in the U.S. Army.

About twenty miles east of Mesquite, on the Nevada-Arizona border, the car radio began to fade. "I am a rock, I am an island" segued into white-noise. The voice of some high-desert broadcaster broke through with the fruit-frost warnings, then Art clicked off the radio. We rode awhile, without speaking, savoring the sound of the Triumph's engine cutting through that thin, desert air. Art, a chain smoker, fired up a Salem and began to tell me about himself.

"Hell, I've been in show business most of my life," he grinned, sucking on that menthol, letting a thick, white plume escape from under the mustache. "My dad, Art Senior, had a traveling rep company in Texas in the 1920s and early 30s. Tent shows were the big thing. We were doing tabs (condensed versions of Broadway plays). By the time I was fifteen, I was doing juvenile leads, opposite my mom."

"And then?"

"And then," he sighed, "and then, the goddamn movies came along and put us out of business."

He was right. Motion pictures and air conditioning had put an end to traveling theater in the United States. No one was going to sit in a tent, sweltering or freezing, when for ten cents they could see four hours of movies, suck Necco wafers, munch buttered popcorn, and luxuriate in fuzzy, climate-controlled bliss.

About two a.m., just after we rolled through a darkened St. George, Utah, I fell asleep. Art shook me awake at sunup. My turn behind the wheel. We exchanged places, and while he dozed, I drove the Triumph up a thin slice of highway that cut through miles of unusual and colorful stone formations. We were following the Virgin River upstream into Zion Canyon, into a landscape grotesquely molded by the consequences of time. Wind, water, and frost had carved out the cliffs and left natural terraces, like giant red and white layer cake. To the right and left of the road, huge limestone fingers sprouted from the canyon floor. The gorge was four thousand feet above sea level, its walls two to three thousand feet high. The road wound and snaked its way to seven thousand eight hundred feet, then spilled onto a large plateau, part of Zion National Park. The map showed us to be thirty miles from our destination, a small village nestled on the other side of the plateau called Kanab.

Once described at the most inaccessible town in the United States, Kanab consisted of one lonely main street, a general store, post office, knick-knack shop, filling station, and a café called Ruby's. At the near end of Main Street as you came into town was a large, white hotel with a spacious lawn, formal dining room, and semi-luxurious suites. At the other end of town, a small stucco motel squatted fifty yards from the highway. It was surrounded by gravel and boasted a postage stamp of a swimming pool and an ancient soda machine. There was no restaurant, no view. There were no telephones or televisions in the rooms. Paul Lewis had cut a deal. This is where we would stay for the six weeks it would take to shoot Jack and Monte's films.

> *If God could do the things we do, He'd be a happy man!*
> —Eli Cross, the messianic director in *The Stunt Man*
> (played by Peter O'Toole)

The crew, the crew, those hearty sons-a-bitches! These are the sorcerers who conjure up the "show" in show-business. Under unusual and frequently impossible circumstances, they make raindrops, teardrops, forest fires, plagues, snow in July, Easter in August, and day into night. They create shadow and light, call up ghosts, and pierce the veil of eternity. They carry within their trucks and trailers, their ditty bags, pouches, kits and kaboodles, the stuff necessary for the weaving of dreams.

An average independent film today may have a crew of fifty or more. Jack's production had twelve. The less money in the budget, the fewer people to do the work. Our twelve enthusiastic souls would haul the equipment, gnarly, cumbersome stuff, with names like brute, spider, barn-door, alligator, and extender, up mountains, down cliffs, across rivers. Once we got the shot, we would take it all down and haul it back to ground zero.

Nicholson was having a swim in the tiny motel pool when Art and I arrived. John Hackett (*Hoffa*), a friend of Jack's and an actor, was with him. John, about thirty-two, was model handsome. He would be playing a lawman in *Ride in the Whirlwind*. Jack beamed at me, seal-like, from just above the water line. The crew was beginning to straggle in from L.A. and he introduced us to each other by shouting our names from pool central.

Gregory Sandor was the director of photography. A round, affable man with a fondness for fine Cuban cigars, he had somehow managed to side-slip the embargo. While smoking one stogie, he always had two or three more poking from the pocket of his Hawaiian shirt, ready for active duty. His professional attire was completed by a Panama porkpie and a freshly washed pair of Black Bear Can't Bust 'Em coveralls. Sandor had previously lensed *Navajo Run* and *Secret File: Hollywood*.

Usually, the director of photography has an operator to work the camera for him. Greg would operate our large 35mm Arriflex himself. His one assistant would load and unload all film magazines, follow focus, keep the slate and the camera reports, and work as camera grip. Greg's assistant was a young, hardworking fellow named Gary Kurtz.

Kurtz was freshly spawned from the pool of cinematic talent at the University of Southern California. His classmate was George Lucas and Kurtz would later produce *American Graffiti*, *Star Wars*, and *The Empire Strikes Back*, all mega-hits directed by Lucas.

Kurtz had a reserved, military bearing, which made him the logical candidate to get us up in the morning. Wearing khakis and engineer's boots, he performed the task with crisp efficiency. I can still remember the sound of those boots. I'm bone-tired, having helped with entertainment at a cruel smelling bar somewhere across the border (Utah being a dry state). About two a.m., some kindred spirit has managed to haul me back to the motel and pour me into bed. Instantly, it seems, the sound begins: *Klomp-klomp-klomp-bang-bang-bang.* "Hello! Time to rise and shine. It's five o'clock."

I had known the art director Wally Moon back in Hollywood. We had worked together for Ted V. Mikels, one of the all-time great characters of low, low budget films. Wally had two assistants, a woolly Scotsman named Jim Campbell, and a slim, blond-haired aristocrat, Brandon Carroll.

Warthogs feed on the decaying fruit of the marula tree, while the ring-tailed lemur sucks the fermenting pods of tamarind.

—Krebs, *Alcohol in Nature*, 1977

Trained in classical theater, Brandon had the voice of an orator, deep and mellifluous, and he used it to his advantage when visiting the Mormon dowagers in search of heirlooms to prop the two movies. He was a striking figure, agile as a bullfighter, head up, back straight, shoulders square to the horizon. A rigging ax and pouches of nails were hooked to his low-slung waist belt, along with a canteen full of whiskey. He never allowed that canteen to reach empty. Now and again, Brandon would secretly pour a nip into his host's tea, just to spice up the day.

Frank Murphy was the sound mixer. Murphy was an enormous man, weighing easily over three hundred pounds. He was an authority on almost any subject. His knowledge of Sherlock Holmes and George Armstrong Custer, in particular, was top drawer. He reminded me of my vision of Mycroft Holmes, Sherlock's mysterious brother, who, too corpulent for the chase, remained comfortably seated at the Diogenes Club, sipping brandy and advising his cocaine-chipping brother on the *real* way of things.

There were two women on the crew. Joyce King was the script supervisor, and Brandon's wife, Vanna, a tall, blonde drink of water, was responsible for wardrobe. Both were hardworking professionals. Joyce would prevail in the business and would later do script on *Easy Rider* and Robert Altman's masterpiece *Nashville* in 1975.

I was shaking hands with my stocky roommate, key grip Russ Namarillo, when a freckled, balding, red-faced dervish whirled into the room accompanied by his terrier, Rex. The dervish was named Ernie, and he would be our Kanab "contact." His energy, enthusiasm, and reputation served as a buffer between ourselves and the local Mormon community. Ernie helped secure difficult locations and negotiated for the livestock, wranglers, etc. The only problem with Ernie was his dog.

Rex the Wonder Dog, as he would come to be known, was a canine obsessive-compulsive, and his compulsion was making love of the carnal variety. He was forever at the ready, tumescent and anxiously trolling for alliances. He was not a large dog, but once his paws were wrapped around the object of his desire, he was impossible to dislodge. Rex's most prestigious score was the lead actress, Millie Perkins. He nailed her one morning when she stopped for an innocent chat with some friendly town-folks.

After cast and crew were introduced, Monte told me that in the morning they would need me to take a horse into the hills a mile or two. Then, I would catch the sun in a hand mirror and cast a series of flashes toward camera, as though sending signals.

Ernie advised us to rethink the schedule. Rain was expected overnight and would likely continue into the next day. "Looks like it's fixin' ta' come one."

This news was as welcome as a train wreck. Most of the first week of shooting had been scheduled for outdoors, to give Wally and the boys time to finish building and dressing what few interiors there were in the script. The budget didn't include room for grouchy weather. There was nothing to do but wait until morning to see if Ernie was wrong. He wasn't.

Searching for the Muse

It was a restless first night. My roommate Nanarillo was a veteran of World War II, Pacific Theater. He had been on those "hot, stinkin' islands with stinkin' jungles full of leeches 'n' shit 'n' fuckin' mosquitoes big as B52s. MacArthur? He was useless as wet bread. Came back when the goddamn war was over!" Russ fell asleep easily, then, in his dreams, would start reliving it all. He would scream at enemies, curse, call to fallen comrades, and weep. His nightmares went on all night, every night.

Breakfast was at Ruby's, a café about the size of a schoolroom. There was nothing upscale about the place except the service. The waitresses, never more than three, were teenage Mormon girls, steeped in the ethics of hard work and courtesy. The food at Ruby's was just right for lumberjacks, lots of pancakes, sausage, and chicken fried steaks big enough to choke a linebacker. No kiwi or granola here. There was an ancient Wurlitzer jukebox against the wall. "Windy" by The Association was the record of preference.

We gathered at the café that first morning, cast and crew, seated in avocado colored booths and at small oilcloth-covered tables. Monte and Jack were trying to decide if there was anything we could shoot in the rain. The mood was less than jolly. Someone threw a quarter into the music machine, "And Windy has stormy eyes that flash at the sound of lies."

Suddenly, the door flew open and in walked a man as big as a house. He was Calvin Johnson, our wrangler. Calvin was a rancher with vast holdings in the area, crop and grazing land, horses and cattle. Paul Lewis had made a deal for him to supply livestock for the film. He and his ranch hands would truck the animals to and from location, look after their well-being, and saddle them when needed.

Calvin stood six five and must have weighed two hundred and sixty pounds. He reminded me of Merlin Olsen, the actor and all-pro tackle for the old Los Angeles Rams. Calvin told Monte the weather was going to stay as ugly as homemade soap most of the day. We were definitely not happy. First day of shooting and we were already behind schedule.

It was decided that Monte, Greg Sandor, and Gary Kurtz would try to get some atmosphere shots on the quick, whenever the sky opened and gave them some light. The rest of us were free to do whatever we wanted as long as we were primed and ready to roll if need be.

My roommate decided to go with Monte as driver. I would have time alone to catch some sleep. I began to feel real friendly toward the rain.

The room was subterranean in spirit. One had to walk down a set of stairs on the outside of the building, past the Coke machine and a broom closet to reach it. It was a homely environment, square, concrete walls, no pictures, no telephone, just two beds with a nightstand between them.

A script for *The Shooting* was on the nightstand. I picked it up, opened it. The screenplay was written by Carole Eastman, who because of Writer's Guild regulations, wrote under the pseudonym Adrien Joyce. She would later write *Five Easy Pieces* with Bob Rafelson, which was nominated for both a Golden Globe and an Oscar.

Once I started reading *The Shooting*, I couldn't put it down. I had entered a world of spare, dreamlike sequences, where communication was reduced to conversation as bleak and barren as the isolated characters in the story. In that vast desert setting, their behavior seemed claustrophobic. Each individual imprisoned in his or her own cynical world was trying to survive as long as possible. The story was unsentimental and starkly honest.

My roommate returned from a fruitless first day, went to bed, and within minutes began reliving the beach assault on Iwo Jima. It was several hours before he finally drifted into a deeper, quieter sleep.

Shortly after midnight, I finished the script. I clicked off the table lamp. In our tiny cellar there wasn't much room for moonlight, still a lone, silver sliver managed to creep through the window, and it bathed the far wall of the room in diffuse light, like a movie screen. I could hear a faint electric purr coming from the Coke machine outside, and way off somewhere, a dog was barking. Just before I fell asleep, I became aware that the rain had stopped.

For the measure of a man's life is the well spending of it, and not the length.

—Plutarch

Morning brought the sun and much mud. Still, we enthusiastically began filming *The Shooting*. Warren Oates was perfect for the part of the bounty hunter, Willett Gashade. He was tall and lean, with a natural country manner and a great Kentucky drawl. He was friendly and unaffected. It was later in the production, when we were alone jaw-jacking, that I began to notice his melancholy side. Warren was a man dealing with memories of bad times and they haunted him like a ghost.

Gashade's horse senses it. A slight disturbance in the heated atmosphere causes the animal to raise its head from the water hole and look back toward the gray hills. Gashade feels it, too. He stands, listens. He hears the thin desert wind, the hum of an insect….

I was leading a mare behind the big red stallion they were using as Gashade's horse. Sure enough, as soon as he heard that lady pass by, Big Red lifted his head from the water hole and looked back over his shoulder to scope out the possibilities.

Warren Oates moved into the shot and turned toward the hills. Those weary, worried eyes searching the horizon. "Cut, print!"

We had been shooting all morning without a hitch. I took the mare over to a little rope corral we'd jerry-rigged and turned her loose. My roommate Russ moseyed over and offered me some of his homemade coffee. He poured it from a large, plaid thermos into a Styrofoam cup. "Take it down before the cold gets to it."

I took his advice. It hit my stomach and brain simultaneously, one-third genuine coffee and two-thirds bourbon. Instantly, I felt goddamn magnanimous. I spotted Warren standing alone by the fence line and took him a cup of Russ's brew. He sniffed it, handed it back. "Kidneys. Doc's orders. Any more alcohol and I'll be pushin' up them daisies. Thanks, anyways."

He fired up a hand-rolled cigarette. I helped myself to his coffee. Things were quiet on the set, camera problems. With time to kill, we just naturally slipped into a quiet confab.

He was born in Kentucky in 1928. He married his sweetheart Teddy when they were both in their mid-teens. Warren joined the Marines, and after discharge he went to school and studied acting on the G.I. Bill. While looking for theater work in New York, he held down a job as a hat check man at the 21 Club. He got to Hollywood in the late 50s.

"I thought one'st I got to L.A., I'd be a happy fella'. Well, I got to L.A. and no siree." Warren, his voice as soft and southern as a Stephen Foster song, looked mostly at the ground while he slipped me bits and pieces of himself. "I got to actin' right away. Good stuff, too. *Ride the High Country, Yellowstone Kelly, Major Dundee.* I was on TV more'n I was home. *Gunsmoke, Twilight Zone, The Fugitive,* then in '62, I landed me a permanent gig on *Stoney Burke.* Worked steady for two years. Only problem was, I was miserable."

He reached forward, scratching the mare beneath her ears. She leaned into his fingers, and he scratched harder, right where the bridle leather had thickened the skin. "I usta' think if I could just make myself fifty thousand dollars in one year, I'd be on top 'a the world, happy as a old coon hound. I made more'n fifty, and it didn't happen. Then I made a hunnerd, hunnerd and fifty thousand, and I was more miserable than ever."

"What seems to be the problem?" I asked. I'd never made fifty thousand dollars. At that time, not even thirty, and, I was happy as a clam at high-tide.

Warren shrugged it off, but after that first talk, every once in a while I would notice that there wasn't a lot of joy hanging out with Warren Oates. I came to know he had marital problems, stuff most of us wrestle with. He had a son with serious medical difficulties, and he had his own health worries. A wonderfully kind man who was never superficial, Warren would die in 1982 at the age of 54. Heart attack.

Revolutionary Shoes

During the course of the Utah shoot, Oates argued repeatedly with Jack Nicholson about gun control and Vietnam. Warren always sided with what he called "the old ways." Nicholson was another situation entirely.

Jack told me with some pride that in 1960 he had played Weary Reilly in *Studs Lonigan*, the movie based on James T. Farrell's tough, street-wise novel. I was impressed. *Studs* and *The Amboy Dukes* were the *Catcher in the Rye* of my time. It was great, full of the angst young city guys were dealing with everyday: sex, violence, fear, brotherhood, and living up to manly bravado. Parents strongly disapproved of the book. I carried a paperback copy in my football helmet for one whole season.

Weary Reilly was one of my fictional heroes. He was born on the wrong side of Chicago, where it's concrete and cold as a gravestone in January. Knowing Jack had played him, from then on, I always saw a little bit of Weary looking out of Jack's eyes.

That morning in Utah, Jack was wearing a black and white Western outfit for his part as Billy Spear, gunfighter. He was good in the role, too. Concentrated and intense, in spite of having to carry on his shoulders all the baggage of being the co-producer on a low budget film.

Nicholson was handy on a horse except for one little habit he had of always looking at the ground when he dismounted, as if he was trying to avoid stepping in horse shit. I mentioned that he might want to look straight ahead, like he knew where he was going. Oops! Those eyes grew colder than a frosted frog. Then he let me have that smile, high beams on, turned his horse over to one of Calvin's wranglers, and sauntered away.

Floyd the wrangler was a living work of art. A mid-size, sinewy fellow, he was the only man I've ever known who could roll a cigarette with one hand while reining a mustang over rough ground with the other. Floyd had a permanent grin etched into the piece of leather he called a face, and he looked at life about as slow and easy as a day in August.

William "Wild Bill" Mackelprang was another Kanabian. He was a husky fellow, six two with a large belly, a jolly nature, and he was distinguished by his eyeglasses. He had broken one lens right down the middle and taped it back together with electrical tape. It was a bit unnerving when he was staring at you, almost as though one of his eyes has been cleaved in two, and each half was having a look. Wild Bill appeared on location one day looking for work. Paul hired him for general labor, and he was so handy he ended up working both films, and even did some acting in *Ride in the Whirlwind*.

In many ways the filming was so simple, no sets, just us, out in the middle of nowhere with four people who were on an exhausting search for a child killer. Much of the time they were on foot, as their horses gradually took sick and died. I got to do my stumbling horse stunt. Actually, I called the local veterinarian. Under his supervision, the animal was doped, then filmed as he slowed, staggered, and gradually lay down to sleep.

Will Hutchins, who was playing the part of Coley, an innocent, vulnerable tagalong, wanted to be a clown, a real clown! It's in the family; his wife Chris is Carol Burnett's sister. After his sojourn in Utah, Hutchins went on to attend a professional clown school. His performance in *The Shooting* was a tragi-comic masterpiece. One of the best scenes in the film is when Coley, abandoned by the others, stumbles across an old man who has been thrown from his horse and lies dying in the desert. Coley, in spite of his own predicament, tries to comfort the man. He ends the scene by giving him his only possessions, a small tin of candy and a toy puzzle.

Coley's generosity is followed by a sequence in which Nicholson, as the evil Billy Spear, taunts him, then shoots him off his horse, killing him. Stunt time!

> *I say it's a darn good day when a man can put on his shoes and go to work.*
>
> —John Burns, detective

They dressed me in Coley's clothes. I mounted his horse and loped around for a minute to get the feel of the animal, then reigned up near camera and waited for my cue. In the stunt business, saddle-falls aren't considered tough duty, but every once in a while, tumbling off a horse goes bad and someone is seriously injured or paralyzed.

What a feeling it is to sit waiting for word to do something difficult and potentially dangerous. Your nerves are keyed, your eyes get clear and bright. Excitement pervades your entire system, your muscles and mind fuse into one. I wasn't thinking about hurting myself; I was wondering how I was going to do something different, a fall that would stand out. Most saddle falls are done by the stuntman peeling off the side of the horse and taking the hit on the strongest part of his body, his back. I decided to throw myself straight to the rear, let my shoulder hit the flank of the horse, spinning my body into mid-air. That way, I would hit the ground face first, making a bigger splat.

Damn, it sure seemed to be taking the crew a long time to get the shot ready. It was getting hot, the clothes were beginning to smell a lot like Will Hutchins, the horse was getting antsy, and inside my boot my foot had started itching. I patted the lathered neck of my mount, calming him. I took a good, deep breath.

"Ready, Gary?" Kurtz shouted from next to the camera. "Standby." Mouth dry, adrenaline rushing, body tensing, then I hear Monte yell, "Action!" I hit that horse's flank so hard it bounced me three feet into the air. The fall to the ground was perfect. I landed rolling, my nose digging a jagged row in the caliche. Everybody applauded.

That night at Ruby's, I felt so good I could hardly eat. In fact, I could hardly sit. During my saddle-fall my gun got twisted underneath my body, and when I hit the ground, it put a bruise on my hip the size of a watermelon.

> *You'll at least have cleaner heartaches.*
>
> —Townes Van Zandt telling a friend why he should quit drinking

Utah being a dry state, those of us who were thirsty, which meant the entire crew with the exception of Gary Kurtz, would finish dinner at Ruby's and head for the Arizona border seventeen miles away. Just as you crossed the state line a bar-pool-hall-juke-joint, appropriately named The Sidewinder, opened its arms to those that were road-weary, friendly, pissed off, or just plain lonely. The place was packed every night.

There was a lot of talk among cast and crew about things that were happening on the West Coast. We brought a lot of New Age sentiment with us to Utah. It filtered to the waitresses at Ruby's, to their customers, then followed a railroad of loose lips all the way to the border. It eventually wound up in the nightly gab of those elbow-calloused citizens at The Sidewinder bar.

We were sitting near that bar, Paul Lewis and I, discussing his respect for the novel *Naked Lunch*, and its zoned out author, William S. Burroughs. Someone kicked up the music. There was an acoustic guitar, fiddle, and a voice, locals all. Once a week there would be a steel guitar and harmonica. The tunes were all Hank Williams stuff, songs about workin', cheatin', and losin' the blues. Things at The Sidewinder were startin' to coil and hiss!

Paul's conversation turned to the hippie phenomenon and its public persona, the flower children. "There wouldn't be any hippies without Kerouac," he insisted. "The Beats set the style ten years ago. I'm talking about guys like Ferlinghetti, Ginsberg—"

"How about Rod McKuen?" I interrupted.

The question pissed him off and I was forced to buy another Smirnoff rocks just to keep the conversation percolating. When I got to the bar, Brandon Carroll was leaning on it, holding some cowboy hostage while he performed a Shakespearean soliloquy. Brandon was so drunk he couldn't scratch himself without falling over, yet he never flubbed a line. The cowpoke applauded and whooped, which got the attention of a gentleman who was sitting all by himself in a corner of the room. The man was dressed in a well-tailored suit, and something about his sloped shoulders and short, curled hair seemed familiar. He turned our way. It was the famous actor, Joseph Cotten.

Cotten had a solitary sip of his cocktail, when what looked like a studio driver arrived. The driver gave the bartender some cash and was handed a brown paper bag. The bag was shaped suspiciously like a bottle. Actor, driver, and bag left the building. We learned Cotten was also staying in Kanab, starring in the movie *Brighty of the Grand Canyon*, along with stars Dick Foran, Pat Conway, and a donkey named Jiggs.

It was starting to get cosmopolitan in Kanab. Fess Parker showed up to shoot some episodes of the television series *Daniel Boone*. Financed by Twentieth Century Fox, the Boone group and their guest stars were put up at the big hotel. Cameron Mitchell arrived in town, along with Harry Dean Stanton and Rupert Crosse. They were principal players in our second film, *Ride in the Whirlwind*.

Whirlwind starts with a stagecoach robbery. As the guard riding shotgun on the stage, I was scheduled to get shot and do another fall. The man they brought in to drive the team of coach horses was Dynamite Harry Woolman.

Dynamite Harry, also known as Three Finger Harry, was older than oatmeal and hard as Texas oak. He had been doing movie action work since the days of silent film. Dynamite walked with a permanent limp. As I was preparing to do my stunt, he informed me his limp was the result of a fall *he* had done off a stagecoach in the 1930s.

Harry Dean Stanton was brought in to play old Blind Dick, an outlaw with a missing eye. On a lonesome western road, miles from anything civilized, Blind Dick starts the movie by taking a pee. He buttons up, then waves his rifle to Indian Joe (Rupert Crosse), a fellow bandit on the opposite hillside. Indian Joe runs down the hill, rallying the other gang members. Here comes the stagecoach.

I was sitting in on the shotgun seat alongside Dynamite Harry. Inside the coach, acting as passengers, were the writer, Charles Eastman, and one of Nicholson's close friends Walter Phelps. It was nine a.m. We had been doing run-bys, atmosphere shots, and horse inserts since six.

The light at mid-morning was all pastels, soft pinks, thin blues, and pale grays. The coach road was bright red clay, hard as a wood floor. As the stagecoach approaches, the outlaws confront it, shoot the guard, and force the vehicle to a halt.

I took the bullet hit from the top of the stage, so I could get up in the air and lay out. It took forever to come down. I could hear the wind whistling past my hair, my shirt was flapping like a waterfront flag, and I almost had time for a nap before I hit the earth. THUD! When I did land, it was a full-body blow that felt like being hit by a car. I didn't hear anything break or snap, so I figured I was still in one piece. Pulling myself painfully to my feet, I discovered the crew already leaving for the next sequence.

Out on the Limb That Breaks

Cameron Mitchell was born in 1918 and was a star on Broadway, television, and in motion pictures through six decades. I remembered him most for his performance in *Monkey on My Back*, portraying champion boxer Barney Ross, whose toughest fight was an addiction to morphine. Cameron was in Utah to play Vern, one of Nicholson's trail riding buddies.

"I ain't even goin' to get started with you today, Vern." Jack's character Wes scowls at Cameron. The cowpokes are camped alongside a line shack, which, unknown to them, is occupied by a gang of stage robbers and murderers. Suddenly, all hell breaks loose. A posse, led by lawman Brandon Carroll, has discovered the hideout and begins firing at the bandits, including the two innocent cowhands and their companion Otis (Tom Filer).

The three innocent men make a run for it. Otis is killed; Wes and Vern flee into the high country. Later, while cornered in a farmyard, Vern steals a horse and is shot attempting to escape.

I was scheduled to double Cameron in the saddle fall. Greg Sandor showed me where he needed me to end up, an imagined circle in the center of the farmyard. I climbed on the back of a mid-size mustang and backed him about fifty feet from the camera, then stopped. Horse and rider ready and waiting. I didn't want a rehearsal.

"Action, Gary!"

The second I had his rein, the mustang took off. I could see my landing area coming up. I slipped my boot out of the left stirrup, took the bullet hit, then, with my right foot, shoved myself out into the air. I hit the ground rolling. Nicholson galloped up on his mount, and though wounded, I (doubling Cameron) jumped on behind him and we hightail it out of there.

The fall went as planned. I was beginning to get a rope on this stunt stuff. Based on my performance in the fall, Millie Perkins agreed to have dinner with me. We dined at Ruby's, seated at the best table in the house. Actually, it was a window booth on the west side, with a view of some gasoline pumps. The rest of our group sat on the east side, giving us some slack, but still able to keep an eye on us.

We stared at the menu. It had been five weeks of pork chops, fried beef, white bread and gravy; we were hoping something new would pop off the page, something we had previously overlooked. I would have paid some serious money for a fresh fruit salad. I settled for a tuna sandwich and iced tea. Millie had the macaroni and cheese.

> *If we do not better our world, there is no use trying to save it with guns and bombs.*
>
> —Grandmother Nixdorff, age 97

We talked about Vietnam and the body count that was broadcast daily into our living rooms by the combat photographers. Millie believed *Ride in the Whirlwind* was strongly anti-gun, and this when the national psyche wasn't concerned with gun control issues.

Through the window of the café, I could see the sun cutting into the horizon, spilling the color of blood over that lonely landscape, covering the desert like a crimson shadow. A soft, pink light began to spread toward us. It seeped into the buildings and bathed the skin of the people. Millie's hands were luminescent, the color of pearl. My eyes caught Nicholson's eyes. They were deep and dark, like well water. He grinned that famous grin and gave me a thumbs up.

Cameron Mitchell, who usually ate at the big hotel, was sitting at a table with Monte Hellman and Monte's wife Jackie. When Cameron saw me, he excused himself and headed my way. He nodded to Millie, then, looking me in the eye and squinting like a gunfighter, rasped, "I been talkin' to the production manager over on the *Daniel Boone* set. Guy goes by the name of Shields. I told him about you. He maybe wants to hire you to work the show. Room 202, Shields. Can't hurt to give him a call." Cameron pinched my arm before sauntering back to his table.

About then, Brandon Carroll, drunk as a barn weasel, entered the café reciting a bawdy rendition of Robert Service's "Dangerous Dan McGrew." His partner, the rollicking Scotsman Jim Campbell, threw some silver into the Wurlitzer: "And everyone knows its Windy...cause Windy has stormy eyes, that flash at the sound of lies."

Jim and our script supervisor, Joyce King, started to dance. All things considered, I remember it as a very romantic evening.

> *I've never known a stuntman who wasn't a little bit mean.*
>
> —Al Jones, stuntman

Ted White is six four and a former star football player for the University of Oklahoma. He has doubled Lee Marvin, Rock Hudson, John Wayne, and Jack Palance in such classics as *Rio Bravo*, *The Alamo*, *Point Blank*, and *City Slickers*. Ted has doubled Jason in *Friday the 13th*, for Christ's sake.

Roy Jenson was also a football player, an all-American tackle at UCLA. Jenson is six two, two hundred and thirty pounds. He became a star in the rough and tumble Canadian leagues before breaking into films as a stuntman. He has done some of the best and most brutal fist-fights in the business, and has acted as well, in pictures like *Harper* with Paul Newman, *Chinatown* with Nicholson, and *The Getaway* and *The Thomas Crown Affair* with Steve McQueen.

Gloomy, muscled Charles Horvath wrote the martial arts manual used by the U.S. Marines for hand-to-hand combat training. During the big war, he was a round-the-clock bodyguard for General Eisenhower. These three men made up the stunt unit on *Daniel Boone*, and that morning in '65, they were looking at me like I was lower than an outhouse rat.

The energetic Mr. Shields had hired me for a week's work in the big leagues. After Jack and Monte gave their okay, I found myself standing in the Twentieth Century Fox stunt trailer, being subjected to the abuse the real articles always heap on the new guy. They knew I was green as a guacamole salad, and they'd been on my case all morning.

"Why in hell," Jenson sneered, "would anyone do a saddle fall without digging up the ground first, and layin' in some sand?" I explained that I didn't know what he was talking about. Charles Horvath, prying the cap off a bottle of Corona with his teeth, snorted gleefully. "That makes you about a bright as a box of rocks, don't it, Kid?" When Horvath moved across the floor, he didn't touch down. He glided on about a half inch of air; he was that smooth. Actually, stealthy would be a better word than smooth. I felt his breath on the back of my neck. For a second, I thought he was going to bite me. Luckily, the door to the trailer flew open and in stepped Daniel Boone.

Just before Fess Parker, dressed as Boone, walked into the trailer, Ted White went into a West Texas cedar fit. His arms were flapping, and he started blowing the air around like a squall off Padre Island. He shoved the cigarette he'd been smoking into my hand and was moving away when Fess came through the door. Ted glared daggers at me. I got the message! I began puffing away on the cigarette. It worked. As I was introduced to Fess Parker, his first words to me were, "You should quit suckin' that cancer stick, Kid!"

It turned out that he and Ted White had a bet down. Two hundred dollars and all the beer the stunt guys could drink if Ted could leave the filthy weed alone for a week. Today was only the second day of the bet. Stuntmen and women protect each other the same as cops do. Your life may depend on your partner. I went to an imaginary wall for my boss and won immediate acceptance.

Gigs and Gags

Before doing a fall, you pad up: elbow pads, knee pads, hip pads, sometimes shoulder pads. Dig up the ground where you intend to land, shovel in a foot of soft sand, or use an inflated airbag. Get rid of anything hard, like a gun! Replace it with rubber or throw it out of the way. You put roll cages in cars, solder on fences instead of barbed wire. Score furniture with a saw to make it break during a fight. Use balsa wood for clubs or bats, and always tickle alligators on the tummy—it hypnotizes them.

I learned these secrets and more from the stunt guys on *Daniel Boone*. They were as safety minded as a crew from EMS. In my first gag on the show, I was doing a fight with burley actor Aldo Ray. In the course of the action, a gun is knocked to the ground. I lunge for it, Aldo pulls a hidden weapon and shoots me. During the take, we somehow got out of position. I lunged for the gun and looked up. Aldo was six inches from me with his weapon pointed right into my face. Ted White lost vertical hold and angrily cut the camera. After a tongue lashing that would have made Bligh's floggings on the Bounty seem like a petting party, Aldo and I redid the scene.

In October 1984, while filming the TV series Cover Up, *actor Jon-Erik Hexum put a gun loaded with blanks to his head and pulled the trigger. The explosion sent the wadding from the blank into his brain, killing him instantly. Hexum was laughing when the gun went off. No one bothered to tell him that up to a distance of five feet, a blank is extremely dangerous.*

After a few days on the television series, I got homesick for Jack and Monte, and our little band of film-making gypsies. It just wasn't as edgy working for a big studio. Yeah, the money was excellent, and the food! It was prepared by white-smocked gourmet chefs cooking in large motorized chuck wagons, then served to us individually by cheery-faced interns. It was too much, reminded me of the Officer's Mess in the goddamn Navy.

I spent most of my time on *Daniel Boone* being chased by Indians, those sneaky red devils, "They can't keep their dirty paws off the wimmin!"

> *The Indians were always portrayed as cruel beasts, sneaking through the grass with knives between their teeth, bent only on destruction. I am six years old, and I'm convinced that Indians are horrible people. I have nightmares about them. In the morning, when I brush my teeth, I see in the mirror the face that terrified me in my dream. Sometimes I cry.*
> —Jamake Highwater on late night TV, *Ritual of the Wind*

The only good Indian on the series was Mingo, Daniel's buddy, and Mingo wasn't even an Indian, he was an Italian. Mingo was played by Ed Ames, a founding member of the famous The Ames Brothers musical group. I rode to the set with Ed, the two of us sitting in the backseat of an escort van. On the twenty-mile drive, Ames would always start singing, filling the vehicle with a marvelous bass-baritone and the overwhelming odor of garlic.

Within a week, I was back across the tracks and glad of it. My sojourn on the series had confirmed the suspicion all movie people carry around in their prejudiced heart of hearts: Film is art; television is a ham and cheese sandwich.

The Indy 500 Blues

We were in the last week of the shoot. Each day had that feverish feel you get when you're on the home leg of the journey. The ritual automobile race to and from location had grown to mythic proportions.

The company rules were to follow each other in a single file to the film site, but that arrangement collapsed after the first few days. It was thirty miles of straight flatland to the site, with a three and a half mile zig-zag along a steep cliff near the end. The race started spontaneously when, after leaving location one evening, a small group of troublemakers, myself included, began to elbow and maneuver our way around each other in an attempt to be the first to arrive at Kanab. Gradually, favorites emerged, a primitive form of dissin' began among drivers, tension increased.

Nicholson refused to take any passenger, he didn't want the extra weight. Paul Lewis complained of having to slow for Joseph Cotten, who, in his personal adventure with alcoholism, always seemed to be walking down the middle of the road at race time. There were mutinies. Riders in the Walter Phelps' vehicle accused him of being too stoned to drive aggressively and replaced Walter with Brandon Carroll, a drinker.

One final grand competition was planned. It was to be called "The Governor's Cup" and was slated to take place during the last week of shooting. As race day grew closer, the madness began to escalate. Bets were placed. Money changed hands. Staunch Mormons like Calvin Johnson and ol' Floyd found themselves reaching for their wallets.

The night before the race, Governor's Cup Eve, I hit the one gas station in Kanab and tanked up the Mack. Nicholson and Lewis were already at the pumps in pre-competition mode. Paul was wearing a French dock-worker's cap, and it had slipped across his forehead, covering all but a slit of his eyeballs. He looked like an assassin. Nicholson refused to acknowledge either of us.

Suddenly, I felt a tap on my shoulder. Actually, more a poke than a tap. I turned and found myself face to face with an irate Monte Hellman. He tore into the three of us like a bull at Pamplona. "How could you guys do this? Jeopardize the entire movie!"

Paul tried to hide under his hat. It didn't work. Monte started to dance around on the balls of his feet, like he was considering throwing a punch. "There will be no fucking Governor's Cup Race as long as I am director of these movies!"

Of course, Monte was right. We never did get to have that one, big, final duke-out, but we did get the films finished without hurting anyone. Jack and Monte took their movies back to Los Angeles, where both the critics and the distributors turned their backs on them. A disheartened Nicholson took the films to the Cannes Festival, carrying the reels through customs in a hat box because he couldn't afford the surcharge for baggage.

In Paris, the films were booked into a theater off The Place de l'Étoile, where they played successfully to a select audience, boosting their notoriety and eventually achieving cult status. In the United States, however, Corman sold the film rights to the Walter Reade Organization, who dumped them into a television package.

In 1971, the two Utah films finally got a limited theatrical release in the United States. The American audience still largely ignored them, but critics loved the movies, lauding them as two of the best Westerns ever made.

> *Ultimately a powerful film, with an offbeat performance by Nicholson as a hired gun, and an incredible, unexpected ending.*
> —Leonard Maltin on *The Shooting*, 1998

In March of 2000, the South by Southwest Film and Music Festival (SXSW 2000), an increasingly important cultural event held in Austin, Texas, began the festivities with an honorarium to director Monte Hellman. Filmmaker Rick Linklater (*Slacker*, *The Newton Boys*), as President of the Austin Film Society, hosted a reception in Hellman's honor and presented a retrospective of his work.

> *Movie people tend to gravitate to Hellman's tough early Westerns, "Ride in the Whirlwind" (1965) and "The Shooting" (1965)—succinct, genre-subverting dramas that move with a skittish, real-time naturalism and a squinty-eyed disengagement that demands a second viewing. You can feel the unfiltered blaze of the sun and taste the tawny dust. Tarantino ranks them with the best Westerns ever made.*
> —Chris Garcia, *Austin American-Statesman*, July 2008

My wife, producer Tomi Barrett (*Rainy Day Friends*), and I attended the reception in Monte's honor. It was a genuinely happy event, watching so many of today's young, pointy-booted filmmakers pay him well deserved homage. During the evening, Monte and I took time to slip off and chuckle about the old days in Kanab and the infamous Governor's Cup Race.

"What happened to you after the shoot?" Monte asked. "Where did all you guys go after Utah?"

Well, after Utah, Paul, Millie, Brandon, Gary Kurtz, Greg Sandor, and I all returned to Los Angeles and jumped barefoot right into the middle of the so-called New Hollywood. In the back-alleys and back lots of the town, independent and exploitation filmmakers were tearing down walls of bigotry and narrow-mindedness that had ruled the industry for more than a quarter century. And, they weren't doing it slowly, stone by stone, but by here-and-now, in your face, total demolition. A new creative breeze was blowing through Hollywood. It would quickly turn into a howling wind of revolution.

Chapter Two

Actor, director, stuntman John "Bud" Cardos. Photo courtesy of the author.

Unscrambling The Egg

For a brief impossible moment, movies stayed connected to the ebb and flow of American culture during its craziest hour.

—Kent Jones, *The Austin Chronicle*, March 2000

The seeds of the American film revolution actually germinated in the uptight atmosphere that prevailed at the close of the 1950s. The decade had produced its share of achievement and wonder. The Korean War ended in '53, the same year *Playboy* magazine debuted with a naked Marilyn Monroe as its centerfold. In '55 Rosa Parks' determined sit-in on an Alabama bus ride led to the end of segregation on public transportation. Jonas Salk cooked up a pot of polio vaccine, and an electrical engineer at Texas Instruments created the future by inventing the micro-chip. In '57, the Space Age began.

Zip guns, bad girls in blue jeans, and the sound of rock and roll upset the country's apple carts in the 50s. We celebrated Kerouac, Salinger, and *Lady Chatterley's Lover*. We lived off TV dinners and Kool-Aid, and a kid from Memphis named Elvis got hotter than a motel honeymoon.

But, for all its accomplishment and frivolity, those of us who made it through the decade remember it as a rather sad time. Except for *I Love Lucy*, it just wasn't very funny in the 1950s. Women earned fifty cents compared to a man's dollar. Southern colleges, drinking fountains, and restrooms were segregated, and the evening news showed us a clear close-up of the hunger gap between rich and poor, between developed and undeveloped.

The big thing in the 1950s was the red scare, the continued deterioration of relations between the free world and communism. The politicians and world media constantly fed us a breakfast of gruesome possibility. The big one is coming. Be prepared!

"Kids, listen up. When they let loose with the seventy-megaton-hydrogen-disintegrator, the one that incinerates cities and micros people into crispy corpses, well, then, quick as a bunny, hop under your desk and cover your ass!"

On the island of Cuba, a cigar-chompin', fatigue-wearin' guerilla jumped out of the closet singing, "I'm a Marxist-Leninist. I'll be one 'til I die," and the old men running our country came right off the spool. Through most of the 50s, a prickly paranoia went rampaging through the psyche of the country in search of un-Americans.

In Hollywood, the film studio publicly sacrificed some of the best and brightest to the infamous blacklist. Friend turned against friend, employer against employee. Careers vanished overnight, families suffered, lives were ruined. In order to survive, artists began to work under assumed names. For the first time in American history, people in the arts in America were forced to hide their identities in a labyrinth of substitute personas.

By the time I arrived in Los Angeles toward the end of the 50s, Hollywood had turned itself into a community shaken by deception and heartbreaking betrayal. Still, it continued the business of making movies, held together by sheer force of talent and a few fierce loyalties.

I pulled into the City of Angels on a Greyhound bus, completing a journey which had started in hot, humid Houston, Texas. Two cramped days and nights rolling along the interstate while sharing a seat with a fidgety young lady from Bossier City, Louisiana. "Yawl goin' ta' Los Angeleeee?" she drawled, scooting her butt around to establish nesting rights for the monotonous miles ahead.

"Yes, ma'am, I am—(dramatic pause)—I'm on my way to Hollywood. I'm an actor!"

Before leaving Houston, I had finished a year as the juvenile lead at the Playhouse Theatre. The ingénue lead was a young Katherine Helmond (winner of Golden Globes for *Soap* and *Who's the Boss?*). Our director was the now-legendary Adrian Hall. I had also performed at the famous Alley Theatre, under Nina Vance, the Grande Dame of Texas theatrics. My list of credits was longer than a one-ended rope: Albee, Ibsen, Inge, Shakespeare, Miller, and Moliere. "You are well prepared," I advised myself, "to begin a career in motion pictures." I was twenty-one years old.

Miss Bossier City wasn't impressed. I asked her about herself and for the next twelve hundred miles she rambled on about her boyfriends and all the times she could have gotten laid and didn't do it. The conversation was as much fun as eating okra.

Pod Peas

The first fellow actor I met in L.A. was a husky, dark-haired cherub named Vic Tayback (winner of two Golden Globes for *Alice*). Vic was the jolliest man I have ever known. His laughter started somewhere between his ample belly and his large, happy heart. It would travel upward, through his barrel chest, gaining speed and power, breaking into rolling waves of pure merriment. If you weren't careful, it would catch you in the crest and toss you around like a rad surf at Malibu. Being with Tayback when he found something amusing was a truly exhilarating experience.

Vic Tayback was born in New York, the son of immigrant Arab parents. He grew up in Burbank, California, and was a star on the high school football team. During his freshman year at Glendale Junior College, he was blindsided by an overzealous defensive end from Cal State Fullerton. The hit put him in the hospital with his knee a mass of shredded lunch meat and broken bones. This ended his dream of playing professional ball, and thus was born a new dream. He would become an actor! In his own words, a "freaking pretender."

The year was 1958. Vic and I were having coffee at the Carolina Pines, a late night hangout at the intersection of Sunset Boulevard and LaBrea Avenue. The area was a Hollywood cornerstone, a few car lengths from the freeway and a gateway to the glamour of the Sunset Strip.

The Pines was a favorite meeting place for unemployed actors and ordinary folks working the graveyard shift at Rocketdyne. It also attracted the normal denizens of night-time Hollywood: con-men, comedians, palm readers, prizefighters, cops, perverts, panhandlers, pimps, hookers, songwriters, playwrights, sycophants, Christian Scientists, Jews, Gentiles, Rastafarians, Jains and Rosecrucians, masochists, misogynists, and night owls of all sexual persuasions.

Vic was having a merry go at rehashing a role he had managed to land on a television show titled *Divorce Court*. He was cast as a soldier from Canada at odds with his wife.

"I'm not really a soldier. Heh, heh heh. I'm just freakin' pretendin' to be a soldier!"

For male actors, the court shows were a godsend. Television's *Court Martial, Day in Court, Divorce Court*—they and the military academy opuses about West Point and Annapolis—provided the rarest of all events in the world of entertainment: employment! There were over thirty thousand members of the Screen Actor's Guild in the 1950s, and only a few hundred jobs.

After I left The Pines that night, I avoided the freeway and drove west on Sunset toward Coldwater Canyon, intending to take that more scenic route over the Beverly Hills to my house in the San Fernando Valley.

The jolliest man in the world, actor Vic Tayback. Photo courtesy of the author.

The beginning of the gossamer area in L.A. known as the Strip starts at the intersection of Laurel Canyon and Sunset Boulevard, right where Schwab's Pharmacy used to sit before the building was demolished and the corner turned into a plastic, day-glo, mini-mall.

For over forty years actors could always get a decent breakfast at Schwab's on the cheap: scrambled eggs with onions, hash browns, buttered toast, and coffee. Plus they could pick up on all of the casting news and plug into the underground scuttlebutt. You could read the showbiz bibles, *Daily Variety* and *The Hollywood Reporter,* for free and have easy access to a bank of public telephones hugging the wall outside the restrooms.

Once in a blue moon there would be a genuine celebrity shopping for gifts at the perfume counter or hunkered in the coffee shop, basking in the envy and admiration of the normal patrons. Mostly, though, Schwab's existed to soothe the souls of the struggling actors, the looking-for-work people. The place teemed with yearning, aching, idealistic wannabes. To those folks, Schwab's was home and hearth.

A block past the pharmacy, at the corner of Crescent Heights, sat the opulent Garden of Allah Hotel, which during its heyday, served as an exotic bedroom community for legendary partiers like actor Humphrey Bogart and Robert Benchley, the celebrated humorist. Benchley, who by his own definition was "not quite a writer and not quite an actor," reportedly did opium poolside while enjoying the succulent G-spots of the Garden: girls and gin.

Across the street was Frascatti's. Its short flight of stairs led to an entrance centered in stone and ivy, like the entrance to a hearty country cottage. Inside, the place was a shadowy watering hole for the town stoics.

Brainfarts

As I drove past those hallowed establishments, it appeared to me they had lost some of their celebrated luster. The Strip seemed a tad gloomy, as though every other light bulb had burned out. There was no traffic. No limousines were lined up in front of The Crescendo, no revelers spilling onto the sidewalks, no red-jacketed car jockeys dashing for motorized status symbols. It could have been winter on a side-street in Seattle, except there wasn't any rain.

By the time I reached La Cienega, I had started a serious conversation with Mr. Boo, the candid little guy who resides permanently inside my corpus callosum.

The problem, as I was hearing it, was that it had been over a year since I had arrived in Los Angeles, weaned on artistic milk and honey from the legitimate theater. I had sashayed into Hollywood hoping to find work that would challenge old assumptions, scratch some skin, and excite change. Instead, I ended up in television, where ratings, commercialism, and one's TVQ called the shots. In TV land, *Gunsmoke*, *Wagon Train*, and an earnest Marlin Perkins running around Nepal looking for Yeti were the popular fare. Folk Art was in; change and revolt were definitely out. "*Film* is where it's all happening!" Boo nagged.

The Cloister nightclub was the only glittery spot on the whole Strip. There was a small crowd gathered in front of the place, gawking at the pudgy-faced man who had just jumped out of a limo. He was clutching the arm of a ravishing, honey-blonde. The two dashed toward the club entrance. A flash bulb went off, and a press photographer yelled out, "Hey, Mick! Over here!"

Man and blonde turned to wave at the crowd. It was Mickey Cohen, L.A.'s most prominent mobster and reputed King of the Strip. The woman was his gal-pal, showgirl/actress Liz Renay (*Date with Death*). For less than a second, our eyes met. Déjà vu? (In two short years I would be stalking leggy Liz through the thorny ravines of Topanga Canyon.) I glanced into the rearview mirror and watched the gangster and his "moll" disappear into the club. By the time I reached Doheny Drive, I had resumed agitating myself.

The Colorful Void

Since I had been in Los Angeles, the film studios had put out such masterpieces as *Paths of Glory*, *Gigi*, *Touch of Evil*, and me? I was doing used car commercials in a smog-pitted parking lot for Channel 9.

I was working in television because when I had been in school (Renton High, Washington State, and the University of Washington in Seattle), my dad, Art Kent, a business agent with the International Brotherhood of Electrical Workers (IBEW), got me a summer job packing steel girders up the sides of mountains so Puget Power could throw up those long-spanned power lines. In order to do the work I had to join the union, IBEW.

In Los Angeles, the IBEW held a contract for stage employees at the television studios. This included stage managers, assistant directors, art directors, electricians, et al. I had arrived in Los Angeles with $500 and a sack full of good intentions. In half-less-than-no-time, I was eating those good intentions for dinner. I needed a job, and I used my union card to land one, as a stage manager at KHJ-TV, Channel 9.

At the time, KHJ was located on the corner of Fountain Avenue and Vine Street. One of my TV tasks was holding the idiot sheets for the grand old man of late-night L.A. news, Ted Meyers. Another was setting up the wrestling remotes from City Coliseum, where the toughest man in town, Judo Gene LeBell, would referee matches between gigs as a movie stuntman. I spent most of my working hours, however, in the parking lot cuing on-camera pitchmen as they hawked rows of used cars to an innocent populace. Not exactly artsy stuff, though there were a few moments of transcendence.

One asphalt-scorched, big-city afternoon, Charlie Stahl, a salesman with a voice like cream soup, was doing an impassioned pitch for an Oldsmobile company. He left the demo auto in the background where the audience couldn't get a good look at it while he approached the camera, propositioning the viewers with that boudoir voice. Comedian George Gobel, who had just won an Emmy for Most Outstanding New Personality in Television, accidentally walked into the shot.

The second it dawned on him that he'd entered a live commercial, Gobel strolled over to the vehicle and gave it the over-once, like a potential customer. The cameraman, realizing there was a famous comedian in the background, zoomed in to a closer shot, whereupon Lonesome George, as he was known to his millions of fans, unzipped his pants, lifted his leg, and urinated on the car's rear tire. Charlie Stahl continued his breathy presentation as though it all made perfect sense.

"Hey, prince of procrastination!" I conjured up Mr. Boo's voice. "You've driven past the turnoff." A silver-winged Mercedes zoomed past then disappeared into the dark wedge of canyon. By the time I reached the Mulholland ridge, I was smack in the middle of a genuine epiphany, "To hell with television!" I could hear it clearly, Boo's demanding chide. It was beginning to sound demanding. *You came to this town to learn about making movies, and damn the torpedoes, Slim, that's what you're gonna do.*" The voice was damned assertive. And, the next morning I answered an advertisement in the *Los Angeles Times* for a position as messenger in the mail room for Allied Artists Picture Corporation.

Fertile Fields of Fibbery

Allied Artists Pictures Corporation was a small movie studio nestled between Sunset Boulevard and Talmadge Street. The area was east of the Hollywood loop, a four hundred-acre rectangle of real estate sloping upward from Sunset into the hills of Los Feliz.

The studio occupied twenty-five acres, the rest of the land was taken with low-income houses, a discount electronics shop, a block of used furniture stores, and a Quonset-hut emporium of cheap Asian imports. There were no boutiques or Beverly Hills bistros within miles, yet, for me, Allied Artists held the secret to the art of moviemaking, and I was inside those big, ornamental gates at last.

Allied was a wholly owned subsidiary of the highly successful B movie programmer, Monogram Pictures Corporation. Monogram's president, Steven Broidy, formed the company to handle production and distribution of high budget, quality pictures, and they were responsible for such films as *Friendly Persuasion* with Gary Cooper, *The Babe Ruth Story* starring William Bendix, and the original *House on Haunted Hill* with the grand master of the macabre, Vincent Price.

Studio manager Eugene Arnstein hired me to run off press releases and the daily call sheets on the mail room mimeograph. Each day, the releases would be copied, then stuffed into envelopes and sent to three hundred and sixty-two media organizations worldwide. The call sheets would be delivered to the set and handed over to the second assistant director.

Once inside the gates, I felt an almost criminal urge to do everything in my power to secure a position on an actual film. I accosted every director on the lot, every production manager, every producer, shamelessly begging for a break. I tried so hard to sell myself, I would actually grunt.

Finally, a courageous director named R.G. Springsteen caved in and gave me a shot. It was nine o'clock, a bright, smogless morning that allowed me to see all the way to the San Bernadino Mountains. I had buttonholed Mr. Springsteen outside of his studio bungalow and forced him to admit he was getting ready to make a movie. It was going to be a Western, *King of the Wild Stallions*, starring George Montgomery (*The Pathfinder*) and a host of established character actors, including silver-haired icon Denver Pyle (*Escape to Witch Mountain*) and Edgar Buchanan (*The Over-the-Hill Gang*).

Cast and crew had already been hired except for the role of one of Montgomery's ranch hands. Springsteen, who had directed the wonderful family film *Come Next Spring* with mega-star Ann Sheridan, consulted his script. "It's only one line of dialogue, and the guy has to do some hard riding." He studied me like I was a poster in the post office. "How about it, Kent? I was going to cast a stuntman. You handy on a horse?"

I spit on the ground, trying to look like a real cowhand. "Handy as pants pockets," I replied. "Course, there ain't no horse that can't be rode, and there ain't no rider that can't be throwed." He hired me, I suppose, just to shut me up.

> *Hey, kid! Put that money away. Didn't anyone tell ya?*
> *In the movies, breakfast is free.*
> —George Montgomery on the set of *King of the Wild Stallions*

I was getting ready to shell out for a bacon and egg sandwich when I heard the voice. I turned around and came face to face with our leading man, George Montgomery. George was so tall he could hunt geese with a rake, and he had the rugged, handsome look of a pioneer. This morning he was dressed in a buckskin shirt, leather boots, and dung-stained jeans. I was wearing pretty much the same thing, only chaps as well. We were in a deserted area forty miles northeast of Los Angeles called Vazquez Rocks.

King of the Wild Stallions was about a ranching widow, her young son, a beautiful wild horse, and the bad guys who try to steal the ranch. Montgomery played a charming drifter who helps the widow run the place. I was his hired hand. This was our first day on the job.

With almost every occupation in the world, short of the military, it is assumed one has had breakfast before leaving the house. If you work construction, teach school, or clock-in at Microsoft, you don't show up in the morning smacking your lips and yelling, "What's to eat?" In motion pictures, however, consuming a large quantity of food is the first order of the day. This cinematic phenomenon was explained to me by Carl Guthrie, the cinematographer of our Western.

"On all exterior shoots, the key budget item is the sun. We need el sol. It's the big light source we use to illuminate everything. Lose the sun, and it costs a fortune to light artificially, juniors, seniors, snoots, scrims, inkies, babies, arcs, generators, cable, extra grips, and electricians. In order to maximize the gratuitous rays of el sol, you start at the crack of dawn. The studios needed a cheap incentive to get the worker ants out of bed and to the set, when for all intents and purposes it was still night. So, they invented free breakfast."

George Montgomery introduced me to the other ranch hands. One was his brother, Michael Letz. Hollywood had changed George's last name for box office reasons. Michael was short and squat as his brother was tall and rangy. Both men were originally from Brady, Montana, where the family was in the cattle business. The Letz boys had been pretty good boxers; George even fought professionally as a heavyweight. In Hollywood, he fell in love with and married singer Dinah Shore. When he made it into the big time as an actor, George made sure his brother always had a job on his pictures.

The other cowhand was stuntman Roy Sickner. A top-notch action man, Sickner would eventually receive an Oscar nomination for co-writing and producing Sam Peckinpah's classic, *The Wild Bunch*, starring William Holden and Warren Oates.

After breakfast, I wandered over to the corral to pick myself a mount. I settled on a big bay with a white sock on his forelock and large, happy eyes.

Once we were mounted, director Springsteen ordered us to ride about a hundred yards up a steep granite slope. On action, we were to gallop down the incline and merge into a herd of stampeding mustangs.

When I got on the rock face and turned to look at the drop, I understood what they meant by *hard riding*. The route down was composed of layered sheets of stone, pitched at sheer angles, no one angle the same, and all slippery as wet moss.

A man would have to be dumb as a stump to run an animal down that incline. "Action!"

I was still thinking it over when I heard the cue. The bay, an experienced movie hand, took off like a Roman candle. Once we got started, the ride was a genuine kicker! I mostly remember the feel of the wind and worrying my hat was going to blow off and ruin the shot. It was over in a heartbeat: a powerful flurry of hooves on rock and the pounding, wild-eyed excitement of the mustangs as we merged into their stampede.

The assistant director signaled the end of the shot by waving a red bandanna. We circled back toward camera. Springsteen was happy. We wouldn't have to do a take two.

> *Lord, strike me bloody fuckin' round!*
> —Dan Sheridan on the set of *King of the Wild Stallions*

Character actor Dan Sheridan (*The Lawman*) was jaw-jacking with fellow thespian Denver Pyle between setups. After the romp down the rocks, I wandered over to eavesdrop on the two old timers. Sheridan, who hailed originally from New Zealand cattle country, spoke in the raunchy patois of a sundowner. His epithets punched colorful holes in the hot air that always accumulates around dressing room trailers. Pyle, a quieter man, began softly reminiscing about his experiences as a kid in Bethune, Colorado. He'd wanted to be a musician, he said, and had left home to become a drummer with a traveling band. "Bang on, mate," Sheridan shouted. "Bang bloody fuckin' on!"

The two old troupers knew and liked each other. They also knew fellow cast member Edgar Buchanan, and all three knew the lead heavy, Emile Meyer (*The Blackboard Jungle*). They had all worked together at some time. In some cases, many times.

It occurred to me then, and I'm convinced of it now, that the American film community is a mobile, surrogate family. Dysfunctional, yes. Bad apples, black sheep, and poisonous uncles abound, but still, we are family. Stuntman Sickner knew all of the wranglers and most of the teamster drivers. Crew members hugged like first cousins at a reunion picnic.

The family of motion picture people, due to their own frenetic hype, seems as swollen and overbearing as the Plantagenets. Actually, the group is not large, and its members filled with a surprising timidity. They cling to each other and to their environs with a gathering instinct comparable to that of the musk ox. Ninety percent of them live and work in the Los Angeles area. Imagine if all carpet layers lived and worked in Savannah, Georgia. Soon, the soul city of the Old South would be up to its juleps in back-slappin' carpet layers. So it is with the family of film.

Late that afternoon, I galloped the bay up to movie star Montgomery and dramatically shouted, "The whole herd's spreadin' out!" Springsteen yelled, "Cut. Print!" The assistant director checked the schedule, then called it a wrap. The juicers tethered the reflectors and got busy coiling the cable. The camera crew struck the huge 33mm Mitchell from its housing and hauled it to a truck. I watched the wranglers lead the horses to water; boots and horseshoes trailing fine, gray dust. The movie folk were packing up their magic, getting ready for the trip back to town. I thought about all of those free breakfasts and grinned. "At last," I said, "I'm home."

Several months after filming *King of the Wild Stallions*, director Springsteen cast me in another role. This time I was U.S. Marine Sergeant Gilchrist. The sergeant is a member of a rifle squad that goes behind North Korean lines to rescue a group of nurses. The picture was titled *Battle Flame* and it starred movie tough guy Scott Brady (*The China Syndrome*).

It was July 1959 and one hundred and three degrees in L.A. However, on Stage #3 at Allied Artists, it was 1952 and winter in Korea. I was dressed in Marine foul weather gear, including wool long johns, a sweater, and a heavy, hooded parka. Worse, I was huddled with several other Marines around a crackling fire.

"Hey, I'm havin' a fuckin' heat stroke here!" The actor squatting alongside me was Robert Blake (*In Cold Blood*, *Baretta*). Ken Miller (*Touch of Evil*) was also in the scene, wrapped in a blanket and lying next to the fire. We were melting like snow cones in a sauna and the makeup girl had to rush in between takes and sop up the sweat.

The scene we were filming took place at an imaginary bivouac near Chosin Reservoir. On the far side of the fire was an enormous cyclorama, a wintry rendering of the Korean highlands. The foreground consisted of steep, ice-covered cliffs and piles of frozen rock. "Action!" As Robert and I began our dialogue, it began to snow.

The creation of a particular scene has always seemed to me a strange and illusory endeavor. The white flakes descend, drifting softly on the air, falling unhurried to earth, covering cliff and rock in a cold, pale carpet. It was so real I began to shiver. The snow landed on the sleeve of my parka; it was Styrofoam. Off camera, special effects supervisor Milt Rice kept his crew busy dropping buckets of the sticky stuff from the overhead grid, and tossing handfuls into the face of portable wind machines.

Between scenes I had time to consider the huge number of people it takes to make a movie, all of the folks the audience never sees. The ones standing right there, just behind the camera. Juicers, grips, makeup, wardrobe, hair, sound, greensmen, bestmen, unit managers, guys like Rice and his crew, stunt people, wranglers, gofers, et al. At the studios, you would have to include the office staff, the executives, their assistants, office managers, secretaries, booking, publicity, editors, musicians, the guards at the gate, as their salaries and expenses are all charged against the movie.

At Allied Artists, the costs included the toilet paper sitting silently on rolls in the studio bathrooms. It is no wonder, then, that the lofty ideals felt at the beginning of a cinematic enterprise all too frequently morph into the lowest common denominator. I am reminded of a cartoon, a black and white sketch in a French film magazine.

A crew is in full swing on a motion picture soundstage. The number of people involved is enormous. They are all clustered near camera. People on ladders holding lights, people with paint brushes in their hands, production assistants talking to executives, still photographers, grips, camera people and more, all intensely focused on the one small bit of color on the page, a can of peas.

"Gary Kent! Who the hell made up that name?" The voice was low and gravelly, like the voice of a line coach at Notre Dame. It was followed through the stage door by a big, beefy man with the bluest, most mischievous eyes I had seen since grade school. It was the star of the movie, Scott Brady, arriving on the set for the first time. He was reading the cast list to see if he knew anyone. Brady was instantly surrounded by friends from the cast and crew. They laughed and greeted each other warmly, like family.

A renowned barroom brawler, Scott Brady was a pussycat to work with. He kept the set amused with his tall tales, practical jokes, and salacious humor. In front of the camera, though, he was perfectly serious in the part of our hard-nosed leader, First Lieutenant Frank Davis. Scott's non-com assistant in *Battle Flame* was nightclub comedian Arthur Walsh. I remembered Walsh from his role as Junior, Spencer Tracy's son in *The Last Hurrah*.

Standing in the Wrong Line

Within a year after starting work at Allied Artists, I was hit with an unexpected malaise, a strange, cloying dissatisfaction that was downright depressing. I should have been happy. Film director Thor Brooks had just cast me in his new movie about the French Foreign Legion, *Legion of the Doomed*.

The lead actor was Bill Williams, who had made his name playing endearing servicemen in classic war movies such as *Back to Bataan* with John Wayne, and Mervyn LeRoy's Oscar-winning masterpiece, *Thirty Seconds Over Tokyo*.

William F. Broidy produced *Legion of the Doomed*. It was shot entirely on a company soundstage and on Allied Artist's back lot. Bill Williams didn't have much to do other than look strong and handsome, a condition bestowed on him naturally. He was cast as an American officer stationed with the Legion and I was playing his radio operator. Our story concerned the trauma Williams undergoes upon learning that his commanding officer is a traitor and in cahoots with the desert tribes. The turncoat officer was portrayed by famed German actor Kurt Krueger (*Sahara*).

We legionnaires sat around our fort mostly; me tweaking the radio while Williams worried about our fickle Commandant and the evil Arab warrior, Karaba (Anthony Caruso). Between takes, Williams talked proudly about his wife, actress Barbara Hale (*Perry Mason*), and their plans to start a family. Kurt Krueger, a handsome blond with the trim, icy style of an Aryan aristocrat, whittled away his off-time playing checkers with the film's extras.

We were bored, the lot of us. The story was formula good-guy, bad-guy, the characters were stereotypes. I had a hard time feeling menaced by our costumed Arabs when the only Arab I knew personally was my friend Vic Tayback, the happiest human in Hollywood. I turned my attention to a young stuntman who had volunteered to teach me how to throw movie punches without hurting anyone. His name was Richard Farnsworth (*The Grey Fox*).

"You gotta hide the air between yourself and the other fella," he drawled. "If the camera can see it, 'magine how that air's gonna look up on the big screen. That miss is gonna look wider'n a mile." Farnsworth explained how important it was for the person taking the punch to *sell it* by reaction: a jerk of the head, snap of the jaw, a doubling of the body at the moment of supposed impact. "Usin' the illusion," he called it.

Late in his life, after forty years as a working stuntman, Richard Farnsworth would become a major movie star. At the age most people are looking to retire, Farnsworth was nominated for two Academy Awards (*The Straight Story, Comes a Horseman*), two Golden Globes for those same pictures, and in March of 2000, he won both the New York Film Critics Award for Best Performance by an Actor and the Independent Spirit Award for Best Male Lead for *The Straight Story*.

Hugging Rosebushes

As the 50s drew to a close, the studios, like the country, were socially indifferent and wallowing in arrogant contentment. Creatively, Hollywood was locked into ways and means from the 40s. No new or unusual chances were to be taken. The town simply did not want to deal with real issues, preferring instead to plant rose gardens and build white picket fences.

In 1958, *Blue Denim*, a terrific play dealing honestly with teenage pregnancy and abortion, debuted on Broadway to rave reviews. The following year, it was made into a hit movie starring Carol Lynley and Brandon De Wilde. In the play, after much soul searching, the teenagers proceed with an abortion. In the movie version, they move to another town, have a baby, and everyone lives happy as hedonists forever after.

Most other arts and artists had taken a front line position, breaking down barriers and opening windows to the shadowy truth. The world of publishing fought heavily through a total of sixty separate court proceedings for the freedom of the written word. Publishers like Olympia Press, The Evergreen Review, and New Directions had defended the sexually explosive works of Ginsberg, Miller, D.H. Lawrence, and Jean Genet and won!

European cinema racked up record grosses with films like *La Dolce Vita* and *Never on Sunday*, both of which had themes of immorality. In the U.S., however, a man and wife could not be shown sleeping together in the same bed. Nobody cursed in our movies, not even sailors. Since the 1934 induction of the Production Code and its ill-natured president Joseph Breen, the world of American Film had become wretchedly sterile.

In New York, theater audiences could slip off Broadway to witness Genet's brilliant dance-drama of racial antagonism, *The Blacks*, or throw on a pipe suit, and skinny tie (ala Sinatra) and cruise uptown to catch Ossie Davis's satire about race relations in the deep south, *Purlie Victorious*. On the West Coast, inside the megalithic movie mills, people of color were being cast only as bellhops, lay-abouts, and poor-folk.

Latin heritage got you a job as a sneering bandito or a few days work as the sidekick with disconnected neurons. Women were either passively dependent or scheming and spidery. Gays were cartoon characters. In an industry that prides itself on visual clarity, life, as seen on the silver screen, was out of focus.

Revolting Developments

My lovely, auburn haired wife Joyce was marveling at how our son Greg, a first-grader, could strut confidently through the parking lot of Sears and rattle off the name of every car simply by observing the grillwork. Daughter Colleen, scarcely over a year old, a bundle of golden locks, pink-pearl skin and laughter, was burrowing deeper into my arms as I twirled us around the den to the music of Glen Yarbrough and The Limeliters.

Joyce was pregnant with our soon to arrive son, Andrew. When Andrew finally appeared in Earth's orbit, he did so with the large, soulful eyes of a mystic and the guts and gusto of an NFL linebacker. As happy as this blissful, domestic scene seemed on the surface, my youthful, idealistic marriage was unraveling with all of the promise and disappointment of a Salvation Army sock at Christmas.

We were all living in the far north end of the San Fernando Valley. I was commuting daily over the back roads and freeways into the metroplex, where I gritted out the nine-to-five in the production office at Allied Artists Studios. At night, I would quaff a quart of black coffee, then hit the theater stages—free of charge. I would arrive home at last, bone-tired and full of shame that I was not achieving anything remotely close to monetary success as an actor in the cutthroat world of show business.

In Los Angeles, a town that defines the motion picture, theater is not a cash crop. As the 60s began, those actors in town who revered the art of performance had been stirring their juices by attending a variety of emotional gymnasiums known as *workshops*. Here, you could hang out the whole shebang, from improvisation to group therapy, from dance, body imaging and voice, to audition preparation, scene reading, and actual performance.

These workshops, located in lofts, garages, and small theaters throughout the city, supplied the answer to the need performers have for in-your-face feedback, and for those gut-wrenching, street level confrontations with the mystical. Jack Nicholson, Dennis Hopper, and Michael Landon were members of The Players' Ring. Jim Raymond (*Gemini Man*), Linda Lavin (*Alice*), and others regularly climbed a set of rickety stairs to the upper level of a two-story garage, The Angel's Company. Vic Tayback and I had joined West Coast Repertory, a workshop that met in the off-hours habitat of an Afro-Cuban dance academy squatting on the corner of Franklin Avenue and Cahuenga Boulevard.

It was the end of October 1960. Late fall is a time in L.A. when the afternoons lose that sweet, summer hangover and begin to chill-up by sunset. The twenty-eight members of West Coast Repertory were inside our building, huddled around a small, electric heater. Actor Gordon Jump (*WKRP in Cincinnati*) was excitedly discussing the future of film. Through the acting underground, he had heard about a daring endeavor pulled off by an acting workshop in New York City. The caper involved the New York group actually shooting a movie, after being informed by everyone in the business of film that it couldn't be, shouldn't be done. In the beleaguered bastions of courageous cinema, it was the shot heard 'round the world.

Shadows *was the beginning of The New Hollywood.*

—Peter Bogdanovich (*Easy Riders, Raging Bulls*)

At the beginning of the year, Lelia Goldoni (*Rainy Day Friends*), a dark-haired, seventeen-year-old dancer from Los Angeles, decided to travel to New York looking for "it," whatever "it" turned out to be. She booked a flight to La Guardia and shortly thereafter found herself engulfed in the frenetic energy of The Big Apple.

A month after arriving, an acquaintance whispered to Lelia that "it" could be found at the Variety Arts Center on 46th Street, where a young firebrand named John Cassavetes was conducting an acting workshop. Rumor was that John had gathered together a volatile, unruly bunch after being rejected by the prestigious Actor's Studio. Lelia decided to check them out.

They turned out to be kind of a lunatic bunch. Seymour Cassells (*Too Late Blues*) was a member, as were Rupert Crosse (*Ride in the Whirlwind*) and William Hurd (*For Love of Ivy*), but to the young dancer from California, they seemed to be doing great things. "Everything was off the cuff. Improvisations would go on for hours. I was fascinated by the whole experience." Not having any money, Lelia struck a deal with Cassavetes to teach dancing in exchange for participating in the acting exercises.

On the surface, nobody in the group seemed to know what they were doing. One Sunday, John engaged them in a secret improvisation, one that involved complicated racial situations. That evening he appeared as a guest on Jean Shepherd's *Night People* show on WOR radio. He mentioned that afternoon's work, and, if he'd had the money, how much he would like to have filmed it. The next day he started receiving monetary contributions from the hard-hearted denizens of night-time New York. In total, the unusual listeners sent in a total of $20,000.

Cassavetes, who Lelia considered an absolutely wonderful con artist, raised another $20,000, grabbed a 16mm camera, ran into the streets and began brazenly filming his actors improvising what would come to be know as the motion picture *Shadows*.

> *John Cassavetes never made a movie that wasn't about love!*
> —Lelia Goldoni

Americans are truest to their best tradition when they are upsetting tradition. In *Shadows*, Cassavetes had the guts to explore the anger and pressure a loving black family feels while struggling to maintain an identity in mid-town Manhattan. The film was spurned by American distributors, so John took the movie to the Cannes Film Festival in France, where it won a special Critic's Award. It was subsequently picked up by England's Lion International and was well-received in Europe.

Years later, *Shadows* finally made its way to the United States, where, to Hollywood's surprise, it became a minor hit. John Cassavetes and his small band of banditos had started a genuine revolution, not only in story content, but in the way a film is filmed, from finance to distribution. The crisp honesty of their work spawned an important new visionary force in American cinema, the *truly independent* motion picture.

Chapter Three

Liz Renay, Gary Kent in The Thrill Killers. *Photo courtesy of the author.*

God Is A Guy Named Jake

Cultural progress only comes about through the fanatical enthusiasm of the revolutionist, whose extreme teaching saves the mass from inertia.

—Edward Stieglitz (in his writings, 1903)

The snake was eighteen-feet long, a python, one of the subspecies *Pythoninae*, constrictors that delight in squeezing their prey to death. The creature was coiled in the bathtub of a luxury suite at the Plaza Hotel in New York, a suite rented mutually by Broadway/movie star Mary Astor (Best Supporting Oscar for *The Great Lie*), and her large, affable fourth husband, Thomas Wheelock. Mary and Tom, both hard partiers, kept the python as a family pet and a conversation piece for their frequent guests, the best and brightest of the Great White Way.

The snake was in the middle of consuming a large rat given to it minutes earlier by a trusted housekeeper, when the door to the bathroom opened and in walked Timothy Sullivan, handsome actor, Broadway raconteur, and merry inebriate. Sullivan was bent on relieving himself as quickly as possible and returning to a rollicking party downstairs. Locked in the sweet lassitude of several straight scotches, Sullivan didn't see the python at first. He unzipped his fly and started his solitary business when his eye caught an ominous slither coming from the direction of the tub. Tim turned, confronting the snake face-to-face. He was so startled and frightened that he continued to urinate all over his trousers and a large portion of the tile floor. It was shortly after the embarrassment of this incident that Sullivan decided to quit his consumption of alcohol, once and for all. He would spend the next seven years in a quest for sobriety.

Footprints

It was a heady, innocent time, the beginning of the 60s. The U.S. was quickly moving away from small town life and becoming a nation of big cities, skyscrapers, and a faster, jet-propelled way of life. In January 1961, John F. Kennedy took office as President of the United States. He was forty-three. He brought with him the youngest cabinet since Andrew Jackson's in 1829. There were young men in Washington, young men in space, young men and women in the Peace Corps.

In Hollywood, the hot ticket was a wagon load of bobby socks flicks, most produced by Roger Corman and aimed at the youth market. The world, it seemed, had suddenly become classically youthful.

Young woman name of Dayle Rodney dropped in the other day to tell our readers about Cinema Workshop. At that, I never heard of anything quite like it. Its members make movies for their own amazement.

—Philip K. Scheuer, *Los Angeles Times*, 1961

Taking inspiration from John Cassavetes and his New York gypsies, we thespians in West Coast Repertory decided we would also make our own movies. After all, Los Angeles was a film town, not a theater town. We pooled our lunch money, changed our name to Cinema Workshop, and got busy making it happen.

Les Green, a fellow Allied Artists employee and a group member, found a 16mm camera at an estate sale and nailed it for our use. (Les would later operate the camera for *Watership Down*, and win an Eddie for his editing of 1986's *Women of Valor* with Susan Sarandon.) We talked the owners of an old commercial warehouse just off Highland Avenue into donating stage space. Eugene Arnstein, Studio Manager at Allied Artists, arranged to have a company truck deliver a supply of lighting equipment free of charge, and Consolidated Film Laboratory gave us a cut-rate deal on processing and developing. Within two weeks we were filming our own improvised scenes.

Some of us, like Les, Vic Tayback, and myself, had enough experience to at least fake professional moviemaking, but for most, those intense evenings in our enclave on Highland Avenue were chock full of mistakes, and only now and then, flashes of insight into the mysterious universe of cinema.

Vic and I were rehearsing a scene from the play *Death of a Salesman* by playwright Arthur Miller, ship-shaping it for our small crew to film. I was directing. Although twenty years too young for the role, Vic was acting the part of the father, a character played on Broadway by his personal hero, Lee J. Cobb.

Les Green was behind camera, while an actress in the group, Dayle Rodney (*Crash Landing*), was holding script.

In those days, all actors smoked cigarettes. It went with the persona of being artistic and high-strung. At the break, Dayle and I lit up, blissfully unaware of the havoc we were wreaking on our lungs. Dayle, a ravishing redhead with a passionate zest for everything cinematic, began to tell me about a motion picture she was going to read for after group ended that evening. "It's an independent," Dayle enthused, letting a white wisp of vapor escape dramatically from lips the color of cherry pops. "It's a mood Western called *Run Home Slow*. A guy named Tim Sullivan is directing."

I had never heard of Sullivan and told Dayle it was not usual for a director to be casting his movie late at night. "Oh, it's perfectly safe," she laughed, grinding out a lip-sticked butt with her stiletto heel. "He's from New York, and besides, he's got to be over sixty." As if in Hollywood that made a difference.

The Money Suit

After group ended that night, it was decided that I should drive Dayle to her appointment, just to be on the safe side. Tim Sullivan lived in a modest house on Lapeer Drive in Beverly Hills. On the drive over, Dayle filled me in on the wherefore of this mysterious man.

Sullivan maintained a modest reputation in the Hollywood loop, having worked a few short years as a dialogue coach. Dayle met him while calling on Beverly Hills film people to tell them about our group. "He's done major work as an actor on Broadway," she said, "during the 40s and early 50s." Now, as he approached the crusty years of late middle age, he had evidently decided to become a movie director.

"Wait 'til you meet him," she enthused. "He's like a man possessed. He's brilliant and wonderful and says all the right things to make an actor care!" She lit a cigarette, reached for the ash tray. "Remember how it felt? When we all really cared?"

Twenty minutes later we were being ushered into Tim Sullivan's living room by his roommate and now Mary Astor's ex-husband, the ursine Thomas Wheelock.

Several other nervous hopefuls were gathered inside, awaiting Sullivan's arrival. We took seats on a long leather couch, Dayle tugging at her skirt and fishing through her handbag for a cigarette. Within seconds the door opened and in walked Mr. Timothy Sullivan, sporting a smile as bright as a pie tin in sunlight. He was unusually handsome, well built, with distinguished gray hair and warm eyes. Green eyes, they were, and they were fairly bursting with merriment. He was dressed in an expensive, well-tailored suit—green, to go with the eyes. He explained that the suit was his "money suit," and that whenever he wore it, people just naturally wanted to give him money. In this case, he'd been out hustling investors for his movie. "We're almost there," he chortled. "One more lunch, one more breakfast, one more handshake, and we'll be rolling the cameras!" Somehow, we all believed him.

Dorothy Parker once credited author Budd Schulberg with capturing the "true shittiness of Hollywood" in his book *What Makes Sammy Run*, a scathing indictment of the town and its populace. However, I must say that in over forty continuous years in the motion picture industry, the vast majority of those I encountered, on or off the set, have been decent, hardworking people. Not much different than folks in any other town. Interesting, yes; a little bonkers, yes; strung tight as a calf-rope at a rodeo, terribly foolish, vain, more than willing to walk to the edge of it all, but essentially, just like you and I.

The one big difference I noticed, even way back then, is that in the world of cinema, they all feel that what *they do* gives dreams somewhere to go, and that dreams are vastly important. I realize this sounds arrogant and presumptuous, but surely in these cynical times dreams are as important as politics, cosmetics, mud-wrestling, playing basketball, or driving monster trucks. One of the most wonderfully tenacious dreamers I met in Hollywood was Tim Sullivan.

> *The status quo movie says everything is okay, don't rock the boat.*
> *I'm the exact opposite. I want to rock the boat.*
>
> —Tim Sullivan, in conversation, 1961

Since the great war and the subsequent communist inquisition, most of the studios avoided truth. They evaded controversy by sinking their collective, timorous teeth into religious epics and sci-fi horror films. Oh, the establishment put out some great films as the 60s began: *Ben-Hur* and *Some Like it Hot* in 1959, a black and white marvel called *The Apartment* with Jack Lemmon and Shirley MacLaine in 1960, *West Side Story* in 1961, and '62 ushered in such diverse delights as *What Ever Happened to Baby Jane* and *The Miracle Worker*. These films were marvelous cinema, but hardly revolutionary.

As the decade began, most of the great movie moguls, men like Jack Warner, Harry Cohn, Sam Goldwyn, David Selznick, were either dead or shriveled into easy chairs, living on past laurels, sipping gin, and watching television. The younger generation and a few fledgling "independents" were making low budget, B versions of the same stuff the majors were making. The revolution that was beginning to simmer in the rest of the arts had stirred nary a ripple in the placid cauldrons of tinseltown.

In 1961, it was unthinkable in Hollywood for an unknown to attempt to raise money from the private sector to shoot a serious movie. Cassavetes and his group in New York had done that very thing, but the studios considered *Shadows* an interesting experiment at best and largely ignored it. Tim Sullivan not only planned to raise his budget free of the movie establishment, but also shoot, edit, promote, and distribute his film himself, and to hell with what those in power thought he should or shouldn't do.

Sullivan was invigorated by a burr of revolutionary zeal planted firmly in the seat of his pants. He wanted to make a Western, one that took chances and challenged the homespun myths of the Hollywood "West." And, he wanted to make it outside of the studio system.

Tim's film, *Run Home Slow*, dealt with the problems of a dysfunctional family wandering aimlessly through a barren desert after the townspeople had lynched their father. Sullivan had taken a shine to me after that first night of readings. He thought my experience with horses and my hurly-burly attitude made me a natural for Ritt Hagen, a sweaty, hot-headed cowpoke and the male lead in his Western. Having gone to the reading with no intention of trying for a part, I was stunned. It was the easiest job I ever got.

The Doppler Effect of Cool

It would take Tim two more years to raise enough money to shoot his film. Two more years of donning the "money suit" and badgering, cajoling, and wheedling just plain folk—firemen, policemen, housewives—into investing their money in his "vision."

It was summer 1963. Coffeehouses were *in*. They were definitely where it was at as the 60s slid into full gear, and most of hip Hollywood was into the coffeehouse scene. I'm not taking about sterile, whip-creamy hangouts like today's Starbucks. The coffee houses in the early 60s were earthy, left-bank kinds of places, like Chez Paulette and Cyrano's on the Strip, or The Renaissance, just east of La Cienega. Avant-garde joints where you could sip your caffeine while enjoying a whiff of something smelling of angst, and now and then the pungent odor of marijuana.

The beat poets and their more colorful offspring, the hippies, were the linchpins of the coffeehouse movement, although once in a while you could catch some comedic guerilla performing, some rebellious skin-scratcher like funnyman Lenny Bruce.

I was sitting at a rickety table inside Fifth Estate, a coffeehouse just west of Crescent Heights, having a cup of joe with Irish Frankie Conway. Irish Frankie was a middle-weight boxer, real name Don Jones, a skinny, cocky kid beginning to tire of the fight game and toying with the idea of a career in show business. In future years, Don would direct several films (*Lethal Pursuit*, *The Forest*), and put in countless hours shooting documentaries for The Discovery Channel, among others.

Don and I were out of work, as usual, and scouring the trade papers for employment opportunities. I decided to check my phone service (at that time, answering machines were non-existent) to see if there was a call from the IBEW. Both Jones and I had been working out of the union part time, on permit, as studio electricians. I had one message. It was from Tim Sullivan. According to the operator at my telephone service, Tim had left a message saying it was urgent that he see me as soon as possible. Within minutes after returning his call, he picked me up in his green, four-door Cadillac.

> *Whatever you can do, or dream you can do, begin it. Boldness has power, creativity, and magic.*
>
> —Grandma Hope, in her musings, 1936

Like most filmmakers, Sullivan was so wrapped up in his project that he was totally oblivious to the fact that the first cultural and social upheaval since the turn of the century was about to begin. Long before he had his financing in place, he began to commit artists and craftsmen to *Run Home Slow*. Talk about confidence! He signed me to play the male lead, then hired an exuberant wannabe stuntman, darkly handsome John "Bud" Cardos, to be production manager, a tall, rangy half-breed named Tom Cloud to wrangle the horses, and a super-young, unknown garage band drummer named Frank Zappa (*200 Motels*, *Uncle Meat*) to supply the music.

As I slid into the front seat of the Cadillac that sunny, summer morning in '63, Tim informed me that we were on our way to Malibu, to take a meeting with actress Mary Astor. He was considering Mary for the part of Nell, the crazy older Hagen sister, and the female lead in his movie.

Once past the Strip, Sunset Boulevard follows a reptilian route through manicured, fluffed up Beverly Hills, the tony suburbs of Brentwood and Pacific Palisades, then tumbles sharply down, onto the Pacific coast continuing north to the surfer havens of Zuma Beach and County Line.

On the long drive to Mary Astor's home, Tim, a heavy smoker, lit up a Chesterfield, then began to ruminate on why Mary and his friend Tom Wheelock had ended their marriage. "Booze had a lot to do with it," he sighed. "Tom and I quit drinking way back in New York." For the first time, I was privy to Tim's astounding tale about how he achieved sobriety with the help of a remarkable apparition named Jake.

Sullivan had been a practicing alcoholic during most of his Broadway career. At first, it was easy to fake sobriety, to even appear clever and articulate; just a talented fellow who liked to party. As the drinking increased, however, it began to savage him in a variety of ways. He would forget his lines, show up late for, at first, rehearsals, then performances. Word got around that he had a problem and he began losing parts.

Tim tried all the available resources for quitting the bottle, including the church and Alcoholics Anonymous. Nothing worked. This man, who had been a shining light on the New York stage, found himself penniless, living in a hovel off Times Square, hungry and sick most of the time.

One morning, after a particular nasty night of handouts and cheap wine, Tim was staggering back to his flat when he collapsed on a bus bench, too sick and drunk to make it across the street. One of New York's finest, a patrolman, was nearby watching him with a jaundiced eye. Tim knew that if he tried to walk, the cop would notice his condition and throw him in jail. Demoralized, out of hope, Tim said out loud, "Ain't this just jake!" *Jake* was an expression used commonly in those days to signify well-being. "Ain't this just jake!" Tim repeated, then heard a voice answer from somewhere in the atmosphere, "This is Jake. What seems to be the problem?"

Tim, too drunk to think clearly, explained his situation out loud, into the thin air. He didn't want to spend another night in jail. He was sure he'd commit suicide if that happened, and yet, he couldn't make it across the street to his bed. Sullivan told me that he could see Jake, a vaporous entity, similar in appearance to Tim's vision of what God must look like. The entity spoke again, loudly, and with an obvious strength. It said, "If I help you, will you give up drinking?" Tim was not a religious man, but he was at his wit's end, so he made the promise. Jake reached toward the drunken actor. "Here, Timothy, give me your hand," he said compassionately. Tim grabbed hold, and Jake walked him across the street without a stumble, without a misstep. Tim smiled warmly as he passed the policeman. By the time he arrived home, he was sober, and his ghostly pal had disappeared. "That was nine years ago," Tim told me. "I haven't had a drink since."

We rode in silence for a few miles. We were quietly gliding past the secluded entrance to Will Rogers State Historic Park when Tim began talking again, "Mary, God bless her, the broad just couldn't leave the booze alone, and then, there were all those damn affairs."

According to Tim, Mary Astor, or as he frequently called her, "the broad," had jumped between the sheets with everyone from mega-star John Barrymore to playwright George S. Kaufman to a respected religious leader at Loyola University. "Tom came home early one day," Tim chuckled. "He was working at Rocketdyne at the time. Came home for lunch, which he didn't usually do. Walked up the path to the house, heard laughter and carrying on coming from the back of the building. Suspicious, because of the broad's past, Tom sneaked around the side and looked in the bedroom window. All he saw were Mary's feet, and in between, the feet of the good Father, shoes and socks still on, and his holy trousers pulled down around his knees." Tim laughed out loud. "The Father and Mary were having a hump right there in broad daylight! That was the end of it. Tom hasn't talked to her since."

Tim said that in spite of standing up for his buddy Wheelock during the divorce proceedings, he and Mary were on good terms. "She's looking forward to our arrival," he assured me.

Mary's house was a rambling, white stucco, perched precariously like an eagle's nest on a cliff overlooking the Pacific Ocean. It was surrounded by bougainvillea, patches of periwinkle and brilliant, scarlet cockscomb. A uniformed maid escorted us through the premises, past a large, airy living room, down a hallway galleried in publicity stills from Mary's varied films, and into the master bedroom. We found the much revered movie star reclining on a huge, silk-sheeted bed, with two giant pillows tilting her in the direction of a window which faced directly into the ocean sky.

Except for wearing oriental lounging pajamas, Mary looked as though she had been made up for an evening on the town. "Timothy," she whispered, "so good to see you."

Classy Ain't

While Sullivan sat on the edge of the bed and pitched his film, I eased into a chair near the window where I could furtively stare at Mary's Oscar. The golden statuette stood at attention on a small pedestal. She had received the award for her best supporting role as Sandra Kovac, a concert pianist, in *The Great Lie*, performing opposite Bette Davis and the suave, sophisticate George Brent.

The critics loved Mary as Kovac. She performed some of her own piano pieces, including a difficult Tchaikovsky concerto and, at the request of designer Orry-Kelly, cut her hair severely into a close-cut, masculine bob. When the film opened, Mary's short haircut became all the rage, and much of the female populace worldwide began to copy the look.

I was awestruck. I remembered Astor as a dynamic screen presence in *The Maltese Falcon, Red Dust, The Prisoner of Zenda*, et al., and now I was sitting in her bedroom, barely a few feet from this marvelous woman. Not wanting to appear the toby, I sneaked a look while she was chatting with Tim. She was, at age 57, still strikingly beautiful, with smooth, cover-girl skin, dark curly hair, a cute, mischievous nose and bright eyes that flirted continuously with everything: Tim, me, her Oscar, the light coming in the window, her own quick, expressive hands, everything!

I was elated when she assured Tim she was interested in the role of Nell. The thought of acting with Mary Astor brought me a feeling of intense pleasure. I, myself, would soon be buying a house in Malibu; I was sure of it. This foolishness was discarded on the ride back to L.A. when Tim informed me that he'd decided she was all wrong for the part. "She's a classy broad, no doubt, but Nell Hagen just ain't no classy broad." I was dumbstruck. Tim fired up a Chesterfield. "I can't picture Mary Astor getting her hands real dirty, can you?" I nodded in agreement, while secretly, inside myself, I was very close to having a cry.

Weevils in the Flour Sack

July and August in L.A. were hotter than hell and dry as face powder. I survived the summer by hanging out on the beach with a tall, blue-eyed cowboy from Texas named Pat Raines. Pat and his sheepdog Rufus would pick me up at my house in the valley, and we would all hightail it to the cooling surf of Redondo. Happy, carefree times for Rufus, Pat, and me.

Since joining the ever-enlarging group attached to *Run Home Slow*, production manager Bud Cardos and I had become close friends. We were the same age, both semi-stuntmen, and we even lived within blocks of each other in the San Fernando Valley. At night, Pat, Bud, and I would escape the swelter by scooting down Wilshire Boulevard to a club in Santa Monica called The Horn. Inside, the waiters, all struggling musical artists, would serve food and drinks while belting out show tunes and current pop hits. Our favorite performer was a shy, hang-dog looking singer with a tremendous baritone voice. His name was Jim Nabors; he would later become famous as TV's Gomer Pyle. Frequently, Nabors would sit at our table and the four of us would discuss whether or not Tim Sullivan would ever get to make his movie.

Nabors was concerned that, at a time when Todd-A.O., Vista Vision, Warner Vision, Cinemascope, and Spectravision were all competing for the audience with a huge palette of brilliantly manipulated color, Tim Sullivan wanted to shoot his movie in black and white. No one had ever heard of musical arranger Frank Zappa, and by now Sullivan had signed a pretty, but unknown actress, Linda Gaye Scott (*Psych-Out*, *West World*) to play my wife, Julie Ann. Worse yet, one of the investors, Allan Richards, an amateur, had been given the role of my hunchback brother Kirby, while other investors, a fireman, truck driver, and housewife, had been signed on as members of the crew. That meant that Tim was getting ready to shoot *Run Home Slow*, a Western without color or name stars, using a haphazard group of complete unknowns for cast and crew. "Things are," Nabors reminded us, "not exactly hunky-dory."

Fadoodling

"Get up, Kent. The game is afoot! We've got places to go and things to do!" The voice came from Tim Sullivan, who was pounding on my door early in the morning. I struggled into a shirt and pair of jeans and met him outside. He was wearing his money suit, so I figured whatever was up was important. Minutes later we were racing over Coldwater Canyon to Sunset, on our way to meet with award-winning actress Mercedes McCambridge.

Miss McCambridge, born in 1916 in Joilet, Illinois, had been a successful stage and radio actress before her sojourn in film. She had a wonderful, full-throated basso voice that delighted listeners of the old *I Love a Mystery* radio serial. Two decades later, that same voice, as the voice of the devil, would send chills up the spines of audiences watching the film *The Exorcist*.

After moving to Hollywood, Mercedes won an Academy Award and a Golden Globe as "Best Supporting Actress" for her performance in *All the King's Men* opposite Broderick Crawford. McCambridge had also picked up a Golden Globe for "Most Promising Newcomer" in 1953.

Mercedes lived in a pristine apartment in upscale Brentwood. She greeted us at the door, a small, stocky, fiftyish woman with a nice smile and intense, intelligent eyes. She invited us into her cozy, pastel colored living room. Tim and I sat on a pale blue couch, she in a chair directly opposite. In between us was a coffee table with three distinct decorations, her Oscar and two Golden Globes.

The meeting that morning consisted mostly of the three of us doing a sixties version of what is now referred to as "bonding." McCambridge was as much into politics and liberal causes as she was acting. One of her heroes at the time was Adlai Stevenson, Illinois Governor. "My little red tomato," she smiled. "He's so humble and contrite, his face turns into a ripe tomato just thinkin' about appearin' before the public." She and Stevenson were close friends; she had campaigned heavily for him in the 1950s during his two bids against Dwight Eisenhower for the presidency of the United States.

We polished off two pots of coffee and several pastries before Tim decided to call it a wrap. We had been with the actress for two hours. It seemed like only thirty minutes. Not once had we talked about the movie. Mercedes finished a story about how embarrassed Adlai was when a press photographer took a picture of him with a large hole in the sole of his shoe. "The picture," she said, "surfaced as a half-page in *Life* magazine."

I could tell by Tim's attitude that he had found his Nell and that his excitement had captivated Mercedes. They talked briefly at the door about costume fittings, shooting schedules, etc. There was much laughter and hugs all around. It crossed my mind that if I felt any better, I'd think it was a set-up. I couldn't wait to get back to the valley and call Bud Cardos.

> *A tension tight tale along a trail of terror!*
> —Ad line for *Run Home Slow*, 1963

The next time I saw Mercedes, it was November. We were on location in California's El Mirage desert flats, a barren, wind-worn area perfectly suited for outlaws, loners, and dreamers. We were there, at last, to begin the filming of *Run Home Slow*.

As production manager, Bud Cardos had decided to save money by having us all stay at a ramshackle cluster of old buildings known as the Taylor Ranch. The ranch was surrounded by Joshua trees, prickly pear, and rattlesnakes. Most of us bunked in the wooden ranch shacks, with outdoor toilet privileges and precious little in the way of creature comforts. Tim, Mercedes, and Linda Gaye Scott were sequestered in spiffy motor homes that Bud had hauled in from Victorville.

Other than a mildly experienced cameraman, Lew Guin, and the professional sound team of Ken Carlson and his boom man, a good natured fellow named Bob Dietz, no one on the crew of *Run Home Slow* had the slightest idea of what they were doing. Not Tim Sullivan, who had never directed before; not Bud Cardos, who'd never managed a production before; not even Pat Raines, my cowboy buddy from Texas. Pat had wrangled the job of key grip. His dog Rufus became the company mascot. Pat was much more at home in the rodeo arena than on a movie set. He knew the front end of a hammer and could manhandle a saw, but that was about it experience-wise. His assistant was Hugo Zimmerman, a happy-go-lucky nebbish and one of the film's major investors. Hugo's wife Neysa, equally pleasant and optimistic, was in charge of props.

Leah Cooper, in her mid-teens, the beautiful, raven-tressed daughter of Doug Cooper, our transportation captain, played a part in the film and also handled wardrobe. A Los Angeles fireman named Jesse Bates was chief electrician, while "Old George," a local and wizened collector of rocks, bits of broken glass, and bones, took charge of preparing lunch and the voicing of complaints.

So, there you have it in a nutshell. We and our inexperienced group of investors, wannabes, and hired desert derelicts set out to film Tim Sullivan's movie. And, film it we did, in spite of every impediment man and nature could hurl into our collective, naive midst.

If you're shooting a Western, don't pick a location near airfields of any kind. We were right next to Edward's Air Force Base, and shot after shot was ruined by the sound of jets screaming overhead.. The heat, the tarantulas, sidewinders, and sand make working conditions in the desert very edgy—should have brought that sunscreen. Forget that director's chair stuff. On location, the director never gets to sit down. On low budget films, neither do the actors. Moviemaking is all start-stop-start-stop-start-stop-start-stop! The best shot of the day is the "martini shot."

Mercedes, or Mercy, as she preferred to be called, was definitely our most experienced hand. She had four simple rules of conduct: relax, concentrate, have patience, have fun. To this end, she carried a purse big as a saddle bag with her on the set. Inside were the items necessary for following those rules: her script, a hairbrush, a hand towel, a copy of Krishnamurti's *Commentaries on Living*, and several tiny bottles of vodka, which she would empty into cups of fruit juice and chug-a-lug without explanation or apology.

As Nell Hagen, the obsessive, half-mad sister to myself and brother Kirby, she wore a tattered vest over a man's undershirt, black work pants, and a pair of old, scuffed up boots. The boots sported a cherished pair of silver-roweled spurs. "Gary Cooper gave me these spurs," she bragged. "I'm wearin' 'em for luck."

Mercy asked each actor to find some piece of bric-a-brac, some talisman, some little something that could have belonged to the character we were portraying. "Stick it in your pocket," she advised. "When you begin to doubt your performance, reach in 'n' grab it. Squeeze it, start rubbin' on it, and that character will come to life, inside your chest, right where your ticker is tickin'. Take my word for it."

When I packed for location, I brought along a small, brown leather coin purse. It had belonged to my grandfather, P.J. Nixdorff, a railroad man. The leather was smooth to the touch, worn thin by time and the constant caress of P.J's fingers probing inside for a buffalo nickel or Indian head penny. I decided the purse would be my ticket to the secret soul of Ritt Hagen. I slipped it into the pocket of my jeans. Allan Richards, playing Kirby, got himself an old bible, and Linda Gay Scott selected a fancy pink parasol.

Her and that puke-pink parasol. If she don't settle down, I'm gonna take that thing and poke it right through her gizzard. Far as I'm concerned, she's a loose shingle, flappin' in the wind.

—Mercedes McCambridge, in *Run Home Slow*, 1963

Good actors, it seems to me, have much of the unabashed spontaneity of childhood going for them, an honesty of emotion, a lack of self-consciousness that gives them freedom to be other than they are—freedom to risk exposing many of the indulgences and frailties we, as adults, are taught to keep hidden.

Brain Breathing

There is something important in this stuff about having the courage to be childlike. It shakes up the mind, opens the head, and lets the brain breathe fresh air. In *Run Home Slow*, both McCambridge and Linda Gaye Scott dared to go over the top with their portrayals. Linda, as the Hagen woman who committed the sin of marrying her cousin Ritt, chose to play Julie Ann as a nitwit, an amalgam of blonde sexuality and stunted intelligence so removed from reality she dressed for the desert as though attending a senior prom in Savannah.

Mercedes, as matriarch Nell, was an incarnation of evil, a repository of madness, full of swagger and strut. She moved through that awful landscape like a truculent drunk, barking orders and talking to the ghost of her recently executed father. I, as Ritt, had been wounded in a gunfight at the beginning of the story, and spent much of my time splayed perilously across the back of a donkey, fading in and out of consciousness. Brother Kirby was a hunchback. The four of us presented one of the strangest foursomes in movie history. Certainly the Old West's most dysfunctional family.

The author, Donald Cerveris, who at one time was Frank Zappa's high school English teacher, had fashioned the story as a mirror of human arrogance and greed. For much of the movie, the Hagens wander aimlessly across the desert, lost, disillusioned, prickly as the Joshua trees, bickering constantly until our hatred and anger turns us against each other. Three of us die, leaving Nell to lope off into a desolate distance, alone, terrified, and tormented by her own disintegrating persona. When the film eventually found distribution, one of the reviewers commented, "Some of the scenes are reminiscent of the work of Spanish master Luis Buñuel, only darker."

At the completion of the shoot, invigorated by the experience, we returned home from the desert wastes only to find that *Run Home Slow*, like Cassavetes's *Shadows*, would be ignored by Hollywood and the major studios. Sullivan's dream, once it was dressed, coiffed, portrayed, and photographed, was casually placed on the shelf of obscure cinema. It took Tim years to find a distributor. Finally, a small company in San Francisco, Emerson Film Enterprises, took the picture, then largely neglected it.

In the first part of this century, movie buffs have mysteriously located copies of *Run Home Slow* via the Internet. They seem intrigued by the weirdness of the story and delighted by the absolute tawdriness of the characters. Unanimously, they laud the early cinematic brilliance of young Zappa's haunting musical score, and cite it as reason alone for seeing the movie.

Cash Flag and the Steckheads

It is impossible to discuss the times and tides of early 60s filmmakers and the seeding of the American film revolution without mention of a colorful character named Ray Dennis "Cash Flag" Steckler (*The Incredibly Strange Creatures who Stopped Living and Became Mixed Up Zombies!!?*). While Tim Sullivan was shooting *Run Home Slow*, Ray Steckler, a balding, Huntz Hall look-a-like, was cavorting on the fringes of legitimate moviemaking by working as a grip at the studios, and as camera operator on several low budget features.

Originally from Reading, Pennsylvania, Steckler began making 8mm shorts when he was fourteen-years old, using the neighborhood kids as actors. After a stint in the army, Ray scurried to L.A., living in his car in a parking lot on Santa Monica Boulevard while he tried to find work in films. He met long-legged dancer Carolyn Brandt on a set of *The Magic of Sinbad*, pursued her until she married him, and shortly thereafter they moved into a modest house on Lemon Grove Avenue and started a family.

One day Ray stuck his hand in his pocket, pulled out some loose change, and figured it was enough money to make his own movie. He rallied his family, wife Carolyn Brandt, his kids, the neighbors and their kids, friends and casual acquaintances, then turned on his camera and began filming. Before he was finished, he would produce, direct, and act in over a dozen motion pictures—all shot on a shoestring, all bizarre, terribly flawed, and all, to some degree, enormously entertaining.

I met Steckler because I was one of those casual acquaintances. At that time, I was married to actress Laura Benedict. We and our two sons, Christopher, three-years old, and newly born Alexander, lived in a quaint redwood house on Coldwater Canyon Avenue, near Moorpark, in the burgeoning San Fernando Valley. Bud Cardos lived several houses away with his wife Pat, their baby girl, a mountain lion, and several tarantulas.

Cardos had a part-time construction business going and in between movie jobs we would strap on our tool belts, grab some two by fours, and start slappin' in those 16-penny nails. Before too long, we would have a house built, an apartment building, a school, and once, even a medical clinic. In the fantasy world of milk and honey, San Fernando Construction paid my rent, kept food on the table, got the kids their tricycles, and as long as we met deadlines, our time was our own. In off hours, we would pound the Hollywood concrete, looking for work in motion pictures.

L. to R. : actors Mercedes McCambridge, Linda Gaye Scott, Gary Kent, and Alan Richards in Run Home Slow. *Photo courtesy of the author.*

Ray Steckler was also a neighbor. One particularly hot, smog-besotted mid-afternoon, when I was in my small yard trying to erect a swing set, Ray approached me and asked if I would like a job in one of his movies. He didn't have a script, could only mumble a vague plot line, but, at the moment, it sounded like a good deal to me. I would make a couple of bucks playing a maniac, get to chase showgirl Liz Renay up and down Topanga Canyon, and fight the film's hero on the lip of a gigantic cliff during the movie's climax.

Liz Renay was fresh out of prison, where she had done three years for refusing to testify against her mobster boyfriend Mickey Cohen. She wanted to change her image, and more pointedly, she needed a job. Steckler offered her employment, and Liz jumped at the offer. I met her over a cup of watery instant coffee in Ray's kitchen. I was impressed by her looks and her attitude. Statuesque wasn't the right word to describe Liz Renay, but it's close. Liz was *statuesque* and then some. That morning she was wearing a tight dress and heels; when she stood to shake my hand she was easily over six feet tall, with a mane of honey-red hair and large, amber colored eyes with small flecks of green in them.

I learned that in the years prior to our introduction and before her sojourn at Terminal Island federal prison, Liz Renay has been a top fashion model for Eileen Ford, a published author, a painter, a nightclub performer, and had dated and reportedly jumped into the sleeping bag with Burt Lancaster, Marlon Brando, Frank Sinatra, Jerry Lewis, and George Raft.

Liz was the first and only connection I ever had with "the mob" or "mafioso" and that aura gave her an exciting mystique. Yet, in spite of her well-publicized links with Albert Anastasia of Murder Incorporated; Mickey Cohen, L.A.'s own resident thug; and gangland bodyguard Tony Cappola, Liz Renay had the cheerfulness and enthusiasm of a yell squad princess at Stephens College.

Director John Waters (*Hairspray*, *Pink Flamingos*), who directed Liz in *Desperate Living*, said she was the happiest person he'd ever met. "She's the happiest person in the whole world. Lovely, kind, nice, and crazy...all in a great way." Waters is dead on. As one of the maniacal murderers in Steckler's tour de terror, I was required to stalk, attack, and maul Miss Renay throughout most of the movie. Much of this manhandling occurred during a horrifying foot chase up hillsides, across rock strewn ledges, through thorny thickets, and over logs and rotting debris in the wild canyons of Topanga. Liz, the whole time, was attired in a skimpy dress and treacherous high heels. She never complained, wimped out, or ruined a take. This may be due to the fact that Liz is part Iroquois.

The picture was titled *The Thrill Killers*. Besides Liz and myself, the film starred a large, puffy actor named Joe Bardo as the good guy, my wife Laura Benedict as an exotic cafe waitress, and acting under the name of "Cash Flag," Ray Steckler himself. I asked him why on earth he would pick such an obviously contrived stage name. "Because," he replied, with his lopsided Steckler grin, "I've been cheated out of my salary so many times, I want producers to know it's cash up front if they want me!"

> *Ray Dennis Steckler is Everyman with a dream. He has demonstrated his unique talent on pocket-change budgets because that's all he had to work with. Yet, no matter what limitations have been placed on him, he has always created entertaining films.*
>
> —Mike Quarles, *Down and Dirty*, 1993

The cinematographer on *The Thrill Killers* was Joseph V. Mascelli. In the film industry, there is a little black book sticking out of the hip pocket of all cinematographers, cameramen, and camera operators. It is called *The Cinematographers Handbook* and it contains all the information necessary to actually run a camera on a movie set—all the lenses available, all apertures, focal lengths, housings, foot-candle info, and tricks of the trade. The book was written by Joe Mascelli. Although shot in black and white to save money, the photography in *Thrill Killers* is superb.

> *Of all of Steckler's movies, none is better cast than* The Thrill Killers. *A lead role features Liz Renay, a Hollywood glamour girl. Other outstanding performances are by Herb Robbins, Gary Kent, and Keith O'Brien, who play three escaped lunatics.*
>
> –Jim Morton, *Incredibly Strange Films*, 1986

Arguably, the best acting in the film is done by Laura Benedict, a soufflé of seductive innuendo, as Liz's cousin Linda, and by Erina Enyo as a street hustler murdered by Cash in a frightening sequence in a run-down hotel room. Mascelli lit the scene with the eerie light from a flashing neon sign outside the room's lone window.

In future years, Ray's fans, known as Steckheads, would refer to *The Thrill Killers* as his best film. The movie also received a hearty endorsement from Bob Dobbs, the mysterious leader of the Church of the SubGenius.

I would end up doing two more pictures for the energetic Ray Steckler, a seriously flawed art piece titled *Sinthia, the Devil's Doll*, and a rollicking detective farce called *Body Fever*. Liz Renay was also in *Body Fever*, and Steckler, who directed, was quite touching as a private eye so down on his luck he had to hitchhike to the scenes of his investigations. Remembering Ray and the shooting of this latter movie, I am reminded of one of the most touching "actor" stories I've ever had the privilege of hearing. This one happens to be true.

During the filming of *Body Fever*, Ray and a buddy went to Hollywood Ranch Market, then an open air market on Vine Street, to pick up a late night snack. As they walked away eating hot dogs, they noticed a big, poorly dressed derelict sitting on a bench. "Hey, isn't that Coleman Francis?" Ray asked. Sure enough, it was Francis, an actor reduced to poverty by old demon rum after many years of commercial success (*This Island Earth, Scarlet Angel*, et al.) Ray greeted the poor fellow warmly and offered him twenty dollars. Not wanting to embarrass him, Ray told Coleman the money was a down payment on a part he wanted Coleman to play the following morning. "Take it and get some chow. Then meet me at nine tomorrow morning at the laundromat on Santa Monica and Vine. I'll give you your lines then." Coleman thanked him, pocketing the twenty bucks. Ray's friend was sure that Coleman would spend the money on booze, but Steckler decided to be at the laundromat the next morning anyway, just in case. At exactly nine, he saw Coleman Francis walking across the street, dressed in a new suit of clothes. Instead of buying liquor, Coleman had taken the twenty dollars, gone to the Salvation Army and bought a suit so he would look good in his new role... whatever it might be.

Who Let the Dogs Out?

What entitles John Cassavetes, Tim Sullivan, and Ray Dennis Steckler to primary mention in any discourse of the American film revolution? What was the "common bond" that bridged these disparate artists together? All three filmmakers, Cassavetes by happenstance, Sullivan by design, Steckler by sheer hubris, managed to do their work completely free of the studio system, and in spite of all the obvious flaws in their endeavors, they managed to get their small, black and white movies reviewed, distributed, and displayed to a worldwide audience. In doing so, they opened the gates to the future of film and illuminated a pathway for the growing army of irascible, energetic, and courageous artisans who lurked impatiently in the alleyways of the town's tomorrows.

The author stalks leggy Liz Renay across the Hills of Topanga.
Photo courtesy of the author.

The Crash of Camelot

The joke goes that Charles Dickens and his agent are having lunch and discussing the newly written *A Tale of Two Cities*. The agent looks at the manuscript briefly, then throws it on the table in front of the noted author. The agent demands, "Come on, make up your mind. Was it the best of times or the worst of times?" Such was the situation in late November 1963.

On the morning of November 22, I was in a good mood. The start of the decade had gone well with the United States under our new president, JFK. He had faced the Russians out of Cuba and single-handedly invigorated the rest of us to shape up. He had a sense of style, a sense of humor, and a positive conviction that tomorrow would be even better than today.

It was about ten thirty in the morning when I walked into the kitchen to pour my kid some orange juice. I'd had friends over the night before; we had been listening to folk songs, an LP by The Limeliters and a new album of Bud and Travis, recorded live during a performance at the Ash Grove on Melrose Avenue. We finished the evening convulsed with laughter over Vaughn Meader's hilarious comedy recording, a spoof of the Kennedys called *The First Family Album*.

There was a radio on top of my refrigerator, tuned to a local station playing music from the Big Band Era, Benny Goodman and some Stan Kenton. The music was suddenly interrupted, the announcer's voice came on the air, breathless, obviously excited. "Oh, my God! The President has been shot! In Dallas, just moments ago, three shots fired…John F. Kennedy was riding in a motorcade… Oh, my God! Blood sprang from his head; he fell face down in the backseat. His wife Jackie screamed, 'Oh, no!' trying to lift his head—"

That fateful morning in 1963 put an instant end to Vaughn Meader's comedy career. More dramatically, it brought Camelot crashing to the ground and ushered in what most of us would refer to thereafter as "the day America lost its innocence."

Chapter Four

Stuntman Bob Ivy flips through an inferno in Warlords.
Photo courtesy of the Ivy Archives.

The Shuck 'N' Jive Of '65

The cultural revolution in cinema was an accident. It was an attempt by Hollywood shysters and money mongers to cash in commercially by reflecting what they considered 'hip.' The idealism and confrontation came from street outlaw-artisans—the independent and hungry writers, directors, actors. The effect on the public was profound.
—Gary Kent, Radio Interview, Austin, Texas, 1997

In 1965, when we returned from Kanab, Utah, we knew we had managed to make ourselves a couple of good movies, *Ride In The Whirlwind* and *The Shooting*. We trudged back to Hollywood exhausted, with several large reels of negative film, three months of dirty laundry, and a healthy exhilaration from a job well done.

The Year That Was

1965 was the year Bob Dylan set aside his acoustic, grabbed a Stratocaster, plugged in with The Paul Butterfield Blues Band at the Newport Folk Festival, and, in one massive surge of wattage, changed the sound of folk and rock music forever. Folk purists were incensed. Rumor has it (wrongly) that folk-singing icon Pete Seeger ran backstage with an ax to cut the power cables so the audience could "at least hear the lyrics!"

It was also the year when Russ Meyer, the self-proclaimed Fellini of Sexual Cinema, embraced his Gothic yearnings and produced a trio of bra-less skin flicks that accentuated his earlier work, *The Immoral Mr. Teas*. Meyer tested the patience of the indecency police and the American Judicial System in matters relating to nudity in film with his best work, *Faster Pussycat, Kill! Kill!* In and out of the Los Angeles courts throughout

75

'65, Meyer finally won. From then on, filmic nudity, in many cases, would be considered "art."

Meyer's triumph opened the sound stage doors to the nudie cuties and to an army of prurient, greedy producers anxious to cash in on the public's thirst for a glimpse of the naked female form beaming down on them from a giant silver screen. That same year the major studios released a wonderful movie that, for the first time in legitimate American cinema, showed a woman's body, naked from the waist up. Directed by Sidney Lumet, the picture won multiple awards: for direction, writing (Mort Fine and David Friedkin), and acting (Rod Steiger). Its title: *The Pawnbroker*.

All that we see or seem, is but a dream within a dream.

—Edgar Allan Poe, 1827

With the hottest days of summer '65 melting the sidewalks, my wife Rose Mary (aka Laura Benedict), our boys Chris and Alex, and I had decided to take an apartment half a block from the sands of Manhattan Beach, twenty-five miles south of Los Angeles. After the stifling dust and rigors of the Utah badlands, the cool breezes of the Pacific were a godsend. I dived into the first roller before the car was unpacked.

By sheer coincidence, Jack Nicholson, his wife (actress and ex-Playboy Playmate, Sandra Knight), and their toddling daughter Jennifer had rented an apartment just across the street, twenty feet nearer the water. The apartment Jack took was on the lower deck of a two-story. The best apartment, top right hand corner, facing the ocean like the captain's quarters on a Navy frigate, was occupied by the stentorian actor Brandon Carroll and his wife Vanna.

So, a goodly portion of our gypsy band from the Utah shoot found ourselves neighbors once again, stepping on each other's beach blankets on a daily basis. We body surfed, hung-out, drank-up, stoned-out, all at once. Since Jack, Brandon, and I had apartments practically on the beach, it quickly became a gathering spot for others from the Utah shoot and our Hollywood pals in general. The handsome John Hackett was a frequent guest, as were Walter Phelps, Don Jones, Harry Dean Stanton, several stuntmen, copious grips, and scores of other film folk.

At first, time spent at Manhattan Beach seemed more tranquil than a Sunday morning on St. Martens. It was, however, an illusion.

Burn, Baby, Burn

In August '65, a large section of Los Angeles known as South Central exploded into red fire and choking smoke, ignited by the long festering rage of the black and minority citizenry of the City of Angels. Dubbed by an excitable and frightened press as "The Watts Riots," the conflagration lasted six days.

The Watts Riots began on August 11, when Lee Minikus, a California Highway Patrol officer, pulled over Marquette Frye, a black man, and his brother Ronald on suspicion of drunk driving. Suddenly, out came the trey-eights, the four-fives, the gages, and the breakdowns. *The attack was on!*

The world at large began to mirror the growing tumult. The riots had ignited people's imaginations, fanning the flames of white fear and black resentment. When the end finally came, thirty-four people were dead and hundreds more injured. Thirty million dollars' worth of property had been destroyed. Over one hundred square blocks of South Central had been decimated.

Jorge, my upstairs neighbor, haunted by the riots across town, bought himself a .22 pistol. "They come after me, homes, I pull my deuce-deuce and start makin' me some jungle-bunny pepperoni, some a' that chongo chow-mien, homes!"

The veil of contented leisure at Manhattan Beach was rapidly disintegrating. Indeed, the entire city of Los Angeles could no longer be considered laid back. By the fall of '65, the most popular song in the nation was "Eve of Destruction" by Barry McGuire. To many of the confused people of the United States, and much of the world at large, '65 was the year the 60s really began.

> *The world has achieved brilliance without wisdom....Ours is a world of nuclear giants and ethical infants.*
>
> —General Omar Bradley, Armistice Day Address

There was something else in the air in the waning days of summer '65. Something besides the odorous fear permeating from the ashes of the Watts Riots. Some other game was afoot, and we all knew it or at least those in the loop did. It resonated in the disdain the young held for "The Corpolopolis," and in the increasing uneasiness and tensions regarding Vietnam; in the lack of voting rights for blacks and minorities in general; and the lack of equality for women at home and in the workplace.

In San Francisco, for instance, social anarchy had hit the streets thinly disguised as a love fest. Centered in Golden Gate Park, it took on the color of tie-dye, beads, and the beat of different drummers. Marijuana and lysergic acid diethylamide

(LSD) were the fuel that energized what appeared to be a genuine artistic and cultural revolution. Radical politics were taking off at Berkeley, "cross the bay." In January of '65, a New Year's Costume Ball was held by the Council on Religion and the Homosexual. Bay Area police harassed the gathering multitudes and thus began the turning point for the Gay Rights Movement.

In May, the San Francisco Civic Auditorium presented an historical concert, offering The Rolling Stones, The Byrds, Paul Revere and the Raiders. In August, the first folk nightclub in San Francisco opened on Fillmore, in the Marine district, with a new band called The Jefferson Airplane. September brought The Beatles to the Cow Palace. Pandemonium broke out, fans rushed the stage. It was the beginning of the biggest musical renaissance of the century, jump-started in the city where singer Tony Bennett had left his heart. The North Beach literary scene and its Beatnik veterans marched across town to a newer and more engaging area, one centered around the crossing of two street signs, Haight and Ashbury.

The San Francisco music, political, and literary scenes exploded into protest, creativity, and drugs. With all of the consumption of weed, the flowers, the hugging, chanting, the burning of incense, it appeared that it was only a matter of days or weeks before some serious confrontation erupted between the hippies and the establishment that would change the world forever, perhaps, even, for the better!

Who Gives a Continental Damn?

In Southern California, however, it was all wrapped in a different cloak, especially in the Hollywood community. At first, the hippies and left-over Beats were given their own space to dance and play. L.A.'s Griffith Park, Venice Beach, and the canyons, Laurel and Topanga, became the playground. They smoked a little pot, gave out free food, and made love with an almost tender poetry connecting their random couplings.

The movie people largely ignored them, writing them off as a colorful curiosity. The hippie flowering that the "suits" of tinsel town did embrace was the recognition that women had breasts concealed under all of those blouses and sweaters. Screenwriters were at last able to include these enticing orbs in their screenplays. To the studios, this was itself a genuine revolution. But, the "New Hollywood" was in fact the "Old Hollywood."

The hit American film of '65 was Julie Andrews, skipping her patent-leathered way across the high meadows to *The Sound of Music*; entertaining, yes, but about as daring and exciting as a bus transfer. With the exception of Stanley Kubrick's riotous look at the cold war in *Dr. Strangelove*, the aforementioned *The Pawnbroker*, and *Cat Ballou*, with Lee Marvin as a hilarious, drunken "black hat," riding into our lives on a sway-backed, equally disabled horse, the major studios were sitting on their bloated behinds. Instead of making great films, they were making starlets and pondering where to go for the evening's dinner/entertainment. Even the "big" stars seemed more concerned with looking "uptown and chic" than they were in lending their looks and talents to the kind of aggressive, challenging, breakthrough cinema coming out of the rest of the world. The stars were available for market openings, magazine articles, cigarette ads, but it seemed that in America, mink stoles, ties, and tuxedos ruled wardrobes, and filming itself was done with an attitude bordering on boredom.

Backbone, Talent, Gumption, and Grit

In Europe, auteur writer/director Ingmar Bergman had already released several of his masterpieces on the travails of the human psyche: *The Virgin Spring*, *The Seventh Seal*, *Through a Glass Darkly*, *Persona*, and my personal favorite, *Wild Strawberries*. Future Hollywood bad boy, Roman Polanski, was hunkered down in Poland, passionately cranking out classics like *Knife In The Water*, and, in '65, *Repulsion*, his chilling tale of sexual repression and a woman's descent into madness. In France, Francois Truffaut surfed the New Wave with *The Four Hundred Blows* and *Soft Skin*; in Japan, Akiro Kurosawa had already produced his masterpieces *Roshoman* (1950) and *Yojimbo* (1961); in Italy, Fellini's *Juliette of The Spirits*, Antonioni's *Three Faces of a Woman, La Notte* (1961), and Francesco Rosi's bloody homage to the art of bullfighting, *The Moment of Truth*, amazed us all. In the UK, gorgeous newcomer Julie Christi set the screen ablaze playing a tramp and a vamp, from platz to palace, in the delectable *Darling*. Everyone, it seemed, was headed into exciting and formerly forbidden terrain in motion pictures, everyone, that is, except the Americans.

> *The heroic lie is a cowardice. There is only one heroism in the world: To see the world as it is, and to love it.*
>
> —Romaine Rolland, *The Geography of Hunger*

I vividly recall being dragged up a warped staircase in the early 60s to a threadbare Hollywood screening room for an "invitation only" viewing. The film was titled *Private Property*, directed by Leslie Stevens. It starred unknowns Corey Allen, Kate Manx, and Warren Oates. The story was a bizarre, frank, and harsh examination of capitalism and sexual ownership with hints of a hidden homosexual relationship thrown in for good measure. It was brilliantly written, acted, and directed. It was also an independent production, mounted by Stevens and his producers for a mere $60,000. It was released in Denmark in 1960 to rave reviews and re-released in that same country in 1965. Almost nobody in the United States has ever seen the film. Hooray for Hollywood?

I'll Have a Double Martini With a Black Olive

According to the public's understanding (achieved primarily through the reading of the prepackaged publicity from Movie Magazines such as *Modern Screen*, *Photoplay*, et al.), all of Hollywood seemed as happy as a banjo and rich as bread buttered on both sides. Hollywood was certainly glamorous. It just was not relevant in a world that, culturally, was bursting at the seams.

There were several watering holes in Hollywood one could always count on in the mid to late 60s to harbor, at any given time, a variety of film folk: producers, agents, directors, stars, etc. Many of the big names and members of the bourgeoisie hung out at the larger clubs and dinner houses, such as Lawry's, The Tail O' The Cock, and Chasen's on La Cienega (where George Burns and The Marx Brothers occupied the same front booth for three decades).

There was The Cloister on Sunset Boulevard, where tinsel town hoydens Jayne Mansfield and Marie MacDonald smiled like lighthouse beacons while their bodyguards hustled them to a table, front and center; The Brown Derby on Vine Street, where Burt Lancaster and partner Harold Hecht frequently took lunch; there was Ciro's, where the town's dream team, Dean Martin and Jerry Lewis, performed every other week for the dressy Beverly Hills crowd. Martin and Lewis would alternate their act with cutting-edge comedian Lenny Bruce. In spite of an audience dressed to the nines, Lenny, ever the rebel, always wore blue jeans while hurling sexual, racial, and political fastballs to his astonished audience.

There was Upstairs At The Downstairs and La Taverna. Further east, on Melrose Avenue, near Paramount and RKO Studios, was Nikodel's, where you could often spy, in my humble opinion, the greatest Sherlock Holmes ever, Basil Rathbone, meeting up with his cohort, Dr. Watson (Nigel Bruce). There were major stars at supermarket openings, Christmas and Easter parades, and footprint implants at Grauman's Chinese Theater on Hollywood Boulevard. Everything in Hollywood was expensive, new and exciting, except for America's largest and most profitable export, the major studio motion picture. Hollywood was just not telling the truth about contemporary life and most of us knew it.

We Are Not You!
—Battle cry of the Independent filmmaker, 1965

Actresses Jayne Mansfield and Marie McDonald arrive at The Cloister with a bevy of assistants and bodyguards. Photo courtesy of the author.

Jack Nicholson was wrestling the freeways daily from Manhattan Beach into Hollywood, where he and director Monte Hellman were splicing together the footage we had shot in Utah. They were also, by sheer hubris, trying to keep Roger Corman's waning interest alive long enough to secure distribution and a few guaranteed play dates before they ran out of gas money. Corman wanted a sure thing and was dubious about these two "difficult" Westerns. The studios controlled most of distribution and exhibition. They ignored the risky films for what they considered the *vox populi*. To Roger, our films were more poppycock than populi.

John Cassavetes' master work, *Shadows*, done years earlier, had not yet found a distributor in spite of Cassavetes winning a special award from the United Nations. His star, Lelia Goldoni, won a BAFTA as "America's Most Promising Newcomer In Leading Film Roles." But the U.S. distributors declared, "No one wants to see black!" Onto the shelf in the backroom it went, where it was soon joined by another genuine independent masterpiece, Michael Roemer's *Nothing But A Man* (1964). Roemer's film, starring Ivan Dixon (*Hogan's Heroes*) and Abbey Lincoln, was a warm, telling story of a black section hand working for the railroad, in love with a preacher's daughter, and the subsequent tribulations of their love for one another. In Europe, *Nothing But A Man* won the San Giorgio Prize as Best Film of 1964. "It's a waste case," American theater owners chided and this beautifully personal film, like Cassavete's *Shadows*, was confined to the dust bin of what might have been.

Tim Sullivan couldn't sell *Run Home Slow*, couldn't give it away even if it were Halloween candy. Ray Steckler's producer, George Morgan, was reduced to stuffing the reels of *Thrill Killers* into the trunk of his car and driving state to state peddling it like Tupperware. Independent movies seemed headed for boot hill when suddenly, everything changed. But, wait, I'm getting ahead of myself. I'm a stuntman, remember?

Big Boned Ideas

By the dog days of summer '65, when our little band of cinematic gypsies came straggling back to Los Angeles from the wilds of Utah, there wasn't a doubt in my mind that I was now a full fledged stuntman! I was convinced that my cajones, if not actually made of brass, were at least brass plated.

Although our infamous Governor's Cup Race had not been allowed to occur in the solitary streets of Kanab, I had managed to do a stagecoach fall, several saddle falls, a free-wheeling fist fight, and get myself chased by Indians through the Utah high desert while dressed in the flowing robes and golden accoutrement of an Aztec priest. Now I had an itch to get back into my elbow pads and fall off something or punch somebody through a window. It was obvious that these stunt folks were superb athletes, and they were the greatest gamblers in the world. The stakes were their bodies and their lives, just the ticket for a small town, country boy from Walla Walla, Washington—a lad raised with cougars, horses, and Huskies for playmates.

The problem for me, as I saw it, was that I needed more juice to get into the roistering world of stunts. In fact, now that I had some real creds, I was anxious to find more independents, films dealing with the real nitty and gritty of life. Also, I badly needed another job, one where I could risk my skin or at least road-rash a bit of it for some greenbacks. Rose Mary and I had just learned we had another little one on the way. I needed a union job to qualify for the Screen Actor's Guild superb maternity care. The rent was due, the boys needed shoes; there was the light bill, the gas bill, the phone bill, all the necessaries of bare bones existence that people face daily.

> *I'm sorry old friend, I got no money to lend,*
> *'cause I'm all in, down and out. If I had the money*
> *I'd be very glad to lend, but if I ever get a hold of*
> *that two-bits again, I'll hold that two bits till the end*
> *'cause I'm all in, down and out"*

—Depression Era Drinking Song, author unknown

It is an indisputable fact that the specter of unemployment attaches itself to the psyche of artists like barnacles to a sperm whale. Many in the movie industry, cast and crew alike, begin hustling their next gigs while still working on their present shoot. The main means of employment, in spite of all of the talk of agents and nepotism, is still word of mouth, conversations held or overheard or tips supplied by good friends who have managed to land a show and are willing to share information. In other words, it's very much who and what you know. Determined to be one of the "Stunt Elite," I decided to hit the streets of Hollywood and stir to life the glowing embers of the stunt fires.

Those looking to score a gig or who were working in or about to work in a motion picture flowed like columns of ants searching for sustenance between certain promising feeding grounds: The Raincheck Room on Santa Monica Boulevard and Barney's Beanery (several blocks west) and then up the hill to the Chez Paulette coffee house on the Strip, where long-legged actress Sally Kellerman, soon to be *M.A.S.H.* star "Hot Lips" Houlihan, worked tables as a waitress.

The Raincheck Room, or simply The Raincheck, as those in the loop called it, catered primarily to New Yorkers, out of work film actors, and crew. It was a bar/bistro where one could grasp a few moments of slack before trundling off to location for another shoot. The place was also a grab-bag of job contacts.

The street rap on The Raincheck was that *"Nobody but people who worked in film even knew it was there."* Located in an unsavory section of West Hollywood, The Raincheck was an easily overlooked small and unattractive greasy spoon. From the outside, it looked like a dump. Yet, during much of the 60s and 70s, it was one of the most popular and best kept secrets in the movie industry. People did not go to The Raincheck to be seen; they went there to not be seen!

Inside, the place was dark and cozy. A row of booths and tables lined one wall, facing a long bar. There was a large mirror and blackboard behind the bar, on which productions and up-coming productions would be listed telling us who was on location and where, who was having a birthday, etc. There was a nightly trivia question on the board and whoever was first to guess it right had free drinks for the night. You could also order an awesome New York steak, baked potato, and salad, all for just $4.95.

Owner Zell Davis, her bartender (Phil Pearl), and the waitresses were film friendly and knew most of the patrons by name. Although most of the clientèle were newbies, it was not unusual to catch a famous face or two on any given night. Liz Taylor and Richard Burton snuggling in a corner booth in the back; Shelly Winters (*Poseidon Adventure, Journey of Fear*), Rod Steiger (*On the Waterfront, Heat of the Night*), and Ben Gazzara (*Voyage of the Damned, The Big Lebowski*) chowing down on a New York strip in a circular booth in the center, while Robert Vaughn (*Man From U.N.C.L.E., Bullitt*), Scott Wilson (*In Cold Blood*), and Chuck Napier (*Silence of the Lambs*) were hugging the bar with Vaughn talking politics and Wilson and Napier heavily into arguing sports.

She-Bear in Tennis Togs

The criteria for admission to The Raincheck was not, however, stardom. It was this: Were you talented at what you did, be it camera, acting, makeup, etc., and could you get along with Zell Davis, the incendiary founder? Paul Lewis, our production manager from the Utah shoots, had been personally thrown out by Zell and "banned forever" at least a dozen times.

Once I was 86'ed from The Raincheck for just walking in with Paul and ordering a Scotch. Before you could say "on the rocks," Zell had us both by the neck, ushering us out of the place. Paul told me it was because of an accidental drenching of an actress with a glass of champagne he had been holding during one of Zell's opening night parties. A couple of weeks after the party, Paul was having lunch with director Paul Harrison (*H.R. Pufnstuf*). Zell came down on him about the champagne spilling incident. Suddenly, things got so quiet you could hear a rat cough. Then Paul exploded! Zell, a one-time pro tennis player, was told to get out of his face or her racquet would be placed assertively up her ample anus sideways! Zell, of course, bounced Paul out of the place. It was just a minor tiff that lasted over twenty years.

Wear Normal Pants but Carry an Awesome Left Hook

There was a small dart room in the back of the joint and an aged pinball machine. A back door led onto a cramped outdoor patio where many of the patrons gathered to catch fresh air (smoking inside and at the bar was still in vogue). It was on this patio that I witnessed Don Jones (Irish Frankie, remember?) whip a bar hound into cowering submission with his deadly left hook. Don was thin, and not overly tall. Many of the drunk clientèle picked Don out as the dude they were going to hassle. One particular evening some Neanderthal with his brains in his back pocket decided Don was just the right size for a beating. He didn't know, of course, that Don was really "Irish Frankie" in disguise. The guy threw a punch, missed. Don got irritated, clouded up, and started "disasterizing" the guy, sending him on an expense paid trip to the floor for some concrete soup and a couple of double hematomas.

Zell immediately manhandled Jones out of The Raincheck, where he joined Paul and I on the front sidewalk. We paused briefly to gather our bearings, then turned our size tens due west to check out the action festering at Barney's Beanery, Paul and Don looking for women or fights…and me…snooping around for word of work on worthwhile projects.

Getting Down in It

To simply get in the business at all is a feat in itself, to continue to work and prosper is an accomplishment worth recognizing, to survive is a miracle.

—Gene Scott Freese, Hollywood Stunt Performers, 1996

On the north side of Santa Monica Boulevard that serendipitous night in late fall of '65, passing time with Paul and Don, outside The Raincheck, all I could think about was grabbing another gig as a stuntman. I knew the odds of injury and death. They had been explained clearly to me by the burly boys from the *Daniel Boone* stunt crew. They might as well have been preaching to a covey of Wiccans. My mind had decided it for me. Hollywood was up to its paparazzi with actors and actresses, but there were not that many stunt people back then, not that

Top: In fighting trim, Don "Irish Frankie" Jones. Photo courtesy of Don Jones.
Bottom: Producer Paul Lewis after working with the author. Photo courtesy
Paul Lewis.

many folks willing to risk it all on split-second timing, the reliability of a super-charged machine, or "jump ramps" stitched together by men you don't know who smell like bar rags! Most of young, male Hollywood wanted to be Tony Curtis or Rock Hudson. The gate to the world of stunts, therefore, was slightly ajar.

The quixotic little guy perched on the edge of my brain, my imaginary childhood pal, Mr. Boo, told me good fortune and serendipity were sitting on a barstool at Barney's. Any good psychotic will tell you to "listen to those voices inside of your head."

We hoboed our way to Barney's, Paul, Don and I, and my cranial crony, Boo. We passed the closed-down filling station, the used furniture store, the hospital supply store, a dark alley or two, then past the used-overhead-fan emporium and the abandoned building that smelled of feral human urine. We ambled by the tire repair shop, skipped over the long-abandoned trolley tracks, once used to ferry Angelenos from downtown L.A. to the beach at Santa Monica, before we began to hear the vocal yin and yang bellowing from Barney's, still a half a block away.

Fagots Stay Out!

—Sign (misspelled) above the bar at Barney's Beanery

Barney's Beanery is better absorbed than described. However, it is such an iconic place for the town's restless humanity, I feel compelled to attempt an explanation of its historic mojo.

Barney's was the rowdy child of John "Barney" Anthony, an ex-Navy man and a boxing manager from the Berkley Bay area of California. It was there that he started his first restaurant, but the lure of a warmer climate drove him to the present location on Santa Monica Boulevard in Southern California. At the time, Santa Monica Boulevard was known as Route 66, an historic thoroughfare in American road lore, at once a cattle trail and a Gold Rush conduit from the West Coast to Chicago.

Barney's carries the arguable reputation of being the second oldest restaurant in Los Angeles. When Barney threw it together with used planks and railroad ties, there were nothing but road-ruts to lure traffic. Barney did well selling his bowls of famous beans to the travelers coming and going on their way to personal nirvanas. Besides beans, Barney was famous for his onion soup, oyster crackers, waffles, pancakes, burgers, and chili.

In spite of the "Fagots Stay Out" sign, that misspelled piece of homophobia tacked above the bar, the customers pretty much ignored the warning, including Barney. He treated everyone like they were his buddies. This semi-tough guy was actually a pussy cat and could always be counted on for a free meal or a little cash, especially for actors, artists, and writers down on their luck. The press called Barney's a "shack," a "shanty," "dinky and dirty" with "soiled pool tables," a "hole, reeking with the odors of cheap liquor, sweat, and greasy food." But the movie star crowd, the artisans, writers, painters, etc., took a shine to Barney and his roughhouse, roadhouse, *laissez faire* behavior. They absolutely loved the place.

Major stars discovered Barney's in "the old, old days." Clara Bow, John Barrymore, Jean Harlow, Clark Gable, Errol Flynn. Later, it was The Doors, who popped in, along with Jimi Hendrix, artists Ed Ruscha, John Altoon, and Dennis Hopper; writers as diverse as Charles Bukowski and Shana Alexander. Janis Joplin is rumored to have had her last drink there; Quentin Tarantino wrote much of his megahit *Pulp Fiction* from a booth at Barney's.

The joint really came alive around two in the morning, when everything else was closing down. That was about the time Paul, Don, Boo, and I strolled in.

I squeezed onto a stool at the bar and ordered my usual Scotch on the rocks. The first sip was as soft and smooth as silk shorts, so I had another one before looking the place over to see what kind of action was coming down. I have always figured that people come to bars for four reasons: to lose themselves; to find themselves; because they're lonely; or because they want to be alone. At Barney's, they came mostly to be part of something—what, I don't know—sort of a creative chaos, I suppose.

Barney's was noisy as a cage full of sun conures. Everyone was talking at once; the jukebox was blaring; the click of pool balls fighting it out on the worn, green tables; waiters and waitresses yelling orders to Barney, who still worked the kitchen; and the constant shuffle of feet, doors opening and closing. Oh, one could think at Barney's, but only if you were very, very good at ignoring civilization in its most haphazard and disorderly state.

I saw Jones throw a quarter down on a pool table side-rail, queuing up for the next game. The place was jammed with the usual artistic hedonists. A restroom door opened and Dennis Hopper emerged, talking and gesturing wildly to no one in particular, wrestling with the zipper on his fly while clasping some kind of devil's brew tightly in his free hand like a baton at a track meet.

From my vantage point at the center of the bar, I could scope the place fairly easily. There were the usual bikers, looking for free women and easy trouble, and the intellectuals, jabbering away about Albert Camus, Heidegger, Sartre, Nietzsche, or Henry Miller. There were beefy weightlifters from the nearby athletic club, and, of course, the movie and art crowd. I saw Paul Lewis, Smirnoff in hand, having a heated discussion with infamous L.A. writer/poet/screenwriter Charles Bukowski.

Bukowski was an unpleasant drunk, a womanizer, a homophobe; unshaven and unbathed; an abusive leftover from the Beat Generation. He was as ugly as a mummy with its wraps off. He was not only constantly commode-hugging, knee-walking plastered, he was also prolific and frequently brilliant as a writer. Much of his stuff was a lot of garbled wordage, but some of his works like *Barfly*; *The Crossing Guard*; *The Post Office*; *Erections, Ejaculations, Exhibitions and General Tales of Ordinary Madness* are exquisite pieces of literature. L.A. embraced him for thirty years. He chronicled for us the winos, the people with the broken dreams and threadbare hearts. He was L.A.'s manic-depressive in residence, unanimously lauded as our own personal, truculent drunk.

Paul Lewis was more refined, a staunch defender of literary facts, and a finalist in the now legendary Governor's Cup Race! In fact, Paul was still struggling to get the high desert dust out of his lungs. It was going to take a few more vodkas to complete the job. With each drink, the talk between him and Bukowski heated up a degree or two. I wasn't worried about Paul, though. The son of a CIO Union organizer, Paul's hard heart was always secretly with the blue collar barn-burner, the guy with his sleeves rolled up. Built stocky and tough, he could have easily passed for a trooper in the Armia Krakow (the Home Army) during the Polish resistance in WW II. The conversation between the two literary *bon vivants* was rapidly approaching fisticuffs. I decided to move to another side of the room to avoid the breaking glass.

"Gar! Hey, buddy!" It was John Hackett, Jack Nicholson's friend, who had worked with us in Kanab. We had become drinking pals at the least, and he had been to my place at the beach a few times for dinner and a swim. John had taken my two boys, Chris and Alex, body surfing. Hackett had been a front-line combat soldier in Korea, which greatly impressed my kids. He had many scary, breathtaking tales to tell involving fear, fighting, and the escaping of death with your ass in your helmet and your bravado in quick retreat.

Forced to stand behind the raucous crowd at the bar, John and I shook hands and began yelling ourselves a conversation. John was a close friend of Robert Vaughn's, the dashing star of one of television's top series, *The Man From U.N.C.L.E.* It turned out that Vaughn's regular stunt double was taking a two-month leave to coordinate the film *What Did You Do In The War, Daddy?* MGM, the studio that produced *U.N.C.L.E*, was looking for someone to double Vaughn and coordinate the stunts on the show until the regular guy returned. Hackett had recommended me to Vaughn for the job.

"What did you say to him?" I asked.

"I told him you had a lot of balls."

Trying to look relaxed, blasé even, I took a strong snort of Scotch before asking the big question, "And what did he say?"

"He said," Hackett motioned for another drink. "He said that he didn't know anyone had more than two."

Kickin' Back on Tunnel Vision

Lunchtime, my second show on *The Man From U.N.C.L.E.* It was less than a month since I had wandered through the gates of MGM Studios in Culver City to be checked out by Robert Vaughn and the director of photography to see if I could pass as Robert's stunt double. The answer was an encouraging yes. I was sent to the makeup department to have my hair cut to match Robert's in its distinct stylishness. I was still shaggy from the Utah Westerns, whereas Vaughn (an Oscar nominee, three-time Golden Globe nominee, and winner of an Emmy) was dapper and suave, more a James Bond than a Jesse James.

The Man From U.N.C.L.E. (United Network Command for Law Enforcement) was in its second season. It started out with a middling following. Shot in black and white, it had a serious demeanor but not much originality. Then, in the season that followed, it changed to color, moved to prime-time Friday nights, and took on a semi-campy patina. Double entendres were allowed, as was Vaughn's sense of comedic irony. *U.N.C.L.E.* producers even came up with an arch nemesis, T.H.R.U.S.H. (The Hierarchy for the Removal of Undesirables and the Subjugation of Humanity). Well known show-biz names were invited on as guests. Soon major stars were queuing up for the chance to appear on what had quickly become a hit show. They usually played the villains and as such were allowed to be as outrageous and flamboyant as they wanted.

My first show had been titled the "Adriatic Express Affair." Besides Robert Vaughn as lead U.N.C.L.E. agent Napoleon Solo, the series starred David McCallum as co-agent Illya Kuryakin, seasoned pro Leo G. Carroll as Chief Waverly, and guest stars Juliet Mills and Jessie Royce Landis. Juliet was an Emmy winner, three-time Golden Globe Nominee, and the sister of actress Hayley Mills. Ms. Landis was an international star, appearing in over a hundred films, including *Airport*, *To Catch a Thief*, and *North By Northwest*.

I was made to feel at home the first time I stepped onto the set. Vaughn himself had established a mood of casual professionalism which resonated through other cast members and the crew. David McCallum was a hoot. Usually in a jolly state of mind, he liked to do his own stunts, the easy stuff, anyway, like jumping out of trees onto people, or diving through windows.

Television is a much faster animal than film. Shoot it, print it, and let's move on: Time is money, honey! That first show had consisted of me doubling Vaughn in a fight inside and on top of a speeding train, The Adriatic Express of the title. I was lucky. Most of the fight took place in a baggage car, so when the bad guy and I knocked each other around, we fell into mail sacks and soft luggage. My sparring partner was George Sawaya, an experienced stuntman and actor. Unfortunately, we had to constantly stop the fight to allow George time to have a cigarette. Everyone seemed more than happy, however, after George and I chased each other over, through, and about the speeding Express. Suddenly, wow, pow! It was lunchtime on my second show, "The Very Important Zombie Affair." Already, I felt like an old *U.N.C.L.E.* hand.

Prime Virginia Ham and Sharp Vermont Cheddar

I was now doing stunts on one of the hottest shows in television. In spite of my previous prejudice, I knew that for me, this one was not going to be an ordinary ham and cheese sandwich. *Man From U.N.C.L.E.* was an American Croque Monsieur. Ham and cheese, yes, but made of the finest ingredients and delicious to the taste.

Sitting at lunch tables erected outside of a Gothic mansion on the MGM back lot, under fake Caribbean foliage, surrounded by extras dressed as zombies, it was easy to forget the turmoil that was building throughout the USA. Rage! Black rage; rage at the machine; young rage; old rage; working class rage. Liberals, college students, iconoclasts were tired of the lies from government, from educators, world leaders, and, worst of all, from their own families. Folks, it seemed, were fed up with the greed, the small, selfish ideas trickling down from the American Corporate Culture.

At night, after the martini shot, when we were wrapped and moving on to various destinations, it was increasingly clear that *"the times, they were a changing."* The hippies and flower children had begun to stray from the parks, from the canyons, and now swirled provocatively up and down the boulevards. The smell of ganja was becoming noticeable in some public places and a new collage of frenetic, psychedelic artwork plastered itself, seemingly overnight, on storefronts, walls, and freeway overpasses. Every other seeker was reading R. Crumb's *Underground Comix*, the *L.A. Free Press*, and *Be Here Now* by former Harvard professor turned New Age guru, Ram Dass. "Peace, brother. Love. Tune in, turn on, drop out!" These became the catch phrases of the times.

The establishment was furious. They saw this as the handiwork of a generation of insignificant malcontents, whereas, the protesters, raised in the shadow of the atomic bomb, considered themselves pioneers and pilgrims seeking the truth! Robert Vaughn was a staunch Democrat and close friend of Robert Kennedy's.

Kennedy was a particular hero of much of the counter culture, incorruptible and not intimidated by the thugs and the scoundrels of business as usual.

In contrast to the chaos, the set of "Zombie Affair" was as steady and smooth as crème brûlée. One of the pleasures of working *U.N.C.L.E.* was the mood, the enthusiasm of cast and crew. It was Christmastime '65, and everyone was in a festive spirit, just like in a Dickens novel, except story wise, we were supposed to be on a lush tropical island. The guest stars for the episode were Claude Akins (*Rawhide, Bonanza*, etc.) and my buxom friend Linda Gaye Scott (who had played my crazed wife Julie Anne in *Run Home Slow*).

Linda was not only beautiful, she was also rich, the heiress to the Scott Paper Company. She was a talented, daring actress, throwing herself into her roles with vivacious, sexual energy and panache. Unfortunately, Linda always seemed to be cast as a ditsy blonde, as though blondes alone have cornered the market on what being "ditsy" is all about. The show itself was campy, unique. David McCallum, I, and several *U.N.C.L.E.* agents got to run around in the jungle attacking zombies, while Linda worked the local hotel as a manicurist and "come on" for Zombie Master, Claude Akins.

I did learn one valuable lesson on "Zombie Affair." After shimmying up a rope to the second story balcony of the mansion, I break in, and as Solo, begin to snoop around. Suddenly, I hear guards approaching, and conveniently duck into a large bedroom. I hide behind the door. A guard enters; he and I get into a brawl, which I, as Solo, of course, win. The problem was that the other stuntman scheduled for the day had called in sick. The director, David Alexander, asked me if I could pick a good fighter from one of the extras, sparing him the task of calling for, and waiting for, another stuntman.

"No problem," I assured Mr. Alexander.

I approached the extras and asked if any of them had athletic experience, thinking that would be a logical choice. An athlete should be able to handle a simple fight. One tall, blond fellow stepped forward. He assured me that he played basketball for UCLA and was handy as a backhoe. I picked him for the fight and together we worked on the staging. After three or four rehearsals, I told the director we were ready.

The minute we got into position and Alexander called "action," the basketball player forgot everything we had worked out. Stumbling over his own feet, he hit me squarely in the face! So I improvised! I grabbed him by his lapels and threw him on the bed. When he tried to get up, I slugged him, whispering, "Lay down, you son of a bitch, you're supposed to be out cold."

"Cut! Print!" Everyone seemed pleased with the fight, so we moved in for close-ups. Mr. Basketball apologized and I learned another valuable outlaw lesson.

Outlaw Rule #5

Never hire amateurs to do the work of a professional, especially for stunts.

I did several more *U.N.C.L.E.s* in 1966, working with Robert Strauss (nominated for an Oscar for *Stalag 17*) and Joyce Jameson, a busty, funny veteran of hundreds of television shows, including *Charlie's Angels*, *Rhoda*, and *Barney Miller*. I also got to work with some of the best stuntmen in the business, guys like Loren Janes, an ex-trigonometry professor and co-founder of The Stuntman's Association, and Jerry Summers, a master at car work. Summers was one of the lead drivers for the spectacular car chase in *The French Connection*. Janes was a stocky, no-nonsense type of guy, very serious in a way befitting ex-trigonometry professors, whereas Summers was more laid back, dark haired and handsome. He could have been a perfect double for teen heartthrob James Darren.

Later, while lounging at the beach with my sons, listening to The Kingston Trio blaring out a sanguine rendition of "Tom Dooley" from a nearby portable perched on our beach blanket, I began to realize, "The Kingston Trio? Wait a minute; it's not them anymore. It's Janis Joplin, The Lovin' Spoonful, The Beatles, Joni Mitchell, Joan Baez, and a Cree Indian chanteuse named Buffy St. Marie. We're getting out of touch here."

Later that day, while driving to MGM Studios to work "The Waverly Ring Affair," it finally sunk in that I was becoming mired in TV again. After those great, ground-breaking Westerns that Jack Nicholson and Monte Hellman had shot in Utah, it had come down to this! *Where were all the daring, zoom, take-a-chance-low-budget-independent movies I had vowed to work on?* They had disappeared. More and more directors and producers were coming from television, and few of them had a well-developed feel for storytelling and the visual sense that is the art of great film-making.

"Is it all over? Has TV conquered the American family, heart and soul?" Good question. If filmic courage was to be redeemed, where would the next generation of daring and dashing filmmakers come from? "Where, oh, where," I hummed, "has our little dog gone?" I, for one, didn't have a clue.

Chapter Five

Actor Bruce Willis receives instruction from director Richard Rush for Color of Night. *Photo courtesy Rush Archives.*

Undoing The Did That Was Done

The very first essential for success is a perpetually constant and regular employment of violence.
———Adolph Hitler, *Mein Kampf*, 1925

The shadow of a huge, burning cross flickered like a phantasm from Hell against the white wood covering the exterior of the church. From another angle, the cross itself looked horrific, reaching upward, with flames shooting up its sides, much like the swastika-draped, searchlight-lit banners that Nazi Albert Speer had mounted to incite the passions of the cheering masses gathered in Berlin to celebrate the dominance of the Third Reich.

In the foreground, clustered around this cruel symbol of the Ku Klux Klan were eerie, white-robed, hooded shapes of people. They shook their fists toward the church, shrieking oaths of belligerence and blood-chilling hatred. Now and again, a dark face would appear at a window, eyes white and wide with terror. Then the face would disappear, yanked quickly away, into the sanctity of the holy house. Just as the flames reached their highest peak, a voice boomed over the scene from a loudspeaker. "Cut. Print."

A medium-sized, well muscled man stepped out of the darkness and walked to the center of activity. He had black, slicked-back hair and an impressive mustache, a real doozy of a handlebar. It gave his chiseled face the appearance of a Prussian cavalry officer. Suspended from a chain around his neck was a 35mm viewfinder and a tusk taken from a wild boar, a tooth he professed to have worn on his helmet when he was "a Viking, in another lifetime." He was a weightlifter, an archer, a champion fencer, accomplished with foils, swords, rapiers, and all things sharp and pointed. He was Ted V. Mikels, director. We were in Bakersfield, California, a muscular town, half Western and half working class. We were filming a movie intriguingly titled *The Black Klansman*.

The Other Half of the Biscuit

The Black Klansman (aka *I Crossed The Color Line*) had been co-authored by my friend, Art Names (who I had ridden with to the Utah shoot) and his partner, John Wilson. The guys had gone to Mikels with a script they had just finished about a bank heist. Mikels liked the work and the three of them took it to Joe Solomon, a producer and financier.

Joe Solomon was a veteran of exploitation. Born in San Francisco, he had worked his way into film distribution and producing through a slick little number titled *Mom and Dad*. Joe took *Mom and Dad* around the states, playing it one territory at a time. He tub-thumped it in the local papers as a "true story of venereal disease and unwanted pregnancy!" Joe would get the word out to the local high schools that the film was a must see if the community wanted to wake the kids up to the horrors of a loose sexual life. He also handed out fliers stating that the picture was so stark in its portrayal of sinful realities that a "registered nurse" would be at each showing.

I was a sophomore in high school when Joe's picture opened in my home town of Renton, Washington. Oh, the buzz that went on! I was tightrope walking along the handrail that escorted the bridge across Cedar River (a feat I felt compelled to do if I was going to replace Burt Lancaster as Hollywood's reigning acrobat), when my pal Darwin McTighe ran up with the breaking news. Rumor had it that "Two girls had passed out at a screening of *Mom and Dad* and had to be taken to the hospital!"

We ate it up, couldn't wait to get to the theater. Although the picture itself was humdrum, naive even, it did great at the box office and Joe Solomon was on his way to a career in the motion picture business.

Ted Mikels pitched Art's caper screenplay to Solomon, whose response was tepid as used bathwater. "Instead," Joe suggested, "let's take advantage of the growing interest in black power. You know, the riots, shootings and the fire hoses? Get me a screenplay centered around that. If I like it, I'll put up the money."

Bombingham

The 60s were definitely in full swing as 1966 continued to unfold. Art and John began to observe the scene. Most of the discordant clamor was centered on a growing resentment of the situation in Vietnam. Other bits and pieces of angst were also spilling out of the closets and filtering through society as a whole. There was women's rights, voting rights, gay issues, contempt for the establishment, concern for the environment, animal rights, a back to nature movement (who can forget *Mother Jones*?), the black power movement, all with their own priorities and champions.

Huey Newton and Bobby Seale, two embittered chums from Merritt College in Oakland, California, got together and formed The Black Panther Party For Self Defense. Later, the name was shortened simply to The Black Panther Party. Militant in its posturing, idealistic in an almost socialist kind of way toward minority communities, The Black Panthers leaned heavily on the fresh memory of the Watts Riots, and even more so, on the bombing by white racists of the 16th Street Bethel Baptist Church in Birmingham, Alabama. Soon, they began attracting sympathy from other minorities and the white liberal community. Marlon Brando, everyone's favorite actor, took up the cause, as did Jane Fonda, Donald Sutherland, and other activists. Art Names and his partner tuned into the turmoil and began to stitch together the essence of their screenplay. They came up with *I Crossed The Color Line* (aka *The Black Klansman*).

The Black Klansman was loosely based on the Birmingham church bombing. In point of fact, between the mid 1940s and 1965, there had been over fifty bombings in the city, hence the menacing sound of the town's nickname, Bombingham. In the 1963 explosion on 16th Street, four young black girls were killed and twenty-three parishioners injured. Our film concerned a young man (Richard Gilden) who is light enough to pass for white. He infiltrates the Klan to find out who is responsible for the death of his daughter and exact revenge.

> *If ever there was a time to use the word 'hoot' to describe a film, then* The Black Klansman *is transcendental material. This film is 1966 exploitation, baby. If you've ever heard the 'N' word, you've still never heard it like this. Shocking today, even though no one has seen it. Beg, borrow, steal and investigate getting a hold of this film—brought to you by the guys who brought you films about zombies and grinding up women in bikinis. 4 out of 5 stars.*

—Internal Review, Internet Movie Data Base, 2007

Bustin' Moves

So, here we were in Bakersfield, getting ready to film the bombing of the church. The assistant directors were clearing all of the extras out of the building, away from the camera for their own safety. All of the extras were black townspeople we had hired for our movie. The Klansmen began to take off their robes and hoods. Hello! They were also black townspeople! Joe had hired them because they needed work, were available, and were actually getting a kick out of portraying white hate mongers. The minute they dropped the hoods over their black faces, they began shouting the "N" word and worse. Sometimes, we could hear righteous laughter coming from underneath the disguises.

We torched the church! Everyone yelled exuberantly as the flames spread throughout the building, crackling and lighting the sky like a Burning Man Festival in the Nevada desert. Sirens! Someone had called the police! Some citizen had told the cops that the Ku Klux Klan was holding a rally in Bakersfield! The fuzz were blown away when, after rounding up the Klansmen and pulling off their hoods, they discovered the hate mongers were all black! It took the influence of the local news crews to settle everyone down and restore a semblance of order to the town.

There were no stunts to speak of in *Klansman*. Mikels asked me to show the actors how to throw a few punches and that was it. I played a small part in a coffee shop scene and helped Three Finger Harry Woolman, who was doing effects, ignite his fireworks. Besides burning the church, Harry, or "Hairbreadth Harry" as he was often called, had to rig a pickup truck to drive headfirst, at full speed, into a large rock thus killing the main villain of the piece. I told Hairbreadth that I would be glad to drive the pickup toward the rock and bail out off camera-side just at the last minute. He would get his crash and his explosion without incident. But noooooo! This is the guy who accidentally set a whole valley on fire when we were filming *Ride In The Whirlwind*. Hairbreadth got his way and rigged the vehicle for the collision with the rock.

It was nighttime, pitch black, the last shot or so of our film. We had all gathered on a wide strip of sand hugging the banks of the Kern River. We were there to film Hairbreadth's gag. In the middle of the beach was a huge rock, as big as a house, lit from head to toe by the crew. Mikels didn't want to miss any of the shot or the accompanying fireworks. In the dark, completely off camera, we could hear the heavy breath of the Kern, its waters flowing swiftly past our staging area.

Everything was ready: camera, crew, director Mikels, and Hairbreadth Harry! The old special effects guru stood outside the pickup, his arms reaching through the window, making sure the steering wheel was tied tightly in position so the vehicle would go in a straight line into the rock. The motor was running. "Camera, marker…Action!" Harry threw the pickup into gear and ran out of the camera's view.

The pickup took off, coughing and spitting, right toward the rock. Then, as if driven by an angry poltergeist, it took a sharp left turn and disappeared into the darkness. A moment later, we heard a loud "kerplunk." The damn thing had headed right into the river. All Ted got on film was the ass-end of the pickup as it was swallowed by the dark. But, wait…the story gets even better. Ted was sure that Woolman was in the pickup, steering it toward the rock. Somehow, in Ted's mind, the old special-effects man had gotten caught in the truck, and was now submerged, gurgling in the black water at the bottom of the Kern. Ted dashed to the riverbank, shouting, "My God, get Harry out!!! Someone get Harry out, he's stuck in the truck! Get him out before he drowns!" Of course, Woolman never was in the pickup! He had just tied it off and aimed it toward the rock. Now Harry slithered up next to Ted, shouting, "Harry! Someone get Harry. Get him out of there. Hurry! Hurry! Somebody get Harry!" Ted and Harry stood next to each other on the bank, shouting out the alarm. It took Ted at least a minute to realize the endangered effects man was not endangered at all. In fact, he was actually standing only a few inches away, shouting for his own rescue.

Outlaw Rule #4

Beware of special effects men with names like "Three Finger" or "Hairbreadth."

Badass Movie Mofos

The Black Klansman accomplished two amazing feats, if nothing else. It raised the opening curtain on what would become known as the era of "blaxploitation," a word most blacks despised. Blaxploitation presented a plethora of action, adventure, and horror films starring mostly black casts that crossed over and were appreciated by white audiences: *Shaft*, *The Mack*, *Sweet Sweetback's Baadasssss Song*, *Blacula*, *Cleopatra Jones*, *Boss Nigger*, *Black Sampson*, etc. *Klansman* also introduced audiences for the first time to a creative bundle of energy by the name of Max Julien. Julien would become not only a force in blaxploitation, but in movies in general. His efforts also provided jobs for a plethora of previously ignored black personnel: crew, extras, stunt people, etc.

Max Julien was tall and lean as a lodge pole, so nice he'd lend you his last pair of long johns. He had an easy smile and possessed a talent that was at once electric and compelling. When we first arrived on the Bakersfield location, several of us rounders, including Max, sashayed ourselves to a local bar to drown our misfortunes and mistakes. Max, who had done stand-up comedy in the East, got up on a little stage and began his routine, just for our amusement.

Max was funny, too. He had us all in stitches. Suddenly, from out of the din and smoke at the back of the bar, a man came staggering toward the stage. He was big as an ox, obviously drunk, and looking for trouble. He reminded me of a used car salesman out for a night on the town. This unfortunate buffoon climbed up on the stage, crept up behind Max, and, leaning over his shoulder, began to sing off key, slobbering all over the microphone and Max's shoulder.

Surprise! There was a lightning fast movement from Max's free arm. Mr. Car Salesman doubled over, fell off the stage into the orchestra pit, landing in a pile of kettle drums. Max had given him a quick, strong elbow jab, right in the solar plexus. It was so fast, so well placed, no one was sure just what had happened. And Max? He didn't miss a beat of his routine, didn't even look at the drunk, coming or going. He laid out those laugh lines, grinning his friendly grin as he lung-crushed the wretched fellow into the timpani. "Cool," I thought. "I didn't even see it coming!"

My roommate on *The Black Klansman* was Bob Maxwell, the lighting director. Tall and sober in demeanor, with an innate decency about him, I had known and liked him from previous low budget films. He reminded me a bit of the famous Broadway star Richard Kiley (*Man of La Mancha*). Bob had that slightly receding hairline and large, intelligent eyes.

Bob's goal was to become an accomplished cinematographer, a dream he would realize when he was picked by Melvin Van Peebles to be the director of photography on the cross-over hit, *Sweet Sweetback's Baadasssss Song*. That film introduced the white audience to Van Peebles and his son Mario.

Maxwell was a quiet man, introspective, fun to converse with. He would listen to my ramblings, interrupting only now and then with some sage comment. I told him about the incident at the bar and how much I had been impressed with Max Julien. Bob's comment? "Why?" I was still pondering my answer when I heard him roll over, face the wall, and make the sounds one makes just before nodding off into deep sleep.

> *Thinking is the hardest work there is, which is the probable reason why so few engage in it.*
>
> —Henry Ford

"Hmmm?" (Me, doing my entree into some serious thinking of my own, a favorite pastime that sometimes got so interesting it consumed hours of valuable time). *Why did I like Max Julien?* I barely knew the man. Just met him a day ago. "Hmmm." Well, because: Max seemed totally himself. He was unpretentious and unimpressed with swagger, stardom, ego, cruelty, and what Texans refer to as "liars, damn liars, and politicians." He was thoughtful, even gracious in a street-smart way. Max was well read and intelligent. Faster than a dust devil, he was also not a physical pushover, as witness his quick dispatch of Mr. Drunk Car Salesman.

I could hear Mr. Boo, the bizarre little fellow that inhabits the thicket surrounding my brain, beginning a rancorous dialog: *"How can you tell about a person in just a day? It takes years to get to know someone!"*

"You are so wrong!" I uttered out loud, and then realized I had disturbed the slumbering Bob Maxwell. He shuffled around beneath his covers, then snorffed off again into dreamland. Good. Now I could continue thinking.

Could I tell much about a man on first meeting? Sure, I could. I was thirty-two-years old; I had spent much of my earlier years intermingling with and quietly observing people, places, and things, especially men. Born into a family of ranchers and wranglers, cavalrymen, soldiers, woodsmen, and barroom brawlers, I had an early education in what that whole "macho" business was all about. I had four sisters and no brothers, big or little. I had spent a good part of my life looking for one. (Hence, I manufactured myself the contumacious Mr. Boo, an imaginary playmate I had cobbled together years ago, when I was about four and playing alone and brotherless in the yard of that hardscrabble ranch in Walla Walla.

I love men; we're so stupid!

—John Cassavetes to Michael Ventura on the set of *Love Streams*

Max Julien and I became good friends on *Klansman* and have remained so for thirty years. We would do two more films together, *The Savage Seven* and *Psych-Out*. Somewhere along the way, he decided to write and star in the first hip, in your face, black-pimp-jivin'-fuck-whitey-flick ever made, one where the black dude is not only the lead, but also, the hero anti/hero, proud of his color and his persona. The picture was titled *The Mack*.

The Mack also starred Juanita Moore (*Imitation of Life*, *The Singing Nun*) and a brash young comedian named Richard Pryor. It was an enormous hit. Max would later write and star in a caper film, *Thomasine and Bushrod*, and write and co-produce *Cleopatra Jones*. He had an enormous influence on hip-hop culture and is frequently referenced by writer/director Quentin Tarantino, as well as in the films *Shaft* and *Foxy Brown*.

WEED!

Paul Lewis once confessed that he couldn't stand smoking pot because it was like getting laid at lunchtime. "It takes the edge off the day, and I gotta' have that edge or I can't do my work." He was somewhat of a minority, because the odor of Acapulco Gold, Panama Red, Maui Wowi, Thai Stick, Skunk, and Michoacan drifted like fog from underneath the closed bathroom doors at Hollywood parties.

It swirled around New Age hangouts like The Source and Cyrano's on the Strip and clung to the clothing of executives doing their business inside luxury suites at the posh hotels of Beverly Hills. Even though the hippies and drop-outs in Griffith Park and Venice Beach were toking openly in the late 60s, it was still a secret activity among the Hollywood community. Don't ask, don't tell!

Then some artistic renegade, some pissed-off cinematic pirate lit up a reefer openly on the Sunset Strip and the carnival, the revolution, and the police confrontations began in earnest.

Black militancy was definitely on the rise in 1966. Every L.A. street corner had a fierce looking, unsmiling, warrior coercing passersby into buying the *Nation of Islam* magazine, or handing out fliers that chronicled their anger. Dashikis and kinky Afros became the style of rebellion.

U.S. forces started the bombing of Cambodia and anti-war activists turned up the volume on their cries for disengagement. The government think-tanks became surly and condemning. On a positive note, Indira Gandhi, a woman, became prime minister of India and began mothering the country created by her father twenty-one years earlier.

In May of 1966, our son, Michael Balfour Kent, stepped into our lives, right along with the blooming of spring's first wild flowers. At the same time, 7/11 came out with the "Slurpee," a fruit flavored sludge of ice in a plastic cup. If you were a teenager in '66, and had your Slurpee and a bag of Doritos, you were hip, man. Can you dig it? Michael preferred mother's milk.

> *There's something happening here,*
> *what it is ain't exactly clear.*
> *There's a man with a gun over there,*
> *telling me I got to beware...."*

—Buffalo Springfield, *For What It's Worth*, 1966

Hollywood Boulevard! If New York's Broadway was the "street of dreams," Hollywood Boulevard was the street of disturbed sleep, of hangover nightmares, and garish neon. I was coming from a lunch at Love's Pit Barbeque with Rose Mary and our boys. Love's was one of the few good places left on the boulevard where a family or a loner would be welcomed and actually served decent food, barbequed beef sandwiches dripping with Love's original sauce, slaw, and a genuine New England pickle, big as a cucumber (ha!), a succulent treat shipped cross-country just for their guests. I had a business meeting further down the boulevard, near Highland Avenue. I decided to walk, letting Rose Mary and the boys get back to the 405 Freeway headed for Manhattan Beach. They would have a forty-five-minute drive at the least.

I glanced at the storefronts and the people on the sidewalk. A plethora of cheap souvenir shops, secondhand stores, and grubby pizza parlors lined this once elegant thoroughfare. There were signs of neglect and urban rot everywhere. It was populated with sad, wannabe starlets, wannabe musicians, runaways, derelicts, fevered traffic, and confused tourists, all looking for Hollywood. Only, Hollywood wasn't there.

The Hollywood they were searching for didn't exist. Ever. It was a gossamer bit of public relations fluff invented to lend mystique and glamor to what actually was a scheming, hard nosed, rough and tumble business, the business of making movies, and that "Hollywood" was in the San Fernando Valley, sequestered behind the walls and gates of Warner Brother's Studios, Universal, and Disney. It was in Culver City, at MGM and Hal Roach Studios; it was in the high-rise offices on the Sunset Strip, Wilshire Boulevard, and in Beverly Hills. It was in the mansions of exclusive, gated Bel Air; in the wedding cake houses hugging the shoreline at Malibu. Hollywood was also on location, almost anywhere in the world but "Hollywood."

It was an unpleasant afternoon, smoggy, with the much envied sun of the Golden State fighting for recognition through the gray, noxious sludge obscuring the tops of the buildings. The smog obliterated any tourist sighting of the famous "HOLLYWOOD" sign which decorated the nearby hills.

"If Brando and Nicholson keep it up, they can do my acting for me," I said out loud. Why not? Nobody was paying attention to me; besides, half of the pedestrians were talking just as loud, if not louder, chatting away their resentments, their dreams, their follies, talking with friends and partners or talking to themselves, as if memorizing lines for an upcoming production.

The area had a few known characters who trekked from one end of the boulevard to the other, caught a second of slack, then repeated the journey the opposite way. They made this trip on a daily basis. They were pretty much objects of curiosity if not downright disdain. Here comes Johnny Fuck Fuck yelling several full throated "fuck its," pumping his arm violently as he bobbed and weaved his way through the human hoard.

It was Don Jones, who frequented the boulevard more often than I, who told me that Johnny Fuck Fuck suffered from Tourette syndrome, a neurological disorder causing tics, involuntary and sudden movements, and repeated vocalizations which were often forbidden and/or obscene. Poor Johnny plied his way along the sidewalk, never making eye contact, but perpetually shouting out his barrage of curse words and flapping his arms like a disoriented duck. I wondered where he lived and if anybody loved him.

There were other strange folk who frequented this forlorn strip leading to nowhere, to the corner of La Brea Avenue, then turning back on itself. I passed the eerie Weird Museum, which had a real human embryo floating around in a bottle and a genuine "shrunken head!" I accepted a leaflet from a man promising redemption and reward through a process called Silva Mind Control, and bumped smack into Boulevard Bill.

Boulevard Bill was a strange character who always appeared on the sidewalk dressed in a buckskin suit, cowboy boots, and ten-gallon hat. He had a trim, white mustache and beard, resembling in many aspects the Buffalo Bill of frontier and Indian fighting fame. This Boulevard Bill, however, was an enigma. He made eye contact, but never spoke, never acknowledged anyone past a slight nod or wink of the eye. No one seemed to know his story. Bill just traversed his way daily from Vine to Highland, scanning the horizon with steel-blue eyes, looking for Indian sign I suppose.

I crossed to the north side of the street. I was nearing my final destination, Musso & Frank's Grill. In the block before the restaurant, I saw The Player, a middle-aged black man wearing a baseball glove and cap. The Player would endlessly catch an imaginary ball, look it over, and then pitch the imaginary ball to an imaginary batter somewhere around an imaginary home plate further up the sidewalk. The Player was usually a fixture in an imaginary ball park just above Sunset, on Western Avenue, an even seedier part of town, with dollar movie emporiums that showed films like *Mondo Cane, Mondo Weirdo*, or a variety of Russ Meyer skin flicks. Rum-dums, derelicts, hookers, and panhandlers abounded. I was overjoyed to see that The Player had been bumped up to the major leagues.

Musso & Frank's! I stood outside those hallowed doors inhaling the aura of old Hollywood. The heavy glass door panels were exquisitely etched in clef swirls and the panels had brightly polished brass door handles. I grabbed one, swung it open, and stepped into film noir, circa 1930.

In what was known as the town's Golden Era, Musso & Frank's Grill was the Hollywood crowd's favorite restaurant. It still is, eighty years later. All of the other legendary restaurants, Chasen's, Romanoff's, The Trocadero, The Brown Derby, have vanished from the scene. Only Musso's is still standing, still serving the artistic, the famous, the elegant, and the romantic. The place, famed for its martinis, serves old-time food: thick steaks, twice baked potatoes, beef stroganoff, sauerbraten, all presented with quiet grace by old school waiters decked out in bright red vests, white shirts, and black bow ties.

The Grill opened for business in 1919. Named after its two owners, John Musso and Frank Toulet, it had an early L.A. décor befitting the mood of the times: subdued lighting, a long, polished wooden bar, dark wood paneling throughout, secluded, high backed booths with soft leather seats perfect for lovers or celebrities who wanted privacy while they conducted their trysts and confidences.

Located on the corner of Hollywood Boulevard and Cherokee Avenue, Musso's was a block away from the Writer's Guild. A natural flow of the town's scribes, who had sold their souls to the movie industry, came there to salve their guilt in having succumbed to so much studio money. Some of the early clientèle included F. Scott Fitzgerald, Raymond Chandler, Dorothy Parker, Dashiell Hammett, and a caustically clever William Faulkner who mixed his own mint juleps behind the bar. The celebrity crowd soon discovered the hangout and people like Charlie Chaplin, Tom Mix, Paulette Goddard, Jayne Mansfield, and Humphrey Bogart picked it as the perfect place for a romantic rendezvous or two.

Today, it would not be unusual to spy Sean Penn, Al Pacino, Woody Allen, Brad Pitt, or Nicholas Cage sitting at the bar enjoying one of the infamous corn-beef sandwiches and washing it down with a cool martini. George Clooney staged some scenes for his movie, *Ocean's Eleven* in Musso's.

Oxymoron: Sad Serendipity

I strolled casually through the dimmed lighting of old, elegant Hollywood, looking for my afternoon cocktail date. Then I saw her. Long blonde tresses catching what light there was and bouncing it back into the atmosphere like water flowing over gold, she was sitting in one of the leather booths, back to the door, puffing anxiously on some long, dramatic cigarette. "Probably a Fatima," I told myself. I slid into the booth. She pulled the cigarette away from pale, full lips, blowing a small stream of smoke over her left shoulder. She leaned forward, kissed me on the cheek. "Hi, Gary."

"Hi, yourself, Vanna," I smiled. "As always, you're looking beautiful."

It was Vanna Carroll, Brandon Carroll's wife, or ex-wife. They were what polite circles referred to as "estranged," but in reality, it was all over. Their dream of marital bliss, gone forever, used up in a few short years, like childhood innocence. Brandon was left alone to contemplate life in his Captain's Quarters at the beach, slugging down Jack Daniels, while Vanna had moved to West Hollywood where she could more easily pursue her career as a wardrobe mistress/costume designer. The parting was a sad affair. I liked them both so much as a team. Brandon, ever the aristocrat, the staunch Shakespearean orator who helped us muddle through the Utah shoots; Vanna, who fussed and worried over the smallest detail in the costuming appearing every evening at the mini-pool in a tiny, brown bikini, golden hair tumbling to her waist, legs as long as bowling alleys, the crew doing everything possible to hide their thoughts of lust and carnal frolicking with another man's wife.

I ordered a vodka martini, straight up, a whisper of vermouth, no olive, just a twist, assuredly the best martini in town. I gulped the first sip like a calf nose-diving into a bucket of milk. God, it tasted good, like manna. I knew in sort of a precognitive way that one martini was not going to cut it. Vanna took my free hand, squeezed it lightly.

"It's great to see you, Gary. It's been awhile."

"Great seeing you, too."

She let her hand slip carefully from mine. No lingering caress, and yet, she left an intimate warmth clinging to my palm, my fingers.

"So, how is the world treating you? You happy? Or just kinda sorta?" She put out her cigarette and immediately picked up the pack, shaking out another one. I was right, Fatimas. I picked up the lighter, flicked it. She cupped my hand, holding it and the flame like one holds a gift too precious to lose back to the universe.

"You know what? I am happy, Vanna. I've been working a lot. I'm not doing what I want, but I'm paying the bills. That's about it. You know the scene. What the hell, who cares, anyhooo?"

"I care." She was looking at me with the largest, most sympathetic, robin's-egg blue eyes I have ever seen. I wanted to change the subject, turn the conversation around, talk about some old times and older memories. Vanna was in the mood for more than memories. She wanted the real skinny, she wanted the future from someone she could believe in, not just a talking head. She expected more from me. So I lied.

> *Work and love—these are the basics.*
> *Without them there is neurosis.*
>
> —Theodore Reik, *Of Love And Lust* (1957)

I didn't tell her that I had been working the past month as a juicer at the major studios, way up on the catwalk, stuck behind an arc light, not part of the action, not involved in the story or the filming of the story, just sitting behind this huge piece of hot metal, waiting for the gaffer (whose name I didn't even know) to give me a signal to turn the arc on or off, or pan it left or right. That was the sum total of my creative output.

I didn't tell her that my last actual movie was the one in Bakersfield, where the special effects man fucked up the closing shot, the money shot, essentially ruining the whole end of the movie, pissing away what "might have been" had they let me do the gag the way it should have been done.

I didn't mention that I had started the walk to our meeting by admitting to myself that I was through with all of the dreams I held about becoming an actor. I was more than willing to let go, leave the emoting up to those more qualified or further along or less hung up with personal problems. My second marriage was on rocky grounds, and yet Rose Mary and I had just welcomed a beautiful new son into our lives. I didn't tell her that I would sell part of my soul to do stunts, fall off things, roll cars, get in fights, as long as I could be a real part of the whole shebang.

Stunt work was a way of connecting with my basic self, the real deal. No pretending here. You could either fight the fight or you couldn't, either crash the car, take the fall, handle the horse, or you couldn't. There was no faking it, which is how I like it: bare-knuckled, bold to the bone! Besides, everyone turned out to watch the stunts! Cast, crew, and extras often grow weary of the acting scenes. Shoot them in a master, shoot them in medium shots, close-ups, reverses. By the end of the day, people are bored, ready for the martini shot. But stunts! At last, something exciting is going to happen to shake up the day. Also, like a good bullfight or rodeo, someone may get hurt: great dinner table conversations!

I signaled the waiter for refills. Vanna was drinking white wine, Chardonnay as I remember, a fancy of the times. The martinis at Musso's are huge, like inverted yarmulkes. When the first one hit my system, the warm glow spread all the way to little buddy Boo, who was in a great mood because he secretly had eyes for Vanna. I decided to take a cue from him and switched the subject from me to her as quickly as possible.

"How do you like West Hollywood? Are they treating you like the princess we all know you to be?" I asked, sounding dumb as plastic underwear.

"Well, fine, except, you know, everyone here is gay."

"Gay? Come on, not everybody. Surely not you."

She giggled a schoolgirl giggle, all bubbly and mischievous. "Of course not me, you doofus. You know that!"

She reached for my hand again, softly pressing hers on top of mine, slowly, as though closing a cover on a cherished book. I was beginning to feel uncomfortable. Was she coming on to me? Boo uttered a silent, *"Yes! Yes, dig it, man. She likes you!"*

The trouble was, I liked her, too, and her husband . . . . and my wife . . . and my kids. The vodka was having an effect. Things were starting to get misty. I asked if I could have a cigarette, knowing that I hated Fatimas, but what the hell, time out. Vanna released my hand, affording me the opportunity to grab the fresh martini and begin inhaling it. I took the cigarette, lit it.

"I think I may have some good news for you." Vanna was smiling now. She looked absolutely gorgeous. Boo whispered that she *"was a vamp, much like Scheherazade."* If I had one more of the huge martinis, I would try something very foolish…like trying to be witty or, worse yet, sophisticated. Vanna reached into a combination purse-carryall and pulled out a slip of paper. She handed it to me teasingly like it was a private number to a very private line.

"This is going to change your future. Yes, and for that you are going to owe me another drink, hot-shot. How do you like them apples?"

I took the paper, turned it over. There was a phone number and name. "Ramsey Thomas." I remembered that Vanna had asked for this meeting, something to do with a possible job offer.

"Ramsey Thomas? I don't think I know him."

"Yeah, but you will. He's the production manager on a new film."

She folded her arms underneath her breasts, lifting them to almost eye level. I squirmed, reached for the martini. She sat there, slight smile, lips remaining slightly open like an entrance to a secret garden. She exhaled a thin wisp of light blue smoke. "The Fatimas!" Boo groaned.

"*A Man Called Dagger*," she continued. "They hired me as the wardrobe designer. It's a great picture, a caper film. Private eye, James Bond kind of stuff. Lots of action." She toyed with a strand of hair, teasing it, twirling it around those long, lovely, lute player fingers.

"Good budget, shooting here in town. Ramsey Thomas is a cool guy. He wants to talk to you."

"Sure, I can do that. What does he want to talk about?"

"He's looking for a stunt coordinator, someone that can also do special effects. I recommended you."

Suddenly, all defenses were down. I loved this lady. *God, she's absolutely delightful, isn't she, Boo?* I chugged about half of my martini before the next lie.

"Well, you know, don't you, Vanna, that I am a special effects guru?"

"I don't know about the effects. I just know you are a good stuntman."

She uncrossed her arms, leaned forward across the table, just inches from my face. "I figure you can start working on the effects after you buy me that other drink." Boo began doing somersaults. "*Yessss!*" he shouted so loudly I was afraid the whole restaurant would hear.

I reminded myself of...

Outlaw Rule #1

Don't put your pistol in another man's holster!

I signaled the waiter. "One more please, Francois, for the old times." Vanna smiled. Me? I melted away into a thin puddle of discarded scruples.

Thin Soup Flicks

There I was, standing rigid as a fence post on the second floor of a set designed for the film *A Man Called Dagger*. I was dressed in a guard uniform. In a minute, my hair was going to be set on fire, after which I would pitch headlong through an observation window and fall two stories into the hard steel of a dentist's chair. Well, actually, the dentist's chair had been removed for the stunt, and I would fall into a pile of cardboard boxes. The window was candy glass and I was wearing a wig for the hair-on-fire effect.

It had been about a month since I had been hired as stunt coordinator and special effects guru after meeting in person with production manager Ramsey Thomas and the film's director, Richard Rush (*The Stunt Man*, *Freebie and the Bean*, *Getting Straight*, *Psych-Out*, etc.). Vanna was right. Ramsey Thomas was a neat little guy with an easygoing style. After an interview in which he explained that the film was chock full of stunts and effects, he called the director in to meet me.

Richard Rush walked briskly into the room holding a script under his arm like a football, he being the star running back. He was tall. He was handsome. He was friendly and he had that glimpse of Easter-candy-kindness hidden just behind the twinkle in his eyes. You knew instantly that this man loved life and he loved what he was doing. *"Probably a Renaissance Man,"* Boo suggested and we hadn't even been introduced.

Rush was in a rush. He had things to do, scenes to stage, actors to rehearse. He asked about my background. I played heavily on the two Utah films, on *Man From U.N.C.L.E.*, etc. He gave me sort of a psychic once over, smiled, and shook my hand. "Welcome aboard." Then he was gone, swallowed up in the shimmering, scintillating veil of his creative energy.

The minute they hired me, I hightailed it to a pay phone and called Paul Lewis. "Paul, this is Gary. Got a minute?"

"Yeah, sure, babe. What's up?"

"I need to talk to a good effects man. Can you help me?"

Paul had turned into a popular production manager. He knew just about every good crew member in town. He was the connection you called when you needed someone with experience in a hurry or if you needed tips on labs, prop houses, film stock emporiums, office space, whatever.

"What's goin' on? What do ya' mean? What kind of effects?"

"Special effects," I answered, looking over my shoulder as though a spy were nearby, clued in on what a phony I really was.

"I just got a gig on a great film as stunt coordinator. They want me to do special effects, too. It's an effects show, for Christ's sake. I don't know anything about effects!"

"OK, you got a pencil?"

"I've got a pen."

He laughed, barely, actually more of a snicker than a laugh. "Don't be a wise ass. Take down this name: Carl Olson. Here's his number. Carl's done a lot of effects. He'll be happy to help. Tell him I told you to call."

I knew Carl Olson. He used to be a roommate of an actor friend of mine. I didn't know he had gone into effects work. I scribbled down the number, thanked Paul, fished out some more pocket change, and called Carl. He wasn't in, so I left a message on his answering machine. That night he returned the call. We made an appointment to meet at his apartment the following morning at eleven.

Carl met me at the door. He was a tall, craggy looking fellow. Disheveled and sleepy, he started mumbling something about being overworked and under-appreciated. He had gone from acting to special effects to the job of assistant director and production manager on several top TV series and independent films (*Magnum, P.I.*; *Flashpoint*; *Return of Count Yorga*). The journey was taking a toll. No sleep for the weary.

After black coffee and some jaw-jacking to catch up on the info loop, he gave me an afternoon of Special Effects 101. Carl showed me how to build pipe bombs, smoke bombs, electrical effects, flame throwers, fire effects, gun shots, bullet hits, and a host of other magical, mind-blowing tricks of the trade. At the end of the day, he offered to loan me his effects kit and gave me instructions on where I could buy black powder, ignition squibs, fake blood, Fuller's earth: all stuff I would need to do the job.

When I left his apartment, my head was crammed with the do's and don'ts of a very complicated, dangerous skill. I also left owing Carl a Kobe fillet and a fifth of good Jack.

Now, here I was, several weeks into the shoot, having blown up a variety of boats, doors, cars, etc., standing on the balcony waiting for my hair to go up in flames after the call for "action." The wig I was wearing had been soaked in rubber cement, a highly flammable liquid. An ignition squib was hidden in the middle of my rug, with the wire running down my shirt, underneath my belt, down my pants leg, and over to Don Jones, who was acting as my assistant for the day. When he heard the cue, Don would touch the wire to a hot lead from a car battery, causing the squib to blow and set my hair on fire. I would panic (for me, an easy acting assignment) while taking a direct hit from a deadly light-ray beamed from below. God willing, I would then fall through the glass to the floor, two stories down. At least that was the plan.

The scene had started with our hero, Dagger, played by Paul Mantee (*Robinson Crusoe on Mars*, *They Shoot Horses Don't They?*), strapped in the dentist's chair one flight down. He is going to be tortured by an electrical current designed to make him behave. The bad guys are all gathered on the second floor to watch the payoff through the observation window. Only, Dagger had a secret weapon, a wrist watch that, if he could turn it just so, would emit a deadly ray of light which could then be focused on the guard (me). I would be instant toast causing my poor, burning body to fall through the observation window. In the confusion and hubbub sure to follow, Dagger would make his escape!

They had already shot the scene of Dagger in the chair, struggling against his bonds with the bad men leering evilly through the window above. With much difficulty, our hero twists his watch around, then pushes a hidden button. A deadly ray of salmon-colored light slices through the window, directly toward me. The company grips had removed the dentist's chair and Don and I had set the boxes in place. Crunch time!

"Ready, Gary?"

I nodded "affirmative," eying the candy glass I was about to crash through. I had picked my spot ahead of time so I wouldn't hit my head on the bulwark, a good way to keep from breaking my neck.

"Roll camera, marker…Action!" I heard the "pop" of the squib, felt a quick jolt of power, then the heat from the wig as it began to burn. My directions were to act electrified and when my head became hot as a depot stove, I was to take my fall. The grips standing below had buckets of water in case I was still burning after the gag. I stood there, simmering and shaking (my version of being zapped) until I felt my scalp begin to heat up. I pitched forward toward the window. For a millisecond, I saw the reflection of my burning head in the glass, coming toward me like a B-movie monster, then everything shattered into a hundred pieces of yellow-red light.

The fall was a piece of cake. I landed squarely in the middle of the boxes, the force of the fall extinguishing the flames. When the grips ran toward me with their water buckets, I was already standing, dusting myself off. Round of applause!

We began to prepare for the electrocution of Don Jones, who was doubling one of the actors. We wired him up. Then Don pretended to be stunned by the same lethal ray that did me in and tumbled through the observation window, into the box bed. (To my credit, I feel obligated to mention that Don's hair was not on fire, and there was no glass in the window when he made his fall.) "Let's be brave, Gary. You go first!" "Cut! Print!" "Move on to the next set." Like I said, a piece of cake.

Inside of the Bubble

On the *Dagger* set, a giant sound stage on Pico Boulevard, we were much removed from the revolutionary turmoil swirling through the atmosphere of the rest of the known world. We had our own territory, our own universe, and it consumed us. The film, a nifty little spy-guy-cannibalism picture, was shot independently, to be released by MGM Studios. In spite of a great director, a talented cast, a superbly enthusiastic crew, and the best new cinematographer in the business, *A Man Called Dagger* hit the screen like a hangover from the 1950s.

The shooting of the movie was a genuine kicker. Richard Rush turned out to be one of the most talented directors I've ever worked for, and I've worked with some great ones. This was only his third film. After *Dagger*, Rush would go on to become an icon in the world of motion picture directors, lauded by the likes of Ingmar Bergman, Francois Truffaut, Stanley Kubrick, and Quentin Tarantino. Many critics credit him with being the filmmaker who started the new wave in American Films.

Richard Rush has been nominated twice for an Oscar as best director, won a Director's Guild award for outstanding achievement in motion pictures, nominated for a Golden Globe, and won the Grand Prix des Ameriques at the Montreal Film Festival. His *The Stunt Man* is considered by critics and worldwide movie fans to be a "masterpiece of cinematic art."

The cameraman on *Dagger* was Laszlo Kovacs. Originally from communist-dominated Hungary, Laszlo was a student at the Film and Drama Academy in Budapest, where he and a fellow student, cinematographer Vilmos Zsigmond, furtively filmed the fighting between the Russian troops and the citizens of the city. In 1956, the two daredevils headed for the Austrian border. Posing as peasants, they hid their revolutionary reels in haystacks during the day, traveling only at night. After making it to Austria, they edited the footage and sold it to a producer. Their documentary, *Ungarn in Flammen* (*Revolt In Hungary*), was finally shown by CBS in 1961.

The Black Hat, or bad guy on our film, Rudolph Kaufman, was played by comedian Jan Murray. Murray was a funny, gracious human being, tall, good looking, easy to work with. He was one of the last of the great Borscht Belt funny boys, a haloed circle of comedians that included Buddy Hackett, Milton Berle, Henny Youngman, etc. Murray was a constant headliner in Las Vegas and a much sought after game show host. He was, however, not a good bad guy. In *Dagger*, he played a mad scientist, an ex-Nazi, intent on taking over the world. He grimaced and punned his way through the film, looking much the vaudevillian and very little like the scary, intimidating villain he was supposed to be.

Award-winning producer/director Richard Rush.
Photo courtesy of Rush Archives.

Like 007, we had a lot of hi-tech tricks: false severed arms, cigarettes that were radio transmitters, pocket pens that fired poison pellets, wheelchairs that turned into flame throwers, meat hooks that gaffed people in the back, suspending them like slabs of beef in a storage locker.

We also had beautiful, talented women to decorate the story: Terry Moore (Oscar nomination for *Come Back Little Sheba* and the purported wife of billionaire Howard Hughes), Sue Ane Langdon (a veteran of *Wild Wild West* and winner of a Golden Globe for best supporting actress for television's *Arnie*), Eileen O'Neill (*I Dream Of Jeannie*), and Maureen Arthur (*Hell Drivers*, *Killers Three*, winner of a Golden Laurel as Best New Female Face, 1967).

There were several wonderful women on the crew: Vanna Carroll as costume designer; dark, gypsy-like Rafaelle Patterson on makeup, and Brianne Murphy

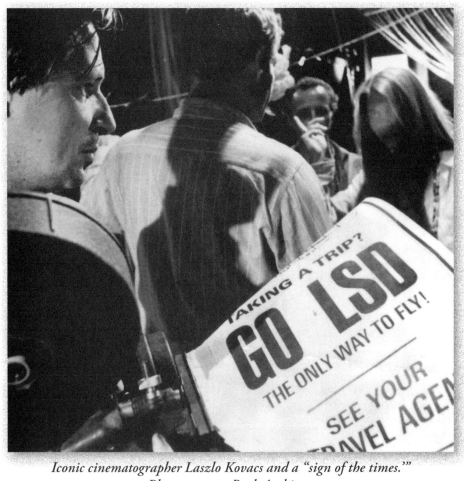

Iconic cinematographer Laszlo Kovacs and a "sign of the times."
Photo courtesy Rush Archives.

as script supervisor. Brianne really wanted to be around the camera. Over the next few years, she would work her way into cinematography, becoming the first woman ever to be cinematographer on a major studio, union film, *Fatso*, with Dom DeLuise and Ann Bancroft. Brianne would eventually be nominated for three Emmys as best cinematographer, win an Oscar for Science and Engineering-Film. In 1984 she won a Crystal Award for *Women In Film*.

The music for the film was co-composed by Steve Allen and Ronald Stein. Allen was a major name in show business, having hosted the original *Tonight Show*, before Jack Parr, Johnny Carson, and Jay Leno. He wrote a lifetime's worth of popular songs before he turned forty. The most well known was the hit "This Could be the Start of Something Big," which came to him, he said, in a dream.

I mention all of these incredible talents and a smattering of their achievements for one reason: to illustrate actor Owen Wilson's theory of harmonic resonance afoot in the psyches of creative people. Wilson tells us that: "There comes a time on all movies, no matter how low budget or how bad, when everyone begins to think, 'You know, I think we've got something here. This could really be something big!'" It is later, when you first see it on the big silver, that's when you want to crawl into your security blanket and weep. Owen is right. We have all done our version of *1941*, Mr. Steven Spielberg's big stinker. In spite of our talent and efforts, by the time it hit the theaters, *A Man Called Dagger* had transformed itself into a turkey the size of a hippo.

Living on Luck

In retrospect, there were some memorable moments on *Dagger*. Sexy Sue Ane Langdon was involved in several scenes requiring special effects. One was a steam bath sequence, where, when ensconced in her private "steam stall," Dagger, who wants information, slips into the outside room and puts a screwdriver through the door latch, essentially locking her in. He turns up the steam. Steam=Effects! To get the proper vapor density, it was necessary for me to be in the stall with Sue Ane, scrunched in the corner with my steam machine. Of course, the glass surrounding the stall was opaque, so she didn't have to be completely nude. Ever the trooper, Sue Ane was as close to nude as you can get without being arrested. (Ambiguity. "Yes, I didn't look.")

Another moment that stands out in my memory bank is when Richard Kiel, who was playing Otto, one of the thug guards, and I (doubling Dagger) are locked inside a set of vertical sliding doors. Kiel (Jaws, the guy with metal teeth in the *Bond* movies) is seven two and probably weighs around three hundred pounds. As stunt coordinator, it was up to me to stage a believable fight between Dagger (six feet and no inches, one hundred seventy pounds, wringing wet) and this surly giant. (When discovered for film, Kiel was working as a bouncer in a Hollywood nightclub.)

We were standing in position. I started to choreograph the fight. I grabbed Kiel by the arm to move him into position. "Hey, stop that!" This at a decibel level equal to the sound of a foghorn. "Don't do that! Don't be yanking on my arm. It will pop right out of its socket!" I was stunned. What the hell did I do wrong? Kiel explained to me that because of his size, his limbs were extremely fragile. Large as fir logs, they were easily dislodged by any sort of tugging or pulling. It once occurred to me that any deficit resulting from being overly huge would be offset by the size of one's wonker. But arms?

In one scene, I am standing behind a huge fake fireplace, one that hides the secret lair of the bad guy! As Paul Mantee's stunt double, I will burst through the fireplace, leap up on a dining table where the bad guy and his cohorts are enjoying dinner. The table is situated on a raised, upper-level kind of stage. Below is a great room, containing, in addition to the large, stuffed furniture, two of Kaufman's guards and across the room, strapped to a giant target, the lovely and helpless Eileen O'Neill. I will leap through the air from the tabletop, grab hold of a giant chandelier, swing across the great room, kicking the guards in the face in the process, and alight in front of the frightened damsel. I am then able to quickly untie her bonds and after a fight with several more guards, the two of us make an escape. Sounds easy enough.

I asked the company grips if the chandelier had been rigged for swinging while holding one hundred and eighty pounds. "No sweat, man, we've got ya' covered." I should have known better. A good way to spot a grip on a movie set is to look for the guy who's knuckles scrape the ground as he moseys to the food truck.

On *Man From U.N.C.L.E.*, a stuntman was scheduled to run and dive through a doorway. Just before the stunt, a grip walked in front of the doorway, accidentally spilling part of an iced Coke on the floor. He neglected to clean it up and didn't inform anyone of its existence. On "Action!" the stuntman ran to the door, slipped on the ice, and dove head first into the door-jam breaking his neck! That was then, however, and this was now.

"Ready, Gary?"

"Ready."

"Roll camera, marker...Action!"

I run through the false fireplace, jump up on the table, and dive for the chandelier. I grasp it and swing out, over the furniture, kicking the two guards in the head, then continue my swing across the room. I drop in front of Ms. O'Neill as planned. "Cut! Print!" Good, they wouldn't need a take two.

While they moved the camera for Mantee's close up, I reached overhead, taking a very light grip on some tassels dangling from the chandelier. I barely touched it, yet in one thunderous roar, it came crashing down on the concrete! Glass, metal, chain, sconces, and bulbs, all mangled into a twisted mess by the force of the fall. If they had needed another take, I would have been upside down, about eight feet over the floor when the thing cut loose. It would have driven my head right into the concrete.

Outlaw Rule #2

Never, ever, trust anybody else when it comes to your safety—not your mommy, not daddy or Uncle Vinny—certainly not a grip in the movie industry.

Well, maybe you could trust yourself or another outlaw if there hasn't been any booze in the area for a couple of days. Whoa, hoss! A fella' can get scraped up doin' this stuff!

After cutting Eileen loose, several more guards rush in. I have to dispense with them in unusual but manly ways. Manly ways? I would need some more stuntmen! I already had ex-boxer Don Jones standing by, but I needed a couple more guys who were experienced enough to remember choreography. Stunt fights are choreographed by the numbers. You move here, and then, on the first beat, I throw a right to your solar plexus, which you block. You counter with a left jab, which I react to and hit the ground. You come toward me and throw a kick to my rib and so on. Anyone who cannot remember the routine runs a danger of hitting someone for real, breaking a nose, a tooth, or even worse, killing someone!

My rodeo pal, Bud Cardos, had been helping with the effects. Bud was handier than rubber shoes when it came to stunts. I also called in a lithe, reclusive actor, John Parker (*Ransom Money*, *Rainy Day Friends*) who had started his career as a dancer. I knew John could nail a routine, so I made him a stuntman for the day. I choreographed the fight. Everybody behaved and moved like we rehearsed, except Don Jones. I told him to be sure and tuck when I threw him over my shoulder. "Otherwise, you'll come down on your heels, and that smarts. If you land on the balls of your feet you'll be just fine." I had learned this interesting fact on *Man From U.N.C.L.E.* when stuntman Loren Janes threw me over his shoulder. I landed on my heels and I thought my teeth had been knocked out. You could hear the "whap" all the way to the San Fernando Valley. I wanted to save Jones that same indignity. "Standby! Roll camera…Action, Gary." Jones came running toward me; I duck, as rehearsed, come up underneath him and flip him into the wild blue. "Whap!" I looked toward the sound. Sure enough, Jones is lying on the floor, grabbing his heel in agony.

Outlaw Rule #3

*Always do exactly what the stunt coordinator tells you
to do. That's why he's the coordinator and you're not!*

I got to do my first "stair fall" on *Dagger*. In the opening sequence, Dagger
is assaulted by a gang of ruffians and responds with unexpected valor. Wearing
an eye patch and a false prosthetic arm, he astounds the bad guys when, like
Superman stepping out of a phone booth, he throws off his disguise and begins
to outwit and outfight the black hats. I play a thug, shooting at Dagger from the
top of a set of vicious looking metal stairs. Dagger ducks and fires back at me
with an AK 47. My whole body explodes with bullet hits and I pitch head first
down the stairs.

Okay, no big deal…except, have you ever stood at the top of a long row of
sharp edged, metal stairs knowing you are about to pitch forward and sacrifice
your ass for the glory of cinema? Broken arms, lacerations, and concussions are
not all that unusual in this stunt. Luckily, I decided to put on a rubber wet suit
underneath my clothes, thus softening the pain of the bumps and lumps on the
way down. Everything went smoothly in this fight sequence, except that John
Parker, the dancer aka the temporary stuntman, got hit in the mouth when he
forgot to duck, leaning right into a punch thrown by Bud Cardos. The film's
producer, Lew Horowitz, begged me to let him participate in some manner, as he
wanted to tell his wife he was "a ballsy son of a bitch." What could I say? He was
the producer. I gave him a task of running around in the middle of the melee,
looking excited, avoiding any real action. Lew got out of position and was hit
directly on top of the head with a metal bar. I cannot say this was deliberate. I
didn't plan it. I swear to it! Thankfully, both Lew and John were exhilarated by
the adrenalin rush. They insisted we all go out for a good old macho drink fest in
celebration of their survival. I agreed and took the whole stunt crew to the nearest
bar, a darkened little operation called the Pleasure Patch that hugged the sidewalk
along Pico Boulevard. We threw open the doors, marching in like the manly men
we obviously were. The place was full of women. What a score! However, there
was something wrong here, something very strange. None of the women seemed
the least bit interested in our arrival. The Pleasure Patch, it turned out, was a gay
bar, the local meet and greet place for the west-side daughters of Lesbos. "Damn
it, I can belly up to the bar just as well as you can!" They did, we did, and everyone
had a *mahvelous* time, all things considered.

Author's Note: When we finished filming *Dagger*, I rode back to base camp
with director Richard Rush in his little green Jaguar. It gave me a chance to

ask him about his background. He told me he had been born in New York, the son of a banker father and a "screaming-liberal" mother, the owner of a New Age bookstore in Los Angeles. Richard attended U.C.L.A., majoring in physics. He had a dream of becoming an astronaut. "I wanted to be the first man on the moon," he laughed. "But math defeated me. I couldn't hack the math, so I transferred to the film department." Inspired by his heroes, directors George Stevens and David Lean, he set his sails toward a new horizon: "I'm going to become a movie director."

After several years spent learning the technical aspects of film by actually working on films, he managed to score a gig directing a low budget flick ($50,000) called *Too Soon To Love*. "When I went to American International for financing, the company was owned by Sam Arkoff and James Nicholson. My first meeting was with Arkoff. An intense little fellow, he leaned into me, growling that they would finance my film, but under one condition. I was never, ever to cast Lola Landers (not her real name). 'If you do not cast Landers, the money is yours!'"

Shortly thereafter, Richard was ushered in to meet Arkoff's partner, James Nicholson. The mini-mogul gestured toward a chair near his large, cherry-wood desk. Nicholson leaned toward Richard and growled. "We are going to finance your movie, but only on one condition. You must cast Lola Landers...no matter what!" Harumph. "If you cast Lola, the money is yours." Such was Rush's introduction into the amazing contradictions of The Hollywood System!

Chapter Six

Kelly Ross and Gary Kent in Hell's Chosen Few, *1968.*
Photo courtesy of Dave Hewitt.

The Blue Bird Of Hippiness

Real cultural revolution should be the flowering of goodness.

—J. Krishnamurti, *"Writings,"* 1956

In the waning light of the 60s, the anti-war movement went front and center in the revolt against the "establishment." Every cultural revolution has to have a "center." In San Francisco, it was Golden Gate Park and the Haight-Ashbury district. In '67, following the highly touted and successful Monterey Pop Festival (in which just about every musician worth their tie-dyes appeared), San Franciscans announced the Summer of Love. The country's gypsies, disaffected teens, beats, hippies, and runaways all headed for San Francisco, convinced that a form of beatific nirvana was waiting, just for them. All would soon be right in their lives and in the world at large.

In The City of Angels the burgeoning protest movement was centered primarily in Venice Beach, Hollywood's Griffith Park, the Sunset Strip, and a twisting, cute, Bohemian kind of canyon called Laurel. Singer/songwriter Joni Mitchell, as poet laureate of the Canyon, held creative, think-tank get-togethers for the idealistic, the freaked out, and the New Age stoners. Musicians, writers, poets, and plain, ordinary citizens were much more involved in the protest movement than we filmmakers. "Hey, man, let's fire up a doobie and mosey over to Joni's place and see what's comin' down!"

The bands on the Sunset Strip were eclipsing the film scene. The plaintive wailings of Bob Dylan and Donovan; the esoteric rantings of Frank Zappa and The Mothers of Invention; the full-throated howls of Janis Joplin: all coursed from Sunset Boulevard through the canyons to the Great San Fernando Valley and southerly to Century City, the Metroplex, and to the circus at the beaches, and beyond.

> *If you're going to San Francisco, be sure to wear some flowers in your hair.*
>
> —Scott McKenzie, "San Francisco (Be Sure to Wear Flowers in Your Hair)," 1967

A tremor of revolt was also rippling through the movie circuit, only we didn't really notice. For us, it was more evolution than revolution. Revolution suggests armed confrontations and violence but things happened at a much calmer pace on the silver screen, not by design, but by the natural inertia of the business end of show business. "Why rock the boat?"

With the exception of the so called "nudie cuties" and the emergence of crossover "blaxploitation," not much had changed in film entertainment for decades. In the late 60s, nostalgia, that "DVD of the mind," was running the thought processes of the suits at the studios and the masses in the audience.

First, the drive-ins swallowed up the family movie-goers (and the teenagers who liked the scene for other reasons), then tunnel-vision lured mom and dad into staying home. After all, TV was free! Art houses and eclectic cinema houses had converted to the profitable "skin flicks," but women wouldn't go to nudie cuties, no matter how artistic they were supposed to be. Despite the obvious money-to-be-made, the major studios were still above playing to the back-seat passion pits, the drive-ins.

We All Need Another Hero

A sickening morbidity gripped the offices and back lots of the major studios as the 60s began to wind down. The old standbys weren't working anymore. The younger movie goers had grown tired of Rock, Rory, Tab, Biff, and the gang. Sure, Brando was still a buzz, but even he had lost some of his box office clout. Furthermore, to the old time moguls, he seemed petulant, arrogant, difficult to control. Paul Newman was nice, of course, but he was always "Paul," and the younger audience was clamoring for a newer, more vibrant persona, someone or something that would set the screen ablaze with the same sort of energy they were seeing in the streets.

Independent producers and filmmakers began to see a crack in the door, a chance to come up with something different and actually get some play dates, albeit in "the drive-ins." Scouting around for fresh meat and hot ideas, they realized they could not have hippie heroes. They were too sedentary, too feminine, too weird! Besides, producers just didn't trust the stuff about "free love," "turn on," and "be here now." It was just too esoteric to make a good slam-banger, which is what they needed to revitalize the box office. Then someone remembered biker Sonny Barger and a letter he had written to President Lyndon Johnson.

Ralph "Sonny" Barger, unarguably the godfather of all outlaw motorcyclists, president of the Oakland Chapter of the Hells Angels M.C., mean as a razor-grazin' water buffalo, patriotic as the fourth of July, was pissed off, angry as hell at the body count pulsing from the news media. High and still rising in Vietnam "the dead are all around . . . there are so many guys killed, maimed, screaming in agony and pain . . . it's terrifying." A Korean army veteran, Barger felt he had to do something!

Letter from Ralph "Sonny" Barger to the President of the USA, 1965:

President Lyndon B. Johnson
1600 Pennsylvania Avenue
Washington, D.C

Dear Mr. President:

On behalf of myself and my associates, I volunteer a group of loyal Americans for behind the line duty in Vietnam.

We feel that a crack group of trained gorillas would demoralize The Viet Cong, and advance the cause of freedom.

We are available for training and duty immediately.

Sincerely,
Ralph Barger Jr.
Oakland, California
President of Hells Angels Motorcycle Club

President Johnson declined Sonny's benevolent offer, but, at the time, its suggestion of noble self-sacrifice caused a small flowering of the press to declare Mr. Barger and entourage heroes.

Could it be? Hells Angels? Wait a minute. Didn't even the greatest actor of the era, Marlon Brando, do a biker flick once? Yeah, *The Wild One*. Did it in the 50s and it made a lot of bucks. Made a lot of noise for its time. Well, why not bring the outlaw biker back? Throw several hundred pounds of hot hog between his legs, stick a human vegematic on the back of the bike, all sexy and leggy, squeezed tight against his butt, her hair blowing in the wind like wheat in a wind storm; rev up the engine and turn 'em all loose on the open highway. "Hot damn, Sherwin, we've got a doozy of an idea here!"

Outlaw Bikers as Heroes?

For most of the next six years (1966-1972) motorcycle movies, or "biker flicks," single-handedly saved the independent movie companies from foreclosure. Scores of them were filmed. Some showed the sweaty, boozy bikers as misunderstood heroes. Others presented a scary persona of psychopathic degenerates, anti-heroes bent on rape, riot, and revolution. Underdogs or rabid mongrels, they were the first to show audiences that the casual use of drugs was already firmly ensconced in the counterculture; they even got us to admit that cursing went on regularly in the everyday life of most men, and frequently, with women as well. Sailors, Marines, and bartenders heaved a collective sigh of relief. The bikers spit in the face of a mean-spirited establishment and ramped up the rancorous debate over the war in Vietnam. Entrenched in the psyche of the public as dangerous brigands, bikers felt free to do just about anything under the umbrella of "freedom."

As Shakespeare's Hamlet would say, "There is something rotten in Denmark." To the bikers and their aficionados, "something rotten" meant contemporary society: the police, the government, the educational system, the morals, and mores of American life in general. During the heyday of their popularity, bikers were simply the hottest, most thrilling on-screen renegades of the time and not one of the motorcycle movies ever lost money.

They Weren't Your Usual Comfort Food

I was still living at Manhattan Beach in 1967, body surfing with sons Chris and Alex; plopping our youngest, Michael, into his stroller for an occasional outdoor jaunt. It was a sweet time, laid back just enough for unfettered living.

One morning we returned from a casual stroll that had taken us from the beach up to pedestrian-packed Manhattan Beach Boulevard, then circled us back to our home turf. *Time for a nap*, Boo suggested. When we entered the apartment, the phone was ringing. It was Paul Lewis. He wanted me to do some effects on a picture he was production managing called *The Born Losers*. Could I be on location early the next morning to fire off some bullet hits in an open courtyard? He casually noted that it was sorta, kind of, a "biker flick."

To me, every time I saw some yahoo racing along the asphalt on the back of a snarling machine, I would immediately think, "There goes a guy who flunked his IQ test, some future organ donor who just doesn't know it yet." I was wrong, but that's another story. I accepted the job. Stuntman/actor/good friend Walt Robles (*The Silence of the Lambs*, *Rainy Day Friends*, *The Stunt Man*) volunteered to be my assistant for the day.

Walt Robles has managed to remain nineteen-years-old for thirty-five years. I don't mean mentally. He's aces high with testy subjects. I'm talking about the body! Walt is built solid, tall with sandy, sunbaked hair, a face like a mountain lion, and he is one of the best athletes I have ever known. Walt can turn upside down, standing on his hands. I mean, his legs and feet are up in the air, his head somewhere in the middle, with only his arms supporting him. Then he throws off about twenty push-ups! Walt can mountain bike with the best, surf the big waves, rock climb (that's Walt in the Campbell Soup commercial, rappelling off the Matterhorn). He flies an airplane, but prefers gliders, and he's an accomplished horseman. Walt has built a miniature railroad that takes up his entire backyard. He has a sense of humor that is clearly around the bend, with a smile that belongs at the Senior Prom. Being with Walt Robles is an exercise in a loss of personal self-esteem.

Early the next morning I grabbed my effects ditty bag and Walt and I drove to location. I have always loved the smell of a movie set. It hits the nostrils all at once, a subtle bouquet of hot lights, makeup, old rubber and sweat, mixed with the odor of the food beginning to ferment on the craft service table. When we arrived, the set of *The Born Losers* was already a beehive of bustle: grips gripping, juicers slapping the paddles of the four-ought cable into hot leads snaking from the generator, setting up the 10ks and juniors; production assistants milling around like freshmen at a frat party; extras and bit players gamadizing their share of the donuts and coffee.

Did I mention that a film shoot is somewhat like a family reunion? There was that industrious redhead, Joyce King, standing by the camera. She was script supervisor. Greg Sandor was the director of photography. Both Joyce and Greg had been on the two Utah Westerns. Bill Pecchi, a husky best-boy grip on *A Man Called Dagger*, was repeating the job on this picture. Joyce and I were just sliding into days-gone-by when Paul walked up. "Hi, Gar. Let me show you the area you have to set up. Oh, who's this?" I introduced Paul to Walt Robles.

> *A film was more powerful when its special effects were cheap and crude, its ideas simple but potently stated.*
>
> —Richard Schickel, paraphrased from *Time*, July 2005.

The plan went like this: I was to rig an open courtyard so that when the film's leading actor (also its director), Tom Laughlin (*Billy Jack, Tea and Sympathy*), came running through the courtyard with the bad guys firing guns at him, you would be able to see bullet hits exploding all around him. Fair enough. The way this is usually done is by taking an ignition squib (a very small explosive device about the size of a horsefly), pack a tiny amount of black powder around it, and then, for added effect, seal the whole shebang inside a packet of Fuller's earth.

> *Fuller's earth: Noun; a mined substance that consists chiefly of clay mineral, but lacks plasticity. Used frequently in kitty litter and garage oil spills because of its absorbency. Cosmetic grade Fuller's is excellent for the removal of oil and impurities from the skin.*
>
> —*Webster's Universal Dictionary*, 1993

In effects work, we use Fuller's earth for boosting the visual impact of explosions, bullet hits or strikes, dust effects, etc. It is very much like a fine, brown powder.

I wired the squibs to a lead that ran to an electrically charged juice box, then packed a little black powder around it and reached in my bag for the Fuller's earth. Yow! It wasn't there. I forgot that I had removed it from the bag to repackage it and neglected to return the stuff to my ditty bag. The sun was beginning to peek into the courtyard. Time was fairly whizzing by. Walt noticed my panicked expression.

"What's the matter, Gar?"

"I forgot the Fuller's earth. I need something to pack the squibs in."

Company grips were now moving large reflectors to the rooftops of surrounding buildings so they could catch the sun and use its rays to softly light the courtyard. Walt ran outside to see what he could find as a Fuller's substitute. Paul showed up, stood over my shoulder, watching my preparations like a math teacher at a final. I fiddled around, trying to look busy. Walt ran back in empty-handed, shouting breathlessly.

"There's nothing out there. The whole place has been swept clean! What are we going to do?"

"*What are you going to do?*" Boo nagged.

"Problems?" Paul scowled.

My eyes darted to a dark glob plopped in a shaded corner of the plaza. "No problems, Paul. Walt, would you please bring me that stuff piled in the corner over there?"

Walt gave the pile the once over and returned. Bending close to my ear, he whispered, "Gar…that's dog poop. You can't use dog poop!"

"Yes, I can. It's exactly what we need. Scoop it up and bring it here. Quickly now."

Walt grabbed a slice of cardboard and went for the odorous pile. Beveling it onto the cardboard, he crossed the courtyard and carefully handed the reeking mess to me. Paul couldn't believe his eyes.

"Come on, Gar, you're not going to…"

"Sure Paul, we've got no choice. We're out of time. This is going to work just great, trust me."

I barely finished hiding my stinking little pouches in the brick flooring when we heard the camera crew approaching. Directly behind them strolled the film's illustrious star, Mr. Tom Laughlin.

Laughlin is a former football star from Minnesota and a master of the difficult but effective martial art Hapkido Karate. Boo pointed out that, behind those squinty, steel eyes, he could not detect even a hint of a requisite kindness. I sure did not want this to go bad! We were introduced. I showed Laughlin where the hits were planted so he wouldn't step on them during the run. Paul Lewis reminded us all that time was money.

"Come on, Gar, are you guys ready?"

"Ready and steady. Let's rock and roll!"

Laughlin took his position. I held the reins to my firing mechanisms. Camera was rolled, slated…"Action."

Tom Laughlin, as the imperturbable Billy Jack, started his dash across the courtyard. I hit the juice. Little explosions, big effects! The air surrounding Tom was dappled with specks of dust, and yes, something else even more colorful: splendiferous chunks of flying dog turds! Flying through the air, flying everywhere. Sticking to the walls, the clothes of the crew, and, yes, even to Mr. Billy Jack himself! "Cut! Print!" High fives from Walt Robles, Paul Lewis, and Mr. Boo. We had succeeded beyond all expectations.

Tom Laughlin qualifies as a genuine outlaw on several filmic fronts. Working both inside and outside of the system, he usually did it all his way, from financing to distribution. He could raise money where there wasn't any money, so he didn't have to answer to the suits. Tom would usually co-script, produce, direct, and star in his own versions of "lone wolf hero on the hoof."

Several times Tom grew disgruntled with the standard means of releasing his films, sued to get them back, then opened them himself in a thousand theaters at once. He would buy out a theater, guaranteeing them their nightly nut; then he was free to keep the profits, a system of distribution referred to as "four-walling." Laughlin insists that he made *Billy Jack* for $800,000 and that the picture made over $60,000,000 at the box office.

As his famous alter ego, Billy Jack, Laughlin starred in a series of action films that found him battling both a numbed establishment indifferent to the needs of the people and the down and dirty bikers, often from the saddle of his own hog.

Every hero becomes a bore at last.

—Ralph Waldo Emerson, *Representative Men*, 1850

It must be nice being a hero: all of that idolization and attention. And the women! Golly! Well, there are many women who have been heroes or heroines, to be correct; women and children, some dogs, maybe even a horse of two. I opt for the kids in the cancer ward at Children's Hospital in Los Angeles. These are my heroes: the kids in the bubble, the ones, like teenager Ryan White (who passed away from the ravages of AIDS, contracted through a blood transfusion). They know they are on the way to an early, unpleasant death, yet they still ennoble the rest of us with their incredible courage and pluck. "Hats off!" I say.

There are many real heroes in life, worthy of kudos, those multitudes suffering gallantly from debilitating or deadly disease, some teachers, single moms and dads, many cops, soldiers, sailors, Marines; those low on the rung of the ladder who still find time for the helping of others even less fortunate. Boo insists that I mention the no-seeums, those dark little bundles of humanity confined to their wheelchairs, spinning along in solitary effort against a world designed for mobility and speed. Do you look away as you pass them by in your Hummer or SUV? Do you smile or salute them?

For some reason, in movies, the heroes are always men, aren't they? And good looking! Wow! They effortlessly stand up against the bad guys, defending civilization from who knows what unspeakable acts. And, oh, they are so handy with guns, fast on the draw, slick as forty crude. Not the sort of fellows to be messed with. They always win, these movie heroes. Stuntmen are always getting shot by the heroes, little heroes, big ones, old heroes, young heroes. They all have commonalities. They all speak in kind of a hushed, threatening, low-throated growl. They shoot the crap out of the bad guys and they always get the girl!

Genuine Imitations

As an audience, Americans have always had a love affair with the heroic, semi-silent, loner-cum-man-of-action. Since the days of the silent screen, they've thrilled us and amazed us. They were, and are, all capable, on screen at least, of fighting five or six guys at once, taking the fall and absorbing the pain for the rest of us wusses. These stars are not really heroes; they just play heroes on TV. They all have *stuntmen* who do the heavy lifting. There are many actors who say that they do their own stunts, but very few actually do. However, taking credit gives them a feeling of manhood in the face of having to do so much "pretending." Of course, there are solid monetary and safety concerns in letting a major star do their own stunts. If they should get hurt, then the film will be held up while the actor or actress recovers. A serious injury could end their careers.

One of the perks of old age is acquiring the skills involved in fine tuning one's perspective. It is my perspective that there are damn few men who can take on several bad guys at once and not get coldcocked rapidly into a major sleep disorder. None of the aforementioned, certainly; life is not a movie! We are all heroes in our dreams, though, aren't we? I would not have wanted to get in a fight with Robert Tessier, however, no matter how many cranky cronies I have on my side. Certainly, dreaming would not mollify the severity of the situation.

Tessier was a real tough character, a legitimate war hero, recipient of several Purple Hearts, and a Silver Star for gallantry in the face of the enemy. There are lots of fellows who play tough guys and heroes in movies, and most of them couldn't carry Tessier's stunt bag, all broth and no beans.

There were, and are, others worthy of mentioning here as long as we are talking about "tough" guys and war heroes. Some are actors, many are stuntmen, and even some are stuntmen/actors. Yakima Canutt, David Sharpe, Lee Marvin, Wayne Morris, Audie Murphy (most decorated American soldier in World War II), Neville Brand, Woody Strode, Henry Fonda, Roy Jenson, James Arness, Charlie Horváth, Carey Loftin, William Smith, Mickey Gilbert, Terry Leonard, Richard Farnsworth, Charles Durning, Clark Gable, Whitey Hughes, Chuck Roberson, Jimmy Stewart, Bobby Hoy, Dean Smith, Ben Johnson, Chuck Norris, Nick Dimitri, John Cardos, Dar Robinson, Jack Palance, just to name a few of the real tough guys who happened to also make movies.

Some of the she-roes, the courageous women who come to mind are: May Boss, Polly Burson, Kitty O'Neil, Sharon Lucas, Patty Elder, Jeannie Epper, Janet Brady, Jeanette MacDonald, Nancy Kulp, Debbie Evans, Heidi von Beltz, Debby Lynn Ross, et al. I am nonplussed at being able to mention only these few.

Together, those listed above represent a Congressional Medal of Honor, the nation's highest award for bravery (Audie Murphy); twenty-seven Purple Hearts; fifteen Silver Stars; twenty Bronze Stars; a Distinguished Flying Cross (Jimmy Stewart); the Navy Cross; numerous combat ribbons; the French Croix de Guerre; the Belgian Croix de Guerre; a plethora of battle stars, National Defense Medals, and Liberation Medals, all given for exceptional valor, self sacrifice, and bravery in the face of the enemy while in defense of their country.

Perspective tells me that stuntmen, stuntwomen, and all of the genuine real-life heroes, including kids and the no-seeums, should automatically qualify as "outlaws." After all, they continually do stuff above and beyond the pale of regular folks. Boo suggests that, *If we are not going to be included in the Oscars, we all ought to at least get 'Outlaw' t-shirts."*

One cannot leave the rugged plains of "rough and tough" without a discussion of two other gentlemen, Gene "Judo Gene" LeBell (*Raging Bull, Men In Black 2, Die Hard 2*) and a tall, mischievous Irishman, spawned in a Pittsburgh row house, named Chuck Bail (*The Stunt Man, Cleopatra Jones, Rainy Day Friends*).

Giving It up for Judo Gene

Gene LeBell, unarguably the toughest man in the world, is the son of Aileen Eaton, a revered boxing promoter and manager at the Olympic Auditorium, a sports arena in downtown Los Angeles, and Dr. Maurice LeBell, an amiable surgeon to the stars. Growing up next to wrestlers and boxers of all sizes and shapes, Gene had his first fight lesson at the age of seven. By the time he reached twenty-one, he had won the National AAU Heavyweight Judo Championship, even though he weighed in at only one hundred and sixty pounds. From then on he was dubbed "Judo Gene" LeBell, a handle that has stuck to him like crazy glue through over sixty years as a martial arts, grappling, and judo champion, as well as a movie stuntman and actor. Judo Gene has done it all, including wrestling bears and defeating Pat O'Conner for the World Heavyweight Wrestling Championship. In over three thousand matches in all martial arts disciplines, Judo Gene has been defeated only once.

Beloved by actors, directors, stuntmen, fighters, and poets, LeBell is known as much for his humor, his teaching, and his writing as he is for his skills with the rough stuff. He will be the first to tell you that, "I am not the toughest man in the world, just the most handsome."

As befits most icons, there are hundreds of Judo Gene tales, most of them hilarious. One that consistently makes the rounds of the Hollywood parties concerns a certain "star" who fancies himself a martial arts expert. This pony-tailed, overweight bully with a penchant for mistreating women was giving the stuntmen assigned to one of his movies a hard time, bragging that there wasn't a man on earth who could take him. As the story goes, Judo Gene, who was in his late sixties at the time, decided to give it a try. In less than a minute, he had this "star" in a choke hold that rendered him unconscious. Gene lowered him gently to the ground. The star insisted he "was not ready," so Gene did it again, this time not so gently. The star's wife, watching from the periphery, happened to notice that at some time during the brief altercation, the star had lost control of his bladder, pissing all over himself and leaving a small, dark stain on the studio floor.

Now in his mid-seventies, Judo Gene is still teaching martial arts and grappling, still writing, and even now and again doing some stuntwork. Gene insists he's still the best looking man in the world.

Whatever we do, let's not make fun of these guys just because they're wearing flowers in their lapels.

—Actor Lee Marvin to the author at the Stuntman's Charity Ball

It is worth noting that all leprechauns are not necessarily short, which may explain why Chuck Bail is six four instead of four six. Chuck weighs in at two hundred and thirty pounds, making him one of the largest leprechauns on record. Tales of derring-do, mishaps, misfortune, amazing achievements, and remarkable courage attach themselves to Chuck Bail like groupies to a rock star. He is perhaps the only legendary producer/director, actor, stuntman who doesn't know he is a legend. He not only qualifies as a cinematic outlaw, he is arguably King of the Outlaws.

Remember, what we are celebrating here, in this book, are the independent filmmakers, gnarly, obscene, obscure, foolish, yes, but a magnificent testament to the freedom and daring of art without consensus, without committee, without numbers that add up to a perfect ten. There is much to be said, after all, for the taker of risks, the person who stands by their convictions in the face of common opinion and common sense. Chuck Bail is a perfect example of such an animal.

Secrets All Good Children Know

The first time I ever heard of Chuck Bail was the last day I drove to Laguna Beach to greet the The Greeter. It was a farewell journey, actually, for myself and sons Chris, Alex, and Mike. My wife and I had reached an impasse in our marriage. We decided that a move from Manhattan Beach back to Hollywood might rekindle the fire before it died out completely. We found a livable apartment in the city and preparations were being made for the exodus. First, however, the kids and I had to see The Greeter one more time.

Eiler Larsen, the Laguna Beach Greeter, was a large, gentle eccentric who stood all day long on a Laguna street corner, waving his cane and/or his hands at passing automobiles. Eiler appeared one day out of the early morning mists and assumed a position at the intersection of Forest Avenue and Pacific Coast Highway. Thus began decades of his welcoming, joyous gyrations. At first, some Laguna residents thought he might be crazy, possibly even dangerous. As the years passed, however, they grew accustomed to the old man with the white hair tumbling over his shoulders, the great, gray beard and the deep tide pools of unconditional love that beamed from those large, sky-blue eyes. Eventually the City Council proclaimed Eiler the "Official Town Greeter."

Not much was known about The Greeter, other than that he was a Dane, a one time sailor, prospector, and vagabond. He lived in a small shack perched in the sunlight on the slope of a nearby hill. He did occasional gardening in town and posed for some portraits, but mostly, Eiler, who much resembled that wise old man of the sea, writer/mariner Peter Freuchen (*The Book of the Seven Seas*), just stood his ground, day and night, greeting people, waving, pointing, smiling, and every once in a while calling out a cheerful, "Hello there!"

Grownups thought of Eiler as a colorful curiosity. Children, however, knew he was much more, a *magic* man, especially in tune with each and every one of them. They loved him more than they did the Easter Bunny, Mickey Mouse, even more than Santa Claus! There was no running to greet The Greeter, no posing with the old man for pictures, no pawing, no questions. Children were just delighted to receive his energetic "wave," after which they would scream with joy, causing no end of consternation to any adults in the immediate vicinity.

The return from Laguna to Manhattan Beach was somewhat melancholy. We stopped at the Victor Hugo Inn (now named Las Brisas) for a late breakfast. Even that peaceful, flower-shrouded restaurant overlooking the sharp cliffs and the shimmering, blue-green Pacific, could not lighten the mood. It was obvious: The boys did not want to move from the beach into the damned city. Young as they were, they were turning into surfer dudes, a persona that slipped easily around their sunbaked little bodies. Mostly though, waving goodbye to The Greeter had put them on a downer. The thought of not having our weekly waving trysts, or even worse, never seeing Eiler again, brought them to a painful plateau of tears.

The Cowboy's Name was Chuckles

We returned to our Manhattan Beach hideaway to discover that wife Rose Mary had left for lunch with friends. The boys dashed for the television. I called my answering service. Answering machines and individual phone messaging were both products of the future. "Teddy's" was the service preferred by all stuntmen. The gaggle of girls on the switchboard were reliable and cheerful; delighted when they could offer you a "work call" from the studios or independents. There was a call from Paul Lewis. "Hey, Gar, got a gig for ya. Chariot race. You and another stunt guy named Chuck Bail will duke it out. It ends with a big crash, horses, chariots, and drivers. You can talk it over with Bail this afternoon. Stage four, LaBrea Studios. Let me know how it goes."

On the drive into town to meet this fellow Chuck Bail, I was privy to a constant, nervous nagging from Mr. Boo. *"Big crash! Chariots, horses, drivers!"* I remember praying that this Bail guy would know what he was doing around a team of spooked horses.

Forty minutes later I was at LaBrea Studios in Hollywood on sound stage number four. I looked for Paul Lewis, but couldn't spot him in the miasma of people who were tripping over electric cables, shouting important stuff to each other, like, "Hey, man. How's it hangin'?" There wasn't a hint of production actually going on, just a sea of "production looking" folk everywhere, some holding scripts,

Chuck Bail, member of The Stuntman's Hall of Fame and a founding member of The Stuntman's Association. Photo courtesy Bail Archives.

others munching donuts and swilling craft service coffee. Then, on the far side of the room, I spotted a gigantic, white cowboy hat rising above the throng like the peak of Mt. Rainier. I headed toward the hat and discovered it was attached to the head of a tall, lanky character sitting on a pile of boxes and twirling a large lariat around in the air. When some unsuspecting person strutted by with his self-importance leading the way, that lariat would suddenly snake out, making a mighty "whooshing" sound, and wrap itself around the ankle of the walker. It would then be snubbed tight, and the person's leg would be lifted, suspended in the atmosphere, hog tied and ready for branding. "Sorry. I just couldn't control myself. Just a habit I can't break." I surmised that this must be Chuck Bail.

No one could start work on the film, as the producers had not deposited the money in the bank. No one could rent props or set dressings, buy raw stock, sign contracts, or pay for lunch. Chuck and I would show up, sit down on the boxes, and exchange stories while waiting for something to happen. We verbally replayed the nation's first Super Bowl, which had taken place in January (Greenbay 35, Kansas City 10); rehashed the hoopla surrounding the First Human Be-In, where twenty thousand Diggers had gathered in San Francisco's Golden Gate Park to protest war, greed, the growing of the Corpolopolis, while celebrating life, love, free expression, and pot. I was in sympathy with the Diggers; Chuck was diametrically opposed.

Bail and I discussed everything but the upcoming production and the chariot race. Every five minutes or so, he would lasso some galoot just for amusement, then turn him loose with the sincerest of apologies. In spite of the flurry of energy around us, we both were beginning to smell a rat in the woodpile. In deference to Paul, we decided to wait the week out and see what would happen. During that time, I learned much about Chuck Bail, all in all a daunting task. After more than forty years, I am still at it.

Bail was born and raised in Pittsburgh, Pennsylvania (The Steel City), an offshoot of a long line of Northeastern Irish men and women. Remnants of the "Olde Sod," the Bails, and on his mother's side, the Freeborns, were as Irish as E Company, and twice as tough. Chuck's grandfather was an Irish cop, Chief of Detectives, actually. His other grandfather was a blacksmith. His uncle was an Irish cop, two cousins were Irish cops. Chuck would have been one, too, except he hated cold weather. He escaped the rigors of Steel City's infamous climate by hiding away at the movies.

He also got an after-school job cleaning riding stables and saddling broncs for the upscale drugstore cowboys. Bail fell in love with horses and motion pictures. He began to dream of a life cloaked in warmth and adventure, anywhere south of

Pittsburgh. He was seventeen-years old, six four, two hundred pounds, and was handsome as an A-list movie star.

> *Mistakes are only horses in disguise. Ain't no need to ride 'em over 'cause we could not ride them different if we tried.*
>
> —Guy Clark, "Ramblin' Jack and Mahan," 1996

Chuck Bail and I had at least one thing in common. We were both ex-Navy men, serving during the Korean War. I was in Naval Air, stationed at Headquarters Flight Unit, Corpus Christi, Texas. Assigned to the Public Information Office, I wrote hometown news releases for the pilots and for the Blue Angels, the Navy's elite precision flying team. Chuck was stationed in California, where he became a heavyweight boxer for the Navy, and also starred on the their swim team. He was assigned to Special Services, where the commanders positioned all of the jocks. Special Services also meant special food, special duty, special treatment.

When Chuck took liberty, he would head for a local airfield to take flying lessons instead of hitting the bars and whorehouses like most of his mates. This all came down in the waning months of the Korean War. President Dwight Eisenhower announced a cease fire between North Korea and the American Forces on July 27, 1953. A shaky truce was signed, and shortly thereafter, Chuck Bail and I were both mustered out of the Navy with honorable discharges.

I accepted a job in Corpus Christi as a newscaster for radio station KSIX. I married my sweetheart, a beautiful young woman named Joyce Marie Peacock. Joyce and I moved to Houston, Texas, where I went to work as an announcer at a slightly more upscale station, KTHT. My bride, a teacher by calling, transferred to the Houston school district. Joyce and I both shared a love of legitimate theater. We had actually met at a community theater in Corpus. I was performing a lead role in the play, *Dear Ruth*, and Joyce was working behind the curtain as a stage manager.

Months later, after our move to Houston, I drove a friend to an audition at the Playhouse Theater, one of the city's more popular legitimate houses.

While waiting for my friend to finish the audition, I was asked by an assistant if I was there to read for a part. On a whim, I answered, "Yes," and ended up reading for legendary director Adrian Hall. Something must have clicked because Mr. Hall asked me to join the company as their juvenile lead. I signed my first professional acting contract at the grand (for the time) salary of $50 a week.

On the West Coast, Chuck Bail was going through a similar benediction. Barely separated from his Navy dress blues, he met a cowboy by the name of Billy Hammond. Hammond was putting together a Wild West Show to travel the orient. Chuck pleaded with Billy to take him along. Billy knew that Chuck was a handy horseman, but felt he needed to put together an act first, something that would give him a special flair, a little bit of pizzazz. Billy taught Chuck to trick rope; Bail taught himself how to shoot a bow and arrow with uncanny precision. Now this dark-haired, handsome athlete could box, fly, swim, ride bucking horses, do trick roping, and shoot Necco Wafers from between a volunteer's fingers with an arrow at a distance of thirty-five feet! Billy added Chuck and his act to the roster, and off they traipsed to the mysterious East.

> *Bad luck is better than no luck at all.*
>
> —Anonymous

Chuck told me that it was in Thailand, on a hot, sweat-drenched night in a cheap hotel spent tossing himself around the bed, that it dawned on him that he was getting winded by all of this cowboy stuff.

"I was riding bucking horses, trick roping, and doing my bow-and-arrow act five times a day, seven days a week. I didn't even have time to change my shorts, let alone enjoy a good meal or get a decent night's sleep. But then, I was young, Gar, and I didn't really need any sleep." The bumps and bruises were another story.

"I didn't really have time to heal before the next son of a bitch would throw me and trample the bejeezus out of me. I would show up for work every morning bent over, barely able to walk, straighten myself up enough to climb into the saddle, then at night I would limp back to some fleabag hotel, and try to grab a couple hours sleep before starting it all over again."

Luckily for Chuck, by the time they set up in Bangkok, the show had run out of money. The cowboys and cowgirls, their horses and their rigging, were abandoned, stuck in the middle of a foreign country without funds or a way back to the States. The American Embassy bought them all tickets to Los Angeles, but no further. Chuck found himself starved, stalled, and stranded in the vast wasteland of Southern California.

"If it had been San Francisco, I would have ended up a fry cook, but since it was Los Angeles, I wound up working as an extra in motion pictures."

There are hundreds of "Chuck Bail" anecdotes, some concerning him and his hilarious adventures, others told by Chuck about those he has known. Equally hilarious stories of superstars, cowboys, tough guys and cowards, horses, dogs, and women. I might as well get started.

FLASHBACK: We are on the back lot of Universal Studios about to witness the birthing of Chuck Bail's movie career! Chuck has been hired as an extra on the television series *Wagon Train* after convincing the casting agent he is more than handy on horseback. They are about to film a big riding scene involving an Indian war party, about twenty-five men, garbed as savages. All of the riding extras, including Bail, have been adorned with fearsome war paint. Shorty, a smallish assistant director, is yelling instructions over a bullhorn. "Okay, boys, listen up. I'm only goin' ta' say this one time!" Chuck wonders if the little fellow is barking at him in particular. "In a minute, you'll all select a horse out of the remuda. You'll mount up and ride to the top of the slope over there." Shorty indicates a steep incline about three hundred yards away. "On 'Action,' you all come trotting down toward camera. Got that?" Mass murmur of agreement from the extras. Shorty approaches the cameraman for a last minute confab.

"Now, boys…" Shorty addresses the extras as "boys," as though they are all a group of Cub scouts. "Now, boys, this here is our star Injun." Shorty indicates a swarthy, Italian looking fellow. "His name is Anthony Caruso. Mr. Caruso, to you. He is the chief Injun and he'll be leadin' the charge. Whatever you do, do not pass or get in front of Mr. Caruso! Got that? Hell or high water, you will always stay behind Mr. Caruso! Okay, boys, mount up and get up the hill."

All of the extras run toward the horses, select their mounts, and take off for the top of the hill. All, that is, except Chuck Bail. Chuck, the new guy in town, notices there is only one horse left, a scruffy looking bay with half of an ear missing. The part of the ear that is still intact is covered in a thick, blue ointment. Medicine from a studio vet, probably. Bail climbs up on the animal's back—there's no saddle since these are supposed to be Indian ponies—and trots up the slope to join the rest of the war party. Every Indian turns his mount to face downhill. Big Chief Anthony Caruso is in the center-front position, scowling evilly, waving a war club. Chuck is hanging in the rear, ready for the charge. He even whoops a few times, quietly, though. He doesn't want to upstage Mr. Caruso. "Whoop, whoop."

The horses know they are going to be rode hard. They fight against the confines of tight reins. They're ready to rumble. Way down below, standing next to the camera, Shorty raises his megaphone, "Stand by!" Shorty shouts. The Indians are already standing by. "Roll camera. Marker. Action!" Twenty-five horses thunder down the slope, while, on their backs, the pretend Indians are yelling and screaming terrible, wild animal sorts of sounds. The scene quickly becomes a cauldron of dust, horses, shouting warriors, with Big Chief Caruso bravely leading the point of the charge. Chuck finds himself suddenly in the center of the mêlée, his horse eating up the slope like a downhill skier. Chuck is elated. He ventures another whoop, this time a bit louder. "Whoop! Whoop!" He brandishes his weapon. This "extra thing" is actually becoming a lot of fun.

Then Chuck notices he is beginning to pass other riders. He decides he had better put on the brakes a little. He pulls back on the reins, but his horse ignores him. Actually, he seems to be speeding up! Chuck pulls again on the reins, harder this time. He looks down to see the headstall has slipped off the horse's head and the bit suddenly drops from the horse's mouth, dangling uselessly like an ornament attached to the animal's frothy lips.

"Damn it, Gar, I was pullin' on nothin', just air. No leverage, nothin' but wind. Now, how was I going to stop the son of a bitch? I slipped the leather straps plow-like around his neck and yanked. It was like he didn't even feel it! He was hell bent for the bottom, and he wasn't gonna play around on the way down."

Chuck notices he has actually passed Mr. Caruso, and is now in the lead, rapidly putting open space between himself and the rest of the war party. "Whoa! Whoa!" Chuck yells. No response from ol' Half-Ear. The horse ignores the command and picks up speed. He's out of control. He hits a reflector and knocks it over. Now Half-Ear heads straight for the camera and camera crew! This terrifies Shorty. He and the crew run for their lives. "Whoa, goddammit! Whoa!!!" He's holding on to Half-Ear's mane like a C-clamp. Ol' Half-Ear doesn't stop until he slides into a squat-down in front of a portable watering trough. Before lowering his head to drink, Half-Ear turns and looks back at Chuck, as if to say, "I did good, didn't I boss?" "Oh, shit!" Chuck can see his career ending before it even begins. He watches as the headstall falls into the murky water.

Shorty comes unglued! You can hear him all the way to the 101, maybe even further. He is shouting a torrent of the most obscene curse words he can think of. "Goddamn son of a bitch holy fuck shit nigger piss spic dago kike limey motherfuckers, why can't they send me someone who knows how ta' ride a fuckin' horse?" Chuck Bail, who is fresh from riding bucking horses five times a day, seven days a week, begins to shrink, becoming smaller and smaller, until eventually his six four frame becomes even shorter than Shorty himself!

Chuck puts the headstall back on Ol' Half-Ear and slips the bit into its mouth. It is time for the Indian war party to attack the wagon train on the dead run. Chuck raises his rifle and pulls the trigger and immediately finds out how Half-Ear had earned his name. Not wanting to lose another ear, the animal throws his head down and begins to buck, providing another show for cast and crew. Welcome, Chuck, to the world of movies.

FLASH FORWARD: We are back on that soundstage on LaBrea Avenue. During our wait time, Chuck has me laughing like Bozo, recounting his intro into the world of film. "I looked down, Gar, and saw that some scissor-bill had slipped the headstall off the bit so it would work loose, just so he and those other yahoos could have a laugh on the new guy. If I'd known who it was, I woulda killed him."

That afternoon, Paul Lewis informs us that he is sorry, but it looks like the picture we are waiting on is a bust. "You might as well write it off, guys. I think it's…I think the whole thing's goin' belly up, including the chariot race."

Chuck and I both knew that "When the fat lady sings, it's over," so we gathered our gear and walked off the lot. On the corner of LaBrea and Sunset, we said our goodbyes. "It's been a hoot chatting with you, Chuck."

"Same to ya', Gar. Maybe we'll bump into each other again sometime."

I cross LaBrea at the traffic light and head for the lot where I'd parked my car. I look back once, just in time to see Chuck Bail heading south, strolling down the sidewalk toward Santa Monica. He is carrying his stunt bag and twirling his lariat over his head, like a hemp halo. He is whistling.

Outside of the Cookie Cutter

Several days later, I am sitting in a black leather booth in The Raincheck, having a few drinks with actor Warren Oates. A Scotch on the rocks for me, and Warren, a Coke. Oates had to quit alcohol some time before, due to his kidney problems. The jukebox in The Raincheck, usually soothing with its stack of oldies-but-goodies and subdued show tunes, is now belching out "White Rabbit" by Jefferson Airplane. Grace Slick getting down! Warren doesn't like the sound. It's "too damned loud!"

I had not seen Oates since our work in Utah several years past. He begins to fill me in on the difficulty Monte Hellman and Jack Nicholson are having getting the films distributed in the United States. "They love 'em overseas. In Paris, we're high-cotton, Kent, 'n' still, Monte can't get us a play-date here in the states. He can't even get us in a porno house!"

Warren continues to fill me in on the trials and tribulations of the distribution business in the United States. I take the opportunity to study his face. In the dim, smoke-cloaked lighting of The Raincheck, I see that Warren has not changed all that much. His whole persona suggests someone who has done too much hard lifting in his time, seen too much bad weather, had too many worries. Oates looked very much like a poor man's "everyman."

Many of Warren's friends, fans, and co-workers insist that he had a face similar to the classic Western-Outdoorsmen stars of movie history. A-list guys, top of the ladder men like Randolph Scott, Gary Cooper, John Wayne, Henry Fonda, Alan Ladd, Robert Mitchum, Joel McCrea. Maybe so, but, to me, Warren looked more real than those fellows. They all seemed too in control, with a slick texture to their faces that belied years spent slumped in the saddle beneath an unforgiving sun; or, as in Warren's case, weeding corn rows and picking strawberries.

The cinematic cowboys all looked like what they were: movie stars. There are only a few film actors, mostly character players, who looked like real cowboys, real workin' men. A handful of fellas' whose looks suggested that they were just ordinary blokes, shop-worn by the difficulties in living a life they could not understand, let alone master. Actor Robert Ryan was one of these men. I would also mention Harry Dean Stanton, Jack Palance, Ben Johnson, Harry Guardino, Lee Marvin, Dan Duryea, and Charles Bronson. Even if they were decked out in a suit or tweed-plus-fours, they still looked like the kind of guys who went to work with a lunch bucket and their sleeves rolled up. Down-and-outers who had already lost whatever it was they were looking for. As far as I can tell, the king of the blue collar everyman was Warren Oates.

"What the Sam-hell is she shouting about?" The bark of Warren's voice yanks me out of my reverie. "'Logic and proportion. Feedin' your head?' Shoot, sounds kinda' like 'rithmetic, don't it?" Warren sneers. "Come on, Kent, you don't like this shit, you know that!" He is referring to the dynamic voice of one of my favorite ladies, Grace Slick.

I explain that "White Rabbit" is a take-off on the classic fairy tale *Alice in Wonderland*, and that the song is suggesting a trip on LSD, lysergic acid diethylamide, known on the streets as simply acid, hence the words about logic and proportion and "feeding your head." This didn't square with Warren.

"What the hell are you doin' readin' *Alice in Wonderland*, anyways? Ain't that for girls 'n' little kids?"

Oates wasn't into drugs, certainly not acid. Nor was he sympathetic to the hippie cum anti-war sentiments that were heating up the "consciousness" kitchens of the late 60s. Warren considered the hippies "wimpies" or, even worse, "pinkos."

What Oates really wanted that evening was to talk about his role of Deputy Sam Wood in *In The Heat Of The Night*, a film he had just finished acting in, and which later would win a Best Actor Oscar for Rod Steiger and multiple awards and nominations for the rest of the cast and crew.

"We shot mosta the film over in Illinois, for political reasons." Warren takes a sip of Coke before continuing. "Man, we got one helluva cast. Rod Steiger playin' the sheriff, I play his deputy. Sidney Poitier's playin' a homicide cop from way up north. That's how come we had to shoot in Illinois. It was supposed to take place in Mississippi, but with Sidney playin' a lead, slappin' a white guy and gettin' away with it? Shoot, Mississippi just ain't ready for that. We woulda had ourselves a necktie party, that's for sure." Warren's voice drifts across the booth slow and easy as buttered rum. "Sidney is gonna be takin' home another one a' them li'l ol' statues for sure—mark my words."

I felt a hand punch my shoulder and turned to discover Don Jones, draft beer in hand, grinning like the proverbial Cheshire cat. "Gar, aren't you gonna scoot over and let a young man sit down?" He didn't wait for an answer, sliding easily into the booth next to Warren, extending his hand, and announcing himself: "Hi, I'm Don Jones! But you can call me Irish Frankie!"

I regard sex as the central problem of life.
—Havelock Ellis, 1936

What I did not know up until that time was that Don had been having an "affaire de coeur" with Warren's estranged wife, Teddy. Childhood sweethearts, Warren and Teddy had just undergone a bitter-sweet separation, and there were evidently some embers still glowing in the fireplace. Oates didn't accept the proffered hand, preferring to just stare at Jonesy, eyes squinting as though he were back in Depoy, hoeing rows under that hot southern sun.

"Well, shoot, if that don't beat all! Don Jones! You're the guy that's been sleepin' with my wife!"

Jonesy jumped like he'd just been bitten by a puma.

"I guess that makes you my fuckin' double then, don't it, Jones?" Warren grinned, sorta kinda friendly like. He took Don's hand and gave it a rough shake. Caught completely off guard, Jonesy didn't know how to respond. Maybe, for the first time in his life, Irish Frankie had been floored.

Songs, Bongs, and Viet Kongs

Half an hour later, I was in my car headed for Manhattan Beach. The dashboard clock read 9:30 p.m. "I'll be home shortly after ten." On went the radio, KHJ 93, the "Real Don Steele rocks and rolls!" The synergistic vocal muscle of The Doors escorts me up the on-ramp, onto the 405 South, "Come on, Baby, light my fire."

Luckily, the head-on between Jonesy and Warren had smoothed out. When I excused myself, having to get home to see my kids off to sleep, the two men, husband and rival, were exchanging tales, giggling like hyenas in the velvet dark of the veldt. I yawned, several times, releasing pockets of leftover tension. Boy, I sure dug that song. It was a screech-out to pure sexuality. It was so, so inciting! I began to sing along.

"Actually, I'm not much of a hippie myself." I mumbled this last aloud, hoping to strike up a conversation with Boo, who had managed to nod off hours earlier, before the serious musing began. "I have to work too hard to 'tune in, turn on, and drop out.' I do, however, agree with much of their philosophy. Boo awoke slowly, stretched lengthwise, yawned, then began his nagging, insinuating whispers, *"Warren Oates has longer hair than you do!"*

"Well, Boo, I'm not one who wants my hair to define who I am."

"*You're so square, man!*" Boo answers. "*You're the only guy who calls himself a rebel who still has short hair.*"

"I have just never taken to the idea of letting my hair speak for me, Boo. I don't want to hear my hair talking, let alone, making a statement. Or my clothes, either. I don't want my clothes chatting it up with anybody!" Silence follows. I may have hurt Boo's feelings. The slurring hum of the freeway traffic and the music from the radio accentuate the solitude.

The Doors have completed their ode to unbridled passion. The airwaves begin to calm with the haunting melody and lyrics of "A Whiter Shade of Pale" by Procol Harum. Hippie or not, I loved the music that was pouring out of the Human Be-Ins, the pop festivals, the current Summer of Love. It was a treasure trove of feelings, poured into a mix-master, then blended into a cocktail of tone poems set to new melodies; cry-outs that were at once spiritual; psychedelic; politically scalding; erotic, up to the nanosecond and streetwise.

Culturally and politically, the world seemed all sixes and sevens, and the leaders of all of that tumult were the music makers. They had the mojo and they carried the message. Acid was the drug of choice, specifically Owsley's Blue Cheer. The *Sergeant Pepper* album by The Beatles was their musical manifesto. "Acid Rock" suddenly became the clarion "call to arms" of the hippies and their worldwide acolytes.

"*To me,*" Boo hisses, "*you are more like a Bohemian-Beatnik-Outlaw-Yuckster than a Hippie!*"

"That sounds fairly accurate to me, Boo." More silence. I entertained myself by reading the large, green and white signs announcing the Freeway off-ramps: "Olympic-Pico-Slauson-La Tijera."

I watched other automobiles turning onto off-ramps, driven by shadow-shapes—dark phantoms on their way to some private destiny—home, hearth, warmth—the love of a spouse, kids, the family dog or cat.

"*I'll bet some of 'em are up to no good—going to meet a lover, cheating on someone, or making a drug deal!*" It was Boo, back in the conversation.

"What would you say, Boo, if I just took the next off-ramp? Took it and disappeared into another time and place, another life altogether? Huh?"

"*I'd say you were losin' it, tiger. Dementia, maybe. Maybe even the Blue Mocus.*"

"Just start the fuck over, brother! Why not? Just begin by being someone else? A complete new life, clean and clear on the edges." After all, I had made a mess of my first marriage to Joyce Peacock, the nicest woman on the planet. "Miss Independent Beauty" from Southwestern University, and now I was about to sabotage my union with actress Laura Benedict, formally "Rose Mary Gallegly."

"Century Boulevard-Los Angeles International Airport."

Hot damn, I could be in Idaho by midnight. Montana, maybe. Riding horses for some wise, grizzled old rancher. We'd sit on the porch, drinking rye whiskey and playing our guitars. "Maybe I could master the harmonica, too, like Dylan."

"*What about the kids?*" Boo scolded. "*You're crazy about those kids.*"

"Give me some slack, Boo! I wouldn't really leave everyone, everyone I know and love. I couldn't do that! I'm just playing around." I reached for the radio dial, gave it a spin. Time for the ten o'clock news.

El Segundo, one mile. I needed to pay attention or I would drive right past my off-ramp like I did my first day directing a movie. I drove right past the off-ramp leading to the set and didn't realize it until I was ten miles down the interstate.

"*You'd better be paying attention, pal,*" Boo sniffed.

"I'm way ahead of ya, kid. Attention wise, I got my high beams on." The voice on the radio began ladling out the body count from Vietnam, "A hundred and fifteen American soldiers were killed today in the fighting around . . . "

"*Fuck! Those Congs are messin' up our guys bad,*" Boo sighed.

"Not funny, huh, Boo? War! War! War!"

I suddenly recall Lt. Commander Rogers, my CO during the Korean War, and his favorite quote: *There never was a time when, in my opinion, some way could not be found to prevent the drawing of the sword.*

"Who said that, Kent?"

"Ulysses S. Grant, sir."

"Hiram Ulysses Grant, that's who said it!" *I hate war as only a soldier who has lived it can.* "General Dwight D. Eisenhower!"

"General Eisenhower. Yes, sir, one of the best, for sure."

I slipped back into the conscious present before Boo could start yammering again, "*Enough of the bloody news.*" I surfed the airwaves until the antennae snatched just the tune to carry us home, Donavan singing, "They call me Mellow Yellow."

"Is it true," I wondered, "that one can get a bitchin' high just from smoking dried banana skins?"

"Rosecrans Avenue-Manhattan Beach."

I cut across two lanes to the off-ramp, hook a right on Rosecrans. Less than a mile, and I'm home. I glide past the mansions of the Manhattan Beach elite, the *beau monde*, so to speak, of the area. I make note of the empty sidewalks. No warmhearted pedestrians on nightly strolls, just walled-off, darkened domains, guarded by angry "No Trespassing" signs and even angrier watch dogs.

I arrive at my home turf and search for a parking spot near the beach. The night's fog is drifting in off the ocean, cutting my vision by half. I'm in luck. An open parking space appears out of that milky mist, like a friendly welcome mat. I cut the engine, roll down the windows and am immediately enveloped by the powerful, always mysterious sound of ocean waves breaking against shoreline. I can feel the ominous gathering of energy, the coiling and cresting, the slight suspension before the fall. When the seas are up, the sound of the break is thunderous, like cannon shot, followed by the hiss of foamy water rolling over sand. I am at once transfixed and humbled.

"Not war, but waves, undulations, ghostly greetings, and mystic movements of energy are what we are all about. Universally, I mean."

I lock the car, then walk slowly toward my apartment, my mind clocking ovetime along the way.

"Hmmm! It seems to me that Warren Oates has waded into a new current of sorts in American film."

The year so far had brought a vault full of remarkable motion pictures to the screen, *Wait Until Dark*, *Bonnie and Clyde*, *The Graduate*, *Cool Hand Luke*, *Guess Who's Coming to Dinner*, and *The Dirty Dozen*, to name just a few. These were marvelous, even stunning examples of cinema, but were they breakthrough works, crafted by daring and chancy cineastes? Hardly! For the most part, the major studios were still pretending there were no homosexuals, that women were just fine with being second-class citizens, and now, with the nudie cuties, they were also allowed to become sexual ornaments. Blacks? What Blacks? Besides the magnificent actor Sydney Poitier, are we talking about Beulah or the butler?

> *Life, happy or unhappy, successful or unsuccessful, is extraordinarily interesting.*
>
> —George Bernard Shaw

The fog has gathered the night into a thin, moisturizing gauze. I feel as though I am moving through the viscous ether from which movies emerge. It is an altogether surreal sensation.

My mind still lingers on the sound of the waves and all of the backwaters, crannies, and coves formed by that energy. Short waves, long waves, tidal waves, waves of greeting, waves of farewell, old waves, new waves. "The New Wave of European cinema," which so far this year, 1967, has carried to the shoreline such delightfully frank and grown-up movies as *Elvira Madigan* (Sweden, director Bo Widerberg), *Hour of the Wolf* (Sweden, director Ingmar Bergman), *I Am Curious (Yellow)* (Denmark, director Vilgot Sjoman), *Far From the Madding Crowd* (England, director John Schlesinger), *Accident* (England, director Joseph Losey), *Mouchette* (France, director Robert Bresson), *La Chinoise* (France, director Jean-Luc Godard), *The Thief of Paris* (France, director Louis Malle), et al.

"There must be, then," I tell myself, "someone in the U.S. who is not afraid to agitate the calm seas of Hollywood commercialism. Some auteur with the know-how and balls to unleash the tide of an American New Wave! Someone like—"

"*Someone like Richard Rush!*" Boo proclaims proudly.

"Exactly." The synchronicity of my/our creative minds seems almost uncanny. "Exactly, Boo." I savor the thought. "Someone like Richard Rush!"

I arrive at the entrance to my apartment flush with the flavor of the evening's reflections. I feel as though I have actually put in a day's work. Taking my house key from a jacket pocket, I insert it into the lock, open the door, and step into the future.

Poster of Satan's Sadists, *courtesy Independent International Pictures Corporation.*

Crotch Rocket Consciousness

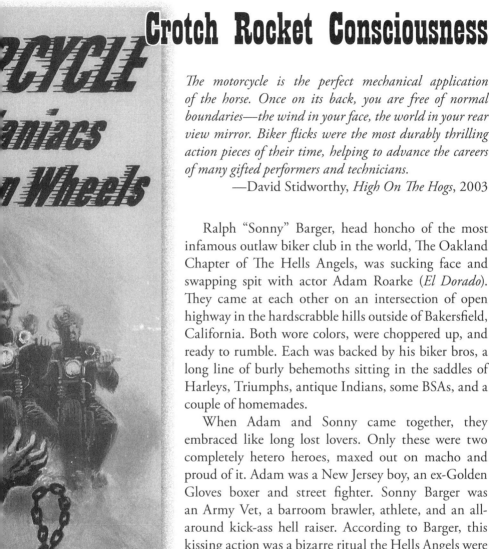

The motorcycle is the perfect mechanical application of the horse. Once on its back, you are free of normal boundaries—the wind in your face, the world in your rear view mirror. Biker flicks were the most durably thrilling action pieces of their time, helping to advance the careers of many gifted performers and technicians.
—David Stidworthy, *High On The Hogs*, 2003

Ralph "Sonny" Barger, head honcho of the most infamous outlaw biker club in the world, The Oakland Chapter of The Hells Angels, was sucking face and swapping spit with actor Adam Roarke (*El Dorado*). They came at each other on an intersection of open highway in the hardscrabble hills outside of Bakersfield, California. Both wore colors, were choppered up, and ready to rumble. Each was backed by his biker bros, a long line of burly behemoths sitting in the saddles of Harleys, Triumphs, antique Indians, some BSAs, and a couple of homemades.

When Adam and Sonny came together, they embraced like long lost lovers. Only these were two completely hetero heroes, maxed out on macho and proud of it. Adam was a New Jersey boy, an ex-Golden Gloves boxer and street fighter. Sonny Barger was an Army Vet, a barroom brawler, athlete, and an all-around kick-ass hell raiser. According to Barger, this kissing action was a bizarre ritual the Hells Angels were required to undergo when greeting the leader of another chapter of the club.

Shout Out for Sonny and the Boys

Roarke and Barger were acting in a new biker flick, *Hells Angels on Wheels*. The movie company was anchored down in Bakersfield and this was the first day of the shoot. Producer Joe Solomon (yes, the *Mom and*

147

Dad Joe Solomon) had gone to Barger and asked him to be in the film. Sonny, who was tired of biker flicks cashing in on the reputation and persona of the real Hells Angels, was cool to the idea. But Solomon could talk the ears off a mule. Joe not only coaxed Barger into agreeing to do the film, but also into acting as technical advisor. Barger also agreed to supply bikes and club members, as needed. Several members of the Hells Angels became actual players in the film's biker gang.

My involvement with *Hells Angels on Wheels* began with a phone call from Paul Lewis. When I had entered our beach apartment several nights before, my wife informed me that Paul had called and wanted a ring back. This was good news. When Paul called, it was usually with a job offer. Sure enough, when I got him on the line, Paul told me he was leaving for Bakersfield, to production manage a biker flick, and he wanted me to coordinate the stunts and double one of the lead actors.

"Who's the actor?"

"Jack Nicholson," Paul answered. "The director needs you there by tomorrow night. Bring a bunch of stunt guys 'cause he's starting with a fight between some bikers and rednecks."

"Who's the director?"

"What? Are you taking notes?" I could hear Paul snort gleefully over the phone line. "The director is Richard Rush. You've worked for him before."

An hour later, when I finally hit the hay, I couldn't sleep. Boo kept going over everything like he was doing a bed check in the Big House. *"Richard and Jack are back!"* he gloated. *"Paul Lewis as production manager, Joe Solomon, yeah, 'Big Joe' producing. How great is that?"* I bounced around all night like a berry in a wagon bed. My mind was already on location, gaffing those stunts.

The next morning, I started rounding up my stunt crew. Bud Cardos, check; Don Jones, check; Walt Robles, check; dancer John Parker for utility choreography. Parker ended up playing a policeman in the film. I also hired a friend of Walt's named Mike Haynes, a likable guy who had done some high work in a live stage show at Las Vegas. In later years, Haynes would make a name for himself as the "Winchester Man," smoking it up for that cigarette company in their TV commercials. He would eventually become president of the International Stuntman's Association.

Spiders, Snakes, and Industrial-Level Dust Devils

That afternoon, we all piled into Bud's arthritic '57 Ford and headed up the highway toward Bakersfield, a town as rough as #4 sandpaper. "Bako" or "B-town" as the Bakersfieldians lovingly refer to it, is a semi-industrial, agricultural hodgepodge situated in California's San Joaquin Valley on the western edge of the vast prairie dustbowl—the one immortalized in John Steinbeck's masterpiece *The Grapes of Wrath*. This is where those hardy, hardened "Oakies" of yore ran out of gas, food, and lodging, and almost ran out of hope.

You can smell the machine oil, the sweat, and the cow shit miles before you make town. I had shot *The Black Klansman* in B-town. If you remember that experience, detailed in an earlier chapter, then you are aware that Bako spoons up a giant helping of fistfights and turmoil most of the time. As you enter city limits, you get an eerie feeling the place seems to have been forgotten by the passage of time. Someone once said B-town is the best place in America to see women with barefoot children in one hundred degree heat.

There are ghosts all over Bako, such as the vaporous visages of some firefighters who had perished while pushing their pants down instead of pulling them up during a holocaust in a local whorehouse; then there are the sad spirits of scores of the town's children who had perished in a yellow fever epidemic early in the 20th century. There is even a much revered ghost, in the upscale Westchester section of town, where a social doyen reputedly offed her philandering husband as he enjoyed a leisurely soak in the tub.

There is more to Bakersfield, however, than foul odors, fights, and murder. There is undoubtedly a sort of whiskey-whiskered charm to the place. It is arguably the Country Music Capital of the West. Here is where honky-tonk icon Buck Owens (*Heehaw*) got his career started and where his hip-swiveling acolyte Dwight Yoakum jump-started Owens' sagging career years later. B-town also spawned famed Western actor Noah Beery, and beloved *Metropolitan Opera* baritone Lawrence Tibbett.

Bakersfield boasts numerous UFO sightings and there have been more than a few direct confrontations with "Bako's Bigfoot," the local abominable snowman. Bakersfield holds an annual Gingerbread House Contest and Festival, during which the baking of gingerbread houses is elevated to an art form. Go figure.

Now I found myself in Bakersfield once again, padded up to double Jack Nicholson, and mingling with Sonny Barger and the Oakland Angels, not a fuzzy, huggy bunch. The town was teeming with bad-boy bikers, all just begging for an ignition switch to kick-start the fireworks.

When I arrived on the set, the first person I saw was director Richard Rush. He was sitting on a worn staircase in an abandoned motel courtyard, directing an intense scene between Nicholson and the female lead, Sabrina Scharf (*Easy Rider*, *The Man From U.N.C.L.E.*).

Sabrina Scharf was a natural beauty, with a storm of tantalizing reddish hair tumbling around her shoulders, flirtatious eyes and prominent, high-set cheekbones. She was tall, with the legs of a prima ballerina. Sabrina, an ex-*Playboy* Playmate, would one day become a California state senator and champion of women's rights.

Director Rush, cinematographer Kovacs in the great Mojave with a gang of make-believe bikers. Photo courtesy Rush Archives.

Wardrobe had poured her into a leopard-print jumpsuit that caressed her figure like Estée Lauder body creme. Of all the young women I have ever met, Sabrina Scharf looked less like a "biker chick" than anyone on the planet. In fact, she looked exactly like a sorority sister, just graduated from Sarah Lawrence—with honors. Sabrina, however, was trying her best to pull off a performance as a "biker mama." She was supposed to be coyly flirting with someone else who also didn't look like a biker, Jack Nicholson.

Jack's character was excused for looking reasonably normal. He was not a real biker. In fact, Jack's character's name was "Poet," not the usual handle of a down-and-dirty motor jock. Poet, it turns out, was a loner, an iconoclast, who just happened to ride a motorcycle, and just happened to accidentally fall in with a gang of cyclists, the Oakland Hells Angels!

It was a night shoot, outdoors. The halo and heat of the 5 and 10 Ks sucked the flying night-critters into the white-hot lenses, incinerating them with a "pop-zing" sound, a bit like a bullet ripping through canvas.

Director of photography Laszlo Kovacs had his face buried in the eyepiece of the big Mitchell camera. My good friend, Joyce King, was holding script, while a pensive, frenetic Wally Moon, a veteran of the Utah Westerns, was scurrying around, fussing over the set dressings. There was seductive, dark-haired, Sheila Scott, Rush's secretary-assistant, bringing him coffee, and Tom Ramsey (*A Man Called Dagger*) was working the perimeter of the set as key grip. *"Another family picnic,"* Boo whispered.

> *We should not forget that our tradition is one of protest and revolt, and it is stultifying to celebrate the rebels of the past while we silence the rebels of the present.*
>
> —Henry Steele Commager, *Freedom, Loyalty, Dissent*, 1954

Do You Smell Something?

If Bakersfield is a symbol of the rough, tough, macho working man, then a spot of gray dirt on the north side of town is the working man's armpit! Named simply "Oildale," it is a place of warts with tattoo parlors on every block, secondhand furniture tucked inside every low-slung-tract-house. Oildale is known for honky-tonk, pool parlors, dust storms, and the sulfuric belch of crude oil. Booze, bikers, bands, and broads—that's Oildale. The favorite joke among the town's citizens goes like this: *Well, you can divorce your wife, but she'll always be your sister.* The Saturday night faux-ruby in the navel of the great San

Joachin Valley, Oildale is one hell of a place. If you can't get in a fight in Oildale, you just aren't trying, pal.

It was nine in the evening. Paul Lewis and I were on our way to Oildale to meet Sonny Barger, head honcho of the Oakland Hells Angels.

Paul was explaining how Joe Solomon had secured the cooperation of Sonny and the boys by buying Barger a new Cadillac. "That was the ticket, Gar. Sonny took the keys and then signed on the dotted line." Somehow, that made perfect sense. If Solomon had offered *me* a new Cadillac, I would have scooted bare-assed across broken glass, if that was what was called for.

Paul lit a cigarette. He was wearing his usual "give ups," the clothes you wear when you don't give a damn about what you look like. Paul is offended if asked to wear a tie or sports coat. If a suit is ever required, Paul vacates the premises. He likes to be comfortable.

"Can I use Barger on the stunt crew?" I asked.

"What? Are you kidding me? Sonny isn't doing any stunts. He's too smart. He's gonna meet with us and suggest which of his guys is able to handle bike jumps or a few fights. Just hear him out, then you make the call."

We slid warily into Oildale and cruised the boulevard looking for a watering trough called Trout's. Suddenly, it appeared—a huge, neon-glowing display of a giant trout, bucking itself upstream over a sign that advertised "Drinks-Dancing." We jimmied our way to a parking spot, locked up, and took a worn footpath to the inside of the joint.

Trout's was loaded for action. First up was a dark, dank bar, then a large lighted area with pool tables. There was a smallish dance floor, backed by a stage supporting a five-piece band. This grizzly ensemble was smack in the middle of twanging out a cow-town tune. If you could see through the haze of cigarette smoke, you could spot some couples in jeans, boots, plaid shirts, and gimme hats, two-stepping around the dance floor, or throwing out some earnest, energetic Western Swing.

Before we had left our motel that night, someone had warned us that Trout's was the worst place in California to meet singles, but the absolute best place to pick up hookers. From the looks of the plus-size derrieres drooping over the bar-stools like melting gummi bears, I assumed the former was spot on. Paul and I sashayed to the bar and ordered up. Paul had his usual Smirnoff rocks, and me, a cheap Scotch on the rocks. Trout's didn't strike me as the kind of place where one needed to put on airs.

Paul went scouting for Barger. I took a trip to the men's room to tidy up before meeting The Big Guy. While attending to business, I took the opportunity to read the usual splay of graffiti one finds adorning the walls of latrines worldwide, an art form synonymous with the odor of urine and sanitary pucks.

"I like to fuck grils!" was scribbled above the commode. "It's g-i-r-l-s, you idiot!" in different, more refined script. Then, "What's wrong with us grils?" underneath it all.

"*That's an old one,*" Boo scoffed. "*I read it on the wall of that can back in Utah. What was the name? Oh, yeah. The Sidewinder.*"

"That was in Arizona, Boo." My eyes focused on a message scribbled just to the right of the urinal. It took a second to make it out, but then: "Drug dealers, please call Ron at 374-6677, or Bobby at 374-9591. Hurry!" Yeah, this had to be Oildale.

Paul had located Sonny Barger and hauled us together for an introduction. It's easy to spot a leader of whatever ilk. They all wear the confidence of their position like a badge. It's in their "'tude," their bearing, and in that world-weary disguise of having a lot of unnecessary shit to deal with. There was no doubt that Sonny was the leader of The Hells Angels, only, his drained appearance, he explained, was due to a hook-up with a young lady from Nogales who "performed chin-ups on my dick all night long. I'm beat, man. Let's get this over with."

Barger was not particularly big, but he was muscled as a cheetah and had those same cat-like moves. He was dark-haired, slight beard and mustache, handsome in a macho "I don't give a shit" kind of way. He was friendly enough, but in his liquored-up eyes, you could see he had his "red-line" drawn. His voice was rough and well-worn, like his boots. Sonny signaled the bartender to keep an eye on our drinks, and we got down to business.

Sonny Barger was not recommending anyone to do stunts. As Paul said, he was too smart to do that. Who wants to have to lawyer-up if it all goes bad! What he was doing was supplying the club members and their bikes to work as atmosphere. He also had a list of guys who were interested in getting in on the stunts. Since there were actually few bike stunts in the film, but a truckload of major fight scenes, I needed men who could take direction easily and follow complicated choreography. We didn't need anyone who would get themselves into a real brawl, or worse, punch out one of the actors just for the hell of it.

"All the guys are good to go, as far as I'm concerned." Sonny glared at the back of a busy bartender until the fellow felt the heat and returned to second up our drinks. "A couple of 'em crashed and burned on the in-land, comin' down the way here." He grinned, looking at me sorta, kinda squinty-eyed. "That ol' Dago Red! It'll kick the shit outta ya, won't it?"

I looked over the names on the list: Terry the Tramp, Dennis "Dirty Denny" Art, Tiny, Magoo. I wanted to get all of them to the set and pick our guys from sight. Since most of them were already signed on as extras, this would be easy to do. We decided to hang it up until morning.

As Paul and I left Trout's that night, Barger was scoping the bar for possible late-night action. The porky plethora of blue jeaned butts overlapping the barstools were winking seductively, an open invitation for some bedroom line dancing.

Paul and I barely talked on the way back to our motel. Actually, I was feeling a little depressed. The afterburn of cheap Scotch lingered in my mouth like the taste and texture of kerosene.

Later, alone in my room, I called the desk for messages. None. I started to call my wife, then thought better of it. She and the kids were probably already asleep. I cradled the phone, turned off the light, sank into the covers.

Lung Crush Boogie

At daybreak, we assembled at an abandoned motel, padding up for a brawl I was staging around an empty swimming pool. There were several main fights in the picture. I had decided to switch stuntmen around, rotate the guys so we never saw the same fellows twice.

Bud Cardos would start the fight. He, Walt, Don, Mike, and I would be playing a group of rednecks, bent on hassling the Angels. Cast and crew were gathered along the lip of a large, empty swimming pool near the abandoned motel. My plan was to follow a loose theme with all of the major fights, something I could hang my hat on creatively and see if anyone noticed. This morning's brawl would start at the top and end up inside the dry bed of the pool. In my mind, a midget Roman Coliseum. The bikers would be the Christians, and we rednecks were the man-eating lions! Our motive? This was our squat, man, our crib. We didn't cotton to the idea of any lowlifes such as The Hells Angels invading our turf.

As is the case with most films, we were shooting out of sequence, not in continuity. Story-wise, this particular fight would occur several scenes into the film, after Jack Nicholson's character, Poet, had formed a fragile bond with the bikers. They were on a "run" and had stopped at the motel for some R&R.

Nicholson was more than willing to do as much of the fighting as we would allow, as was "Buddy" the leader of the bikers, played by Adam Roarke. Adam was, in fact, a direct offspring of the gangs and the streets of Brooklyn, New York. He grew up meaner than a cold snake. It took a hitch in the U.S. Army to settle him down. He retained that great, grungy, street chutzpah, however, and wasn't afraid to flaunt it. Adam was about five ten and maybe weighed in at about one sixty-five. He had close cropped, brownish hair, a stubble of beard groping his chin, and wild, intense eyes. These two actors were so handy, I could have gone to Fiji, lay on the beach drinking gin-slings, and phoned in the fight.

I pulled several potential gladiators from the host of real bikers, notably a tall, redheaded half-Native American named Gary Littlejohn (*Color of Night*,

The Born Losers). Littlejohn would become an actor and stuntman of note, and eventually be inducted into the Harley Davidson Hall of Fame. I also tagged Tex Hall (*Easy Rider*, *The Savage Seven*), a loner, a vagabond, a hellacious bike-rider and mechanic; Dirty Denny, who wore the same old soiled peacoat every day of the shoot. Dirty would reach in the pocket, pull out a much gamadized pork-chop, blow off the lint and clothes critters, take a good chew, then return it to his pocket. I also had the services of those ultimate Angels, Terry the Tramp (Terry always armed himself with a bullwhip), Fuzzy, Doug "The Thug" Orr, Magoo, Zorro, and Hi Ho Steve, an eclectic hodgepodge that oozed motor oil, machismo, and mayhem. Somehow, I managed to choreograph the fight, then we all got down in it for the camera.

The Hells Angels pull into a motel. One of their members, Daryll (James Oliver, *Lethal Weapon 3* and *4*) has just tied the knot. He and his bride, Abigail (Jana Taylor, *Dreamscape*, *A Cold Wind In August*), rent a room in which to consummate the union. Buddy (Roarke), Poet (Nicholson), and the rest of the gang head for the bar for some liquid lubrication. On the way, they are stopped by Bud Cardos, myself, and the "redneck boys."

"Well, well, looky here. If it ain't Jesse James and his outlaws." Cardos steps in front of Buddy, blocking his path. Small talk and lip-shit-disrespect passes back and forth. Cardos reaches out and strokes Buddy's facial hair. "Ain't that a nice little beard, though." Buddy slams a vicious punch to Cardos' stomach, doubling him over, then follows with an uppercut that drives him backwards, away from the gate.

As a redneck in waiting, I dive on the back of Biker "Jocko," played by John Garwood. (John was a set-builder for Dick Rush on *A Man Called Dagger*, and he would appear in several more of Rush's films as an actor, including *The Savage Seven* and *The Stunt Man*.) Jocko throws me with a hip flip, following up with a kick to the head. Now the whole herd is outta the chute. Cardos grabs hold of a flagpole, swings through the air, and mule-kicks Jocko, putting him out of commission. "Bull," played by husky actor Richard Anders (*World on Fire*, *The Adventures of Huck Finn*), throws several quick blows into Cardos' kidney, then pushes him off the edge of the empty pool. Bud falls onto the concrete bottom, a good twelve feet below. Don Jones pulls Bull into him, knees him in the crotch, then unleashes a roundhouse that puts him out of the fight. Poet charges from the sidelines, leaps through the air, landing on the backs of Haynes and me, taking us to the ground.

FLASH CUT: Love in Black Lace

The scene shifts quickly into the interior of a motel room where the two newlyweds are preparing to make love. Abigail is wearing a black lace bra and panties, covered demurely by a see-through lace top. Daryll has stripped off his "colors" and his shirt. His motorcycle lurks in the background like a voyeur. The approach to this scene is gentle, sweet even, when contrasted with the vicious fight we witness going on outside of the window. Rush uses this back and forth POV between love and violence several times during the fight.

When the camera does settle back on the poolside rampage, Mike Haynes and I have armed ourselves with tire irons and are menacing Buddy, backing him toward the pool edge. He trips and falls into the crevasse. Haynes, another no-neck, and I stand at the top of the pool, looking down at the unconscious Cardos, then to the lone gladiator, Buddy. We slowly slide down the grab-ladders at pool's edge. Using our tire irons as prods, we back Buddy against the bare pool wall. Suddenly, a motorcycle drive-chain hit's the ground with a loud thud, right at Buddy's feet. The camera tilts up to discover Poet, just as he leaps from the pool rim to the bottom, landing alongside his pal.

Nicholson had pulled me aside before shooting the scene, "Hey, Kent, remember what you told me in Utah? When I was getting down off a' that horse? You told me not to look down. 'Look straight ahead,' you said. Remember? 'Like you know where you're goin'! Well, just watch this jump, kid!"

When he did the leap, Jack walked straight to the lip of the pool and jumped, never once looking down to scope his landing. "Oh, shit!" Boo gushed, convinced that Jack was going to drive his knees up through his chin. There is a lot of difference between the two feet or so one encounters on a horse dismount, and the fourteen feet down onto the bare concrete of a pool bottom.

Jack landed perfectly on the balls of his feet, bending his knees to absorb the shock. You could hear the clank of those brass balls all the way to the makeup trailer.

Although the subject of nudity in American film had pretty much been settled with the advent of the nudie cuties, scenes of unbridled, bare-naked passion were still missing from the legitimate screens and drive-ins. To their credit the "biker flicks" began to tear down that last forbidden wall, albeit, most of them showed sex between couples as a feast of gang rape and male dominance, lacking any pretense of romance, sensitivity, or feeling. Richard Rush, under the free reign of the medium, endeavored to bring some taste and genuine honesty to the coupling condition. In the love scene with Abigail and Daryll, the camera lingers on their faces, on the kisses and cuddling, making no attempt to exploit the event for the sake of prurient pandering. Besides, contrasting the tenderness, the slowly building rivulets of consensual sex, with the brutal gang fight going on outside of the room, gave the audience double their pleasure. Sex and violence. What could be more American?

Cut to: The Pool Bottom

Poet and Buddy, back to back, take on the rednecks for survival rights at the coliseum (swimming pool). Buddy swings the chain, keeping two of the thugs occupied. Poet drives into redneck Haynes, throwing a series of quick body jabs until I swing on him with the tire iron. Poet ducks, puts his back into my gut, flipping me over onto the concrete. I bounce to my feet. Cardos is recovered, up and ready. We quickly surround the two bikers. Victory is within our meaty grasp when, suddenly, the sound of police sirens slams into the scene. Buddy and Poet push through our lines and stride triumphantly toward the shallow end of the pool, where a unit from Bakersfield's finest have taken up positions on the steps. The fight is officially over. Bikers, for once, have been saved by the boys in blue!

Oxymoron: Clearly Misunderstood

In the waning years of the 1960s, the biker gangs had risen in stature. They were now perceived by the naive and uninformed as counterculture heroes, patriotic, free from the mores and morals of civilization. They presented a picture of masculine bravado and camaraderie far removed from reality. A grungy group, indeed, but a group to be admired, nonetheless. My experience with them was somewhat south of that. A vast majority of motorcycle enthusiasts, even many biker groups, are law abiding, respectable citizenry. The outlaw or fringe clubs, however, were far from the wholesome freedom riders they were pictured as. They were, and still are, a contentious, drug addled, booze swilling, lawbreaking bunch of roughhouse rowdies.

My job on *Hells Angels on Wheels* was to keep their heroic image alive, at least as far as stunts were concerned. The Angels were to never back down from a fight. Never start one, just end it, and end it by winning! They were to be brave, coordinated, handy to the hilt when it came to motorcycle derring-do. They were to be generally misunderstood by the establishment and empathized with by the ordinary citizenry, courageous rough-riders with admirable *bon ami*. That's what the script called for, anyway.

The next fight in the film called for Poet to be gang-jumped by several sailors. They beat Poet up and the Angels decide to exact revenge. For this brawl, I had to stuff my pride in my backpack. I had been a U.S. Sailor, serving honorably during the Korean War. I still carry an affinity for all things Navy. Causing shipmates to be defeated by a bunch of unshaven cycle jocks was hard on my patriotic psyche.

The fight was to be staged in a real live amusement park, complete with rides, cotton candy, freak shows, etc. A massive crowd of extras had been hired as atmosphere for the night. I had brought two buddies from Los Angeles to sailor-up for the fight. One was Jim Raymond (stuntman, *Most Wanted*, *The Bionic Woman*). The other was Jerry "Flush" Fitzpatrick. Flush was six three, an ex-Marine, one of the youngest jarheads to serve in combat in the front lines of Korea. He was fifteen at that time and had lied his way into the Corps.

I must digress here and share some inside information. Heretofore unknown, but worth mentioning in passing, I had met Jerry Fitzpatrick several years earlier, when we both adorned the cast of a low budget feature titled *One Shocking Moment*. The film was directed by the illustrious Ted V. Mikels. These were pre-*Black Klansman* days. Jerry and I were both green as jalapeños and hungrier than a hibernating bear. We had answered an ad in *Daily Variety* announcing open casting. We both ended up getting parts. I was the lead, Cliff Newhall, and Fitzpatrick was my office buddy, Rick.

One Shocking Moment was a tame precursor of the nudie cuties, a turgid tale of marital infidelity and a young marriage on the edge of unraveling. The minute Jerry and I heard there would be nudity (always on the part of the female cast members), a whipping scene, etc., we thought, *What have we gotten ourselves into?* But, it was Christmas. We needed money for the holidays, and after all, acting is acting. As I was a union member and this was a non-union picture, I decided to change my name for the credits. Indeed, I am billed in the credits as "Phillip Brady." Fitzpatrick suggested that, as a lark and due to the prurient nature of the script, we should adopt appropriate assumed names for the duration of the shoot. He decided his would be "Flush Toilet," and I decided on the more pertinent stage name of "Crack Widener."

Brazenly exploited as "the most sensuous movie picture ever made," *One Shocking Moment* enjoyed a wide release, eventually garnering some decent reviews. Film historian Christopher Curry, in his biography of Mikels titled *Film Alchemy*, writes: "By design or by accident, *One Shocking Moment* was, and still is, a topical film. Not only does it capture a believable Los Angeles of the mid-sixties, but it also lays out a time in American history when women were largely second class citizens. This is a fascinating feature of independent cinema; it's as though the film is a sort of time capsule, with not only real-life locations, fashion and décor captured within the frame of the movie, but also a mind-set, with all of its good and bad nuances." It is interesting to note that, more than forty years after the making of the film, Fitzpatrick and I still address each other as "Flush" and "Crack."

I picked "Flush" and Jim Raymond to play my sailors as they were the right age, experienced, and best of all, had short, military-style hair in an era of long hair on most males. Both Flush and Jim could pull off a fight and act as well, which served Rush's purposes, as they would be required to exchange some dialogue with Jack Nicholson.

The Angels arrive at the crowded park, then take off in various directions looking for amusement. Poet wanders away by himself. Grooving on the flash of neon, the juice of the music, he accidentally bumps into a pod of sailors. Poet apologizes, but they will have none of it. The sailors are on shore leave (What ship docks in landlocked Bakersfield?) and, as usual with beached swabbies, they are looking for action. Jim is eating from a bag of popcorn, which he throws in Poet's face. Poet reacts and the fight begins.

Poet is outnumbered and slammed against a chain-link fence. Flush pins his arms while Jim works him over. It is important to note here that, like in *A Man Called Dagger*, a producer chooses a fight to make his appearance on film. In this case, producer Joe Solomon plays a bystander who tries to interfere on Poet's behalf. He dashes into the scene, grabbing Jim by the arm, saying, "Hey, those are pretty lousy odds!"

Jim tells him, "Back off or you'll get some, too!" The sailors leave Poet bloodied, nearly unconscious, clinging to the fence to keep from falling. Buddy's bikers find him and take him to their leader. Revenge is called for; the bikers search the fairgrounds for the sailors. They finally locate them, riding on a stand-up merry-go-round.

I had the bike gang split into two separate lines leading up to the exit of the ride. As the sailors leave, laughing and carrying on, they see the motley "gauntlet" stretching out before them. There's no retreat, no way to avoid an altercation. Jim dashes forward, picking up an Angel, and gives him a shoulder spin before tossing him to the ground. The rumble begins!

Punches, kicks, tosses, throws, all happen in a split second. Bull knocks Jim to the ground and sits on him. Flush, now facing the gang alone, pulls a knife. As the circle of opponents slowly closes around him, he desperately parries and feints with the opened blade. Someone hands Buddy a chain and he fakes to the right. Flush lunges. Buddy hammers him to the ground with a stiff arm throw, then administers the coup de grâce, one final blow to the head with the chain. Jocko kneels next to the prostrate body. "Jeez, Buddy. I think he's dead!" End of fight!

I have described in detail much of the fight direction herein to illustrate the importance of choreography when staging for the screen. If one punch is off center, timed wrong, or one kick out of control, someone could be seriously hurt. We do much of our work by the numbers, i.e., one, two, punch, three, four, kick, etc. I was pleased to say that during the fights I staged so far, nobody was injured, nobody harmed, nobody even got their feelings hurt. The stunt guys did a great job and were free to return to Los Angeles.

I had a few days of leisure before staging the big barroom brawl that would set the violent tone for the entire movie. I decided to watch some of the scenes being shot, a chance to study Richard's directing. Most great directors accomplish their mysterious magic by casting a spell over cast and crew that keeps them spellbound until the film wraps. Richard's particular spell consisted of his strong sense of purpose and an enchanting gravitas.

He was not a screamer nor an egocentric maniac. He was the older brother-father you always admired, and hence, wanted to listen to.

Rush and his ensemble were filming a party sequence inside of one of the motel's largest rooms. They must have had at least twenty-five extras, along with the crew and most of the major cast.

Fortune is a woman, and if you wish to master her, you must strike and beat her.

—Niccolo Machiavelli, *The Prince (Il Principe)*

I could smell the marijuana and incense before I ever got to the party room. I could hear the sound of laughter, yelling, shouting, the maxed-out ribaldry. The first thing I encountered upon entering was a 36 DD woman's breast in a black lace brassier. Less than an inch away, its fleshy partner had escaped the confines of its cup, and was now the recipient of some highly creative body painting. The breast belonged to the chest of a female extra, and the artist involved in the painting project was actor/director Bob Kelljan (*Count Yorga, Vampire*; *Return of Count Yorga*).

The room was a cauldron of hard-partying Hells Angels, their mamas, sundry groupies, and "wanna-be" Angels. It is of some importance to note here that Cass Elliot, the eloquent voice of an increasingly popular singing group, had been watching a biker movie on television with her musician friends. She heard the bikers calling their female cohorts their *mamas*. It was quickly adopted by this quintessential group of the late sixties, early seventies, and thereafter; they would be known as The Mamas and The Papas.

That night, in the party room in B-town, most of the women were in stages of undress or no-dress. Whiskey, wine, and beer were passed freely between the revelers, along with hand-rolled doobies. Since the "biker flicks" were considered "outlaw" by their very nature, the independent exhibitors and drive-ins were willing to display behavior far outside the sanctions of normal society. Hence, the smoking of marijuana and parade of female nudity was ramped up in these potboilers. To their credit, these films were able to admit to a lifestyle already rampant in the counterculture, and in the escalating world of rock-music, but largely ignored by the Majors. The biker flick's open portrayal of the use of drugs, especially pot, was the first honest admission of its everyday use since the infamous and highly misleading portrayal of the drug in a 1936 motion picture titled *Reefer Madness!* (Original title: *Tell Your Children.*)

In Rush's *Hells Angels on Wheels*, the party-people were toking at will, passing a joint or two around the loop for the mutual enjoyment of "friends and neighbors," a ritual easily recognized by most of the young people of the world, and certainly, by the hippie culture. Kelljan continued his artwork, demonstrably influenced by the smoke swirling through the crowd and the mass swilling of alcohol. In this one sequence alone, Rush managed to squeeze in hints of murder, bi-sexuality, random coupling, male dominance, extensive use of the aforementioned drugs, while still allowing his audience to retain a gritty empathy for his subjects.

Shill, Buddy's main squeeze, starts flirting with everyone, male or female, teasing the crowd and the artist. She lifts her skirt above her waist. Kelljan begins to paint a small flower just above her panty line. Moments later, she and Poet are in a back room, making love. The party has descended into an orgy of paint, pot, bodies, and booze. A biker suddenly rushes in yelling, "Bingham is coming! He's outside, now!"

Enter one of the premiere talents in the cinema of the period, actor/director Jack Starrett. A country boy from Refugio, Texas, Starrett was of medium height, husky build, with mischievous eyes and a voice as low and gravelly as a Baytown backroad. In *Hells Angels on Wheels*, he was playing Police Sergeant Bingham, a cop with a hard-on toward the gang, anxious to pin something on them and put them away. Starrett was an excellent actor, more than believable in every role he played, in movies as diverse as *Blazing Saddles*, *Rambo: First Blood*, and a half-dozen biker films. He also had a promising career as a director (*Cleopatra Jones*, *Run, Angel, Run*). He was built like a center-fielder, think Mickey Mantle, with a thinning thatch of brown hair and sported a menacing mustache. Starrett and I would end up working four more films together. Each time, I found him to be good humored, professional, and an incredible party-animal.

After the martini shot, it was as though the pressure from keeping all of the emotions he had bottled up during his splendid, subdued performances, would bubble to the surface. His self-control would go AWOL for the rest of the day. In 1989, Starrett passed away prematurely, at age fifty-two, from cancer of the liver.

Sgt. Bingham, cool as a snow goose, manages to out-macho Buddy in a one-on-one. Buddy moves into his face. Bingham stands his ground. Unwrapping a cigarillo, he fires up and blows the smoke in Buddy's mug. He's experienced enough to know not to tip over the outhouse. He's just there to drop a warning. "I'm gonna be watchin' ya, Buddy, several times a day, so don't be spittin' on any sidewalks."

Necessary Baggage

"I just want to meet a man who doesn't need a co-signer." The voice behind the plea was Joyce King's, script supervisor on *Hells Angels On Wheels*. Joyce and I had become close friends ever since the two Monte Hellman Westerns. We were sharing dinner and drinks after a long day of filming in B-town, a place not particularly known for haute cuisine. In this case, it was a barbeque joint, with a sawdust floor, a salt lick, genuine paper towels for napkins, a bustling bar crowd, and a row of noble heads from decapitated deer adorning the walls. Country icon Lefty Frizzell was belting out, "If you've got the money, Honey, I've got the time" on the jukebox.

Joyce was the script supervisor of choice for most of Hollywood's daring, independent directors of the period, from Robert Altman. Richard Rush, Joel Schumacher, Dennis Hopper and Peter Bogdanovich to Henry Jaglom, Jack Hill, Curtis Harrington, Burt Topper, and Al Adamson, a veritable list of Who's Who in independent film. She was also sister-in-arms for most of the crew people, providing a kind word, a good laugh, even performing a near-professional back rub when the going got rough. Always sanguine in the most dire of times, Joyce was, and is, an endearing friend to much of the Los Angeles film community.

Joyce King was born in Hollywood, the only daughter of a prizefighter, a suspected rum-runner, and a school teacher. Her mother, who lived to age ninety-six, was the founder of the Driver's Ed programs in the American School System. Joyce had intentions of becoming an actress, but the desire to just belong to a career in film, plus the practical problem of making a living, soon led her away from the stage to behind the camera.

Her first job in motion pictures was as company cook on a picture called *Hell Squad*. A war movie, *Hell Squad* was produced and directed by Burt Topper (*The Devil's 8*, *The Hard Ride*), and shot mainly on weekends with short-ends. She then hooked a gig on a low budget pot-boiler centered around crop dusting, its pilots and their airplanes. Titled *No Place to Land*, this plane-crash of a movie actually starred film stars John Ireland (*Red River*), Gail Russell (*The Uninvited*), Jackie Coogan (*The Prize Fighter*), and the exotic, if not talented, Mari Blanchard (*Breaking Point*, *Twice Told Tales*). Joyce was hired as stunt double for Blanchard and spent most of the shoot freezing to death in the open cockpit of a bi-plane.

Shortly thereafter, she found her niche in the industry of making films, cuddled comfortably next to the camera, holding script.

During our dinner in Bakos, Joyce and I exchanged the latest cinematic scuttlebutt. While trying to develop his own projects, director Monte Hellman was keeping bread on the table editing for Roger Corman, Colombia, and Universal Studios. Jack Nicholson, besides starring in *Hells Angels on Wheels*, had separated from his wife, Sandra. He had also written another screenplay, which Corman was producing. Appropriately titled *The Trip* ("Touch the scream that crawls the walls!"), the film was a bit of psychedelic experimentation starring Peter Fonda, Bruce Dern, Dennis Hopper, and Susan Strasberg.

Will Hutchins had quit movies and had enrolled in a school for clowns! Brandon Carroll was still holed up at Manhattan Beach, writing the great American screenplay, with occasional forays into town to act in episodic television. Warren Oates had finished shooting *In The Heat of The Night* and was immersed up to his sideburns in major roles in popular Western TV serials such as *Gunsmoke* and *Cimmaron Strip*. Cameron Mitchell had just finished co-starring in *Hombre* with Paul Newman and had left for Europe. He would spend the next ten years working on films of lesser quality, in Germany and Italy.

David McCallum had also gone to Europe, where he gave a wonderful performance as a simple, kindly bus driver yearning for the love of a beautiful, unattainable woman, played by Italian star Sylvia Koscina. The picture, titled *Three Bites of The Apple*, although well received by critics, quickly disappeared into the haunted archives of forgotten gems.

The Man From U.N.C.L.E. Robert Vaughn journeyed to Cambridge, Massachusetts, in May 1967, where he presented a brilliant speech at Harvard University, critiquing America's policy in Vietnam. (Given at Dunster House Forum, May 5, 1967.)

Laszlo Kovacs and most of the crew from *A Man Called Dagger* had reassembled in Bakersfield for *Hells Angels On Wheels*. As Joyce and I moved into our dessert phase, some of the crew, key grip Tom Ramsey (*Bottle Rocket*), set dresser Wally Moon (*The Astro-Zombies*), and lighting gaffer Richard "Aggi" Aguilar (*My Best Friend's Wedding, Sleepless In Seattle*) joined us at the table. The conversation slid easily into who had seen the latest, greatest motion picture. Hands down, all of the kudos went to *The Graduate*, starring a relative newcomer, Dustin Hoffman (*Little Big Man, Midnight Cowboy*), *The Dirty Dozen* with Lee Marvin was a close second, followed by *Guess Who's Coming To Dinner*.

In a recent discussion, actor/director George Clooney observed that in his opinion, "the great decade of film was 1964 to 1975." In that light, 1967 would end as a banner year for cinema. Besides the aforementioned flicks, Hollywood released *Barefoot in the Park, Casino Royale, Reflections in a Golden Eye, Cool Hand*

Luke, Bonnie and Clyde, In the Heat of the Night, and *In Cold Blood*, damn near masterworks, all.

It didn't take long for our gab-fest in Bakos to get around to a discussion of sex, in cinema, that is. The nudie cuties, of course, had opened the window on the naked body and discovered a cash cow with unlimited possibilities. The studios were anxious to somehow get in on the action without appearing immoral. Unfortunately, in my opinion, they chose to enter the fray with an inferior movie, and with only material motives, *Valley of the Dolls*.

Our gaffer, Aggi Aguilar, knew the director of photography on *Dolls*, William Daniels, former president of the American Society of Cinematographers and Oscar winner for *The Naked City*. Although still in production, the hype on *Dolls* was already being overcooked. "This was the one! It tells the real story." Directed by multi-award nominee Mark Robson (*Champion, The Harder They Fall*), it had a superlative cast of award winners and nominees, from the powerful talents of Patty Duke and Susan Hayward to Sharon Tate, Paul Burke, Barbara Parkins, and the uncredited screen debut of future Oscar winner Richard Dreyfuss. The screenplay was adapted from Jacqueline Susann's novel, "the Nation's most startling and hotly discussed best-seller now on the screen, with every shock and sensation intact!"

The story centers on three women seeking their way to stardom in the licentious and mean-spirited world of high-glam and showbiz. The titular *Dolls* are prescription drugs, the "downers" used to fight off the highs of alcohol and perturbation surrounding their fragile lives. In spite of an excellent cast, director, composer (John Williams, most Oscars of anyone else in film, forty-five nominations, five wins), etc., the picture was a mordant bore. It made beaucoups bucks at the box office, thinly disguised as an important and "breakthrough" film. However, to the critics and most serious moviegoers, it was a big disappointment, neither important nor breakthrough. Hollywood, for all of its desire to be hip, still could not get over the myth that, to them, sex was dirty! From some murky myopia, they could not separate sex from nudity. If someone took their clothes off, preferably a woman, why then, they had to fuck, or be raped, or spied upon, or suffer all number of vile, even cruel acts.

The naked female body was shown in a much more creative and honest way in a new film being shot in Sweden. Titled *I Am Curious (Yellow)* this picture was more of an examination of political activism, socialist agendas, relationships, and even a "movie within a movie," than of sex per se. In fact, the lead female of the story, Lena Lyman, wasn't really the American ideal of a sex symbol. To her credit, Lena was a bit chunky, hardly seductive, and entirely believable in her role as a young woman experimenting with life in all of its generalities. It dealt with meditation, love, politics. Her work won her the Guldbagge Award (Beetle Award) for Best Actress. The award is Sweden's highest honor for work in film.

What was so wonderful about *I Am Curious (Yellow)* was that it did not live up to American expectations. Of course, the cinematic grapevine put out the worldwide skinny that this film managed to pull back the covers on sexual coupling. We were promised lots of full frontal nudity, both male and female, and word had it that several times they "actually did it" for the camera. Although filmed and released in 1967, it did not make the rounds of international movie houses until 1968, and was, in fact, seized by U.S. Customs agents in that year under obscenity charges. The subsequent trial and eventual release of *I Am Curious (Yellow)* changed forever the U.S. obscenity codes in regard to motion pictures.

When we finally got to see this "evil" work, however, it was actually quite tepid. And, rightfully so, portraying its characters as people, not sex objects, although they were randy enough when the situation called for it.

Well, then, all of this promise of bare skin and the "reality" of drug use offered by *Valley of the Dolls* had already been examined in the nudie cuties and the biker flicks and foreign films, at least a hundred times, and in more honest detail. In fact, at the time of the filming of *Valley of the Dolls*, the drug of interest on the streets was definitely pot (weed, maryjane, ganja, bud) and its more exotic cousins, Thai-stick and hash (from the Arabic *hashsha* meaning to become dry). Hash is a little more potent than straight pot. In fact, it gave rise to the name *assassin*, as those bent on killing used to consume the narcotic to increase their stamina and sense of purpose.

While marijuana was by far the most used and abused, other, stronger psychedelics were rapidly gaining popularity. Acid, mushrooms, peyote, angel dust, MDMA, etc., were popping their way into the mouths and digestive tracts of the seekers and shakers. However, no self-respecting hippie or New Age provocateur was that interested in popping pills. That had temporarily gone out of style. The sojourners of the 60s and 70s were looking for spiritual affirmation and expansion of the mind, not a quick trip to oblivion.

Oh, some of the bikers, the real ruffians, kept pharmacies of exotic tabs on hand to wash down with their booze. Heavy-duty stuff like Christmas Trees, Black Mollies, speed, co-pilots, yellow jackets, V's, percs, biscuits; the old stand-bys, Benzedrine (Bennies), and goofballs. This made it difficult for me to use these bikers in stunts, as they were often too bloody wasted to perform.

Hells Angels On Wheels, like the other biker films, openly flaunted it all, without fear of censorship or public disdain. These films, the independents and skin flicks, continued to be where it was at, as the decade entered the last stages of existence.

All of us at the table in B-town that night felt we were in the middle of something important, albeit a mystery of what that importance was. Me? I was anxious to return to L.A., to put together a stunt crew for the last glorious fight of the picture. This one, I knew, was going to have to be a knockout.

Steel Belted Cojones

To pull off the bar brawl I had in mind, I was going to need at least a couple of new guys. The script called for a real donnybrook; a pier-six-near-riot, one that would rough up the sensibilities of an audience inured to violence. I immediately thought of Chuck Bail. If anyone could help me pull this thing off, it would be him. I tried all morning to get Chuck on the phone, but no answer. I left a message on his answering service, no response. Deciding to be a bit more aggressive, I cranked up my wagon, grabbed my sons for company, and headed for those L.A. freeways.

It was about forty minutes north on the 99, then another twenty on the Pasadena East, to reach Chuck Bail's place. He was hunkered down on several acres out in the west end of the San Fernando Valley with a house, barn, high-fall tower, riding arena, and several falling horses he was training to rent to the studios.

When I arrived, no one answered the door. Nobody home except the dog, a big German shepherd, howling from the backyard like a timber wolf. "Come on, boy. It's nice to be nice." "Boy" eyed me like he was starving and I was a fresh filet.

I wrote Chuck a note asking him to call and slipped it inside the screen door. Now the dog really went postal. He figured I was trying to force an entry and he was having none of it. "Boy" continued to harass me even after I left. I could hear his bark all the way to the freeway entrance ramp.

On the trip home, the kids started begging me to buy them a dog, maybe even two or three. "Maybe even a horse!" Never mind that we lived in a tiny apartment smack in the middle of other tiny apartments, surrounded by sand and sidewalks. "We want a horse!"

"*Promise them a turtle,*" Boo whispered, before losing himself back into my subconscious.

Later that afternoon, Chuck Bail telephoned me. Chuck had been doing mostly major studio stuff and a lot of television. "Independent" sounded to him like a lot of hard work on Chinese overtime, low wages or no pay. After much wheedling and cajoling, I got him to agree to do the show. I asked him to meet me at Bud Cardos' later that evening, then wondered if he knew another stuntman that he could bring along for the fight. He suggested his friend, Eddy Donno.

Eddy Donno turned out to be a roly-poly tough guy from Philadelphia, with a shuck of blonde hair and a sardonic wit. He was an excellent stuntman. Eventually, Eddie would end up as one of the best stunt coordinators in the business. (*Californication*, *The 40 Year Old Virgin*, *Die Hard 2*; nominated for an Emmy as stunt coordinator on Kiefer Sutherland's hit series *24*.)

We all met at Bud's place in Reseda. We decided to take two separate cars to location, Chuck and Eddie in Bail's gull-wing Mercedes, Bud and I in Bud's

'63 Ford pickup. Naturally, we decided to race each other to Bakersfield. They won, but only because Cardos and I elected to make a pit stop along the way. The drive takes almost two hours, even pushing the sound barrier. Bud and I were both thirsty. It was, after all, a long haul. I was standing outside the parked pickup, pouring a shot into a Styrofoam cup and following it down my throat with a short toast to the pursuit of anything interesting, when I caught glimpse of Chuck's Mercedes tearing up the 99 like a top seed at Le Mans. Donno and Bail (a teetotaler) beat us to Bakos by, at best, only forty minutes.

The next morning we assembled in a vacant barroom to work out the fight. Done! That evening we were ready to rumble! Buddy (Roarke) tells Poet (Nicholson) to wait outside of a bar while the club takes care of some old business inside. He tells Poet, "If anyone runs out, you can have 'em."

Chuck, Eddie, Bud, and I were playing rival bikers. Inside of our bar hangout, things are getting down. Several girls in mini-dresses are on stage, frugging furiously. One of the freak-out ladies is I.J. Jefferson, aka "Mimi Machu" (*Drive, He Said*; *Psych-Out*), Nicholson's off-camera girl friend. Long-legged, wild-haired, wearing a hot yellow mini, Mimi is lost in the dance and the music when The Angels enter the bar. They are about as welcome as a busload of screwworms. Jocko pulls the plug on the electricity to the jukebox. Mimi stops in mid-frug. "Hey!"

"Why don't you take five, baby?" Jocko smirks.

Buddy slides up to the bar, next to Eddy Donno. He accuses him of "messin' up one of the Angels." As Buddy turns to call the injured Angel over to demonstrate, Donno grabs a bottle and smashes Buddy over the head. The battle begins! Bull knocks Cardos through a saloon portico. I leap over the bar, punching Bull in the gut, then throw a left hook that sends him crashing to the sawdust floor. Now things really heat up. The Angels are on me like ugly on a hippo. Tiny pins my arms behind my back, while Jocko pummels me with body jabs; I cave in, slumping to the ground. Chuck Bail is pinned in a corner of the bar, fighting for his life. Angels are bouncing off of him like basketballs. A biker is tossed from the saloon; Poet chases him back inside and into the men's room, where he sticks the guy's head in a toilet. Imagine every outrageous barroom brawl from the old Westerns, and you get a pretty good fix on our fight. It was a real "dog-biting, nut-cutting, rib-breaking brouhaha."

My boys are losing! Chuck is pounded into submission underneath a stack of bar stools; Donno is unconscious; Cardos has done a ghost, and that leaves just me, alone, on top of the bar. Suddenly, some no-good snake knocks my legs out from under me and I sail into the mirror and the booze bottles on the back counter. Glass shatters, the mirror breaks, and I plummet to the floor! I was padded-up for this fall, but, somehow, my forearm protection had slipped past my elbow. As I headed for the floor, I saw all of the broken glass, lying on my fall pad, with the glistening shards sticking straight up, winking at me sorta evil like. Hard to back-peddle in this situation and praying was not an option. By instinct, I threw my arm in front of my face before I hit. I felt the glass slice my arm open, blood begins to squirt everywhere! There are spilled drinks, broken bottles, tables overturned, chairs busted. It's getting messy as a room full of used condoms.

Sutures in My Future

Thirty minutes later, I am sitting in Emergency at Bakersfield Presbyterian. Bud Cardos has driven me over. We have arrived to put the kibosh on my bleeding arm. It was probably inopportune, but we had stopped for a drink along the way and now were feeling pain free. Well, actually, Bud wasn't feeling any to begin with, but, nonetheless, the liquid lull helped in his commiseration. Me? I was aces high. The fight was finished, well done, actually, in spite of my accident. The booze had tempered any thought of remorse and I began to actually comprehend:

Outlaw Rule #7

When there is a risk of real broken glass being involved, use candy glass, or call in sick!

What I remember most about the hospital visit was that Bud Cardos seemed to be incredibly funny. Yes, that's right, Bud Cardos. He was throwing out imitations of me like bathwater and somehow he had me in stitches. The good kind. Moments later, when the doctor arrived to sew up my arm, I was laughing so hard that when asked to put my arm out on a sleeve of the gurney I was lying on, I misunderstood. I sort of slid my whole self out on the sleeve, and in the process, turned the whole damned thing over, dumping my poor, bleeding body on the hospital floor. To my way of thinking, this disaster was even funnier than Bud's imitations.

Thirty-six stitches in my arm and several hours later, I was back at that trusty sanctuary, Trout's Bar and Grill. I felt reasonably well considering I had just been carved up like a Thanksgiving turkey. But then, I was on pain killers which I had washed down with a glass of straight Cutty Sark. We had staked out a table, Bud and I, Paul Lewis, Chuck Bail, and Eddy Donno. On stage, a hot six-piece was laying down the latest and greatest tunes of the day. Chuck Bail, usually a perfect study in decorum, shouted out, "We want to hear Eddy Donno! Come on, folks, let's hear it for Eddy Donno. He's the best singer to ever leave the East Coast for the Old West. As luck would have it, we have him here in person, tonight! Come on, Eddy, give us a treat!" (Applause, applause, applause.)

Eddy stood and strolled confidently to the bandstand. He whispered to the musicians. They nodded to each other in that secret exchange that goes on among musicians before something magic happens. Eddie grabbed up a hand mic; the band played an upbeat intro, and, "Surprise!" Eddie slid effortlessly into a rousing rendition of "Mack the Knife" (made famous by Bobby Darin). Eddie was so good, so hot, even the band applauded. A stuntman who could really sing? Who knew? Well, Chuck knew. Back in Philly, Eddie had made a name for himself as a singer, even appearing on Dick Clark's *American Bandstand*.

The next evening, Cardos and I were scheduled to double Adam Roarke and Jack Nicholson in the last big fight of the film. The mano-a-mano starts at a campfire, escalates into a duke-out up and down some stairs, across a rooftop, and back to ground level with the two rivals pummeling themselves in and out of the bonfire, kicking, yelling, carrying on, etc. Shill throws a lug-wrench to Buddy. Poet is stunned. He had gotten into the fight in the first place by defending her; now, even she has turned on him. Disgusted by it all, he turns and starts to walk away. An enraged Buddy jumps on his bike, chasing after Poet and accidentally crashes through a plate glass window. His bike explodes, turning Buddy into a crispy-critter. Ad infinitum!

Cardos and I pad up, then slip into our characters' clothes. Bud is doubling Adam; I am doubling Jack.

"Whatever you do, Bud, don't grab my left forearm where the bandage is. It'll rip out the stitches."

"Gotcha," Bud answers, but, like he didn't really hear me.

"*Yeah, right!*" Boo hisses.

Ready Gary? Ready Bud? The assistant director is anxious to get it on.

"*Time is money; money is time!*" Boo parrots. I clip his lip and stuff him away, inside of my shoulda-woulda-coulda vault.

"Roll camera. Marker…Action!"

The rumble begins and all goes well. We punch each other around, throw a bunch of unkind words back and forth, then Bud swings a chain at me, after I kick him in the head, backing me up the stairs. If you have never been in a real fist fight, a one-on-one-or-two brawl, on the street, in a club, or the back of an alley, I will inform you that all rules and regulations are off. It is not the Marquis of Queensberry attitude of polite fisticuffs, nor the karate combat you see in movies, where one vanquishes all with perfectly timed moves. Street combat is more a rain of blows, of hair-pulling, knife-wielding, sucker-punching, kneeing, gouging, biting. An exchange of quick and violent effort, in which right and wrong are relative to who is winning, who is losing. I tried to stage this fight with that fact in mind, the body language of the street.

Bud and I battled across the rooftops, and now, back on ground level, we wrestle each other through the fire, slamming each other with burning boards, trying to jam anything hot or glowing into the other's face or genitals. I pick up a burning shard; Bud stops me by grabbing my arm. Yeah, the arm with all of the stitches. Riiippppp!!! I feel it and hear it at the same time. Damn, that smarts! "*Told ya' so,*" Boo smirks. Blood soaks through my jacket sleeve, but what the hell. We are almost finished. "Onward, then, into that good, vicious night!"

Minutes later, Jack and Adam are back in the clothes, doing the close-ups. I examine my arm. All the stitches have been torn lose and the wound is hanging open like a torn shutter. I could care less. The fights are over, finis!

A quick touch up, a nice, hot shower, and I was good to go. Back to Los Angeles. "Bye-bye, B-town! It's been good to know ya."

Reflections in a Jaundiced Eye

I was all set to drive a company car back to L.A. when the AD informed me that Nicholson and Mimi wanted to ride along. I ambled over to their motel room and knocked. Jack opened the door. I was almost bowled over by the cloud of smoke escaping from the room. A light-blue haze, wafting its way seductively into the high-desert sky. Marijuana! It was so potent that, momentarily, I forgot why I was there. Jack and Mimi were as stoned as sinners in a Pilgrim Platz.

Machu was tired; she immediately bogarted the back seat, and, once nested, slept all of the way to Hollywood. Jack, however, was wired, elated from finishing the long, arduous shoot. He wanted to drive. I slid into the passenger seat, riding shotgun. "So, what's up, Jack? What's next on your slate?"

Nicholson took his time answering, and then, in that slow, distinct voice that served him so handily throughout his career, "I want to try doin' what Dick's doing."

"Directing?"

"Yeah. I'm about ready to take the plunge. I've got a couple of projects I think I can get Corman to spring for. One's a basketball story. I really dig basketball. You know what I mean?

"Yeah."

"How about you?"

"Oh, I love basketball."

"No," Jack checked the speedometer, eased up on the gas, "I mean what are you going do next?"

"Me? I'm thinking' about doing another film with Bud Cardos. I'll be playing a bad guy, as usual, and doing some stunts. Director is a guy named Al Adamson. (pause) Ever heard of him?"

"Nope, never heard the name."

Jack turned on the radio and channel surfed until he found The Beatles' *Sgt. Pepper's Lonely Hearts Club Band*. For a full minute, he finger-bopped along with the tune.

I was tempted to tell Nicholson that I, too, harbored a desire to direct motion pictures, but my artistic timidity got the upper hand. After all, what actor or actress of any skill would accept direction from a stuntman? Especially one who carried on actual conversations with an imaginary pal named Boo, a buddy who inhabited some disorderly, low-rent domicile inside my head? *No one*, I convinced myself, then decided to pretend I was falling asleep.

I began to examine my not at all unique habit of talking to an imaginary being. "*It is not always,*" Boo pontificated, "*a condition of psychosis nor does it cling disproportionately to the ids of serial killers.*"

Boo was right, of course. A bit of a know it all. History tells us there have been scores, yea, thousands, of perfectly formed, normal beings, who have carried on conversations with themselves. Albert Einstein, Charles Darwin, Julius Caesar, William Shakespeare, for example. My favorite mariner, a salty old seaman named Joshua Slocum, was himself a known solitary linguist. Slocum was the first human to successfully sail around the world alone. He accomplished this dangerously daunting task aboard his jerry-rigged sloop, the *Spray*. After weeks at sea, Joshua found himself lonely as a Tristan Cock, and he bore this unbearable solitude by giving himself an imaginary shipmate. He would frequently shout commands to him. "How goes she here, mate?" he would call to his phantom friend at the helm.

"Steady on, Captain, and strong!" he would reply to himself.

This conversation became routine for the good skipper, and he continued the practice throughout a lifetime at sea, shouting out orders, and then repeatedly answering himself.

Revered French songwriter Serge Gainsbourg ("*Je t'aime…moi non plus*") invented a delightful alter-ego that he named "Gainsbarre." This "other guy" allowed him to say whatever he wished, usually outlandish or risqué, in public, on TV, etc., and never take the blame. It was always "Gainsbarre" who did the dirty deed. What a wonderful freedom from responsibility, "Know what I'm sayin', Boo?"

Could we all, I wondered, *actually just be lonely?*

Jack Nicholson turned off the radio. He wanted to talk. The dark cloak of nighttime on the 99, a combination of dulled lighting and lingering smog, draped our speeding little chariot like a mucky pergola. Jack took his soulful eyes from the road, looking at me dead on. A question? "It's kinda hard knowin' there's a revolution goin' on when you're right in the middle of it, huh, Kent?" For miles, it seemed, we drifted through the atmosphere in complete silence. Just as we reached the north end of the San Fernando Valley, it began to rain.

Pithy Reputations

Several months later, *Hells Angels on Wheels* opened nationwide.

> *Using, in many cases, a handheld camera, Leslie Kovacks captures in some fascinating angles and shots, the sweaty, boozy, grimy characters.*
> —George McKinnon, *Boston Globe*

> *The film frequently erupts into a lyrical feeling that gives it a sort of sadness and melancholy.*
> —Joan Fox, *Toronto Globe-Mail*

To my jaundiced eye, the best review, reprinted in *Daily Variety* said simply:

> *The Angels cavort in fights, brilliantly done!"*
> —Linda Scarborough, *New York Daily News*

Yes, Alice, there is a wonderland!

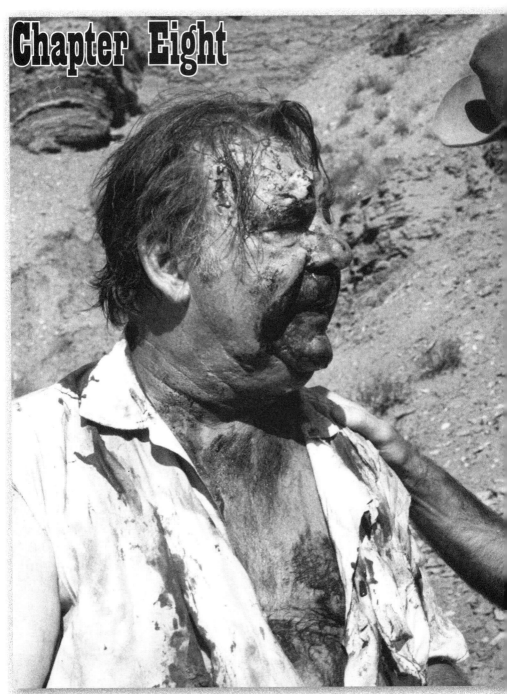

Chapter Eight

Two old pals, Lon Chaney Jr. and Al Adamson, hard at the work of making movies. Photo courtesy of Sam Sherman.

Scratching The Angry Itch

Fear is an instructor of great sagacity and the herald of all revolutions. One thing he teaches, that there is rottenness where he appears.

—Ralph Waldo Emerson, *Compensation*

Memories and Whiskey

Bud Cardos found me sitting in the back seat of a Yellow Cab, drinking straight up out of a bottle of booze with actor Lee Marvin. Marvin was discussing the possibility of his punching out my dad, six four Art Kent.

From my conversations about my childhood, Lee figured my dad had not shown me enough respect. The taxi was parked in the back lot of a popular Hollywood restaurant named the Fog Cutter. I had worked at the Fog Cutter, part-time, as a quasi-bouncer/doorman and in that capacity had been befriended by a motley group of elite Hollywood night crawlers, including the irascible Mr. Marvin.

During my time at the Fog Cutter, I was privy to the best and worst of the celebrity night-style, close up. Celebs would arrive at this marvelous, red velvet-walled, uptown eating emporium in their Caddys, Lincolns, and sometimes, more exotic vehicles like Mercedes, D-Jags, and Bentleys. This was not the Barney's Beanery crowd. These were the major stars, studio heads, their representatives, relatives, and agents. They would arrive as evening began, and by evenings end, they would pour from the restaurant, usually plastered, mostly in a good mood, but also often cantankerous and suffering from a serious loss of cool.

175

There were a few loners worth a mention here, as, considering their renown in the public arena, it made their aloneness all the more pronounced.

First and foremost was America's most decorated war hero, Audie Murphy. Amidst a cackling swarm of the usual meet-and-greeters, Audie would always arrive alone. Out of respect, I would have his car parked up front for easy access when he was ready to leave. He would offer a polite, "Good evening," as I held the door for him. Once inside, he would eat alone, and when he was ready to call it a night, he would leave alone. *Such a small, solitary fellow*, I thought. *There is something rather sad going on here.* At the time, this sensitive, incredibly courageous man, was suffering from severe depression and facing personal bankruptcy. He also carried with him, much like the M1 he used to strap up during WWII, a constant specter of guilt, guilt over surviving the war, when so many of his fellow combatants did not; guilt at the brouhaha accorded his battlefield bravado; and, yes, even guilt over the hundreds of German soldiers who greeted the unfortunate end of their days by appearing in the sights of his formidable weapon. Who knew? Audie Murphy was not a talkative man.

Another loner was America's most popular TV host ever, Johnny Carson. He would arrive just before dark, tooling into the back lot in the pilot seat of a new Jaguar XKE. Like Audie, he would throw out a quiet, "Good evening," before entering the restaurant. Sometimes he would dine with another person or two, but often as not, he dined alone. Upon leaving, he would always bid adieu to Fog Cutter's glamorous, convivial owner, Edna Earle, flip me a fiver on the way to his car, and toodle off, alone inside of that spiffy Jag. "*There goes Johnny,*" Boo would declare. "*The country's funniest man.*"

My favorite solitary persona from Fog Cutter's nights had to be actor, decorated WWII combat veteran, and ebullient raconteur, Lee Marvin. Lee would always arrive as a guest in a carload of people. Everyone would be excited, bursting with laughter and small talk as they made their jolly way into the restaurant. Marvin was always in the middle of the merriment, seemingly among good friends. About an hour later, he would exit the restaurant alone, either pissed off, bored, or both, and ask me to call him a cab. We would chat casually until the cab arrived, then he would jump in and off he would go, just him and the cabbie, into who knows what mischief in the exotic environs of Tinsel Town.

About the fourth time this unusual ritual occurred, Marvin suggested I join him in a short quaff, one for the road so to speak. He pulled a flask of hooch from inside of his jacket pocket, unscrewed it, handed it to me, "Go ahead, kid, put some hair on it." Being young, naive, and thirsty, I accepted his offer.

During this spirited exchange of joie de vivre, which was repeated several times, it did not take long for a casual bond to develop. Thereafter, when the taxi arrived, Marvin would have the driver park to the side of the lot, and invite me inside for a few straight slugs and a friendly chat. The night Bud Cardos tracked me down, Lee and I had been discussing everything from H-bombs to UFOs and the recent passing of Sherlock Holmes (actor Basil Rathbone). "So long, Sherlock." Gulp, gulp! We segued neatly from the death of Rathbone into a critique of the wildly popular comedy duo, The Smothers Brothers. Lee had bumped into the two comedians inside the restaurant. Tom Smothers had been wearing a red velvet dinner jacket, and Lee mistook him for a waiter. "Ya' know, Kent, actually, he looked even more like one of those guys that operates elevators." During these tête-à-têtes, the meter would be chalking up bucks like crazy. Once in a while, however, when the moon was just right, the driver would kill the meter and the engine, pull off his hat, and join in the festivities.

Hanging with My Homies

Bud Cardos opened a door of the taxi. He had tracked me down to sign me up for a picture he was production managing/stunt coordinating called *The Fakers* (aka *Hell's Bloody Devils*, *Operation M*, etc.). "Hey, Gary, are you gonna come down to Marineland and do some stunts for us? It's a crime caper. They got Broderick Crawford (Academy Award and Golden Globe for *All The King's Men*, Hollywood Walk of Fame), Scott Brady, Keith Andes (*Clash By Night*, *The Farmer's Daughter*), and remember Kent Taylor? Ol' Boston Blackie? Well, he's in this one, too. Plays a Nazi big shot. And oh, yeah, we've got Colonel Sanders."

"Colonel who?" This from Lee Marvin, who was running interference.

"Colonel Sanders, the chicken guy. He's got a part in the picture," Bud enthused. He paused to light a cigarette. "Come on, Gary, we'll do a little car work, some foot chases, and then, you get killed by the good guys about a quarter of the way through. You'll be one of the thugs." Since I had started doing stunts, Thug #1 or #2 had become cornerstones of my acting career.

> *In this world, you've got Hitchcock, you've got Roger Corman. But, there are fanatical, avid, ardent fans of Al Adamson.*
>
> —Joe Franklin, New York talk show host

Going to work on an Al Adamson set was like being in a movie by the grand Italian illusionist, Federico Fellini and/or working in a cheap seat, cut-rate carnival. There were bikers, midgets, acrobats, ex-mobsters, and classical performers. There were Oscar winners and porno stars. There were usually deadly snakes around, lots of horses, dogs, donkeys, and sometimes cougars. The morning I arrived on the set at Marineland, it was dolphins and singing seals.

The Fakers was in its second week of filming. Cast and crew were sequestered in a small holding area near the main entrance to the West Coast's largest oceanic amusement park. I was introduced to Mr. Adamson, who enthusiastically informed me that, as soon as the cameras were ready, I, as Thug #1, and my partner, William Bonner, Thug #2, were going to chase the lead actress Ann Randall (*Westworld*, *Stacey*, ex-Playmate of the Month) through all of the photogenic areas of the park. The chase would include a cat and mouse stalk through thousands of spectators gathered in the amphitheater to watch the morning show. "This," according to Adamson, "will give the picture a 'big budget' look."

"It's gonna be great! You two wise guys go after the dame. She darts into the crowd and you lose her. We got two thousand people, for Christ's sake. You go into the crowd, you shove people outta the way, but don't shove too hard, cause we don't havva permit to film the crowd. In the background, the seals'll be singing away, and the dolphins will be jumping around. It'll be fantastic!" That was Al Adamson, directing. When he turned toward Ann to give her instructions, I took the opportunity to study him. Al was a likable character, about six two, reed thin, with big, blue eyes, a boxer's nose, and a prominent chin. He didn't look like a director. He looked like someone who worked in a hardware store in Fresno. His pants were too short, and he was what we used to call a "white-socker," the guy who was the last minute desperation date for the prom.

Al was not a social or political revolutionary. He never attended a concert of any kind. He never grew his hair past his ears, never smoked a joint, never wore an ankh or hugged a tree or marched in a peace rally. He was against sex and drugs, and he seldom drank. Maybe a beer or two in a month. He wore polyester and liked both the police and the Marines. Al was so square he qualified as a counterrevolutionary. And yet, Al made those movies!

The Adamson Family

The first crew member who I recognized that morning was director of cinematography Laszlo (Leslie) Kovacs. He was giving orders to his loader, a young man with neat blond hair and intense enthusiasm. His name was Gary Graver (*Trick or Treats*, *Stagecoach*). Graver looked more like a Princeton cheerleader than a grown-up member of a camera crew. He was handsome in a boyish way and extremely charismatic. During my time on the shoot, I learned some of his background.

Gary Graver had just arrived in Hollywood from Portland, Oregon, when he received his draft notice—Class 1-A, Vietnam cannon fodder! He immediately began to scheme, "If I quickly enlist in the Navy, I won't have to go to war. Better yet, if I tell them I'm a photographer (which he wasn't), how bad can it get?"

The Navy greeted Gary with open arms and immediately sent him into the thick of the fighting as a combat photographer. He spent his part of the war next to a 70mm cannon, on the bow of a Navy gunboat, hunting VC in the Mekong Delta. For two years he dodged enemy incoming and fired back with a battered 16mm Arriflex motion picture camera.

That morning at Marineland, Graver was constantly in the changing-bag, loading short ends. This was his first professional job and he wanted to do well. Adamson was impressed and he also found Gary's dry sense of humor appealing. Al ran out of money before he could finish *The Fakers* and cameraman Kovacs had to move on to another job. When filming was resumed, Al asked Gary if he wanted to photograph the rest of the picture. Graver shot at least the last twenty minutes of the film. It got him director of photography credit, and started a relationship with Al that would last through twelve more movies including *Lost*, the last picture Al ever directed.

It was downright delightful to see that Joyce King was on as script supervisor, and there was Richard "Aggi" Aguilar, Kovac's gifted gaffer. Several years earlier, I had watched Aguilar light an entire feature (*Machismo*) all by himself and never even get his clothes dirty, an impossible feat for anyone but Aggie.

The sound mixer on the shoot turned out to be Bob Dietz; his wife Hedy was the still photographer. Although truly a surrogate family, movie set inhabitants are not really that in a Norman Rockwell, home and hearth, kind of way. Theirs is more a dysfunctional/functional kinship, owing no loyalty except to the film and a peculiar adulation of film directors, who is usually Daddy, or God, or the Devil, or a combination of the three.

Producers are usually thought of as mere carrion: suspect older uncles, interlopers and meddlers, a malevolent cluster of money managers bent on sacrificing the integrity of "the family" in their pursuit of the almighty dollar. The actors, crew people, etc., all assume the roles of brothers, sisters, cousins, and treat each other in a haphazard, though respectfully familial, manner. Then there were Bob and Hedy Dietz. "*Oh, boy, cookies!*" It was Boo, trading off his usual cynicism for the possibility of food.

"We was getting ready for some coffee, Garrry." Hedy Dietz spoke with a lilted German accent, stretching out the r in my name with a Roman roll, giving it a slight European flavor. I rather fancied the sound of it. "We haff some pastry; Bob eats two already. You should haff some, Garrry, before de are disappeared."

Hedy and her husband Bob were always a welcome sight. On every shoot, they would bring their own blend of coffee and a supply of homemade pastries that they would share with whomever needed a little TLC. Hedy showed me a bag of red raspberry tarts. I declined, explaining that I didn't want anything in my stomach, as they were about to call for the stunts.

"Lunch!" They set the catering tables up on the lawn next to Marineland proper, so the ocean breeze would offer respite from the bounced heat of the reflectors and the direct roast of the 10Ks. Most of the cast were already seated and eating when the crew and I arrived. As we were walking to the area, a loud, raucous voice came rolling across the lawn, trailing obscenities, euphemisms, and punch lines, all delivered rapid fire, without a pause for breath, "So, she reaches under the bed, grabs that familiar bit of crockery, opens the window and pours a pot of piss down on the bugger's head. 'Here's yer half-n-half, darlin'. It's half mine, and its half Harry's! Now go on the hell home!' Heaaah! Hah de bloody har har!" The laugh was unmistakable. It was actor Scott Brady.

Comfortable Trousers

I had worked with Scott Brady before, on *Battle Flame*, at Allied Artists. He was a walking contradiction then, raunchy as a sailor on shore leave one minute, and reverent as a Catholic Cardinal the next. In spite of his reputation as a boozer and a brawler, I had found him easy to work with. Now this burly bear of a man was sitting at the lunch table, exchanging tall tales with old time movie star, Kent Taylor. When Scott saw me, his large, Irish face curved into a smile. "I'll be damned, if it isn't Clark Kent! Get over here, Clark, and give us a shake." Scott's hands were big and beefy, like the hands of a heavyweight boxer. "Kent, say hello to Kent. Jesus Christ, what a phony sounding name."

Suddenly, I found myself shaking hands with one of my childhood heroes, Kent Taylor. He had been starring in movies before I was born: *Husband's Holiday* in 1931, *The Sign of The Cross* in 1932, *Death Takes A Holiday*, and *Limehouse Blues* in 1934. He had been a major star in the 40s and 50s, headlining in *Bomber's Moon*, *The Daltons Ride Again*, *Ghost Town*, *Payment on Demand*, et al. He is best remembered though, as the tough talking detective, Boston Blackie. Taylor had to be in his seventies, yet he was as handsome and fit as someone half his age, dark, flashing eyes, black hair thinning a bit. He had retained that chiseled, Ronald Coleman movie star perfection. The two old pros invited me to join them for lunch. It was like having an audience with two popes at the same time, yet I felt totally at ease, like I was hangin' with my homeboys.

There were other old pros at the lunch table that day. Broderick Crawford had been hired to play Inspector Gavin, head of an FBI field office, and the Carradine family patriarch, John, had been cast as the owner of a pet shop. Both men began their careers in the 1930s. Carradine was in *Tol'able David* ('30), and Broderick appeared in *Woman Chases Man* ('37). In 1949, Crawford's performance as Willie Stark in *All The King's Men* won him an Oscar for Best Actor. Carradine should have won Best Supporting actor for his portrayal of Henry Fonda's friend, Casey, in John Ford's masterpiece *Grapes of Wrath*.

I had watched guys like Carradine, Crawford, and Brady from the balcony of the Roxy Theater when I was in junior high, wearing penny loafers and corduroy pants. Back then, Saturday morning was always chore time, cleaning the barn, shoveling horseshit, and pulling thistle out of the vegetable garden. But Saturday afternoons were all mine. My good buddy, Darwin McTighe and I would hitch a ride into town to catch the matinée.

It was an idyllic, enchanting time. A box of Black Crows, Pepsi, popcorn, and Dar and I would spend the afternoon mesmerized by Scott Brady as Tony Regan in *Undertow*, framed for murder, hiding from the cops while struggling to clear his name. Powerful stuff! Or jeering Carradine as the slimy Jesse Wick in Jean Renoir's first American film *Swamp Water*. In those days, you would see a double feature, a cartoon, *The Pathe Newsreel*, and sometimes even a twenty-minute serial, like *Boston Blackie* or *Sabu, King of the Jungle*. These adventurous actors, along with Boo and Darwin McTighe, were my constant companions throughout my "formative years."

> *Ain't that the best chicken you've ever eaten?*
> —Colonel Sanders, in *Hell's Bloody Devils*

The noon meal consisted of all of the Kentucky Fried Chicken we could eat, served to us by the Colonel himself. Adamson had cut a deal. He gave Colonel a line in the film in exchange for free lunches. It was coleslaw, biscuits, and fried chicken every day for three and a half weeks. Gary Graver told me that ever since *Hell's Bloody Devils* he hasn't been able to look a chicken in the beady little chicken eye, let alone eat one.

After lunch, we filmed the chase sequence in a series of shots that brought me out of the Marineland Amphitheater onto a grassy bluff overlooking the Pacific Ocean. There, in full consort with that magnificent expanse of blue on blue, water and sky, Thug #1 met his demise, a *fait accompli*. Shot to death by the FBI just as I was about to nab the dame!

> *It was sort of a multi-demential experience,*
> *going to the drive-ins.*
> —Sam Sherman, *Independent International*

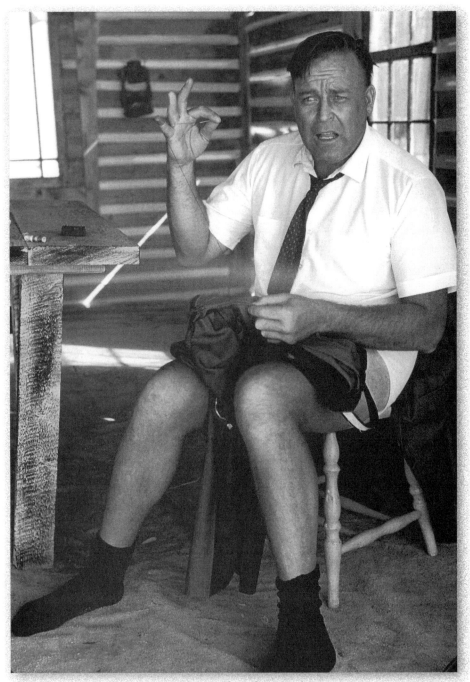

Scott Brady doing double duty for Al Adamson's movies.
Photo courtesy of the author.

During the late 60s and early 70s much of The American Film Revolution was being fought in the trenches of the drive-in movie theaters. Always a mainstay of family entertainment, the drive-ins began to lose mom, dad, and the kids to television. TV was, after all, free, and it was serving up a veritable picnic of programming for everybody in the household: *Gomer Pyle, Bonanza, Mayberry RFD, Gunsmoke, The Smothers Brothers, Ed Sullivan, The Beverly Hillbillies, I Love Lucy, The Man From U.N.C.L.E.*, all in the preferred window for family entertainment. On the other hand, the major studios felt insulted if their films played the drive-ins. They would only book in their worst movies, or their second and third runs.

When the family abandoned the outdoor movie theaters, high school and college kids replaced them, seeking a cultural Mecca they could call their own. When the majors gave the drive-ins, or passion pits, as the teenyboppers called them, the cold shoulder, the exhibitors turned to independent and exploitation filmmakers. This volatile mix of rebellious youth and daring moviemaking began to challenge the newly created rating system and led to an explosion of seat of

L. to R. actor John Gabriel, Colonel Harland Sanders, actress Anne Randall.
"Ain't that the best chicken you've ever eatin'?"Photo courtesy Sam Sherman.

the pants cinema. Biker films, blaxploitation, nudie cuties, and cutting edge comedies, all set new ground rules for what was socially, politically, and personally acceptable. The undisputed King of the Drive-in moviemakers was Al Adamson.

Al Adamson and his partner, Sam Sherman, more than any other filmmakers of their time, gave employment to actors and actresses, who, having once been at the top of their profession, now found themselves out of the loop, drinking too much coffee, reading trade papers full of unfamiliar names, and waiting beside telephones that never rang. Al hired them. He paid them enough to get their health benefits, treating them like they were still important, helping them feel like movie stars one more time. And to Al's credit, he didn't see them as has-beens on the way down. They were performers that he'd loved and admired since he was a kid, hanging around movie sets with his dad, silent era movie actor Denver Dixon.

Adamson also enjoyed working with young, developing talent, like Vilmos Zsigmond and Laszlo Kovacs. Both later became outstanding, much respected cinematographers, lensing some of the most memorable motion pictures of the past thirty years. Bud Cardos, myself, Greydon Clark, and Jack Starrett went on to make our own films. Gary Graver became a successful moviemaker and for fifteen years was cinematographer, magic act stooge, and best friend of the Grand Master himself, Orson Welles.

After *Hell's Bloody Devils*, I would make five more pictures for Al and Sam, each one as bizarre and convoluted as Hollywood Boulevard on Halloween. They were mostly mayhem exaggerated into comic book nonsense. To Al and Sam, violence overdone to the point of being ridiculous was violence robbed of its power, and therefore, forced to exist only as entertainment, an hour and a half of thrills, chills and belly laughs viewed on a drive-in movie screen from the back seat of a Chevy.

"There's no excuse for beauty, honesty, and love."

It was a cocky, double-dare ya time in a dangerous, double-dare ya world. Boundaries were ignored or cast aside, in music, decor, apparel, political viewpoints, home, hearth, and commitments or lack of commitments. People were changing their minds and their lovers as fast as they changed their sheets. The windows of the mind were thrown wide open by a gaggle of diverse pioneers, journeying into the psyche. New, psychedelic territory was being explored. Uncharted seas were sailed in search of a newer, more available God. Urban Pilgrims were rejuvenating the spirit, and declaring a brighter, more honest glimpse into the human heart.

My family and I moved back to Hollywood. Adieu Manhattan Beach, adieu fresh air and sunshine. Hello smog, hello town that moves at a pace too fast for my feet to follow! L.A. is laid back, my ass!

Rose Mary, the boys, and I had taken an apartment near Normandy and Fountain Avenue. It was one of those complexes where you not only know your neighbors, you know what they're eating and what they're talking about. A dozen different accents, salutations, seasonings, and slogans commingled in the hallways day and night. One's senses were overwhelmed by the odor of Paella Valenciana, Acapulco Gold, and patchouli, coalesced into one exotic nose-numbing bouillabaisse.

Upstairs, five doors to the right, Mrs. Weary would be threatening to hit her husband Mr. Weary "widda broom!" Sherry Stewart, beautiful, exotic, with a face lovely as an ivory cameo, occupied Apt. 207. Ms. Stewart loved the music of The Beatles and The Rolling Stones and played them at unbearable decibels, night and day. Directly opposite 207, one could hear L.A. newscaster Jerry Dunphy announcing Lyndon Johnson's commitment of another fifty thousand troops to Vietnam.

I lived on the ground floor, Apt. 110. I was inside, quacking like a duck. It was my son Alexander's fifth birthday party. He, his brothers, and some of their pals were gathered in our darkened living room, watching a black and white, 8mm projection of Daffy Duck cartoons. I was supplying the sound effects. There wasn't a kid in the room who wouldn't rather have been outside in the parking lot playing dodge ball, or down the street at the old concrete schoolyard, playing war. The phone rang! It was Paul Lewis advising me "the game was afoot." Richard Rush was getting ready to make a psychedelic motion picture appropriately titled *Psych-Out*. Paul wanted me to do the special effects and coordinate the stunts. Richard wanted me to play a part. That's right: Thugs' Leader! I ended up doing all three. It turned out to be one of the best efforts of my career, such as it is.

> *Drugs are like grooving on the scenery while driving in the fast lane of the freeway.*
> —The author

Our first production meeting was held at an office adjacent to The First National Bank on Sunset Boulevard, very near the start of the Strip. I remember as I entered the building, the raspy, nasal voice of Dylan seeping like granulated syrup from the Musak, "The times, they are a changing…." I opened the door of the meeting room and stepped into the amazing, colorful, brazen, audacious new world of psychedelia. First off, there was Jack Nicholson, wearing a Royal Canadian Mounted Policeman's Uniform, all black and red, like a Queen's Grenadier. Boo cautioned me, "*Go easy. We might be in the wrong room.*"

Richard Rush had been offered another motorcycle movie to direct, based on the success of *Hells Angels On Wheels*. The proffer came from music icon Dick Clark (*American Bandstand*, *Times Square Rockin' New Year's Eve*). Rush was not anxious to do another biker film. He'd been there, done that. But, he agreed to the project if, first, Clark would produce a bizarre bit of pop-prurience called *Psych-Out*. It was an idea brought to him by Jack Nicholson. Its mind-blowing images and storyline were centered in and around the Love Generation, which mainly habituated the Haight-Ashbury area of San Francisco.

Dick Clark is a very savvy man. Although far removed from the so-called "hippie mentality," which he knew was fueled in large part by drugs, he also knew better than anyone the incredibly eclectic, energetic, and talented music scene that seemed to be carrying the message of the movement. I am reminded of a line from Noel Coward's *Private Lives*, in which Amanda says, "Extraordinary, how potent cheap music is." Dick had started his career in the mailroom at WRUN in Utica, New York, and quickly worked his way up to his own show, the iconic *American Bandstand* on ABC. He is a member of the Rock and Roll Hall of Fame, the Radio Hall of Fame, is the winner of five daytime Emmys, and has a star on the Hollywood Boulevard Walk of Fame. Dick Clark figured if he let Richard do this "hippie homage," he could call in enough musical IOUs to sell the film. Clark agreed to finance the film through his music company and American International Pictures.

> *This early entry from auteur director Richard Rush is a colorful, exciting time capsule from the era of flower power. The fact that it still holds up to this day is mainly due to the sheer amount of the talent involved.*
>
> —Donald Guarisco, *All Movie Guide*

In attendance at that first production meeting on Sunset Boulevard were enough artistic outlaws and revolutionaries to overthrow a small country. Many of them were already icons, others on their way to becoming so. Besides Nicholson, the cast included Bruce Dern, who would one day be nominated for an Oscar (*Coming Home*), nominated for two Golden Globes (*Coming Home*, *The Great Gatsby*), and win Best Supporting Actor Award from the National Society of Film Critics for his role in the Nicholson directed basketball film, *Drive, He Said*. Dean Stockwell was nominated for an Oscar for *Married To The Mob*, won Best Actor twice at the Cannes Film Festival for *Long Days Journey Into Night* and *Compulsion*, was nominated for five Emmys, won two Golden Globes and was nominated for four others. Stockwell also has his star on the Hollywood Boulevard Walk of Fame.

Cast member Henry Jaglom would go on to become a brilliant director in his own right, helming such delicious film fare as *Eating*, *Baby Fever*, and *Last Summer in The Hamptons*. In 1997, his film about people yearning to find their soul mates, *Deja Vu*, won the Jury Prize at the prestigious Cannes Film Festival.

Jennie, the deaf girl searching for her older brother (played by Dern) through the noisy, bustling environment of the Haight, was brilliantly played by Susan Strasberg, daughter of famed drama coach Lee Strasberg. Susan had been nominated for a BAFTA as Most Promising Newcomer, in 1955, for her role in *Picnic*. She was nominated for a Golden Globe in 1962, as best actress in *Hemingway's Adventures of a Young Man*. Actor/director Garry Marshall, brother of actress/director Penny Marshall, would go on to win a Golden Globe as Filmmaker of the Year in 2004. Garry has also received four Emmy nominations, and has won an Honorary Lifetime Membership in The Producers Guild, and received his star on Hollywood's Walk of Fame.

Intense, endearing actor Adam Roarke was back, along with my friends, the tall, good-natured Max Julien, and the beautiful blonde, Linda Gaye Scott. The crew included Laszlo Kovacs on camera, Aggi Aguilar as gaffer, Joyce King holding script, and Tom Ramsey as key grip. Old family friends, each and every one.

That evening everybody got the chance to meet everybody else. I seem to recall finger sandwiches and white wine, but I couldn't swear to it. Then Paul Lewis gave us our scripts and we got down to business. We had a brief run-through, Richard discussing how he visualized the scenes.

Although the vibrant cultural revolution was carried aloft by all of the arts combined, it was the music and its haunting, driving call to arms against the cruel, stagnant mainstream that carried the message most clearly. Musicians involved in *Psych-Out* included Jimi Hendrix, Strawberry Alarm Clock, The Seeds, Boenzee Cryque, Sky Saxon, and musical director Ronald Stein.

The story concerns a young deaf girl who travels to Haight-Ashbury in search of her brother, who has sent her a postcard reading, "Jess Saes: God is alive and well and living in a sugar cube." Not much to go on. It is interesting to note, however, that she is introduced to the whole flower-power-hippie-music scene that was re-defining San Francisco while being unable to hear.

Chapter Nine

Illustration by Michael Gallegly

Killing And All That Jazz

"Smell the color of purple."

—advertising slogan for *Psych-Out*

The screenplay for *Psych-Out* was swollen with all of the accouterments of living theater playing out 24/7 in San Francisco, especially the happenings in the Haight. Nicholson was playing Stoney, the leader of a psychedelic band called Mumbling Jim. His band mates were Adam Roarke as Ben, Max Julien as Elwood, and Linda Gaye Scott as Lynn.

Everybody lived and slept together communally in a big old rambling house that was decorated like an original Salvador Dali after a bad storm, beads trailing off to nowhere, crepe streamers leading to lofts and lairs, giant blobs of contrasting color splashed across the walls, screaming parrots screaming. And washed over all of it, the seductive, obvious glaze of marijuana and LSD (acid).

We had almost finished the run-through; everyone, including myself, seemed up to the task. I had a fight or two to stage, one in an automobile junkyard where I would get a chance to actually act with Jack Nicholson!

Boo gave a timorous, *"Huzzah,"* preferring that I stick to pretending rather than actually getting involved in anything resembling danger. There would be an effects scene involving a fired up furnace and a young girl vomiting black ooze. *"Should be no problem,"* this, again, from Mr. Boo. *"Over the years, you've gotten that barfing bit down, haven't you, lad?"*

The last few pages of the script, actually, the entire ending of the movie, called for one big acid trip. A bad one, involving stunts, fireballs, freakish cars on freeways, houses burning, walls and staircases smoking in psychedelic suggestions of devils and dragons, and a

189

full-on body hit by several speeding vehicles that does in Dean Stockwell, one of our heroes. Hmmmm! Sounded like stunts and effects to me. Richard Rush and Dick Clark had never taken acid, so the scenery was going to be pretty much up to me. The only problem? I had never taken the stuff either and had no idea what a trip gone bad would look like. Every acid freak I consulted gave me the same advice, "You aren't gonna know by askin', dude. If you're gonna run with the wolves, you need to learn how to howl." Outlaw translation: *Strap up, mount up, and rendezvous behind the bank.*

By the following morning I had made up my mind. I was going to take some LSD, in the interest of art, mind you, and a desire to be spot on in creating the event for Richard and his camera. I called my new friend, cinematographer Gary Graver, and asked if he could assist me in my first real psychedelic experience. I knew that Graver had done the drug several times. He offered to help and even suggested I arrange to spend an entire afternoon and evening at his apartment. "It will last about eight hours."

"*Watch it,*" Boo warned. "*People have nose-dived off of the roofs of buildings while on this stuff!*"

"Hey, listen, Graver, is your apartment on the ground floor?" I asked.

"Nah, top floor, four flights up. Why?"

A half hour later, I was eating breakfast with my kids when Alex pointed out that I was about to pour orange juice on my cereal. Upstairs, Ms. Stewart was playing Nancy and Frank Sinatra, "Something Stupid" cranked to the max. Not a good sign.

Around ten-thirty in the morning, I drove to visit actor John Parker. John, I knew, had taken several acid trips, so I hoped for a couple of inside tips before I personally embarked. The smog that morning was so thick I could taste it inside the car, a noxious mix of chalk and rusting metal. Parker lived off of East Sunset, in the Silver Lake district, an area sculpted with low hills and quaint, 50s-style houses that stuck to the side-slopes like birds nests. On very smoggy days, you couldn't see twenty feet in front of you. When it was clear, you could easily view the area's contour for miles, rolling, colorful buttes and smooth knolls that dropped into a southern leg of the San Fernando Valley. You could also make out the glint of the city of Glendale, nestled against the deep, purple shoulder of Mt. Washington. Eastward, far off in the distance, were the snow-spackled peaks of the San Gabriel Mountains. It was this view, this sweeping vista of pure gorgeousness, that led one to believe that Los Angeles was indeed the City of Angels.

I nosed the car next to the curb above John's apartment and moments later, was inside, canoodling while he threw together a pot of coffee. I had called ahead, told him what I wanted. John was delighted that he was being given the opportunity to be The Big Kahuna, psychedelically speaking. He was used to being the nondescript guy, the one making the least noise on a low-budget crew as he hustled props and decorated sets.

"Coffee's ready!" John and I filled our cups and adjourned to the living room to discuss my approaching journey via LSD.

Parker told me to relax and "go with the flow," wherever it took me. I shouldn't worry about jumping from the roof, as others were going to be there, including the much responsible Gary Graver, and they would make sure I was having a nice, safe trip. He even advised me to prepare for the event by selecting some of my favorite music to explore while under the influence, and to take along some books and articles I wanted to read in particular.

That evening I started preparing for my first experience with acid. The big A! First came the music. Bob Dylan was everyone's poet/musician of choice, the guy hip to trip with. However, I just didn't get Dylan. His lyrics were okay, sometimes clever, but not romantic enough for me, and his voice had such an off-key, nasal drip to it that it put me in mind of a math professor with a serious sinus infection. No, not for me, not for my mind-altering excursion into the unknown. Instead, I decided on the sadder, more esoteric music just in from a Canadian singer/songwriter/poet/mystic-monk of a man named Leonard Cohen. I had bumped into Cohen's hauntingly lovely "Suzanne" while sunbathing at the beach, eavesdropping on a bevy of Canuck stewardesses who were catching some rays before a return flight to our neighbor North of the Line. The lyrics of "Suzanne" blew me away, as did the mellow, beautifully melancholic voice of Cohen himself. "*Perfect,*" Boo interjected. "*Perfect for a bout of deep depression!*"

For the inclusion of sheer joy, I packed some music by folk-singer, environmentalist, peace activist, and to me, hero, Pete Seeger. I had caught Pete at the Ash Grove, a folk-blues club on Santa Monica Boulevard. When he lit into "This Land is Your Land" I was forever hooked. Pete had a way of throwing back his head when he sang, opening up his throat so that his magnificent voice came out pure, strong as a new day, a new beginning, a clear, clarion call of hope. "*Good choice,*" Boo announced.

I decided against The Beatles, everyone's go-to group for a gavotte with the psyche. I was afraid that, if by chance I did achieve a meet-up with my inner self, I didn't want to arrive there in a dippy, teenybopper yellow submarine. Group-wise, it was either going to be the sexual thumpings of Creedence Clearwater Revival or the grander, subtler sensuousness of a little recognized band from Britain, Barclay James Harvest. I decided on the latter, as BJH had achieved a magnificent orchestral sound in their music by adding the mysterious mellotron to the usual guitar, bass, and drums. What could be more fitting for *La Grande Voyage* than a full-throated symphony orchestra?

Next on my acid list was reading material. I was in the process of reading Richard Brautigan's *Trout Fishing In America*. To me, this book was a profound treasure, a whimsical series of stories, observations, and recollections, a poetic musing on how greed and social decomposition were eroding the rural life. I preferred this North Beach writer to his peers, Ginsberg and Ferlinghetti. For those serious acid moments, I decided to revisit Sartre, Kant, and Heidegger, so I also stuffed editions of their work into my psychedelic ditty bag.

At the last, I decided to include an LP of Paul Robeson, the great black singer, athlete, actor, writer, and political activist. Robeson was one of my childhood idols. The sound of that incredibly deep, thundering voice of his, rumbling its way through work songs, field calls, and spirituals, always inspired the hell out of me.

I surveyed my accouterments for the afternoon's departure. Boo suggested I might want to take along a bag of cookies, a banana, and a bottle of water. "Goddamn, what am I getting ready to do? What am I thinking? What if I injure an innocent while doing a sailor-dive off a rooftop? What if the innocent is me?" But, then, did I consider canceling my trip? Not for a second. This was, after all, a journey in the interests of cinematic purity!

Arriving at Gary Graver's apartment ten minutes late, I was greeted by his then girlfriend, Ms. Misty, a tall, lithe woman with a cascade of long, dark hair and a seductive, bedroom aura. Also in the room were Don Jones, there just for the observing, and marginal moviemaker Ed De Priest. Ed was accompanied by his constant shadow, girlfriend-nymph, Merrilyn Rabbit. Graver was on the telephone. Ms. Misty told me, "Relax, get comfy. Graver will be with you in a minute."

I took a seat in a respectable looking armchair with thick, crimson upholstery. Nothing too busy or artsy for me. I wanted a decent, solid, safe chair, with room for a body to squirm if need be. I opened my bag and began to unpack the stuff I had brought for my personal enjoyment. Graver's beautiful Irish setter, Siddhartha, stopped by for a pet, decided to stay, and sat next to me on the floor, assuming what seemed to the "yogic" equivalent of a canine mudra. "*This is going to be a piece of cake,*" Boo whispered.

Ms. Misty vamped her voluptuous body across the room like a modern day Salome. She handed me a large glass of green liquid and a small, yellowish pill. "Here Gar, wash it down with this."

"What is it?"

"It's wheat grass, alfalfa, amaranth sprouts, buckwheat, adzuki bean…"

"No, I mean the pill. Is this the acid?" I turned it over in my palm. It was so small, lying there against my skin like an innocent M&M.

"Yes, it's the acid, Studikins. Orange Sunshine." She held one of the little fellows in her fingers, touched it against mine. "*Bon voyage, Gar,*" and she pelicaned it through her lips like a Christmas candy.

"Well, here we go, kid, balls to the wall!" I popped the acid into my mouth washing it down with a huge gulp of the green stuff. Yuck! It was the worst tasting drink I'd encountered since arriving on the planet. I almost puked. Gary Graver, wearing his schoolboy grin, moseyed my way slow as a sloth covered in syrup. He motioned toward the nauseating, greenish goop. "Isn't that stuff great? I was lucky. I ran into Gypsy Boots this afternoon, and figured I better stock up for tonight. I got us a couple of quarts."

Boo acerbically mutters, "*Oh, goody!*"

Robert Bootzin, aka "Gypsy Boots," was Southern California's favorite health guru and nature boy. He scooted around Los Angeles in a van painted in psychedelic graffiti, selling homegrown vegetables, herbs, spices, magic potions, and purified spring waters. His nickname was a combo of his last name *Bootzin*, and the fact that he always dressed in denim cut-offs and old cowboy boots. Of undetermined age, Boots was a heart-full of charisma and good humor. I was very fond of Gypsy. If this gooey green liquid with the obscene taste came from him, it had to be the real unky-dunk.

An hour and a quart of green stuff later, I was beginning to think there was nothing to LSD and its reputation for being a mind-blowing experience. Other than a small tingling of anxiety, I was feeling bloody chipper.

Ms. Misty was twirling like a Sufi, only in slow motion, to a recording of Frank Sinatra's, for Christ's sake, "Strangers in the Night." Ed De Priest and Merrilyn were making out on the couch. Gary Graver had positioned himself directly under a ceiling lamp with a Tiffany shade. "Wow!" Graver was obviously seeing something remarkable, something invisible to the rest of us. "Wow. Oh, wow! Look at that! Oh, man, wow!" The situation did not appear particularly mind-blowing to me.

John Parker had promised me I would likely have a trip of "quiet study, a journey of intellectual expansion, an examination of my spiritual self." To that end, Don Jones and I had been discussing everything from the discovery by astrophysicists of a small particle of energy they labeled a "quark," to South African heart surgeon Dr. Christiaan Barnard's performance of the world's first heart transplant, segueing to sax player John Coltrane and his free jazz album *Interstellar Space*, ending in a happy reflection on the contraceptive gizmo, "The Pill," which Jonesy informed me was now available in seven select varieties. Boo was falling asleep, actually, out of boredom.

I considered leaving earlier than anticipated. I was hungry. If I left now I could stop by a bistro for a little pub-grub before calling the night fini. "Yeah, that would be the ticket," Jones snickered. "Maybe they can fry you up one of them quarks.

As I arose from the chair, all of the red from the upholstery clung to my body, then began a slow, syrupy drip off of me and onto the floor. "Holy Toledo!"

"What?" Jones yelled. His words hit the walls like bullets fired from the chamber of an over-and-under street-sweeper. Why was he screaming?

"Wow," Graver sighed, louder than necessary, while staring, transfixed by the electric colors in the Tiffany of the lamp above his head.

"Hoobijahdihah," said Ms. Misty, mid-swirl, and then, "Hoobijahdihah!" again.

Siddhartha, Graver's ever faithful Irish setter, followed me into the bathroom, where I intended to splash cold water on my rapidly melting face and put a stop to this nonsense. I stood above the sink, looking down, way down. Way, way down! The sink appeared to be about twelve yards away from me, near the bottom of a very distant floor. "Holy shit! I must be ten feet tall." Somehow, I managed to douse water about my head, face, and neck. This restored a semblance of perspective. I bid everyone *hasta luego* and headed for the door. God, the door now seemed over a block away. "Gar? Are you okay to drive?" This from Jonesy, who appeared concerned about me even though he was starting to shrink in size!

"Roger that!" Why did my voice sound so wimpy all of a sudden? I'm a stuntman. I mustn't appear wimpy in the least. I opened the door and stepped onto the balcony.

"*Don't jump!*" Boo was awake now, and very nervous. I couldn't blame him; I was nervous myself, being privy to the rapid disintegration of reality in any form that I could recognize.

"I am not going to jump!" I said aloud, and then realized I was talking to Graver's dog, who had followed me from the apartment, perhaps concerned in his own little Irish way. I opened the door and shooed him back inside where producer Ed De Priest and Merrilyn Rabbit seemed to be disappearing into the couch.

"Wow!" exclaimed Gary Graver.

"What?" yelled Don Jones.

"Hoobijahdihah," cooed Ms. Misty.

Somehow, I made it down the stairs and into my car. Then came the difficult part: driving home!

I had only a few short blocks left to go, but panic was setting in with a swiftness reserved for pickpockets at the Cannes Film Festival. The street in front of me, festooned with automobiles, trucks, motorcycles, et al., was a bucking wraith of concrete road-flesh, twisted in the middle, like taffy, and then, it snapped off, into a night sky populated with a zillion stars that pulsed, throbbed, ignited, and spun, all within reach of my hand. By the time I made Sunset and Gower, I was seriously considering surrender. I was going to pull to the curb and wait for the police, at which time I intended to break down, confess all sins, and plead for hospitalization. Boo thought it was a good idea. I noticed, however, that if I opened my window, and looked directly at the road two feet or so in front of me, the concrete was not performing those frightening gymnastics. Also, if I ignored the sky, the pulsing lights, the humming sound of the universal, "Ohmnmmmm," and Boo's hysterical shriek, I was actually in good shape. I opted to try and make a run for it, arriving home shortly thereafter, safe and reasonably sound.

I lay awake most of the night, listening to the sound of my heart trying to kick its way through my chest! I promised God that if he would just let me live, I would never, ever take acid again. "Excuse me, God, I know that I'm a sinner! Could you, please, just give me a little slack?"

By early morn, the stuff began to wear off, and I was left with a feeling of genuine elation at having survived. Everything seemed brighter, clearer, cleaner. More in place and centered than usual. I stepped outside, inhaling the sunshine. What a beautiful day! Plus, I now knew exactly how I would accomplish the special effects for *Psych-Out* sound and visual. "Hallelujah!" I shouted to the newborn world. "I am sanctified!"

Later, as I wolfed down a breakfast waffle topped with honey, bacon "crisp," orange juice, coffee, and, after digesting the *L.A. Times* morning edition, it dawned on me that I had not once gotten into any of the items I had packed for my trip. Oh, well. I began to plot a psychedelic experience for Richard Rush's cameras. The script required it to be a bad trip. Well, I could handle that. I had pumped up my street creds, gotten mean and fried. I was raring to skank the bank, do me a Clyde, and boogie on over to a wilder side.

LSD, STP, and Psilocybin

The Haight-Ashbury district of San Francisco was not only the Mecca for the growing peace movement, but also the nexus for the emergence of all things psychedelic. It was an open-air zoo, so to speak, and director Richard Rush used it all to illuminate his film.

With *Psych-Out*, Rush and his merry band remained true to the requirements of outlawry. Although produced by straight arrow Dick Clark, the film displayed an almost blasé attitude toward the profligate use of marijuana, at the time, a highly illegal substance. In some states, getting caught with a doobie would get you twenty years in the slammer. LSD had been declared an illegal, dangerous substance since 1966, yet it was a large part of the open cultural scene in Rush's film. The psychogenic was even recommended by many in the cast as a pleasant gateway to spiritual discovery.

After some shots of the cast wandering around San Francisco to establish the film's locale as Haight-Ashbury, production manager Paul Lewis moved cast and crew back to Los Angeles, where the major part of the movie was to be filmed.

Going Commando, L.A. Style

I'm redneck, thug leader #1, perched on top of a pile of car carcasses stacked in an automotive junkyard. From here I witness Stoney (Nicholson), Elwood (Max Julien), Ben (Adam Roarke), and Jenny (Susan Strasberg) arrive at the yard to search for her missing brother. Through the grapevine, they have ascertained he is living in an abandoned car in this junkyard. Me and my fellow thugs, Bud Cardos, Don Jones, William Bonner, Pat Raines, et al., are hovering over the yard waiting for the missing brother to reappear. We want a piece of him ourselves. I was never sure why, as the script did not explain the motive for our hatred, just that we were thugs, spawn, I suppose, of urban decay.

Stoney and his entourage pull next to an abandoned vehicle, the one with all of the right signs, and get out to investigate. Thug Time! Loud crunching sound as I leap from the top of the pile of ravaged metal to the hood of a lower level car. My fellow rednecks appear on top of surrounding autos and perch there, like vultures, scouting carrion. Stoney and I get into a verbal shoving match, culminating in a junkyard duke-out. Cardos goes head first through a car window; I grab Ben and give him a jaw job. Stoney hits Jones over the head with a bottle, and on and on, ad-fisticum. Finally, Max Julien, as Elwood, drops some acid, sees himself as a knight in shining armor, and takes me and the boys to the ground with the assistance of a two-by-four wooden plank. Game over. Hippies 4, rednecks 0.

Next, Richard Rush had us all assemble at The Cheetah, a wildly popular dance-rock emporium on the pier at Santa Monica's now defunct Pacific Ocean Park. In the 40s and 50s, before a fire wiped out P.O.P., the club had been a huge ballroom where the sophisticates of Los Angeles would migrate to dance to the music of Guy Lombardo, Sammy Kaye, Les Brown and the Band of Renown, and especially Lawrence Welk and his Champagne Music Makers.

After the fire, the pier was closed except for a few suspicious outdoor foodstalls, and the ballroom (sold and renamed The Cheetah). It is interesting to note that it took a holocaust to convert the syrupy sound of Lawrence Welk and his band into the psychedelic wailings of the new house band, Alice Cooper (aka The Nazz).

Alice and The Nazz were nodding out during daylight hours in a spare room at the house of actor John Phillip Law, who I would later cast and direct in my homage to cancer survival, *Rainy Day Friends*. John's pad was just above the Strip, on Sunset. Come nighttime, the band would boogey from Sunset out to the beach, where they would open the house for such mind-blowing guest artists

The bad guys vs. the good guys. L. to R. Don Jones, Gary Kent, Adam Roarke,
Susan Strasberg, Jack Nicholson, and Bud Cardos in Psych-Out.
Photo courtesy of the author.

as Jim Morrison and The Doors, Buffalo Springfield, Jimi Hendrix, Frank Zappa
and The Mothers of Invention, GTO, and the marvelously energetic, extremely
popular Watts 103rd Street Rhythm Band. Remember "Express Yourself" and
"Spreadin' Honey?"

In *Psych-Out*, Stoney and his Mumbling Jim band have at long last scored a
gig at The Cheetah. They are laying down licks for a stoned, mesmerized crowd.
Jenny is sitting in the audience, and, though deaf, she can feel the vibrations of
the music while losing herself into the beauty of the accompanying light show.
Suddenly, the camera discovers her long lost brother Steve (Bruce Dern) edging
his way through the crowd. He is wearing a long, white smock, has long hair down
past his shoulder line, quite resembling an apparition from an early Dickens novel,

or some ghost freshly escaped from a story by Edgar Allen Poe. Steve is trying to make his way through the throng to reunite with his sister.

In *Psych-out*, Rush explained that my job as Thug Leader was to chase Dern through much of the film. Now, Bruce had been a top notch speed skater when he was barely big enough to burp, and it gets worse; he had been a champion runner most of his life, in prep school, in college, and he continued to run throughout his career. A half-mile or mile was a walk in the park to Bruce. He was now into distance running, marathons and ultra-marathons, fifty-milers, for Christ's sake.

I, as Thug #1, am hanging out at The Cheetah, grooving on the young chicks, when I spot Steve in the crowd and make for him with the intention of punching him out. He sees me and dashes for the exit. Now comes the hard part. I have to chase him!

"Ready, Bruce? Ready, Gary?" Richard Rush asks. We are standing outside the nightclub, toeing down for the event. Laszlo Kovacs is in the camera eyepiece and the crew is standing by. Joyce King, Paul Lewis, Aggi, et al., assemble to watch the chase. "Roll camera. Marker. Action!" Bruce takes off. Rush has asked me to wait a beat or so before I give chase, to give him a chance. Give him a chance! Are you friggin' out of your tree?

Bruce Dern has legs like a racehorse and the speed of a Ferrari. By the time I began my lope after him, he was several blocks away, and almost out of sight. This was the case throughout the entire movie. I mean, I didn't even come close, in spite of Rush suggesting that he might want to slow down a little and give *me* a chance!

Several days later, I actually found myself doubling Dern in a hairy little break-in at an art museum. It was one of the numerous times in my stunt career when I almost bought the bullet. The sequence involves Bruce's character, Steve, breaking into the building to reclaim a piece of his sculpture. It is nighttime, and the museum, a humongous bulb of a structure, is closed to the public. To gain entrance, Steve is forced to climb to the top of the dome, where he breaks a skylight, lowers himself through the opening, and then swings his body out into the air, lets go of his grip, and manages to propel himself over the balustrade of a balcony. He then descends the stairs to the rotunda. That is the plan as explained to me by director Rush.

So, here I am, dressed in Dern's wardrobe, including the white smock and the long, straggly wig he wears throughout the film. I crawl out on top of the building and find the hole punched through the skylight by the crew. Because of the nature of the camera coverage, a straight up shot from three stories directly below, I was unable to place fall pads down there, in case I slipped and took a header. It had to work, or lights out for this poor, humble country boy. I find a small piece of molding to use as a handhold, and yell to Richard that I am ready. "Roll camera. Marker. Action, Gary!"

I crawl through the opening and find myself dangling in mid-air, three stories up, gripping with just the tips of my fingers holding my weight (a hundred and eighty pounds), with nothing below me but the 3 Cs: camera, crew, and concrete. I could feel my fingers slipping, so I start my swing. When I feel the time is right, I hurtle out into space and let go. From down below, it doesn't look like much, but from up top, it was downright scary! I make it over the railing, but barely! Deep sigh of relief, and then I'm off, bounding down the stairs, impersonating the runner! Whew! Somebody say, *Amen*!

Next afternoon, we're all gathered on a soundstage in Hollywood, where we are going to do a special effects sequence of Jenny as a little girl (played by Susan Bushman) going through a traumatic, horrible scene with her mother. Supposedly it's the event that led to her losing the ability to hear. We are in a makeshift basement, with a large furnace set up on stage, containing a roaring fire.

Jenny begins to cry hysterically, a sound that wakes her sleeping brother. He creeps to the basement door and peeks in. The cruel mother is teasing Jenny, holding a box over her head, one that contains knickknacks and keepsakes very important to the little girl. Jenny is pleading with her mother to give her back the box. Behind them, the fire in the furnace has reached the intensity of an inferno. Suddenly the mother turns and throws the box into the fire. Jenny goes into a seizure, and then it happens, the Black Ooze Experience!

The script calls for Jenny to vomit a "black ooze," with repulsive tendrils escaping her mouth "like the hideous legs of a large spider." Okay, I'm the effects guy. This is not the usual stuff of pyro and powder, fire and smoke. This calls for something much more artistic. Some magic thing-a-ma-bob from the ditty bag of delights that every good effects guy has glued to his person like a second skin.

I open the bag and out jumps my bottle of powdered Alka-Seltzer, the stuff I put on an actress's face for a Gary Graver Sci-Fi. You cover it with make up, and when the face sweats under the hot lights, the powder begins to sizzle and boil, leaving the effect of the skin disintegrating under some sort of acid. Next, I extracted a coil of soft solder, the kind I could snip and twist around a length of smooth wire, turning it into instant barbwire. An actor or a horse could run into it, look like they were being ripped apart, while actually, they were safe as Sunday School. I used this to good effect in Don Jones' chiller *Abducted*.

Reaching further into the bag, I pulled out a grease gun and several packs of licorice from a convenience store candy counter. I shredded the licorice into long, black strands, and packed the grease gun with a good forty weight. Rush was ready, Laszlo was ready, and little Susan was ready. When the camera rolled, Susan fed the strands of dark licorice out of her mouth. I was on the off-camera side, squirting the grease so that it blended visually with the licorice. Hola! The Black Ooze Effect! Did it work? Well, here's a review of that exact sequence, penned by Harold Clarke for *Ecco Magazine*:

> *The horrific impact of this moment is amplified when black venom, the manifestation of years of abuse, oozes from little Jenny's mouth. This repulsive act, which is reminiscent of the tongue dislodging scene from H.G. Lewis'* Blood Feast, *and Linda Blair's satanic retching in* The Exorcist, *lingers in the psyche long after* Psych-Out's *conclusion.*

Scoring and Then, Tweaking

In Richard's film, the real dangerous stuff was Dom or "STP," as it was known on the streets. DOM was a form of petroleum waste that was also a highly powerful hallucinogenic. Its street name stood for "Stop The Police," "Serenity, Tranquility, Peace," or "Super Terrific Psychedelic," depending on who is calling the shots. It first became popular with street space cadets in 1967. It was the cause of a lot of brain damage and even death before hospitals knew exactly what it was, or how to treat it.

In *Psych-Out*, it is after downing a glass of STP that the adult Jenny begins her frightening, eventually deadly, sojourn through the treacherous environs of "The Haight." This particularly long, frightening sequence starts with fire effects that dog her through a nightmare of flame, houses, streets, walls, stairs, small explosions that smoke, curl, and snarl as Jennie dashes, panicked, through a phantasmagoria of her worst dreams. Her bad trip ends with her almost comatose, as fireballs whiz past, dangerously close to her face. Gradually the fireballs morph into the headlights of speeding vehicles, and she finds herself standing in the middle of a heavily trafficked freeway.

Richard Rush and the gang all assembled on a side street in crowded downtown Los Angeles. I was going to do a controlled burn inside of an old house. For this undertaking, I had assembled my usual effects crew, Don Jones and John Parker, and a couple of new guys, a slim, borderline pyromaniac named Gary Heacock (*The Astro-Zombies*, *The Time Travelers*) and the bear-like, taciturn effects guru, Roger George (*The Terminator*, *Repo Man*).

The morning would start after two coffees and three chocolate éclairs from craft service, my usual. Things would get started with actor Bruce Dern standing against a large, flaming cross at the far end of a burning hallway. So, all that's required is a controlled burn, inside an old, dry wooden house, circa 1940s, in which the walls and ceiling are on fire, as well as an eight-foot blazing cross at the far end of a hallway. Got it!

The crew brought out all of the company fire extinguishers. Paul Lewis had two hook and ladder outfits from LAFD on standby, just in case. The Brucer (Dern) was pumped, ready to rumble. You could feel the excitement building. Everyone, and I mean *everyone*, was crowding forward to get close to the action. For maybe a millisecond, I had second thoughts. I could hear Walter Cronkite on the news break, "Failed actor Gary Kent, masquerading as a special effects expert, outdoes Ms. O'Leary's infamous Chicago cow by burning down Los Angeles! Updates on the hour!"

Actually, the scene came off swimmingly. Walls were burning, big chunks of flaming beams fell from the ceiling; Bruce writhed and gesticulated in front of the massive, incinerating cross. Heavenly, if I must say so myself. When Rush called, "Cut," my boys just squeezed off the gas jets leading to the "dustpans" that fed out masses of flame, and we used an extinguisher on the gelled walls. Mission accomplished. One could now actually lean against those wooden walls without so much as a tingle. Please remember, this was long before CGI, the entire conflagration was pulled out of my ditty bag of secret tricks. Thanks be to Zoroaster!

Boot Scooting

I am standing in the middle of a closed off section of California Freeway 405, dressed in Dean Stockwell's clothes, white hippie suit, headband, beads, the works. I am also wearing pads underneath the clothes, as I am about to be hit by a speeding car. What the hell is going down? Well, I am doubling Stockwell, that's what, and this is his death scene. I, doubling him, have dashed onto the freeway to rescue Susan Strasberg, who stands, frozen with fear in the midst of whizzing interstate traffic. I picked Don "Irish Frankie" Jones to drive the hit car. You can depend on Jonesy to nail his marks. I'd rather ride with him when he's drunk than with most people when they're sober.

Kovacs is ready on camera; Joyce King hugs her script. Paul Lewis has hired a bunch of extras to drive atmosphere to and fro on the freeway. It is a night shoot, and the lights are somewhat disorienting. Jones is waiting, about a hundred yards down the highway, motor on, foot hovering atop the gas pedal.

Richard Rush rolls the camera, and calls, "Action!" Of the cars hurtling toward me, I have to pick out the one Jones is driving, a '65 white Ford four-door, and prepare myself for the hit. The timing has to be spot on, or I will break my legs, or worse, my precious and graceful neck! Here comes Jonesy, head on. I take my time, waiting for the last millisecond before impact, then throw myself up, onto the hood and roll into the windshield. Brakes screech, Jones kills the engine. It worked just as if was planned by somebody intelligent.

The next shot is of me bouncing off the sides of other vehicles. "Cut!" The final shot requires me to climb to the top rung of a step ladder, where my intent is to do a back flip onto the hood of a passing car, roll off the opposite side, strike my head on the concrete curbing, crushing my skull. Again, it is Jonesy doing the driving. Since I am going off backwards, the car has to be always at the same speed, or I run the possibility of pitching onto the concrete, backwards, head first from a height of about eight feet.

"Ready, Gary?" asks the assistant director. "Let's do it!" I am calm, centered. All apprehension dissipated long ago, before I began countdown. Boo has squeezed his eyes tightly closed after being rudely dismissed from my consciousness. Company grips hold the ladder legs to keep them steady. I nod to the AD. "Roll camera. Marker." Rush yells, "Action!" and the automobile, a sleek station wagon, slides through traffic, headed my way. I spot it out of the corner of my eye. At just the right moment, I throw myself off the ladder, landing on my back and shoulders directly in the middle of the hood. I roll across the hood, do another ass-backward tuck, and pretend to slam my head into the pavement. "Cut." Applause! I have survived.

Who Closed the Gate to the Garden?

We thought we were making an important statement with *Psych-Out*. Unlike the iconoclastic *Easy Rider*, which focused mainly on a pair of outsiders, our movie reflected the attitudes of a much larger group of individuals. We dealt, not only with the tapestry and timbre of the times, but specifically, communal living: virtual strangers, united only by a common humanity, taking care of each other genuinely, thoughtful of one another in a new, unfettered sort of way.

Jack Nicholson's character, Stoney, was a stand up guy, one you wouldn't mind having as your brother even if you lived in Olathe, Kansas. Stoney had ethics: "You take care of your neighbor; you don't roll over on a friend; and you are willing to sacrifice, fight even, for what you believe in." Stoney cared about his job and his band mates; he showed up for rehearsals on time, and applied a good, old fashioned attitude toward his work. Stoney had the ability to respond to whatever situation confronted him, whether it was a frightened, deaf girl, or a freaked out druggie who could not regain control of his disintegrating faculties. What could be more All-American than that?

In a very real sense, the structure of *Psych-Out* mirrored the structure of the everyday lives of real people everywhere. At the time, Rush thought the film did too much *sloganeering*, and yet, sloganeering was indicative of the times. "Peace, brother, peace." "Make love, not war." "We shall overcome." *Psych-Out* had it all, including an eerie forewarning of darker, more sinister days right around the corner.

We had shot a scene of a mock funeral in L.A.'s Griffith Park, with the popular music group Strawberry Alarm Clock playing their megahit "Incense and Peppermint," while Stoney and the gang carried a coffin containing the supposed corpse of band mate Ben. Suddenly, the "corpse" sits up, grinning and kissing all and sundry in a marvelous suggestion of death followed by the rebirthing of life. However, while the festivities continued, Bud Cardos and I, as the Thugs, can be seen stalking poor, deaf Jennie. We are waiting, wolf-like, for the chance to devour her innocence. Remind you of anything? That evening, just at wrap time, word arrived on set that the spiritual leader of the Civil Rights Movement, Reverend Martin Luther King, Jr., had been assassinated. Shot to death by a rabid racist named James Earl Ray. King had been speaking to a small gathering from a balcony outside his motel room in Memphis, Tennessee, when the life of this so devout, so peaceful man, was snuffed out instantly, like blowing out a candle.

A couple of months later, while I was enjoying a steamy dance with my provocative and stunningly beautiful neighbor, Ms. Sherry Stewart, someone burst through the door shouting, "Robert Kennedy has just been shot to death!" Only blocks away, in a crowded foyer of the famed Ambassador Hotel, my presidential candidate, a knight in shining armor of the young and the hopeful, had been taken down by a disgruntled young Palestinian named Sirhan Sirhan. Sherry began to cry. I, however, was not all that surprised. Mankind, it seemed to me, was just satisfying his innate craving to kill.

Psych-Out and the 60s, then, were almost finished. Over and done with. Rush's film, in its way, was a warning not to get caught up in it all: the dugs, the free sex, the abandonment of the conscience to randomness. It is, as they say, a wild and dangerous world sometimes, and all of the flowers, the love-ins, the be-ins, the "peace is power" movements didn't really work. "Life is a plastic bubble, man. Reality is a trip" (from *Psych-Out*). Well, what really happens is a guy gets hit by a car and dies, and the flower children disappear into the foothills, or slip into neckties instead of tie-dyes and go to work at the Corpolopolis. Ad nauseum.

The era of the psychedelic movie was a thin soup lasting only around two years. To the American mainstream audience, the hippie culture was just too strange, too dangerous, and too drug-addled to last. The USA morphed quickly into a bloated bag of blathering humanoids, lusting after creature comfort and personal, instead of spiritual, gain. By the time Rush's film opened in theaters in places like Dallas, Texas or Seepage, Wisconsin, there was no longer a psychedelic movement. By far, the most evocative film of the year was *In Cold Blood*, a disturbing account of the horrible slaughter of a farm family in, of all places, Kansas.

After all of the flowers withered and died, society was more screwed up than ever, certainly meaner, more petty, seemingly caring about only its leather britches, faux celebrity, Saturday night, and the paycheck. It was no longer "peace and love." It was "grunge" and "punk" and me, me, me. I ponder the question, how bad a place would the planet have been if we had all really loved one another? Surely, it could not be any worse than it is now.

Chogs and Cool Beans

On a typical Los Angeles evening, after the sidewalks cool and most of the automobiles have gone to bed, the atmosphere clears enough to allow the odor of the foliage to break through. Sage, lemon, honeysuckle, the fragrant frangipani, all contribute to a superb olfactory experience, one not available in those other giant metroplexes: New York, Chicago, Houston, or Dallas. This is late evening, Southern California style.

I had just closed the door on John Parker's smoke-filled apartment. Our drama group West Coast Repertory was meeting inside, and the artsy-crafty habitués were overwhelming my nostrils with their phlegmatic puffings. I stepped outdoors to inhale fresh ozone and the seductive aroma of night-blooming jasmine. Standing on a landing in the midst of a staircase zigzagging downward from street parking two levels above, I suddenly saw a dark shadow, an alarming silhouette hurtling toward me from the top of the stairs. Whatever it was, it was full speed, out of control. I stepped to the side, just managing to grab a coat lapel as "it" tumbled past. A second later and the shadow-shape would have done a header over the railing, into a thorny, rat-infested arroyo.

Ignoring the fact that he had just tripped and tumbled down two flights of stairs, "the shape," now recognizable as a man, set about retrieving a fist full of his papers, dislodged during the fall. "Hello," and "Thanks," he announced cheerily, while pocketing a set of keys. "My name is Peter, Peter Bogdanovich, and I'm looking for the apartment of a Mr. John Parker."

Wearing slightly askew, horn-rimmed eyeglasses, there was something almost professorial about the fellow. He was dressed in a sports coat, well pressed chinos, and cordovan moccasins, penny loafers, actually. It was possible to deduce from his dress and high-spirited demeanor that he was on the trail of becoming important in some fashion, and indeed, he would shortly be hailed as one of the most respected new directors in American cinema, eventually nominated for several Oscars as both a writer and director, three nominations for a Golden Globe, and winner of a New York Film Critics Circle award, among other awards too numerous to mention.

Over time, I would learn that, as a young man, Peter had worked as programmer of movies for New York's Museum of Modern Art. While still in his teens, Bogdanovich had written articles and reviews for the prestigious *Cahiers du cinéma* and *Esquire*. Other than cinematographer Gary Graver, Peter Bogdanovich probably knew more about film and film history than anyone else in the business, here and abroad. *"Oh, yeah,"* Boo reminds me, *"don't forget film fanatic Quentin Tarantino!"*

I introduce myself to Peter, and then escort him to the proper apartment. Bogdanovich had arrived in response to an ad our drama group had run in *Daily Variety*, seeking directors for the workshop. I cannot recall the reason, but Bogdanovich and West Coast Repertory did not come to an agreement. I thought that was the last of it.

Several days later, however, I got a call from Peter. He was about to direct a film for Roger Corman, and he would like to audition group members for some of the parts. Boo was ecstatic. *"Perhaps,"* he enthused, *"there will be a little something for me in the picture."* Yeah, right. An invisible, nagging drone, an imaginary, pesky presence, at best. Not bloody likely!

Auditions were held at Pete's house in the San Fernando Valley, a trim, bungalow on Saticoy Street, in Van Nuys, a not the least pretentious domicile. Pete's wife, Polly Platt (*Bottle Rocket, The War of the Roses*, et al.), a multi-Oscar nominee and winner of a Women In Film Crystal Award, was hosting the readings from a nookish area of her kitchen. Polly Platt has that Joni Mitchell, sexy-waif persona, but back then she was much too busy to give it reins: wife, nursemaid, chief-cook and bottle-washer, producer, actress, writer, art director, assistant, secretary, costumer. I was even more impressed when I later learned that Polly had actually been a stunt double for Nancy Sinatra on Roger Corman's biker flick *The Wild Angels*.

Polly and Peter were as pleasant and preoccupied as pickers of peas in the Willamette Valley. They were not just husband and wife; they were collaborators, cine-souls on the fast track of becoming. They had met as young, dedicated idealists in the luministic swirl of the New York film loop, circa 1961. It was, at first, a romantic coupling, centered around a never ending schedule of screenings and all night cinematic tête-à-têtes.

In his early 20s at the time, Peter had landed a gig as programmer for The New York Theater. (Author's note: One of his first bookings was John Cassavetes' *Shadows*.) Polly, fresh from Carnegie Mellon University, where she had studied scenic design, advised Peter that she was going to be working with him in summer stock productions. He, the attractive, slightly arrogant film nerd, she the free spirited exotic from the Southwest, soon bonded like high school sweethearts. They were seemingly meant for each other. Together they trekked to Hollywood, where Peter knew the real deal of cinema was taking place. Peter and Polly quickly became fixtures in the newly awakened L.A. film scene, a scene largely financed and encouraged by Roger Corman.

Putting the Pump in the Pond

"No, there's no way I can go that high. Look, here's where it stands. I like the kid. I'll cast him in the lead role, but it pays Guild minimum, that's it! I won't go a penny over." It was Peter Bogdanovich on the telephone negotiating with an agent for the services of his client, actor Tim O'Kelly (*For Pete's Sake*, *The Mod Squad*). Polly gestured me toward a kitchen chair, whispering, "Peter will be with you in just a minute. Coffee?" Damn, in her dancing crinoline skirt, knee-high rawhides, silver conchos and bright Southwestern buttons, longish blonde hair flipping around her face like a flamenco fan, Polly was so cute, so "down with it," and so, well, so busy!

Executive producer Roger Corman laid out only a couple of absolutes. Peter would have to stay within his meager budget, $60,000, and he would have to use the services of the much beloved horror icon, actor Boris Karloff (*House of Frankenstein*, *The Body Snatcher*, et al.). Karloff owed Roger another film, and because of his failing health, Corman wanted to call in the debt before it was too late.

Agreeing to the conditions, Peter was free to make his film, a story he and Polly had cobbled together, a story loosely based on the tragic killing of students, faculty, and passersby by a deranged, troubled young man, a sniper, so to speak, firing from the parapet of the Observation Tower at the University of Texas. In their script, Peter and Polly had placed Boris Karloff, as Byron Orlock, an aged horror movie star. Much of the film concerns efforts by Bogdanovich as a movie director, to talk Orlock into making a personal appearance at a drive-in screening of one of his films. Orlock insists that he is outmoded, rendered silly, even, by today's standards of real life horror, for example the shootings of Martin Luther King and Bobby Kennedy, the seemingly endless slaughter endemic to the Vietnam War, and the massacre from the Texas tower. It seemed only appropriate that the next film to hit the streets with a big buzz should be titled *Targets*.

Having successfully completed his telephonic negotiations, Peter was in an exuberant mood. He was always, it seemed to me, energized by some inner glee, a marvelous, childlike appreciation for life and for his participation in it.

"Gary, how would you like to play a part, and do the special effects for my film?" This came more as the offer of a sacred gift, than as a legitimate job offer. I accepted it as such, anyway, and found myself serendipitously attached to what turned out to be another one of those magical journeys into the world of make-believe, albeit a journey centered on mass murder, madness, and the foul, black heart of humanity in general.

> *Now o'er the one half-world*
> *Nature seems dead, and wicked dreams abuse*
> *The curtain'd sleep; witchcraft celebrates*
> *Pale Hecate's offerings; and wither'd Murder,*
> *Alarum'd by his sentinel, the wolf,*
> *Whose howl's his watch, thus with his stealthy pace,*
> *With Tarquin's ravishing strides, towards his design*
> *Moves like a ghost.*

—William Shakespeare, *MacBeth*, Act II, Scene I

That night, I put on a meditative LP, a sitar instrumental, *Taba Sawari* by Ravi Shankar, the great Hindustani musician. Very mantric, very calming. I brewed a cup of fine Indian tea. I was after a peaceful, Nirvanic plateau from which to settle into the screenplay of *Targets*. This, I knew, was going to be a heavy read.

Written primarily by Peter, with expert assistance from Polly and close friend, writer/director Sam Fuller (*The Big Red One, Street of No Return*), the story was rock-solid. It followed a mentally unstable young man, Bobby Thompson, from his seemingly placid, pleasant life in a typically middle-class, humdrum neighborhood, through his gradual disintegration into a killing machine. He eventually ends up at (genius afoot here) a drive-in movie theater. The fellow climbs up the rafters behind the massive screen, punches a hole through the canvass, and begins to shoot, randomly killing the innocent movie goers, who are mostly just sitting in their cars, grooving out on this night's entertainment, which just happens to be a horror movie, starring that most frightening of horror stars, Byron Orlock (Boris Karloff).

As the special effects guy and munitions expert, it would be my job to do all of the shooting, starting with the surprise slaughter of the young man's family, then a grocery delivery boy, drivers whizzing along a freeway, and end with the mass killing at the drive-in. "*Oh, goody!*" Boo enthused, no longer rancorous that he had been eliminated from any casting possibilities. "*Goody, the climax of the* film *shall be yours, and you get to end the picture by killing everybody. What an amazing raison des temps!*"

We started filming in the Valley (San Fernando) at a gun shop where Bobby casually buys ammo, preparing for his onslaught. The gun shop clerk was played by my buddy and West Coast Repertory member Stafford "Pots and Pans" Morgan (*Rainy Day Friends, The Capture of Bigfoot*). Pots and Pans received that nickname through the connective tissue of superb salesmanship. After refusing to let his wife and kids suffer the niggardly existence befalling families of most out of work actors, Stafford took a position that sent him door-to-bloody-door, hawking all manner of dinnerware, especially the clanking, clinking, pots and pans variety.

After killing his parents, Bobby shoots the grocery delivery boy, played by another of our group members, Warren White (*Wildfire, Farmer & Chase*).

The killing of the delivery boy is followed with a shot of a corpse (Bobby's mother's body) being dragged through the house, through the living room, into the bedroom, where she is tenderly placed on the covers, as though enjoying a small nap. Life in the suburbs, gone a bit amuck, I'd say.

Blam! Kapow! Zing, Spling! The sound of gunshots. Rapid fire! I, dressed as an oilfield worker, have just left a small storage shed carrying a large battery on my shoulder. I am halfway across the work yard when I hear the sound. It seems to be coming from the top of a large water tank, which crouches like a giant daddy long legs in the center of the yard.

Blam! Kapow! I set the battery on the ground and start a climb up the long flight of metal stairs hugging the outside tank-wall. As I curl around the last twenty feet of stairs, nearing the top, I suddenly see him, an ordinary looking young man, squatting on the roof, holding a rifle. He is firing at will on vehicles flowing past on the 405 freeway.

"What the hell?" I yell. "Hey, what's going..." The sniper turns, shooting me in mid-sentence. I do a header off the stairs, dead as a peeled egg.

Minutes later, I am behind the wheel of a snappy '65 Ford Mustang, tooling along that same stretch of 99. On a cue from the AD, who is on a walkie-talkie on top of the water tank, I feign being fired upon, then wheel the Mustang perilously through the traffic flow, seemingly out of control. Cut! Now I transfer to another vehicle, a Ford Woody, and, with Don Jones as a passenger, I swerve the Woody off onto the shoulder of the freeway and skid to a stop. Don, who is dressed in drag, jumps from the passenger side and starts a panicked run along the side of the highway. Suddenly, his body jerks upright, then tumbles to the ground. Dead, you wicked wench. Dead as beef jerky.

Of course, this was all being filmed by Peter and the gang, who were hunkered down on top of the water tower, filming the sequence from the sniper's point of view. As we were stealing the shot, we had no permits to shoot on or to cordon off the 99; fellow travelers hadn't a clue as to what was going on. They called the police, saying they had just witnessed a woman being shot while running alongside the freeway. Faster than a New York minute, the cops were there, cuffing Jonesy and I, and tossing us into the back of a squad car, Boo saying, *"Hey, come on, we're just part of a movie!"*

Witnessing all of the police work from their vantage point atop the tower, Peter and the crew grabbed their equipment and did a ghost, vanishing into the afternoon vapors of the North Valley. *"Like the cinematic cowards they all are,"* Boo hisses. In spite of our excuses, Jones and I received hefty fines for reckless endangerment and had our licenses suspended for six months.

It was eerie, uncanny to say the least, how closely this all followed the Texas tower tragedy in sequence of events. Scarcely three years earlier, young Charles Whitman, a cherubic, blond all-American boy, who was suffering from a glioblastoma brain tumor and years of bottled up anger and resentment, had moved like a deadly snake through these same procedures.

Around midnight on July 31, 1966, Whitman stabbed his own mother through the heart, killing her instantly. Later that same night, he killed his wife Kathleen, stabbing her three times as she lay sleeping in their modest West Austin home. Kathleen was exhausted from working the swing shift at Bell Telephone. She was already fast asleep when her husband entered the room with murder on his mind.

The next morning, August 1, Whitman stopped at a local hardware store in Austin and purchased an M1 carbine "to hunt wild hogs," he told the clerk. Later, at a Sears store, he purchased a shotgun and a bolt action Remington 700 hunting rifle with a 4x Leupold scope. He stocked up on a bag full of ammo and headed for the University of Texas. His guns were stuffed into his old Marine footlocker, which he lugged, along with a sack full of sandwiches and soda pop, to the top of the observation deck of the tower of the Student Administration Building. The first person he killed at the university was a receptionist, who he hit over the head with the butt of one of his rifles. She was knocked unconscious and died several hours later. Whitman then blocked the door to the parapet, made himself comfortable as possible, pulled out the rest of his guns, and prepared for some hard partying, *Psycho* style.

My very good friend, recently deceased actor Robert Burns (*The Texas Chain Saw Massacre, Confessions of a Serial Killer*), was a UT student at the time. He was crossing campus just as the rampage began. In Robert's words, then, exactly as told to me:

"It was a bright, cheerfully sunny day. I was shuffling along on the way to journalism class, when I head a loud *Blamp!* sound. As there was much construction going on at the time, I just assumed that some workers had dropped a twelve-by-ten plank onto the concrete. *Blamp!* I heard it again, this time louder, and closer. Out of the corner of my eye, I noticed a foxy looking young lady, dressed in white short-shorts, walking west across the esplanade. I hear the "plank dropping" sound again, and the girl sank to the ground. A large, red stain began to spread across the cloth of her white shorts. 'My God,' I thought, 'She's been shot!' Some brave soul ran to her, covered her with his body to protect her, and then, he himself jerked violently, collapsing across the girl like the deflating bellows on an accordion.

"I ran to a student union coffee shop, and burst in yelling, 'Everyone, stay away from the windows! Get under the tables! Someone is shooting at the students.' Well, everyone ignored the warning and dashed outside to see what was going on. Some of them were shot immediately, others took cover wherever they could find it: lampposts, automobiles, statuary, etc.

"It seemed an eternity before the police arrived. In actuality, it was only a matter of minutes. Before the arrival of the fuzz, however, scores of students flooded the campus with their hunting rifles and all manner of personal weaponry. Determining the shots were coming from the top of the tower, they began a personal barrage of gunfire that helped pin the sniper down until the police could decide on action. I stayed in the coffee shop. I was terrified, certain the world was coming to an end. The gunfire was horrific! Even with the return fire from police and students, the sniper continued to find easy targets, picking them off one by one, like carnival ducks."

The slaughter belching from the Texas tower finally came to an end when two Austin police officers, Ramiro Martinez and Houston McCoy, worked their way up the stairwell and forced open the tower door. Spotting Whitman crouched in a corner of the parapet, they drew down on him, shooting to kill. Within seconds, poor Charlie Whitman was pushing up them daisies.

Now, here we were, three years later, preparing to do our own tower scene, only this one was from the high side of an outdoor drive-in movie screen. Our sniper, Bobby Thompson, has hauled his bag of weapons across the parking lot, entered a utility door, and climbed a ladder behind the giant screen to a small scaffold near the top. He punches a hole in the screen, affording a wide-angle view of the entire drive-in area. He checks his guns to make sure they are ready, then settles in to wait for dark, and the arrival of the viewing crowd, when the carnage will begin.

Production manager Paul Lewis and I took charge of hiring the extras, the ones who would be under the gun, so to speak. Besides personal friends and acquaintances, I brought along three of my boys, Chris, Alex, and Mike, not only to appear as kids in cars with the folks, but to also help me schlep my equipment around while I performed the shooting.

For the close shots of the people getting hit, I would use squibs, attached to the body in front of a metal protection plate. The clothing was scored, allowing a blood pouch to squirt through the cloth on cue. Peter and cameraman Laszlo Kovacs had planned a series of shots where the camera would zoom in, following the sound of gunfire to a close-up of a bullet impact on glass, metal, etc. For this effect, I used a compressed air rifle, loaded with a Vaseline pellet in which a small, round piece of black felt had been inserted. When the pellet hit its mark, the Vaseline would splatter and spread, giving the look of shattered glass. The dark round felt would look exactly like a bullet hole.

Most of us on the film knew the story of the Texas Tower Massacre, in detail. As cars began to pull into the drive-in for the pretend slaughter, an eerie feeling of dread spread slowly through cast and crew. As the saying goes, it was *déjà vu*. There had been too much real killing, in such a few short years (supposedly the years of peace and love), to feel relaxed around gunfire, make-believe or not. We were still suffering shell shock from starting the year with the Tet Offensive in Vietnam, a surprise conflagration by the North Vietnamese that demoralized the U.S.A., both at the front and at home, continuing with the shootings of Bobby Kennedy and Martin Luther King, Jr., and then, there was a little number called the My Lai Massacre which trickled in mid-semester from the front in Vietnam. A bunch of rogue American GIs, led by a glutinous asshole named Lt. William Calley, went on a rampage of looting, rape, and murder, eventually killing as many as four hundred innocent, unarmed Vietnamese civilians. There were those in the U.S. who felt the abominable action was justified, a natural by-product of war. "Not responsible for collateral damage," they said. "*Really?*" the usually lachrymose Boo snorted, "*Then who the fuck is responsible?*"

Boris Karloff, aka Frankenstein's monster, The Body Snatcher, Captain Hook, the face at the window, the dark shape under the streetlight, all of these phantasms, and yet, he was one of the sweetest individuals I have ever known, male or female.

Boris and I were sitting on a bench at the Reseda Drive-In, waiting for filming to begin. Jim Morris, a likeable, more than capable production assistant, had just brought us a sack full of McDonald's hamburgers laden with their recent coup de grâce, the Big Mac: two all beef patties, lettuce, cheese, pickles, onion, and special sauce. The Big Mac would soon replace home cooking as America's meal of choice and kick start the junk food revolution. Why, you could even order up a mess of gut bustin' fries, and a piping hot slice of Mom's apple pie along with your Big Mac.

All of these things considered, Mr. Karloff was not hungry. Actually, he was in ill health, suffering from severe back pain and emphysema. Walking, or even standing, was a painful ritual for Boris, involving leg braces and use of a cane. He'd had several back operations, trying to relieve the pain of old injuries, and also, the partial removal of lung tissue had left him breathless, and frequently attached to a portable oxygen tank. Yet, here he was, on a movie set once more, friendly, charming, and gracious, especially to the kids crowding around to see Frankenstein. Boris adored children, and championed them always, them and their causes.

There was a twinkle, a veritable bonfire of kindness lighting up Karloff's eyes. When he looked directly at you, you were immediately immersed in a flare of sunshine. This then was the famous movie monster who terrified folks in their darkest hours. "Roses are my life now," Boris exclaimed. "Roses and Bedlington Terriers. I raise them, you know, and have actually achieved some notoriety in the cultivation of my little beauties."

So Karloff and I sat and chatted, the old, revered actor from Camberwell, London, England, and the young stuntman from Walla Walla, Washington. Everything I know about the cultivation of roses, which is extensive, I learned from *The Body Snatcher*. While waiting for Bogdanovich to call for the start of the mass slaughter, when my work would begin, Boris entertained the boys and I with droll stories of his early days in theater. "Yes," said the stage manager, as he watched the handsome newcomer exit the theater arm in arm with several beautiful ingénues, "But can he act?"

At dusk, the boys and I hauled my rifle and air compressor (ala Javier Bardem in *No Country For Old Men*) to different positions in the drive-in lot, where I would proceed to fire on certain targets selected by Bogdanovich, i.e., a man in a phone booth, the projectionist in his projection room, an usher scrambling among the cars to see what was going on, moviegoers and their children sitting placidly in their automobiles as their lives are snuffed out on the whim of a psychotic sniper.

There was an especially chilling moment when I was required to take aim and shoot at my own son, Michael, who, as a baby boy extra, was sharing the front seat of a Volvo alongside the film's dolly grip, Jack Oliver. For just that one, brief moment in time, when I saw Michael's face through the scope of a rifle, I grew physically sick, struck nauseous by the horror of knowing that there were actually people walking among us who could do this, shoot their own loved ones, family, innocent strangers, without hesitation or remorse. I shift my aim to Oliver, squeeze the trigger, and Jack slumps over in the seat, supposedly dead. And Michael begins to cry. He is hungry, it seems, for a Big Mac. The shooting sequence at the Reseda Drive-In goes perfectly. I manage to fire my rifle and Vaseline pellets at least fifty times, without actually hitting or hurting anyone.

The sequence ends when Karloff, who is at the movie to make a personal appearance, grows weary of the hysterical fear engendered by some crazed man (Bobby Thompson) hidden behind a movie screen. He grabs his cane and stalks toward the sound of the gunfire. Sniper Thompson has run out of ammo, and, after dropping his last remaining weapon into a crevasse, suddenly sees what to him, for all intents, is the evil Baron Victor Von Leppe, stepped freshly from his own flickering image on the screen. There follows a brilliantly edited series of quick cuts between Von Leppe, on screen, Bobby, and the rapidly approaching horror star, Byron Orlock (Karloff), in person.

I watched, fascinated, as the courageous old thespian hobbled up to a now quivering sniper and strikes him with the cane, sneering in disgust, "Is that what I was afraid of?" So then, *Targets* ends, not with a bang, but with a whimper, as the cowed Bobby Thompson writhes on the ground, groveling at the feet of the grand old man of make-believe horror.

The reviews for *Targets* ran the gamut of "brilliant" to "overwrought and self serving."

> *Incredibly suspenseful, with a sweat inducing climax at the drive-in theater. Excellent photography by Lazslo Kovacs.*
>
> —Leonard Maltin, 1998

Mostly, the film was especially embraced by the moviegoers themselves:

> *Small budget films do not get any better than this…neither do most larger budgets. Give it ten stars.*
>
> —Funkyfry, Oakland, CA

> *It strikingly captures the texture of a particular time, the cars, clothes, signs, the drive-in, the suburban houses. It is nothing short of a neural map of time.*
>
> —Tostinati, IMDB

> *A first rate thriller, with remarkable power. Bravo to Bogdanovich and company for this one.*
>
> —Raegan Butcher, Raincity, WA

Bogdanovich and company? This, then, would have to include Peter's wife, Polly, production manager Paul Lewis, cinematographer Laszlo Kovacs, script supervisor Joyce King, a young actor named Frank Marshall who played a ticket taker at the drive-in (Marshall would later distinguish himself as producer of *Jurassic Park*, *The Bourne Ultimatum*, *Snow Falling on Cedars*, *Back To The Future*, *Raiders of The Lost Ark*, et al., as well as four Oscar nominations, three Saturn Award nominations, winning a Lifetime Achievement Award from the Producers Guild, plus other awards and nominations too numerous to mention), and Mike Farrell, the man I shot in the phone booth (*Desperate Housewives*, *M.A.S.H.*, etc., winner of a Crystal Humanitarian Award, nominations for two Golden Globes, two Emmys, and a nomination from the Directors Guild for Outstanding Directorial Achievement).

One would have to also mention the sound editor, Verna Fields, who later distinguished herself by editing such great films as *American Graffiti*, *Paper Moon*, *Medium Cool*, *Jaws*, and would eventually be appointed to an executive position at Universal Studios. Lastly, and humbly, I would add myself, Gary Kent (*The Pyramid, Rainy Day Friends*, winner of Best Special Stunt in a Motion Picture, International Stuntman Awards), just for doing all of that shooting without killing anyone. "Hats off, then, each and every one."

Largely disapproved by the American Rifle Association and the gun lobby, *Targets* has been lauded as the first movie ever to speak out for gun control and reformation of the laws governing possession of firearms. Whether intentional or not, that distinction alone elevates Peter Bogdanovich and Polly Platt to the top of the heap of Hollywood Outlaws.

Chapter Ten

Gary Kent and his "squaw" actress Penny Marshall in The Savage Seven.
Photo courtesy of the author.

The Apple Butter Hits The Fan

Power does not corrupt. Fear corrupts, perhaps the fear of a loss of power.
—John Steinbeck, *The Short Reign of Pippin IV*

The late 60s were our last chance to get it right. I mean us, we, humankind, and we blew it. Oh, on the surface, it was a marvelous time. Who can ever decry the exhilaration of witnessing the birth of real civil rights, the airing out the attics of prejudice, of homophobia, of entrenched misogyny, the blooming of the intellect and the strength of the arts in the shaping of a dynamic new culture? Wow! Beam me up, buttercup! Yet, there was so much death. The death of innocence, death of an idealistic future, death of purity of heart, of ideas, belief, hope, and possibilities, and then, the actual, bloodletting butchery. For the sake of the reader's enjoyment, however, let's begin with the magical, the mystical, and the mundane.

In the middle of the decade, the young moviegoing public was fed up with safe, clean celebrities. They wanted a wild man, an outsider, someone reckless and without conscience. Hence, the embracing of the "biker." For the years that it lasted, about five in all, there wasn't a biker film that lost money. However, the whole image was wearing a bit thin at the end of the decade. Still, there were several last, glorious gasps from the genre.

I had just returned from a game of football, a bare-knuckle duke-out involving a group of stuntmen and actors, too antsy and testosterone-fueled to let an off-duty day pass without a bruising of some sort. On this particular day, I was rotating at quarterback with a tough, talented guy from the New York scene, named Robert "Bobby" Duval. Not only was Duval a good football player, he was a slap in the face to all

217

that prissy, proper decorum the gussied up male Hollywood actors were wont to display throughout "the loop."

Duval was somewhat challenged, hair-wise. He was close to bald at a very young age. This didn't bother him in the least, however, or his libido. When he went on acting interviews, he would go *au naturel*, carrying his toupee along in a brown-paper bag. "This," he would announce, "is me without hair. And this..." he would pull his rug out of the sack and place it on his head, "this is me with hair. Take your pick."

Bobby Duval also showed little regard for the hallowed Hollywood tradition of having just the "right pictures" to leave with casting agents. It is a known fact in the biz that most out of work actors use "I'm waiting for my new pictures" as an excuse for their unemployment. Duval, however, just dropped by one of the kiosks that pop out a small strip of photos for a couple of quarters. He would take the narrow band with him on interviews, and when asked to leave a picture, he would take out the strip, tear off a likeness, and hand it to them along with his resume. My kinda guy: outlaw to the bone.

> *It's not whether you win or lose, but how you play the game.*
> —Fielding Yost, Yale, 1936

On the particular day in mention, our ragtag team had just finished a squeaker against the team of actor Robert Conrad (*Wild, Wild West*; *Baa Baa Black Sheep*, a Golden Globe nomination, winner of a People's Choice Award for Favorite Male Performer, 1977). Conrad and his boys were as close to a professional ball team as you could get without breaking the rules of amateur athletics. Conrad was himself a gifted athlete, and he would surround himself with stunt men from *Wild, Wild West*, and actual players from the Los Angeles Rams (who just happened to drop by for a visit).

We always dreaded the meet-ups with Conrad. Someone was usually going to get hurt and it would not be anyone on his team. In fact, this day's game began with our wide receiver, actor/stuntman Jim Raymond, breaking his thumb on the opening kick-off. Others on our team were my Marine buddy, Jerry "Flush" Fitzpatrick, a three-pack-a-day smoker who would be winded and graying by the third set of downs, and Don "Irish Frankie" Jones. Jonesy, a respectable tight end, would arrive at our madcap encounters dressed in leisure slacks, loafers, and sunglasses, carrying a cup of coffee. More like a junior bank manager than a football player.

The game finished with us winning. Duval had simply out-dodged, and out-ran, the best of Conrad's defenders. Tie score. Shortly thereafter, I faked those same Conradites out of their jockstraps by charging the line like I was doing a "Duval," only, at the last minute, I tossed a flea flicker to Jones, who hauled it in and raced to the goal line (an imaginary boundary between two telephone poles). Final score, 18-12, us.

When the game ended Bob Conrad endeared himself to all athletes involved by having a car arrive loaded with a tub full of iced beer. This thoughtful gesture on his part was a clear demonstration of Conrad's ability, in spite of his "stardom," to just be "one of the boys."

Returning home from the game was an ordeal for me, in that "home" was now a small room in a rooming house owned and operated by my former neighbor, the deliciously difficult Sherry Stewart. Rosemary and I had decided on a break in our marriage, and loaded down with guilt and a few paltry belongings, I moved out. Since this was my second failed marriage, I felt that quite possibly I just was not meant for the institution. Of course, Boo assured me that it was all my fault, "*It's impossible, champ, to love a man who is never there.*"

Sherry Stewart knocked on my door, handing me a small slip of paper. It was a message from Chuck Bail, asking me to give him a call. I did. Chuck and Richard Rush were getting ready to pay off a debt to impresario Dick Clark by adjourning to the Nevada desert to film another biker epic, *The Savage Seven*. This was music to my ears, just what I needed, a chance to get out of town, someplace where one could ignore one's mistakes and once again feel like somebody, albeit, in a Godforsaken, unappetizing, desolate, remote area of the country, where feeling like somebody was a solemn, solitary, frequently bitter affair.

According to Chuck, Bud Cardos and I would be playing parts as well as handling action. Richard's idea was to cast stuntmen in lead roles, thus lending an edgy persona to the diverse groups involved. I would play "Rodeo Lansford," a bike gang member. Our leader was the indefatigable Adam Roarke. His sidekicks, besides myself, were Walt Robles, Eddy Donno, Gary Littlejohn, Tex Hall, Alan Gibbs (*Crocodile Dundee, Scarface*), Richard Anders, iconic singer/songwriter Duane Eddy (*"Forty Miles of Bad Road," "Rebel Rouser"*) and Larry Bishop (*Kill Bill: Vol. 2, Angel Unchained*), son of Rat Pack comedian Joey Bishop.

The bikers descend on a small Indian village in the middle of nowhere, in search of fun and some slack time. What they find is an impoverished village being cheated out of its dignity and resources by a large consortium of corporate power grabbers. The "Corps" were bent on stealing large energy reserves from the unsuspecting natives. The "suits" hire the bikers to harass the Indians, in hopes of driving them off their land. Playing the Indian leader was Robert Walker, Jr. (*Evil Town, The Passover Plot*, Golden Globe Winner as Most Promising Male

Newcomer, 1963, son of actress Jennifer Jones and actor Robert Walker). My good friends John "Bud" Cardos, as Running Buck, and Max Julien, as Grey Wolf, were part of the Indian tribe resisting the takeover.

The Indian women, or "squaws," as the bikers referred to them, were Marcia, played by Joanna Frank (*The Young Animals*; *America, America*, sister of TV's iconic producer Steven Bochco), Penny Marshall (who would gain fame as Laverne in the hilarious TV comedy *Laverne and Shirley* and garner acclaim as the director of such films as *A League of Their Own* and *Big*) playing Tina, and my friend Susannah Darrow (*Death Wish*, *CHiPs*) playing Nancy.

The corporate bad guys were corpulent Mel Berger (*Deadly Hero, Bad Charleston Charlie*), Billy Green Bush (*The Reivers, Five Easy Pieces*), and the stunt maestro himself, Chuck Bail. Chuck would be coordinating stunts and appearing on camera as Taggert, the obnoxious head henchman for the boys from the Corpolopolis.

Adding to this unusual gathering of talent in the desert wastes would be the producing talents of Dick Clark, the film's theme song "Anyone For Tennis?," co-written by Eric Clapton and performed by Cream, and the classic "Iron Butterfly Theme," performed by Iron Butterfly.

A Filmic Farrago–Who? Us?

Actress Goldie Hawn once stated she judged a movie by the experience she had making it. Such is the case with me. The actual incidences, planned or happenstance, that occur during the making of a film far outshine the impact of the completed product. *The Savage Seven*, then, is memorable in that regard for a variety of unusual, endearing, and nearly calamitous incidents. I will start with the improbable but true UFO adventure!

Richard Rush had selected for the movie's location a gathering of shanties and rundown trailers on the edge of the Great Mojave, outside of Searchlight, Nevada. This was an area populated largely by scorpions, diamondbacks, tarantulas, and a few scruffy dropouts, their women, and dogs. Although we stayed in comfortable lodgings, a low-slung motel near the shooting site, there was damned little to do at night but read or sleep.

There was a gambling casino a stone's throw down the interstate, but for those of us not into throwing our money away, entertainment was almost non-existent. In that light, on an off weekend, Max Julien, Penny Marshall, and I decided to make a run back to L.A. in Max's '59 Caddy Eldorado. We would visit our families and return late Sunday in time for the Monday morning call.

The large part of the trip went as planned. We hummed along at about seventy per, singing songs and telling tales until we reached L.A., where we split forces until time to return. The journey back was dramatically different.

While in town, Max had scored some killer weed, sinsemilla, as I recall. We were about twenty miles out of L.A. when we fired up. Max and I toked pretty much through eastern California and on into the Nevada desert. Penny had slept very little while in town, so she zonked out in the back seat the entire journey, waking only now and then to see if we were still in shape to drive, then slipping quietly back into the sweet arms of Morpheus, a sleep deepened by wisps of ganja floating over the headrests from the activity in the front seat.

About ten miles from our destination, Max's Caddy gave up the ghost: coughed, spit a bit, rolled over, and died. Max eased the vehicle gently to the side of the highway. It was around three in the morning, not a light in sight, dark as the inside of a coffin. After several attempts to restart the engine, we shut her down and began to consider our situation. It was obvious we were out where the buses don't run, ten miles to water and three miles from Hell. What to do? We decided that, since neither of us was mechanically inclined, firing up another spliff seemed the proper thing to do, so we did.

My mind drifted through the windshield, across the automobile hood, bounced into the night sky, and was scooting around the celestial playing fields of Andromeda when I heard Max say in a soft, serious voice, "It's like our whole culture is invisible, baby!"

"Whose culture? Our culture?"

 "No, baby, *my* culture. See, in the movies, at the end of the day, when the black guy goes home, you never see where he goes. Dig? You never see what his home looks like, never see his kids greet him, what they have for supper, what paintings are on the wall…"

My consciousness completed a breathtaking high-dive from the backwaters of that neighborly galaxy to the front seat of the Caddy.

"You never hear the music in the black guy's house," Max continued, "Because the movie always goes home with the white guy. Dig? It's like, at the end of the day, the black guy goes back to the prop department."

The approaching era of blaxploitation would soon change all that. For the first time in history, American movie audiences would be privy to a potpourri of clothing, color, language, and events they had never seen before. Like all exploitation films, many of these were just bad movies, yet within their props and set dressings, their locations, their dialogue, in their trials and tribulations, the world finally began to glimpse a bit of what it was like being black in America. Max Julien would become one of the founding fathers.

While Penny slept, Max and I settled into some far-out conversation, covering everything but the price of goat milk and soy. Soon the talk trickled down to a few potent exclamations, then stopped altogether. Max rolled down his window, and we sat listening to that incredible desert silence.

"Must be pretty quiet out here since the buffalo died, huh?" Max observed, and then, we saw it. Just above the horizon, a slow-spinning circle of light, translucent, bluish in color. Nothing like either of us had ever seen before. "Hey, Gary, look at that," Max whispered.

"I see it. What the hell is it, a helicopter? Nah, too stationary, no sound. Out here we'd hear a chopper for miles."

"It isn't a plane either. Planes just don't act like that," Max said, stepping out of the car for a cleaner look.

The object began to pop vertically up and down, a space we gathered to be at least a hundred feet, and yet, it covered the area instantly, somewhat like a bouncing celestial basketball, only this ball was much larger than NBA standards. The blue lights were pulsing, as though sending or receiving a message. Then they just shut off, like a switch had been thrown. Where before there had been something large, looming, mobile and colorful, there was nothing but dark, empty sky.

We decided not to wake Penny. As our apparition had disappeared, she would surely think we were just two stoners, vegged out on herb, and perhaps we were. By morning, a passerby delivered a message to the film company, who immediately sent a van to pick us up and tow the Caddy in for repairs, and that would have been the end of it, a mere private moment of synchronicity between two fanciful beings, tripping on the edge of reality, had it not been for a very slick segue that shunted our psyches from the Adventure of the UFO into the Adventure of The Broken Body.

It has to be more than coincidence that ever since that night in the desert, Max Julien and I have retained a sort of psychic simpatico, an ability to tune in to one another's feelings, thoughts, and well-being that defies time and place. For instance, shortly after rejoining the film company, I was working with the second unit on traveling shots, shots of the biker gang having a go at a bit of frivolity on the open highway. This ride was done to the sound of Eric Clapton and Cream, performing the theme song "Anyone for Tennis?" Just your usual hazy, lazy, routine outing for a bunch of grizzled blokes on Harleys.

The stunt guys were in the lead of the pack, with the actors following close behind. Tex Hall, one of the better riders, was standing on his seat, weaving his bike back and forth by steering with his body English. One of my favorite stuntmen, Alan Gibbs, thought that Tex looked real spiffy, standing up there in the sun while hurtling along the highway at about forty per, so Gibbs, who, despite his years of experience as a stuntman had never attempted a seat stand before, attempted to leap up on the saddle. Big mistake! Gibbs lost his balance and fell. His left foot kicked the peg on the way down, throwing his bike directly into mine.

One moment I was riding along the highway, digging on Clapton, feeling quite groovy, the next moment I was bikeless, turned inside out, end over end, falling head first with nothing between me and the concrete but my jeans. I hit the pavement hard, like being head butted by a water buffalo. Whump! I skidded about twenty feet before coming to a stop. I had thrown my arm in front of my head to keep from crushing my skull. I considered myself lucky, just a little road rash, and then, Larry Bishop and the rest of the actors plowed into me with their cycles, full speed. I felt the air leave my lungs. Actually, I heard the air leave my lungs. Whooofff! I have never, ever, been hit that hard in my life. Pulling myself to my feet, I struggled to the side of the road and then collapsed.

Producer Dick Clark was on scene, and he and a P.A. drove Alan and I to the nearest hospital in Boulder, Colorado. Alan had a few scratches. I actually felt okay, a little shaken, that's all. Boo wasn't so sure, *"Let's wait, Big Guy, and hear what the doc has to say before we plan any dance moves."*

I was sitting on the business end of a hospital examining table when everything began to turn yellow and swirly. Just as I started to pass out, a burly technician grabbed me. "Are you alright?" Mr. Burly asks. His voice is echoing at me from the far end of a long, nauseating tunnel of pain. *"Does he look alright to you?"* Boo sneers. Of course, no one could hear Boo but me, and I was hurting too bad to pay attention.

A young, bookish looking doctor entered the room, holding my X-rays. "Son, you're going to be our guest for a while. You've got four broken ribs, a broken ankle, and multiple lacerations. Welcome to your new home."

The first cast member to visit me in Boulder Community Hospital was guitarist and actor Duane Eddy. Duane, a tall, humble fellow, entered the room laden with magazines, bags of candy, and cans of soda pop, all brought for my enjoyment. I will never forget his act of kindness. I scarcely knew Duane. He was just one of the "bikers" hangin' in the back of the pack. He kept pretty much to himself and never participated in the wild shenanigans, the hard partying that most of the cast and crew engaged in nightly. Eddy was without question a musical genius. Legendary rocker John Fogerty, in an article in *Rolling Stone Magazine*, called Duane the "first rock and roll Guitar God." In 2004, he would receive the Legend Award from *Guitar Player Magazine*, win a Grammy for co-authoring the theme for TV's hit series *Peter Gunn*, and, in 1994, was inducted into the Rock and Roll Hall of Fame.

Duane Eddy is the only guitar picker to have ten top singles in four separate decades. I will mention only some of my personal favorites: "Rebel Rouser," "Forty Miles of Bad Road," "Boss Guitar," "The Lonely One," "Ramrod," and "Movin' n' Groovin." During our pleasant, albeit subdued conversation, bonded by the sharing of Hershey bars and RC cola, Eddy told me the following story:

"I was working the other film unit with some of the major actors about six miles from your group when word came through that there had been an accident on the stunt unit. They said Chuck Bail had been badly hurt. Well, suddenly Max Julien interrupted, saying, 'Nah, it wasn't Chuck Bail. It was Gary Kent.' Now, how do you suppose ol' Max knew that, Gary?"

Later, when Max got a chance to visit me in the hospital, I asked him that same question. "I don't know. I just knew. Know what I mean? I just knew—here." Max pointed to his heart. Yeah, I guess I knew, exactly.

Rosy Palm and Her Five Sleazy Sisters

"Here it is! I see it now!" This from actor John Garwood, who was on his knees in front of Adam Roarke. Adam had his pants unzipped, with an index finger protruding through his fly like a miniature phallus. John, Adam, Larry Bishop, and the boys had come to visit me in my little room at Boulder Community. As usual, all of their humor was based on a common denominator of sexual innuendo in its most infantile form. The finger through the fly routine was one they had developed to an art form, and they used it constantly throughout filming, mostly for their own amusement.

I was delighted to see them, in spite of the noise and commotion they brought to the quiet confines of a place of healing. They were still dressed in their biker regalia, chains, buckles, shit-kickers, and all. They had also managed to smuggle in an ounce of grass. They rolled a joint and we all had a toke just to say we'd done it. "Here, Gar," Adam said, handing me the baggie and a pack of rolling papers. "Stash this, and when you feel like the rage is getting to you, fire up a doob and you'll be just fine."

Adam and the boys finished off the last of Duane Eddy's candy and soda, had a few laughs, told a few lies, and then waved adieu. As they disappeared into the labyrinth of hospital hallways, I could hear their laughter, their whoops and cattle calls long after they had left the vicinity. Later that evening, a winsome woman, dressed as a nurse, came into my room, and pulling back the sheets, announced, "Hi, Mr. Kent. My name is Rose and I am here to give you your massage."

"Massage? What massage?"

Boo advised me to just shut up and go with the flow. Rose's fingers crawled sensuously up my leg, coming to rest on my private parts. "Oh, my," she whispered, huskily, "we're gonna need a little wake-up call, aren't we?" She leaned forward, kissed me, jamming her tongue into my mouth like a spatula turning pancakes. Her hand began a casual pumping motion on "ol' Tommyhawk," who had retreated into his shell like a snail dropped into a bucket of beer.

"I'm very sorry, dear heart," I sighed, "ol' Tommyhawk is away for the night." Actually, I was so high on pot and Percodan, I was having an out-of-body experience, observing the proceedings from somewhere above the overhead light fixture.

"Just try, damn it!" Boo implored. *"Just give it a damned try…for me!"*

To my credit, I did try. I squeezed my eyes shut, and t-r-i-e-d. I tried so hard, I grunted, a small, quack-like sound, like a duck with stomach flu. No luck. I was much too drugged. Rose needed a "woody" to complete the deed and all I could offer her was a "wordy." I later learned this had all been arranged by Adam, Garwood, Duane Eddy, and the gang out of pure compassion, I suppose. I handed Rose a couple of twenties, and as she left the room, she killed the overheads. Within seconds, I was sound asleep, back in the celestial galaxies, running, jumping, gliding around heaven like a bloody archangel. "God bless us, Boo," I smiled, channeling Tiny Tim, "God bless us each and every one."

Please Pass the Cool Breeze

Robert Walker, Jr., was sitting in front of his motel room in complete zazen posture, full lotus position, eating air. Bud Cardos and I, who were roomies on *The Savage Seven*, stopped next door to pick up Chuck Bail. The three of us would then walk three blocks to the casino/café that provided meals for cast and crew. In doing so, we passed right by Walker. If he noticed us, he didn't show it. His eyes were shut, hands connected in the cosmic mudra, breathing deeply in-out-in-out, forgetting self, I suppose, and just being one with the all of all.

Robert had informed cast and crew that he was on his way to spiritual enlightenment and was presently cleansing his body by eating only ozone, air, wind, slight breezes, whimsies, whatever wafted his way. At the time, we were convinced he had perhaps taken one tab too many of Owsley's Blue Cheer and was now paying the piper.

"Hey, Robert," Chuck called out. "There's a nor'easter blowing in later. I hear they're delicious. If you like, I'll loan you a knife and fork so you can slice up a gust or two."

The small café squatting in the middle of the desert where we all ate and canoodled daily also housed a gambling area: slots, one-armed bandits, and a couple of blackjack tables. Bud Cardos was a slot machine junkie. He would sit for hours feeding precious coins into the hungry mouth of the contraptions. I also noticed that people engaged in playing the slots always talk to the device, as though it can hear them. If you passed anywhere near Cardos while he was playing, you would hear so much cajoling, pleading, demanding, and praying you would think he was pleading directly to God, or, possibly, his ex-wife.

I am definitely not a gambler, not with money, anyway. I kind of figured that every time I did a stunt, it was a gamble, more or less, and I never fancied pushing my luck further for mere amusement or, worse, for filthy lucre. However, I enjoyed standing around the blackjack table, watching the rest of the gang hand over their hard earned cash to the house.

One evening, Walt Robles, Bob O'Neill, (our property master, later director of *Angel, Blood Mania*), and Dick Compton (our assistant property master, director of *Macon County Line, Angels Die Hard*) were sitting at the table, trying to coerce the cards into behaving themselves. Chuck Bail, also not a gambler, walked up, and for some reason known only to he and the devil, pulled out a stool and joined the game. The jukebox was playing an old classic by Bob Nolan and The Sons of the Pioneers, "Cool Water." I was shuffling around, enjoying the deep harmonies of pioneers Hugh and Karl Farr, when I noticed a desert-rat-drifter enter the bar. He was dressed for the cattle drive, including worn chaps, and, slung across his hips, a pair of pearl-handled six-shooters. His eyes were red and squinty from too much sun, or too much liquor. I've seen trouble on two legs before, and this rounder was packing a load of it. He eyeballed the game for a minute or two, and then sidled up behind Walt Robles.

"That's a fool's hand, you're holdin' there, buddy. You better learn how to play this game 'cause it ain't no game for sissies!"

Robles, certainly no sissy, was taken aback, not sure how to react. Chuck Bail, however, solved the problem for him. Without ever looking up from his cards, without ever taking the measure of the man, Chuck just tipped his hat back and muttered, "Shut up. Get the hell out of here or I'll break your fuckin' back."

Now, as I have mentioned, Bail is six four and he has the dangerous look of a Black-Irishman and the persona of an enforcer for the Black and Tans. When the roadhouse rowdy got a good look at Chuck, he evidently surmised that if Bail wasn't even going to look up from his playing hand, then maybe he wasn't feeling intimidated. Without another word, the poor fellow grinned sheepishly and backed out of the saloon, just like in a Western movie. A few minutes later, the cocktail waitress told Chuck that the guns the guy had on his hips were real Colts and loaded with live ammunition. In the opinion of the mighty Mr. Boo, *"Chuck Bail has the luck o' the Irish and the balls of a mountain gorilla!"* Damned straight, Boo.

All Jacked Up

Every day of the shoot, Chuck and Eddy Donno would race Bud Cardos and me from the motel to the location and back again, Chuck driving his gull-wing Mercedes, Bud and I in Bud's 182 Cessna. Usually, by the time we got the plane un-chocked and airborne, the Mercedes was way ahead of the game. One morning, while the fellows were eating breakfast, Bud and I jacked the Mercedes up, took off one of the tires and hid it. When it was time for the race, we were airborne and halfway to the set while they were still trying to figure out where the hell the tire was. Sometimes you have to think outside of the box to make your statement in this world.

There were so many fights, stunts, altercations, etc. on *The Savage Seven* we needed a permanent medic on set. I was never quite sure what the storyline was, other than to show that, in the grasp of the Corpolopolis, mere mortals are mere globs of goo, and as such, can be cleverly turned against one another, coerced into seemingly random violence, unleashed on the misguided and the thoughtless.

From the film's beginning, Chuck had designed a constant assault on the senses with non-stop action, primarily stunt sequences and fights between the Indians and the bikers. Meanwhile, Richard Rush would keep the audience guessing at what seemed to be obvious outcomes, only to twist things sideways, bending the loyalties and psyches of the storyline like an afternoon at a bizarre amusement park. Just when you think the bikers have sympathy for the Indians (vis-a-vis a love connection between Adam Roarke (as Kissum) and Joanna Frank (as Marcia), there's a reversal. A killing is staged by the corporation's henchmen to make it look like the Indians have double-crossed the bikers. The film ends with a vast panorama of brutality so broad in terror and scope it makes Custer's last stand look like a childish game at a schoolyard.

Bail is a master at large, intricately woven action sequences that make his work a notch above the rest of the action directors. In this almost operatic climax of roiling anger between Indians and bikers, he and cameraman Laszlo Kovacs lend a lyrical sweep to the violence, a *sturm und drang* that, one minute is close up on two men reduced to the lowest denominator of human endeavor by pounding one another to death, to a series of exquisitely staged wide shots, overhead shots, POVs removed from the immediacy of battle, allowing a perspective at once both beautiful, if battle can be so, and terribly, terribly sad.

It is easy to view *The Savage Seven* as metaphor for the bloodshed of the 1960s (i.e., Vietnam, political and private assassinations, little murders, serial killings, the Chicago Riots, etc.). Unfortunately, it was only going to get worse. As titles roll, Kissum and Marcia are left alone, surveying the devastation, as if to say, "What have we done?" And more pertinently, "Where do we go from here?"

"Be Here Now, but Maybe not Tomorrow or Tuesday"

Why do we have war? Is there a God? If so, is he sitting around inside all of us? Is there a collective soul that goes beyond the mere discovery of personal consciousness? Is there such a thing as a real social conscience, and if so, where is it hiding? These are just some of the questions we thought would be answered by the turmoil, the foment, the shakeup of the psyche, the drug experimentation, and the opening of moral floodgates that loosed the revolutionary minds of the 1960s. Indeed, there were moments of great joy, of magnificent journeys into new domains, a new grasp of the previously ungraspable, and yet, anger, suspicion, resentment, and greed continued to rule and even multiply, drowning out the mantra of "Peace and Love."

One of the big mistakes of the 60s revolution was in not understanding how complicated the contemplative, communal life could be. For one, a progressive community is in the habit of anointing gurus. Well, unfortunately, gurus morph into narcissists, interested in gaining and retaining power, less "power for the people" than "power over the people." There were just too many of these spiritual mechanics running around; it was all too bizarre. Everyone was getting deep tissue massages, primal screaming, diving head first into EST and Esalan, adoring Timothy Leary, Werner Erhard, and Baba Ram Dass. Me? I didn't believe in following gurus except, maybe, the original head honcho of the gurus, Jesus Christ, who said basically only three things: live simply, love thy neighbor, and judge not lest ye be judged.

It is important to remember that, for decades, hovering over the spiritual yearnings of the world's populace like a mushroom cloud, was the dark specter of the H-bomb. To many of us, it wasn't just something governments threatened to use; it was more a question of "Who's first, and when?" This ghastly apparition haunted mankind daily, stifling creative efforts for peace, and drawing the shades on open dialogue. All governments, it seemed, were playing defense.

To the 'more' of life—the real revolution.

—Trina Paulus, *Hope for the Flowers*

The idealistic, the flower children, the Beats, hippies, and New Agers were all losing ground to the more militant revolutionists. The Weathermen, the Black Panthers, the SDS, the SLA, etc., began making bombs and robbing banks in the name of change. The "Establishment" reacted quickly, arresting and taking to trial many of the ringleaders, and also, the simply disaffected and disillusioned. This latter was clearly illustrated at the Chicago Democratic Convention in August

Actor John Parker salutes the "Age of Aquarius'"and the rest of the world, 1969.
Photo courtesy of the author.

1968. Here, the rubber met the road, so to speak, and the overly brutal police response to throngs of protesters became of a symbol of the oppressive practices of governments everywhere.

Good God! I've Been Graped!

I was on a soundstage in West Hollywood, lying on a bed of soft velvets and lush linens. I was pretty much naked, except for a leather headband, a breechcloth of animal-hide, and deerskin moccasins. Maria Lease, a lovely actress/director (*The Scavengers, Silk Stalkings*), was sitting on my chest, dropping fresh grapes teasingly into my mouth. This action would be followed by some serious making-out, interrupted only for rapacious gulps from a nearby flagon of wine. Ms. Lease was also bared-down in a scanty arrangement of animal skins. Her near perfect breasts, barely confined in a skimpy bra, brushed tantalizingly across my cheek, my lips, and then hung there, in mid-air, much like ripening fruit, or, as Boo suggested, *"A cluster of grapes."*

Minutes earlier we had entered our rocky bedroom singing, "We're off to see the Lizard." The "lizard" in this case, I suppose, was my much-shrunken little buddy, Tommyhawk, who lay curled inside my animal breeches like a frightened dormouse. Yes, Lease and I were starring in a nudie cutie, acting our little hearts out as debauched cave dwellers in a scurrilous little number titled *One Million AC/DC*. The film was being directed by Gary Graver, from a script written by the master of bad movies himself, Ed Wood, Jr. (*Plan 9 from Outer Space, Orgy of the Dead*).

Sex, that wet and wiggly little monster, had been unleashed on the puritan public in a variety of new and unusual ways by the end of the 60s. On the surface, we Americans were not talking about sex; we talked about intellectual, big-headed things, like raising one's children, one's rhubarb, and one's consciousness. Sex seldom entered the conversation. We didn't talk about it; we just did it, with more abandon and frequency than usual.

For many, the "Sexual Revolution" was more a guise for licentious self-indulgence than a respecting of freedom of choice, women's rights, and personal responsibility. It is important to note that this part of the cultural revolution would later spawn hard core pornography, AIDS, and a smudging down of much of the romance, glamour, tenderness, fidelity, and real sensuality that had previously been a large part of the sexual experience.

The subject of sex in all its persuasions had been amply covered in most of the arts: music, sculpting, fine art, literature, and legitimate theater. In film, however, it was more a matter of uncovering rather than covering.

The sole purpose of the nudie cutie seemed to be to satisfy once and for all the demand of a newly liberated populace to catch a glimpse of the naked female body. We were, after all, a country largely descended from puritans. Lest we forget, Richard Nixon (a Quaker) had been elected president in 1968, in spite of what appeared to be a spiritual and cultural revolution. In fact, it was during his tenure that the catchphrase "cover-up" took on such ominous potency.

Of course, sex was not necessarily nudity, nor was nudity necessarily sex. The advent of the nudie cutie brought home that conundrum magnificently. Actors and actresses were running around half-clothed all over the place and the public could not get enough of it. Hence, a steady source of financing was immediately available for any filmmaker willing to strip his performers somewhere in the midst of the movie.

At first, most of the folk who got involved in making these movies were the outlaws and wanna-be filmmakers who needed a hook to raise financing or distribution. Mostly, they had the artistic morals and attitudes of pirates, in that they felt they shouldn't have to answer to anyone in the creation of their "masterpiece." The money guys offered the least interference, "We don't care about the story, just get a girl in there and get her clothes off!"

On that little sound stage in West Hollywood, we were all convinced that *One Million AC/DC* was so badly written and the budget so miserly it would never see the daylight of distribution. Screenwriter Ed Wood, Jr., had even changed his screen credit to read Akdov Telmig (vodka gimlet spelled backwards). Ed was in his waning years as Hollywood's worst director, and, sadly, the demon drink had become his best friend and constant companion.

Wood did not show up on the set as I remember, but I did chance to meet him one day in the editing room. He was sitting on a stool, talking to Don Jones. He was by that time a shadow of his former self: frail, losing his hair, eyesight strained and watery. He was holding a plastic cup, half full of vodka; he spilled a portion attempting to shake my hand. Still, there was humor and humanity pouring from those weary eyes.

Had Ed known then that, years later, distinguished actor Johnny Depp (*Pirates of The Caribbean, Edward Scissorhands*) would bring his life to the legitimate screen and in the process garner a Best Supporting Actor Oscar for Martin Landau, win another for Best Make-up, collect a New York Film Critics Circle Award, a National Society of Film Critics Award, a Golden Globe and two Golden Palms, would he have thrown the vodka aside, and leapt atop the movieola to dance a gavotte to the sheer joy of life? *"Yeah,"* Boo sighed, *"Probably, he woulda."*

Back on the soundstage, I was pulled from beneath the succulent body of Ms. Lease, and asked to perform a song. My first and only chance to actually sing solo in a movie and the damned song was "The Spear Goes into the Monster."

"The Spear goes into the monster, and the monster blows his mind." I think you grasp the metaphor, eh?

It would take someone with the warped sensitivity of an Ed Wood or a Gary Graver to concoct such a film as *One Million AC/DC*. Cave babes and buff bros orgying out on libertine behavior while fighting off a prehistoric monster. The "monster" in question was a toy lizard Gary picked up at the five and dime. Every other shot or so, Gary would sneak the fellow up over a small boulder, then later, during foley, he would add raging animal sounds, and lo and behold, he had his monster.

Much of the film was shot on location at the Bronson Caves. The caves, created by the Union Rock Company in 1903, sit atop the western slope of L.A.'s Griffith Park. The Union Company quarried crushed rock from the area to create the streets of a burgeoning new community known as Hollywood. When the company stopped operation, they left their excavation caves behind. The main cave is actually a cavernous, but short, tunnel. It has been used in countless movies and TV serials, most notably serving as the Bat Cave in the *Batman* TV series.

Imagine, if you will, a cave with Don "Irish Frankie" Jones working as sound mixer; Gary Graver as director; Ed De Priest as producer; myself as Mota, the Mighty Warlord; Maria Lease as Vela, the voluptuous cave babe; and Ron Foreman (production designer, *Rocky 3*, *Colors*) as art director, all surrounded by a plethora of skinny cave gals and guys stirring up the burbling plot of a movie drunkenly penned by Ed Wood, Jr. It is a wonder, really, that we were not deported. In retrospect, I did get to do a great fight, (using war clubs, fists, tooth, and nail) with another caveman, Louis Ojena (*Machismo*, *The Hanging of Jake Ellis*). Made my day, actually, considering I was starring in unquestionably one of the worst movies ever made. "Please, Vela, hurry with the flagon of chardonnay!"

We accepted work on these low budget wonkers not because of the material, but because of the filmmaker, who, more often than not, was a close friend. In this case, it was Gary Graver, an outlaw to the bone, and proud of it. Gary just wanted to make movies, period. I did several nudies, or "skin flicks," as they were called on the Boulevard, for Graver. I did several as a production manager (*The Hard Road*; *Sandra, the Making of a Woman*), and again, as an actor, in a semi-glossed tale of girls, guns, and gangsters gone wild in the days of prohibition, *The Fabulous Bastard From Chicago*.

The Fabulous Bastard From Chicago actually had a budget, and a good thing, too, since the film was set in the late 1920s, with all of the costumes, scenery, automobiles of the era demanding meticulous recreation. Greg Corarito (*The Bikini Keys*, *Carnal Madness*) would direct from a screenplay by producer/director/writer Richard Compton (*Welcome Home, Soldier Boys*, *A Small Town In Texas*). Gary Graver was the cinematographer.

The film concerned a dapper bootlegger, John Alderman (*The Stunt Man*, *The Hard Road*), and his moll, Maria Lease, trying to outwit and outmaneuver the rapidly closing noose of the booze police. Alderman's chief bodyguard-gofer was played by my good friend, Walt Robles. The really, really bad guy was played by corpulent actor/writer James Myers, who is perhaps best known for co-writing, under his nom de plume Jimmy DeKnight, the megahit "Rock Around the Clock." The song, recorded by Bill Haley and His Comets in the late 1950s, sold over twenty-five million records and kick-started the era of Rock and Roll.

I played the chief good guy, a Chicago police detective named Wes Thompson, and for once I got to keep my clothes on!

As usual, Gary Graver's sense of humor kept the set alive with laughter. He had a habit of, when running camera, covering himself with a barney (a furniture pad thrown over camera and operator to muffle noise), and then, when the director would call "cut," there would be no movement from underneath the cloth. When the blanket was pulled off, there would be Gary, still stuck to the eyepiece, pretending he was sound asleep.

The vintage automobiles and delivery trucks were a veritable feast for car enthusiasts worldwide. Walt Robles got the thrill of driving one of these relics in a chase scene. During this hound-pursuing-the-hare sequence, the camera would cut to the interior of a 1928 Model A taxi cab, where actor John Alderman and I were involved in a verbal joust that allowed us room to exercise our acting chops. Corarito and Graver had the patience to let the scene "happen," a visual and verbal squeeze back through time, creating one of those moments that scoops you up in the magic and holds you, however briefly, in an achingly real atmosphere that transcends make-believe. For John and I, it *was* 1928.

That particular scene ends with Robles bailing out of the truck while it is still in motion, rolling down an embankment, and then getting his brains blown out by rival gangster James Meyer's henchmen.

Although providing more than its share of nudity, *The Fabulous Bastard From Chicago* contained enough good acting and production value to attract some uptown attention. I quote, paraphrased, from an article by Kevin Thomas, dean of Los Angeles film reviewers, in the *Los Angeles Times*, November 7, 1969:

> *A lot of the acting by supporting players is amateurish around the edges, but John Alderman, an actor of considerable charm and versatility, the lovely Miss Maria Lease, and virile Gary Kent, the film's Eliot Ness, are talented and thoroughly professional. Color photography by Gary Graver is very good indeed. These filmmakers, in the not too distant future, may be turning out the kind of pictures everyone stands in line to see.*

You Can't Put the Cat Back in the Bag

Once filmmaker Russ Meyer unleashed the nudie cutie onto the American movie audience, there was no going back. It would only get more daring and only increase in demand. Even the major studios took advantage of the newly formed MP code to include adult situations and subject matter into grown-up, legitimate productions. Still, it took the brilliance of filmmakers such as Francis Ford Coppola (*Tonight For Sure*, *The Bellhop and the Playgirls*), and the brothers Denis and Terry Sanders (*Invasion of The Bee Girls*; *Crime & Punishment, USA*) to cinematically elevate the underbelly of American behavior beyond mere voyeurism.

Due to the efforts of these early raconteurs, American Cinema finally began to grow up and catch up with the rest of the civilized world in regard to its treatment of adult, sexually explicit material. I remember Graver, Don Jones, John Parker, myself, and other film cohorts rushing to view *Bob & Carol & Ted & Alice*, Paul Mazursky's droll examination of free love and mate swapping, starring Natalie Wood, Robert Culp, Elliott Gould, and Dyan Cannon. Presented by one of the best directors in the business, this mini-masterpiece crossed the boundaries of what the public considered "proper" entertainment.

Several actors of prominence turned down roles in the film, fearing a backlash by the mainstream audience, among them: Steve McQueen, Jane Fonda, Robert Redford, Faye Dunaway, and Warren Beatty. After its release, *Bob & Carol & Ted & Alice* received four Oscar nominations, two Golden Globe nominations, and won two New York Film Critic's Circle Awards, and a Writer's Guild Award for Best Screenplay.

It is hard to explain the sheer euphoria experienced by the curious, more adventurous cinophiles, when we at last had easy access to movies that brilliantly covered subject matter previously verboten—*Candy*, a farce-comedy written by Terry Southern, in which a teenage high school girl searches for meaning in a variety of kinky adventures. A loose parody of Voltaire's *Candide*, it includes multi-racial sex, sex with a hunchback, a Hindi guru, a hermit, and ultimately, a tryst between our heroine and her own father. The film, though rated X, still attracted a stalwart cast, including Marlon Brando, Richard Burton, James Coburn, John Huston, Walter Matthau, and Ringo Starr.

Midnight Cowboy, directed by John Schlesinger, is the story of a small-time Texas hustler and would-be gigolo played by Jon Voight, and his misadventures while seeking his fortune in New York. The film deals with homosexuality, male prostitution, and infidelity. Still, it won three Oscars, for Best Director, Best Picture, and Best Screenplay. Its two stars, Voight and Dustin Hoffman, both received Best Actor nominations. The first and only X-rated film to ever win an

Oscar, *Midnight Cowboy* also won a Golden Globe and numerous other industry awards and nominations.

Brian De Palma's *Greetings* was the first film ever to receive an X rating. De Palma's film introduced a very young Robert De Nero, playing a Peeping Tom and would-be filmmaker. Director Roman Polanski shocked and chilled us with scenes of bestiality in his classy *Rosemary's Baby*, in which a struggling Mia Farrow is impregnated by Satan while a coven of onlookers watch, just as enthralled as the movie audience.

Homosexuality, both male and female, was for once treated with intelligence and respect by major filmmakers in works like *The Killing of Sister George*, *The Sergeant*, *The Boys in the Band*, *The Fox*, and *Norman...Is That You?* Although the legitimate stage, literature, and, at long last, motion pictures had opened the closet on matters regarding homosexuality, musicians, the unabashed leaders of the cultural revolution, continued to shy away from the subject, and, with rare exception, do so to this day. I suppose it is difficult to write a song about coming out or announcing one's sexual preference melodically.

Drugs: those affable, delirious, often lethal companions of the twisted psyche ever since Mota the Warlord first sucked a marula pod many BC years ago, were always a furtive presence in American film. Pictures like *Reefer Madness* deceptively approached the subject of drug use way back in the 1930s. Later, *Monkey on My Back*, *The Gene Krupa Story*, *The Man with the Golden Arm*, and *Valley of The Dolls* dealt more truthfully with the ravages of morphine, alcohol, heroin, and prescription addiction.

The biker and psychedelic films of the 60s and 70s openly suggested marijuana, acid, and other mood-changers were not necessarily products from The Evil One himself.

Major movie moguls finally embraced the casual use of marijuana as a relatively harmless, often funny, immoderation. *I Love You, Alice B. Toklas!*, starring iconic comedian Peter Sellers (*The Pink Panther*, *Dr. Strangelove*), offered up a corporate man who, after eating marijuana-laced brownies, decides to try the hippie lifestyle. The picture, adored by the movie mainstream, was nominated for a Golden Globe, several Golden Laurels, and garnered a Writer's Guild nomination for Best Screenplay.

Jack Nicholson's "turn-on" scene in *Easy Rider* set the bar for "tripping out" on film, and Cheech Marin and Tommy Chong made fame and fortune filming their frequently hilarious high jinks with the devil weed. In fact, none of these eclectic, drug-infested works had difficulty getting worldwide distribution or attracting an audience.

The movie-drug experience in the 60s and 70s, however, more likely included one's ingesting, inhaling, or chowing down on some illegal substance, loading up on munchies, and hauling your semi-comatose self off to view a select group of films recommended on the street as "must see this on drugs." The buzz, frequently in error, was that the films contained "hidden messages" buried in the movie's tapestry, especially for the "hip" crowd.

It was just such an event that lured my former neighbor, Sherry Stewart, and I to the theater to see Stanley Kubrick's (*The Shining, The Killing*) brilliant and mystifying *2001: A Space Odyssey*. We got higher than a Gemini flight before attending the screening. Once inside the theater, we bumped into just about everyone we knew from the West End movie crowd, and they all seemed to be smoking joints, right out in the open lobby. All acid heads considered *2001* their personal interpretation of what rebirth, celestially speaking, was all about. The film simply *blew us away*. Kubrick's masterwork won an Oscar for Best Visual Effects, plus numerous other award wins and nominations including a Hugo and a Golden Laurel.

Other films demanding chemical preparation were The Beatles' *Yellow Submarine* and Disney's *Fantasia*. Rumors swirled along the boulevard that the Disney people had inserted new, drug-oriented material into this childhood classic, just for us. Watching *Fantasia* on blue-blotter was akin to three weeks on the Magic Mountain roller coaster, with no timeouts or bathroom breaks.

A later favorite of the over-medicated counterculture was *A Clockwork Orange*, Stanley Kubrick's homage to ultra violence, drugs, sex, and petty crime, which received four Oscar nominations, won Kubrick the New York Film Critic's Circle Award for Best Director, and further advanced the career of Britain's brilliant actor, Malcolm McDowell (*If...*, *Caligula*). It was increasingly apparent that "drugs" were helping people feel connected in a variety of ways.

Illusion appears, but does not exist.

—Buddha

The illusion was that I was in the boxcar of a train, crossing the severity of the Russian steppes in winter, bound for a fateful meeting with other revolutionaries in Tiflis, a smoky, dour city in the USSR. I was Joseph Stalin, peasant, future leader of the Soviet Union, and I needed to pee. There were other peasants sharing the boxcar. I stood, weaving my way into a corner of the car, and pissed into a communal bucket. The sound of liquid splashing in the bottom of the bucket completed the illusion. The audience was at once repelled and titillated; never have the plinkity sounds of urination by one of the most infamous leaders of the Cold War fallen on the ears of so many, and so artistically.

Actually, I was on stage at a legitimate theater on Fountain Avenue, in Hollywood, and my fellow thespians and I were in the opening act of "The Passion of Josef D." by famed playwright Paddy Chayefsky (*Marty*, *Network*; three Oscars, two Golden Globes, many others, including four from the Writers Guild of America). This was Chayefsky's brilliant drama about the Russian Revolution and "Stalinism." It dealt with the rise of the man of steel—the murderous Joseph—to a supreme power that held the Soviet Union, its citizenry, their dreams, aspirations, and liberties in a vice-like grip for over thirty years. It just seemed right, somehow, to our little theater group, to do something apropos to the times.

We at West Coast Repertory considered ourselves cutting edge, and as such, we were determined to stay topical, informative, even offensive if the moment called for it. A ragtag pudding of working and barely working actors, we shared one commonality in particular—a love of live theater. After the indignity actors frequently undergo during the making of a motion picture, redemption only came from the body of experience provided by performing live. To this end, we had formed our company.

Our first full-blown production was *The Hostage* by Brendan Behan, a story centered around what the Irish still refer to as "The Troubles." The setting was a rooming house in Dublin, where Catholics and Protestants were forced to coexist, and even thrive. To make sure the audience enjoyed the play, we served Irish coffee during intermission. I, as lead curmudgeon Pat, started the last act by approaching the audience, singing a favorite Irish ditty, "The Hound that Caught the Pubic Hair." Our first production, then, was a rowdy, rollicking success.

For Chayefsky's play, we opted for serving Black Russians at intermission, as the show had a certain Bolshevik brutishness, starting with the urination scene in the crowded boxcar. Actually, the lighting was dimmed and I turned my back to the audience, pouring a small tube of water into the bucket. The audience however, believed it was really happening. I could clearly hear an uncomfortable wave of discreet laughter passing front to back of the auditorium.

The violence occurring during the Russian Revolution, the blood-curdling cries of the mounted Cossacks and the angry revolutionaries as they slaughtered everyone in their path resonated with the sights and sounds we saw every night on the evening news broadcasts from Vietnam. We felt our production, on that dusty, squat proscenium on Fountain Avenue, was somehow, terribly important to everyone, everywhere. All theater people do, though. In the course of performing a stage production, they actually sustain themselves with only the crushing, creative nourishment of it all. They are, after all, the self-appointed aristocracy of the performing arts. Still, in Los Angeles, it was motion pictures that was carrying the big stick and calling all of the shots. We fought like rabid badgers to attract an audience to our play, while down the street, there would be a line a block long, waiting to see some dog-eared film promising passion, pathos, entertainment, or enlightenment.

Chapter Eleven

A stunt goes terribly wrong on the set of Hi Riders, *Lake Casitas, 1979.*
Photos courtesy Hedy Dietz.

Movies, Mayhem, And Murder

Violence is as American as apple pie.
—H. Rap Brown, Black Activist

Charles Manson's handshake felt like a dead trout and he wouldn't look me in the eye. We were on the Spahn Ranch, the hangout for Manson and his creepy-crawlies. It was seven in the morning. The sun, up since six, had followed me from the great flat basin of the San Fernando Valley through the Santa Susanna Pass to the ranch, a dilapidated cluster of wooden buildings hugging the highway into Simi Valley.

I was there to do a saddle fall on an exploitative Western titled *Lash of Lust*. The production manager, my friend Bud Cardos, had hired Manson the night before to fix a dune buggy we used to haul heavy camera gear. It wasn't fixed; the morning was starting to heat up and we needed the buggy on the set.

To me, Manson was as shifty and full of hot air as a corn-eating cow. I listened to him rap out a line of barely audible bullshit as to why the job wasn't done. When he was scamming, he would stare at the ground, stirring the dust around with his bare feet. At the last moment, he'd look sort of sideways and up, to see if I was buying his story. That morning, his eyes were nothing like the large, hypnotic orbs that months later would flash from the front pages of the world press when he was busted for multiple murders. They were small, narrow eyes, like the eyes of a shoplifter.

"A flake and a loser," Boo whispered, and yet I felt sorry for the guy. He was in need of a bath, his hair was long and caked with mud and grease; he wasn't wearing a shirt or shoes. Charlie only stood about five four. He weighed about as much as bag full of whistles and looked as lethal as a pill bug. "If you spent his money, and didn't fix the buggy, Cardos is gonna tear

you a new asshole," I threatened. Manson suddenly got real busy under the hood of the vehicle.

It was the first week of August 1969, the week before the Tate-LaBianca murders. Richard Nixon was sitting in the Oval Office, paranoid and pissed off. In spite of his overwhelming support at the ballot box, a large, vocally demanding group of citizens comprised of anti-war liberals, new-left intellectuals, what was left of the hippies, upstart New Agers, Blacks, free thinkers, homosexuals, and things that go bump in the night just wouldn't behave. Laws were passed, police were unleashed, raids began, and still the pox continued to spread.

San Francisco, however, the spiritual center of the Love Generation, had turned downright ugly. Pushers, pimps, and hustlers were preying on the naive and innocent who continued to flock to the city in search of Nirvana. Hard drugs, needles, and the damage done were clogging the arteries and neuronal pathways of the Haight and its zoned-out population. The flower children packed up their good intentions, their poets, pets, and peyote, their hash stash, Donavan albums and window-pane and moved en masse to Los Angeles. Included in the exodus was an elfish, delusional ex-con named Charles Manson and a busload of his fanatical followers.

Sure I'm crazy—mad as a hatter. What difference does that make? You know, a long time ago being crazy meant something. Now, everybody's crazy.

—Charles Manson, in an interview with Diane Sawyer

The Spahn Ranch was a sometime location site for low budget and independent film companies. It had a ramshackle Western street, complete with board sidewalk, an ancient water tower, and a stable of horses. There were also acres of dry, rolling hills, an occasional wagon track going nowhere, some abandoned shacks, lots of scrub oak, agaves, and prickly pear. The owner, George Spahn, was a semi-invalid. Old and blind, he was looked after by his partner, a woman named Pearl. Between location rentals, Pearl and George made a living by hiring out the horses.

Pearl's job was made easier when Manson showed up. In return for allowing them to stay on the property, Charlie and the girls agreed to help run the place. It is reported that one of the gang, a slight young runaway named Lynette "Squeaky" Fromme, was assigned to have sex with Old George, to keep him in a constant state of bliss. Manson finally managed to get the dune buggy running just before Cardos arrived to see what was taking so long.

I walked over to the barn to select a horse for the stunt. I had just settled on a medium-sized Morgan, a pretty animal, dark brown, with one white stocking, when a strange apparition drifted through the background. It was Tex Watson, Manson's second in command. Watson was dressed in black and carried a six-gun on each hip. He was strutting past the horse stalls, mumbling to himself, throwing macho, fantasy feints into the empty air. The horses ignored him. I thought he looked rather comical—about as dashing as a hoe.

I mounted the Morgan and rode her to the movie set so she could get a fix on all of the excitement and clamor. I was going to get shot off her back, and she knew it. She could tell by my body language and the odor of gun powder. I ran her into a nearby field to work off some energy. When I returned to the set, I found Bud Cardos tossing Tex Watson into the boonies. Watson had been hanging around, twirling his six-guns and bothering the female members of the crew. The film's director, the prolific Al Adamson, asked Cardos to remove Watson from the set. Cardos asked him to leave, but Watson reappeared and began practicing his fast draw on the hairdresser. Bud grabbed him by the arm and turned him around, which is somewhat like being turned around by a small tornado. "I told ya once. I'm not gonna tell ya again. Get your ass outta here. You're botherin' everybody."

Bud propelled Mr. Watson to the edge of the set and gave him a shove. Tex stumbled several feet, almost falling, and then lumbered away, a bundle of seething resentment and self-pity. As we were wrapping the set later that afternoon, we heard the sound of gunfire coming from a valley a ridge or two away. Pearl told us that the guns Watson wore on his hip were real, and that he was armed with live ammunition. This was the second time I had been privy to that same experience. Ships that pass in the night?

At lunchtime, I took a box from the caterer and, avoiding the tables set up for the movie people, walked about a hundred yards to a cluster of scrub oak and sat down. Before I could open the box, I heard the sound of someone laughing. Patricia Krenwinkel, one of the Manson girls, was coming toward me out of the sun, all rustling gingham and soft laughter, like a spirit from a long forgotten summer. She appeared over a rise of parched California stubble, shooing a flock of chickens in front of her, scolding them, and then breaking into girlish giggles when the frustrated fowls protested. She stopped about six feet from me, peering into the shadow of the oaks. She called out in a thin, friendly voice, "Hello, isn't this a gorgeous day?"

Krenwinkel shuffled forward into my shade. Now I could see her clearly—in her twenties, five four, with frizzled brown hair falling to her waist. She wore a long dress, was barefoot, and carried a small bouquet of wild flowers.

"Are you with the movie people?" she asked, her eyes openly flirting. Her mouth formed a perfect little "o" after the question.

"I sure am," I answered.

"Can I have your leftovers? From lunch, I mean?"

That had been the way of the Manson clan. Every time we filmed at the ranch, lunchtime would bring out the girls. They would pop up, one by one, from behind the rocks and abandoned farm vehicles. There they would squat, staring. Then, like refugees, they would start begging for food, for some discarded bit of baloney or a cupcake remnant. I wasn't going to feel like eating until after the stunt, so I gave Patricia my lunch.

We hired one of Charlie's guys to work on our crew, a tall, curly-haired youngster named Juan Flynn. Flynn was from Panama, a vaquero, a hard worker experienced around horses. He had an innocent, enthusiastic attitude and a smile as big as Yosemite. Later that afternoon, after I had done my saddle fall, I headed for the grip truck to grab a cold beer. Juan trudged past me, looking sad, like someone had run over his dog. I invited him to join me. There are few wrongs committed under the brain-frying California sun that an ice-cold beer cannot cure.

By the second drink, Juan, usually as shy as a crocus, opened up and began telling me his troubles. He was unhappy with his situation at the ranch. He had to sleep in the barn, eat garbage the Manson clan had rummaged out of restaurant dumpsters, and worse, neither Charlie nor Tex knew their ass from a stump when it came to handling horses.

"They stickin' me with alla the work, man."

"Why don't you just leave?"

"I'm gonna, man, soon's he pays me up."

Juan finished a beer, crunched the can with one hand, hooking it expertly into an empty barrel about eight feet away.

"I don't like Charlie," he confided. "You can't trust him. When he pays up, I'm makin' my move. I'm doin' me a ghost, man."

Months later, the City of Angels took Manson, Krenwinkel, Leslie Van Houton, Susan Atkins, and Tex Watson to court, eventually convicting them of the multiple murders of actress Sharon Tate, hairdresser Jay Sebring, coffee heiress Abigail Folger, her friend Wojciech Frykowski, and the elderly LaBiancas, Rosemary and Leno. Juan Flynn appeared as a witness for the prosecution. Like everyone else in L.A., I watched the daily coverage of the trial. When he took the stand, Juan's testimony was brave and straightforward. It turned out that the handsome Argentine cowboy was the only member of the Manson family who wasn't afraid of Charlie.

I would make several more films on the Spahn Ranch while the Manson Family occupied the premises. The murders had already occurred by the time I arrived on the ranch, or at least several had, yet no one had fingered Manson. The cops were looking for some devil worshipping hippie cult, more sophisticated in design and purpose than Charlie, Tex, and the girls.

The Northern Lights have seen queer sights,
But the queerest they ever did see
Was that night on the marge of Lake Lebarge
I cremated Sam McGee

—Robert Service, "The Cremation of Sam McGee"

I, too, have seen more than my share of the weird and unusual. The film industry alone could fill several large books with experiences both outré and super-strange. I am reminded of a time when Gary Graver used a "Maternity Pillow" to give actress Connie Nelson a swollen tummy for her pregnancy scenes in *The Hard Road*, and then, slipped that same stuffing on the shoulder of actor Gene Clark, to turn him into a hunchback for the horror film, *Trick or Treats*. In those days, you made do with what you had. In both cases, the illusion worked perfectly. Near the top of my bizarre list, however, would have to be the uncanny stunt performances in the short, eerie life of "Shorty" Shea.

I first met Donald "Shorty" Shea on the picture, *The Fabulous Bastard From Chicago*. He was working as an extra, and participated in the chase scene where mobsters followed a fleeing Walt Robles through the dirt roads of the Spahn Ranch backcountry. Shorty was indeed short—about five six, a hundred and forty-five pounds. He had longish, brown, thinning hair, and an anxious, jaw-wide smile. Shorty fancied himself a stuntman and introduced himself as such. In reality, he was a wrangler at the Spahn Ranch and a sometime movie extra.

I was shooting a film on the ranch, *The Girls From Thunder Strip*, when Shorty, always anxious to make an impression, asked if I'd like to see one of his "stunts?"

"Sure," I said, "let's have a look."

He pulled a large, brown gelding from the corral, threw a saddle on him and cinched up. He winked at me from under his weathered Stetson. Shorty then took a long coil of rope, tied one end off to the saddle horn, and tied the other end around his neck! He led the horse over to open ground, humming loudly what sounded to me a lot like the tune "Jenny Got a Hoecake."

Shorty bent down, picked up a fist-sized stone, then, sinking to the ground, he lay in a prone position and threw the stone at the horse, yelling "Hey, giddy-yup, you!"

That old Brownie took off galloping like he was in the Belmont. The rope zinged tight, almost yanking poor Shorty's head off. *"What the hell?!"* Boo shouted. The horse dragged Shorty about a hundred yards before we could catch up and stop the animal. Shea climbed slowly to his feet, nursing a bad rope burn and a set of soiled trousers; otherwise, he was in fairly decent condition, considering.

"Boy, howdy, that wuz a good un', wouldn't ya say?"

Shorty Shea had another "stunt" he was proud of. He would take a couple of cardboard boxes, stack them on top of one another at ground level, then climb to the roof of a building. He would wave that old Stetson, then peel off, diving headfirst into the boxes. He didn't come in on his back, which is usual, or his side, stomach, feet; he just plowed into those boxes head first, like a duck diving for dinner. I surmised that Shorty was not going to be with us for long, but then, Charlie Manson and the gang put an end to Shorty before his "stunts" got a chance to.

The cast and crew of *The Girls From Thunder Strip* were taking lunch break way out in the boonies on the Spahn ranch, hunkered down in the shade of a scrub oak, when someone mentioned that Shorty Shea had not been around for days. *Thunder Strip* was directed by David L. Hewitt, a likeable independent who I had worked with before on a picture called *The Mighty Gorga*. Hewitt was easy going, adept at special effects and camera, and let his actors do the acting. As long as you hit your marks and remembered your lines you were pretty much okay with David.

As was usual with the outlaws and independents, money was short, enthusiasm and esprit were high. I was playing Teach, a psychopathic biker who raped young women and shot older women through the head—an evil son of a bitch, so to speak. My two biker buddies were William Bonner (*Satan's Sadists, Angels' Wild Women*) and Mick Mehas (*Pink Garter Gang, Hell's Chosen Few*). We play three wild bikers who cozy up with several women involved in selling illegal whiskey, including Maray Ayres (*Dirty Dingus Magee, The Cycle Savages*) and Megan Timothy (*The Mighty Gorga, Charro!*).

Hewitt filled out the remainder of the major cast with supertalented disc-jockey/actor/music icon Casey Kasem (*Scooby-Doo, The Gumball Rally*) and the sons of two of Hollywood's most glamorous and glittering superstars, Jody McCrea (son of Francis Dee and Joel McCrea) and Lindsay Crosby (son of crooner Bing Crosby). Jack Starrett completed the cast as the cool, Juicy Fruit-chewing sheriff. Hewitt hired Shorty Shea as an extra and to help with hauling equipment. "Anyone seen Shorty lately?" he asked.

Hmmmm? We all stopped mid-sandwich, looking at each other, counting coup, then scoped our surroundings. There was an abandoned well about twenty feet away, where we elected to throw our sandwich wrappings and empty soda cans. I may be imagining this, but I recall feeling a strange sort of psychic foreboding emanating from the well. Shorty himself was nowhere to be seen.

We continued filming *Thunder Strip*. Highlights for me were the high jinks between Jack Starrett and Casey Kasem. They had the feel of an old time comedy team from the Borscht circuit. Casey, as an inept federal revenue agent, would screw things up, and Starrett, as the small town sheriff, was always able to calm the chaos with a stick of Juicy Fruit. I got to be terribly mean and dangerous until shot to death by good guy Jody McCrea. Tall, rangy, and good-looking like his dad Joel, one of the most beloved Western actors ever, Jody was easy-going and pleasant to work with. He seemed totally unimpressed with the business of acting or being the offspring of such revered parents. His mom, actress Francis Dee, has her star on the Walk of Fame; dad Joel not only has his star on that same walk, but also received a Golden Boot award, a Los Angeles Film Critics Association Lifetime Achievement Award, and a Western Heritage Award. Jody always seemed like he was a bit uncomfortable wearing such big shoes, like he'd rather be sitting around the barn, jaw-jacking with the hands.

Gary Graver played the hometown mechanic, as well as photographing the film. Bing Crosby's son, Lindsay, played the small part of a deputy. Boo had an interesting observation regarding certain cast and crew members. It occurred to him that there was a pronounced, almost desperate "urge to merge" coming from both Crosby and missing stuntman Shorty Shea. I agreed. Lindsay Crosby seemed a bit lost, over anxious to be liked and to belong. These same qualities clung to Shorty like saran wrap. It translated loosely into, "Please, somebody notice me, hug me, love me." Crosby, who I scarcely knew, insisted that I take his brand new Cadillac convertible and keep it for a few days, just for the hell of it. I did, mainly to show off to my then paramour, Sherry Stewart. Also, I felt a little sorry for both Shorty and Lindsay; I wanted to please them.

Sad to say, Boo turned out to be right. Although Shorty worked for George Spahn as a wrangler, he would hang out with Charlie and his "family" just out of loneliness, I suppose. Still, he didn't care much for Charlie and the feeling was mutual.

In total, I did five films at the Spahn ranch, and each time Charlie, Tex, and the Family generally were always around. Shorty Shea was still absent, but no one had a real answer as to what happened to him. On some of the films (like Al Adamson's *Angels' Wild Women*), several of The Family were hired as extras. And then, suddenly, everyone was gone, fading into the California desert like Bedouins.

Charles Manson and Band of Hippies Arrested in Tate-LaBianca Murders

The entire city of Los Angeles, and especially the show business community, heaved a collective sigh of relief. They had been wrapped in a cloak of intense fear ever since actress Sharon Tate, wife of director Roman Polanski, and her friends had been brutally slaughtered at the Polanski home on Cielo Drive, a stone's throw from the trim abodes of many of the Hollywood elite. Now, it seemed, the danger was gone, and the killers at last had faces: a band of drug-addled hippies who had been hiding out at a desolate abandoned ranch in the middle of the Mojave called Barker Ranch. That made sense, drugs and hippies, and yet, there remained a cloying paranoia throughout the trial, and indeed, for years after the word "hippie" had faded from the common vernacular.

Of course, it never was as simple as it seemed. Charlie Manson held a messianic thrall over his "Family," and many of his Family on the outside remained loyal to Charlie, posing at the least a potential threat to the traumatized citizens of Los Angeles. The impact of the murders was so pronounced that to this day people see Manson and his followers as the personification of evil. Me? I remember Charlie as this little barefoot guy in need of a bath, a decent meal, and possibly a good spanking.

It was almost only a footnote to the sensational trial when Bruce Davis, a Manson lieutenant, admitted that he, Family member Clem Grogan, and Manson himself had taken the unfortunate Shorty Shea to a secluded area on the Spahn Ranch, where they proceeded to torture him and then stab him to death. Manson, Davis testified, believed Shea was a snitch, and was feeding information on the Family's activities to the police. Eventually Davis led authorities to Shorty's remains, some of which, it is rumored, had been tossed down an abandoned well near a cluster of scrub oaks.

I cannot end my disturbing account of the Spahn Ranch and the filming of *Thunder Strip* without mentioning that in December of 1989, a wonderful, friendly fellow—one of the world's good guys—took a shotgun and put a blast through his head, committing suicide. It happened in a Las Vegas hotel room. This seemingly happy little elf was only fifty-one years old. His name was Lindsay Crosby.

Baptized by the Rain

Before it all came down, before the vultures beating against the windows broke through and feasted on the rotting corpse of the Love Generation, before smut went from "good, healthy fun" to degeneracy and disease, before the slogan Black Power morphed into "Get Whitey, get even, get yours," before the shaming of America, its politics and its people, there was one last hurrah, one final, glorious glimpse of what might have been. It was known simply as Woodstock.

Sherry Stewart and I were standing on a landing outside of John Parker's apartment, arguing about Richard Nixon, when it began to rain. At first a trickle, then a downpour. In a few seconds, we were completely drenched, yet we didn't move except to sway slightly toward one another. Before you could say "parangareecutitimiquaro," we embraced. The argument (her for Nixon, me vehemently against) was instantly forgotten. We stood there in the rain, holding each other, and then, as if on cue, we both began to weep. Why? I'm not sure. It had something to do with washing sins away, becoming clean again, losing the muck and mire of existence as we knew it. All I know is we both felt it simultaneously and we couldn't stop. Now we were crying and laughing at the same time. It was startling, really, in retrospect. It continued for some time. It was one of the happiest moments of my life.

John Parker opened the door and shooed us into his apartment. It was August. We had arrived to watch news of the festivities at the huge concert occurring on Max Yasgur's farm in upstate New York, an area known locally as Woodstock. Everybody that was anybody had either gone to see it personally or were following it enviously on TV news segments. Woodstock boasted an incredible menu of the era's finest musicians: Joan Baez; The Grateful Dead; Jefferson Airplane; Joe Cocker; Country Joe and the Fish; Richie Havens; Santana; The Who; Arlo Guthrie; Blood, Sweat & Tears; Canned Heat; Crosby, Stills, Nash & Young; Sha Na Na; Creedence Clearwater Revival; Jimi Hendrix; Janis Joplin; and many more.

Suddenly we became aware that it was raining at Woodstock, a veritable deluge, and yet, the festivities continued. The crowd was overwhelming, three or four times the amount anticipated. People wandered around in various stages of dress or undress, all grooving simultaneously on the music, the moment. What started out as a paid event now turned suddenly into a free concert. Candles were passed around, and as dark set in, the TV camera pulled up and away, displaying a vast field of small, flickering lights, twinkling and moving in time to the music. It was more than enchanting—it was magic!

California's own Clown of Consciousness, Wavy Gravy (aka Hugh Romney), was, along with his cohorts, in charge of security. Instead of calling themselves the police, they called themselves The Please. Soon, it was evident that the food, water, and toilet facilities were totally inadequate, and the whole of Yasgur's pastureland turned instantly into a quagmire. Wavy got on the speakers and told the crowd, "This is our chance to show the world how it could be if we ran the show." The performers, the people, the cops—everyone pulled themselves together. United by some universal, spontaneous energy, they turned a potential disaster into a beautiful celebration of life.

Sherry, John, Boo, and I were all crying, huddled together in John's darkish little apartment in the Silver Lake district of Los Angeles, deeply moved by this last, great burst of innocence, of peace and love coming over the TV screen. Society as a whole had gone quite mad. Too much pushing and shoving, too much yelling, too many lies, deceits, cruel acts, and murders—and now, it seemed, "candles in the rain" were healing the nation. It was August 1969. Just across the valley, Charles

Manson was killing Shorty Shea. Hard drugs, the deaths of Joplin, Hendrix, and Morrison were right around the corner, as was Altamont: the blow that finally put a brutal end to the joy of "coming together." But who knew? For just one, small, shining moment, we actually believed everything was going to be all right, and the world would actually become a better place.

Wavy Gravy, already a counterculture icon, returned to the West Coast a hero for helping to pull off the success of Woodstock. Wavy owns and runs The Hog Farm, a communal house he lovingly calls "the hippie Hyannis Port." It is here he throws his annual "pignic" for the disadvantaged and those in need of easing the heavy luggage of their lives. Wavy is the co-founder of the Seva Foundation, an organization dedicated to ending worldwide poverty, supplying preventive medicine to help eliminate blindness and eye disease in India, Nepal, Tibet, and supporting Native Americans in health care, community development, and cultural preservation.

Wavy Gravy, who in his eclectic lifetime has called such diverse personalities as Albert Einstein, Bob Dylan, Al and Tipper Gore, Bill Graham, Jerry Garcia, et al., his friends, also founded and still runs Camp Winnarainbow, a performing arts camp for children and adults in need of laughter, exuberance, and unfettered creative expression. *The Village Voice* has called Wavy Gravy "one of the better people on this earth."

I first met Wavy at a restaurant in Los Angeles called The Fred C. Dobbs, owned and operated by his paramour, actress/restaurateur Bonnie Jean Beecher. Gravy and Bonnie Jean were man and wife, soul mates and business partners.

"It's evil, wicked, mean, and nasty. Don't step on the grass, Sam." "Boh-dah...boh-doh...bah." The sagacious lyrics and throbbing guitar of Steppenwolf accompanied Don Jones and I as we cruised the Strip, searching for a parking space. From Fairfax to Doheny it was wall-to-wall traffic, both automobile and pedestrian. Even before the infamous curfew riot of 1966 (*Riot On Sunset Strip*), the Strip had gained a mostly defiant pedestrian popularity. Much like an upscale Times Square, no person walking the Strip bothered to heed traffic lights or street signs. It was open territory. Maneuvering your way along the route at night was an almost death-defying endeavor.

"*That John Kay sure has a set of lungs,*" Boo riffed, referring to the lead singer-songwriter of Steppenwolf.

"You said it, Boo," I answered out loud.

"Huh?" Jonesy asked, unaware that I was talking to myself.

"There, Jones! Pull into Ben Frank's lot. I see a car pulling out."

Ben Frank's was an all-night coffee shop near the end of the Strip where the action was non-stop. Its menu was about as bland as cafeteria pudding, but when stoned, drunk, sobering up, famished, or just hanging out, who cared? Jonesy pulled into the lot and we raced others to the one open parking spot. Success. Off went the engine, the radio, and the pounding sounds of Steppenwolf.

We could barely shoulder our way through the crowds of pedestrians packing the sidewalks, thousands of people, it seemed, dog-paddling along through the stream of "what is," in some cases, well in over their heads all looking for something or someone, truth, beauty, love, or a chance to do some parallel parking on a Simmons Beauty Rest. Jones and I knew what we were looking for: The Fred C. Dobbs, that eccentric watering hole recommended by somebody who knew somebody who knew owner Bonnie Jean.

The name "Fred C. Dobbs" was filched from the Humphrey Bogart character in John Huston's *The Treasure of the Sierra Madre*. The restaurant was set about fifty yards off Sunset Boulevard, a long, narrow building partially covered in shrubbery. You would not know it was even there if you were strolling along the boulevard, trolling for action. It was unlike the other Sunset Strip clubs in that you didn't go there to dance, be seen, make out, or make trouble. You went there because you were obsessed with poetry, music, paintings, philosophy, argument, books, history, politics, and karma.

Once inside, we were greeted by a long, wood-topped bar and a large room full of tables and people. The place fairly overflowed with a kind of hippie-happiness. The motif was definitely psychedelic and everyone seemed in a joyous mood. Jones made a beeline for a section of the room where a medium sized man, dressed in clown garb, was telling jokes to a cameraman that Jones knew. I was called over and introduced to Wavy Gravy.

Wavy had a face like an oblong balloon, hair like a pissed off briar patch, bunny rabbit eyes, and a smile that belongs in a hall of fame. He was everything they said he was and more. Extremely intelligent, obviously well read, poetic, versatile in conversation, leaping from politics to humor to abstract theory in one deep, yogic breath. Mostly, he was just a very nice, overly energetic guy, heavy on the side of kindness and love. He remains, to this day, a lifelong advocate for peace and personal empowerment.

I worked my way to the bar, and, sliding onto a stool, ordered a Cutty and water. "*Easy on the water,*" Boo exclaimed. There was a large, black gentleman sitting a stool away from me, hunched into himself like a mother bear. He was dressed like he was headed into the African bush: khaki shorts, hiking boots, and one of those outback hats with the brim pinned up on one side. He was puffing away contentedly on a corncob pipe. I had not seen anyone suck a corncob since 1950, when my high school buddy Darwin McTighe and I had stood on a street corner in Renton, Washington, to watch General Douglas MacArthur pass by. I said so to my bar neighbor. He gave me a quick once-over, then pushed his pipe toward me. "Here, brother, have a toke."

I was sure the pipe contained weed and I glanced around for a glimpse of the "narcs." Rumor had it that the The Fred C. Dobbs had juice with the LAPD. "As long as you behave," the rumor said, "the cops will ignore your dope scene." Not true, but still, if I went down, half of the room would go down with me. I accepted the offer and took a slow, deep tug on the end of the pipe stem. I could feel the bowl heat in my hand, the top glowing red, like an ember caught by the wind. Pow! What a taste, instantly something sweet and cloying began to crawl around inside of my body.

"Indica?" I asked the bear.

"Nah. Opium. Afghani!"

"*Oh, shit!*" Boo stammered. "*Now we've stepped in it. We're hooked!*"

I returned the pipe to its owner, nervously overstating my appreciation: "Thank you, Bro, I mean, thanks a lot. I am pleased, I mean, I'm happy…ah, delighted…more than that, even. More than delighted, I mean. Wow! I'm really stoned. Thanks, brother.

"No sweat. Enjoy your life." He returned to his original, hunched, solitary position, staring off into the "nothingness" of everything. Right before I slid off the stool, I had a curious sensation that the dark and solitary bear was a famous Olympic athlete. Nah, couldn't be. I'm sure I was mistaken, but still, he closely resembled a certain gold medal decathlete.

"*Drugs and athletics don't mix,*" Boo scolded. "*You know that.*" Hmmmm. I'm not so sure, Boo. And still, there was that curious sensation of recognition.

I continued my side-slip from the bar stool, wobbling my way toward the center of the room where an artist had stretched a canvas across two chair backs, and was creating a lovely pastoral, all flowers and fields and sky. I pulled up a chair, seating myself at an empty table. Within seconds, handsome French movie star Jean-Pierre Aumont (*Castle Keep*, *A Tale of Two Cities*) appeared out of the crowd, and, to my delight, took a seat next to mine. Aumont, besides being a famous international film star, was also a genuine French war hero, awarded the Croix de Guerre with two palms, and The Legion of Honor for his gallantry while fighting with the Free French in North Africa and Italy during WW II.

Jean-Pierre was delighted, he informed me, by the music. "It's Bach, of course, Johann Sebastian, Mass in B Minor! Do you like it?" I assured him that I did, although, to be honest, I had hardly noticed until he so charmingly pointed it out. Classical music blaring from a P.A. system was a bit much for me, even on The Big O. Jean-Pierre was smoking a joint. He took a hit, smiled that wonderful, French movie star smile, all incredibly white, perfect sized teeth, and large, sparkly eyes. He handed me the joint, "*S'il vous plaît.*" I took a long, deep drag, nice, like elephant shit. About that time, I spotted Bunk Gardner, Frank Zappa's main man, sitting by a window, carrying on a conversation with a dog. I mean a real dog, the four-legged, furry kind. Wow! I was beginning to take a real shine to The Fred C. Dobbs.

Jazz: Five Thousand Variations on a Theme

Vito Paulekas was a hippie Renaissance man. A sculptor by trade, an elfin, chunky-monkey-dancing muse by twilight. I didn't know Vito well, only that he appeared frequently at The Fred C. Dobbs, followed and surrounded by a gathering of slim, attractive, and highly eccentric young acid poppers, men and women dressed in a variety of costumes, some as mimes, others as jesters, princes, Queens of the May, if you will. Vito and his entourage would twirl around the inside of the restaurant like a small Mummers parade and then vanish into the night going hither and yon.

Vito was one of those magical sprites that others seem to follow automatically like a pied piper, or a sane, safer Charlie Manson: "Vito knows where 'it's' at!" One night, after several straight Scotches with an Amaretto chaser, Jones and I decided to join his groupies and see where the hell Vito was leading everyone. He took us east, along the Strip, chanting, singing, striking gongs, and flipping tambourines, a veritable mélange of the curved, coiled, and straight, loosed on the night's environs like a dragon on Chinese New Year.

Vito was our leader, and he led us down, down, over the hill into West Los Angeles. Finally we came to a stop in front of a two story Normandy villa. The house itself was dark as printer's ink. *"Nobody home,"* Boo snuffed. "Quiet down, Boo," I whispered, trying my best to avoid the disturbed looks directed my way from several wild looking ladies in tank tops and tie-dyed huggers. "Huh?" Jones asked. Vito mounted the steps, rang the bell several times. The door swung open and we were motioned inside.

The living room was dimly lit by multicolored forty-watt bulbs sitting in a row of wall sconces. A soft glow from a chandelier mounted over a table in a formal dining room illuminated our small crowd. The shape of a large, black woman materialized and her ham hock arms enveloped Vito like a hug from a grizzly. You could hear the sound of music seeping through the walls, wafting through the A/C outlets over the doorways. Somewhere inside the house someone was playing jazz, cool jazz—West Coast jazz!

Vito introduced us to Mama Lou, evidently the owner/mother lioness of the place. Mama Lou led us down a short flight of stairs, and then opened the door to a smoke-hazed room rife with a mix of exotic aromas. When my eyes adjusted to the low light, I could just make out the shadowy shapes of the people inside. There were musicians and groovers. The groovers, all of whom seemed on the nod, were splayed across a collection of sofas arranged around the edges of the room.

The sofas rested on the floor, having had their legs removed. The musicians, about eight in all, were sitting on folding chairs in a makeshift stage area. There were no amps, just the instruments and the folks that played them. I found an empty section of couch, eased into place, and began to get my groove on. Gradually, I became aware of someone sitting next to me, slumped into the pillows, eyes closed, fingers tapping out some secret rhythm not necessarily connected to the present time and place. It was obvious that he was on the nod, tarred out, high on horse. He looked vaguely familiar. I leaned closer…and then I recognized him. It was Chet Baker, who was, to me, the greatest horn player in the world.

Le Jazz Hot

Most people rode out of the 60s on the backs of the movies and folk/rock music. It would be unconscionable, however, to leave the era without paying homage to the jazz scene. Flashback: When I first arrived in L.A., I wandered into a small bistro on the corner of Hollywood Boulevard and Western Avenue. The name escapes me. Nothing about the place was unusual, just your normal, dark neighborhood hangout kind of place. I struck up a conversation with another loner, a fellow named Murphy. Murphy had a slight build, a pencil mustache, smallish eyes. He looked a bit like a tall ferret, Murphy did. He was dressed in neatly pressed khakis, both shirt and trousers. He had a slight lisp which I attributed to a set of ill fitting false teeth, which he would take out now and then, dunk in a glass of whiskey, then return them to his mouth with a most appalling sucking sound.

It turned out that Murphy was an ex-convict. He did five years at Chino for pulling down on a guy with a forty-five. "He fooled me out, Bub, burned me on an eight-ball." Murphy was also a singer, Blues mostly. He joyously recalled the times he had stood alone on the prison stage, bowing, as his captive audience shouted his name for encores. Murphy was also into jazz and knew everyone and everything about it. "What time you get off work, Bub?" he asked.

I was working an evening shift at a TV station as a stage manager, and generally wouldn't be finished work until midnight. "Perfect," Murphy said.

"Meet me tomorrow night, twelve thirty, corner of Cahuenga and Hollywood Boulevard."

I arrived at the appointed hour to find Murphy dressed in his khakis, smelling of Barbasol and Brylcreem, pacing impatiently. "We just got time for a coupla sets, Bub," he said, taking my arm and hustling me along the east side of Cahuenga. Minutes later, we were inside a percolating jazz club filled to the rafters with aficionados and celebrities. A quintet was laying down licks, a jiving five. Murphy and I slid into an empty booth near the door. The waitress, a long, cool redhead, seemed to know Murphy, greeting him like family. "You singing tonight, Murph?" she asked.

"Nah, I'm just here showin' off my new pal. Adrianne, say hello to Mr. Gary Can't..."

"Kent" I corrected

"Don't make a scene!" Boo whispered. *"At least he didn't call you Bub!"*

"Well, hello, Mr. Can't. Welcome to Shelly's."

So then, this was it. The famous Shelly's Manne-Hole, owned and operated by one of the founding fathers of the West Coast jazz scene, drummer/musician Shelly Manne. Shelly Manne had scored, appeared in, and played for some of my favorite films, notably *Daktari, Trader Horn, The Gene Krupa Story,* and he also taught Frank "Chairman of the Board" Sinatra how to play the drums for the masterful *The Man with the Golden Arm.* I had gone to a screening of that film with an actor friend named Jered Barclay, who played a junkie going through detox while sharing a cell with Sinatra's character, Frankie Machine. Filmed in black and white, the picture was a stark portrayal of a man struggling with drug addiction, among other problems. *The Man with the Golden Arm* was at first refused a Seal by the Motion Picture Association. Eventually, the restriction was lifted, allowing movies to deal honestly with issues such as drug addiction, alcoholism, abortion, etc.

Now, here I was, sitting in a booth in The Manne-Hole, Shelly's own personal jazz club. I don't know whether it was because I was excited or happy, but I began to feel the booze long before seconds arrived, compliments of the house. *"That Murphy, he's the one, isn't he?"* Boo smiled. I lit up a Kool and proceeded to tell Murphy all about jazz, what it was, who founded, fostered, played it, who was cool, who was not. He looked at me out of those squinty little ferret eyes and then helped himself to one of my cigarettes. "Who made you Mr. Bejeez Jazzbo? Huh, Bub? Mr. Bejeez Jazzbo?"

Well, then, I had to tell him about that time in sixth grade in Renton, Washington, when I, an expert in the art of playing hooky, skipped school and hitchhiked into Big Time Seattle to the Orpheum Theater to catch the great Louis Armstrong in person. I had sat in the second row, chewing a Big Hunk candy bar, while Armstrong commanded the stage, wiping his brow with that ever-present white handkerchief. He belted out jazz, blues, Sunday go to meetin' spirituals, sometimes singing, always blowing heaven through his magic horn. He was the music man long before such a man existed.

I told Murphy about whipping out to The Lighthouse at Hermosa Beach with my cousin DeHugh, to catch Stan Kenton and The Misty Miss Christy (singer June Christy), The Lighthouse All Stars, Shorty Rogers, Miles Davis, and others. I was about to tell him about my friend, Jered Barclay, and the screening of *The Man with the Golden Arm,* when I felt ol' Murph suddenly tune me out. "Heya,

Bub!" Murphy said. I looked up, directly into the sad, sweet eyes of one of my all-time heroes.

"Hey, yourself, Murph," the hero said, vigorously shaking Murphy's hand. Murphy scooted a bit on the seat, offering the hero a place to sit.

"Shake five, Bub, with my new buddy; this here is Gary "Bejeez Jazzbo" Can't. Jazzbo, say hello to Chet Baker."

Chet Baker!!! It was hard to keep from trembling when we shook hands. "Kent," I managed to stammer. "Gary Kent. K-E-N-T." It was important that we get the name right. Baker smiled, and then in a surprisingly soft voice, said, "Like Superman!"

"Yeah," I answered, "just like my cousin Clark…" (weak smile).

"Or like them sissy cigarettes." Murphy snorted. "Can't stand those girly things. Made outta fiberglass 'stead a' tobacco."

"*Chet Baker,*" Boo swooned, "*our idol!*" There had been a time when I actually wanted to be Chet Baker. Back when I had just gotten out of Navy boot camp, me and my friend Roger "The Dodger" Goodspeed grabbed a Greyhound from San Diego to Los Angeles, hitting every club and gin joint along the PCH. Somewhere in La Jolla we checked into a jazz event at UCSD, and behold, Chet Baker and Gerry Mulligan were making a guest appearance. I couldn't believe the music—that horn, as clear and tender as a sigh directly from the soul. Gerry and Chet played opposing riffs, Mulligan on sax and Chet on his trumpet. Then Chet Baker sang and played, "My Funny Valentine," one of his favorites. You've never really been melancholy unless you've listened to Chet singing "My Funny Valentine." The man's voice was intimate, soft and sweet, like a June afternoon, then, suddenly vibrant, full of gusto and bravado. He was also smashingly good-looking, like the actor James Dean, only more masculine, a bit sullen, but more intriguing than Dean. I was hooked forever on Chet Baker.

Flash forward to the night Chet Baker and I met, introduced by Murphy, while occupying a booth at Shelly's Manne-Hole in Hollywood. "Hello, Gary. How's it?"

I returned often to the Manne-Hole, sitting with Murphy while the jazz greats of the day/night did their sets. If he was in town, Chet would sit with us when not playing or singing. The nights Murphy couldn't make it, Baker would frequently leave the bar and join me in the booth, always giving me a friendly handshake, followed by a polite, "How's it, Gary?" Not "Buddy," or "Bub," or "Can't" or even "Kent," always "Gary."

Chet Baker drank a lot, talked a lot about his addiction to heroin, which is what landed him in the slammer. That was, in fact, how he had met Murphy. After they had both done their time, they came together playing a gig at a sort of Synanon/Al-Anon kind of place that writer Charles Bukowski was pushing.

Chet loved hearing me talk about the horses, cows, International Harvesters, combines, hired hands, roundups, pea pie, rhubarb pie and milkmaids that had been such a memorable part of my childhood. Chet was originally from Yale, Oklahoma, but was not really a country boy. He was in the worldwide fast lane before puberty. I think, in some small way, he missed the simplicity and seeming purity of a country life.

Baker had lost some of the gloss he had affected back at the show in La Jolla. Sometimes he would come into Shelly's hungover or strung out and seedy as a hobo or an ex-con. I figured it was the drugs, and the time spent in prison that had given him that slightly used appearance, that quiet look of desperation in his eyes. There were rumors that, in spite of his popularity, some were beginning to consider him a pain in the ass, a problem instead of a legend. I began to feel sorry for my new friend. After several months playing gigs in and around Los Angeles, Chet left for Europe and I didn't see him again until that night when Vito Paulekas lured Jones and I into Mama Lou's den of inequity in West Hollywood.

Flash Forward: "Gary? Gary-Gary-Gary...is that you?" He reached for my hand. "How's it, man?" "How's it?"

Even in the dim light, I could tell that Baker was a shadow of his former self. His face was drawn and gray, his cheekbones like knife scars, the white t-shirt he always wore under his sport coat was frayed at the neck, spotted with booze or blood. He was wearing slacks and loafers but no socks. I talked him into walking up the hill to Ben Frank's to grab some vittles, but the noise, the lights, the whole anxious ambiance of Frank's irritated him, so we adjourned to a bus bench on the Boulevard.

It was a bit surreal, the two of us, sitting on a bus bench, going nowhere. We didn't talk at first—just watched the L.A. nightlife pass us by. A bus stopped, the doors opened, I waved it on. The driver shrugged. "Must be a couple of fags or alkies." Well, if that was his thinking, he would have been wrong. We actually were a couple of kids playing a game, Chet and I. Just kids, waving to cars as they passed, smiling at the late night pedestrians, even giving a thumbs up to The Fuzz as they cruised past, looking for trouble, or maybe free donuts and coffee at Ben Frank's.

Slowly, Chet began to talk, in a melancholy monotone, listing all of his mistakes and heartaches over the past few years. He had been incarcerated several times for his addiction. He tried kicking, cold turkey, in-house, in the hospital, he even locked himself for a week in a motel room; nothing was working for him. In San Francisco, a drug deal went wrong and some thugs rearranged his teeth with a knuckle sandwich. Eventually, he had to settle for dentures, which he felt affected his playing for the worse. Now he was just doing gigs to survive until the next score: popping horse, injecting it just under the skin, until "I can get straight."

He told me he had made a bunch of movies, notably *Hell's Horizon* with John Ireland (*Red River, House of Seven Corpses*). Chet played "Jockey," a crew member on a B29, flying into certain danger during the Korean War. He had played for, or been featured musician on, at least a dozen more films. He had even turned down the offer of a studio contract. "You can have all of it, Gary, all that glamor and all of that free love."

"*What free love?*" Boo murmured.

When it came time to go, I tried to talk Chet into returning with me to Frank's parking lot. Jones would show up and give him a ride wherever he wanted to go. Baker said no, he was just going to hang for a while on the bench, maybe mosey back to Mama Lou's and sit in. "Thanks for the company, Gary. I'll see you in the funny papers."

The last memory I have of Chet Baker is of him sitting on that bus bench. He looked so alone, so helpless, like a wounded eagle. It broke my heart. I wondered if the people in the passing cars, the limos and Benzos, if they noticed him, were they seeing a derelict, a nobody, a junkie? Or were they, like me, seeing the greatest horn player in the world?

AFTERSHOCK

In May 1988, Chet Baker died after a fall from his hotel room in Amsterdam, The Netherlands. Some pundits called it suicide, some murder. As far as I'm concerned, they are both wrong. It was an accident. Chet was simply doing a "Belushi," a speedball—heroin and cocaine. Both were found in his system. The window was open, he lost his balance and fell, hitting his head on the concrete. How do I know? Boo told me.

Since the late 70s, Chet had returned to Europe, with occasional side trips to Japan. During the period, he did some of his best work, including the haunting "In Tokyo," recorded the year before his death. "*Suicide?*" Boo scoffed. "*Your pal Chet had been killing himself most of his sad, frenetic, fantastic life.*" To tap an old jazz phrase, "*The man was just too hip for the room.*"

Jazz Wise, It's a Wrap

In the fall of 2007, I picked up a tape of a film titled *Sweet Love, Bitter* (aka *It Won't Rub Off, Baby*). Highly recommended to me by Joe Kane, the inspiring, eclectic columnist ("Phantom of the Movies") and publisher/editor of *Videoscope Magazine*. He had caught the movie quite by accident, during a pot-fueled trip from the East to West Coast before beginning his junior year at Queen's College. The film was an independent, shot in 1967. It starred Don Murray (*Bus Stop,*

Scorpion) and comedian/activist Dick Gregory (*Panther, Children of The Struggle*) in his movie debut. Gregory was brilliant as Richie "Eagle" Stokes, a down-and-out, self-destructive jazzman.

Stokes meets Don Murray, an alcoholic, at a pawnshop. They are both there to hock a precious item in order to survive. They form a tenuous friendship, this Black, used-car of a jazzman, and Murray, the white intellectual losing his way to oblivion. Sound depressing? Well, it is, sort of. The film is beautifully shot in black and white, highlighting the grit and drama of street life. The performances are spot on, especially Gregory's.

Like so many of the independents that were made with passion and heart for a budget, *Sweet Love, Bitter* never received the distribution or recognition it deserved. Not romantic, no punches pulled, honest to the bone, it was nonetheless endearing, a touching, emotionally accurate reminder of all of those fragile and wounded fellow travelers for whom the fever of life and living is just too much to handle. Moral of the story? There isn't one, only the haunting questions, "Where are we all going? And, who, pray tell, will survive?"

Chapter Twelve

A typical Al Adamson gang, L. to R. Rebecca Blumberg, Gary Kent, director Adamson, actor Jack Elam, Gary Graver, Harvey Wheeler, 1984.
Photo courtesy of the author.

My Pal, Al

Not everything that counts can be counted, and not everything that can be counted counts.

—Albert Einstein

"We were filming some monuments in this park, Wupatki, just north of Flagstaff, Arizona. We were stoned out of our minds. You could smell pot everywhere. Dennis and Peter were high; I was high; the whole crew was high. There was so much grass you could smell it for half a mile."

It was Paul Lewis talking. I had joined him for dinner on the patio of The Melting Pot, a natural foods (fondue) restaurant on the corner of Melrose and La Cienega in West Los Angeles. He was recalling his adventures production managing a film called *Easy Rider*, with Dennis Hopper, Peter Fonda, Jack Nicholson, and Luke Askew (*The Newton Boys*, *Wanda Nevada*).

"Luke was into something about Mickey Mouse, or something like that, I don't remember." Paul reached for a dinner roll, tore off the crust, then rolled the remainder into little balls of dough, which he would then dunk in olive oil and eat. "We were filming at night, and a park ranger had been assigned to keep an eye on us. Luke was going on and on about this mouse, or duck, whatever—the smell of pot was just overwhelming."

"This was where? Arizona?" I asked, incredulous. This was '69. The use of marijuana was still a serious crime. In Arizona, it could get you twenty years.

"We were next to the reservation, you know, the big Navajo one."

"Four Corners." I had spent some time there location scouting another picture.

"That's it."

259

Paul dunked another dough ball, followed by a sip of a deeply fruited Cabernet. "We were right on the edge of the Indian reservation; everyone was getting high, and suddenly, out of the corner of my eye, I saw this ranger coming toward me. He looked fucking furious. Luke swallowed the joint we were smoking but we couldn't do anything about the smell."

"The ranger stormed up to me and said, 'Looks like I'm going to have to close you guys down.' "I thought, 'Oh, shit, it's all over, we're going to jail.' I tried my best to act innocent."

"What's the trouble officer?"

"Your people are climbing all over our monuments!"

"What?"

"Our monuments. Your people are climbing around on them. We can't have that. If it continues, I'm going to have to close you down!"

"Luke and I were shocked. We couldn't believe our luck. 'I'll take care of it right away, officer. I promise. I won't let it happen again.'"

The hot ticket for venting youthful angst during the last of the 60s continued to be the "biker flick." The motorcycle movie just would not go away. In most of these films, the bad guys (bikers) were the good guys, and the squares, the police, the establishment, were the bad guys. The popularity of the biker flick carried over to the nighttime film crowd at Barney's and The Raincheck Room, and to the hungry newbies and wanna-bes gamadizing breakfast at Schwab's Drug Store every morning.

Everyone, it seemed, had just gotten a role in, or just finished a "'cycle film." A partial list of top performers who worked one or more of the genre includes Karen Black, Gary Busey, John Cassavetes, Bruce Dern, Peter Fonda, Scott Glenn, Dennis Hopper, Casey Kasem, Diane Ladd, Ann-Margret, Cameron Mitchell, Jack Nicholson, Michael J. Pollard, Jane Russell, Harry Dean Stanton, Adam Roarke, Max Julien, Jeremy Slate, football player Joe Namath, and the daughter of "The Chairman of the Board," Nancy Sinatra.

Some of these films have even managed to achieve classic "cult" status; Roger Corman's *The Wild Angels*, Tom Laughlin's *The Born Losers*, Richard Rush's *Hells Angels On Wheels* come to mind. But the piéce de résistance, the biker film that really caught the world's attention was *Easy Rider*. Even during filming, this small, low-budget effort by Lewis, Hopper, Nicholson, and Fonda seemed to mirror the contrasting idealism and raging hysteria of the times.

When Paul motored the cast and crew through Dallas, Texas, it was the morning after the shooting of Bobby Kennedy in Los Angeles. People on the sidewalks and freeway overpasses threw rocks and other, more dangerous debris at them, shouting, "Murderers! Killers!" Paul told me they were attacked simply because the company vehicles had California license plates.

Easy Rider, made for a few hundred thousand dollars, was a box office bonanza. It breathed new life into the independent movie market, and continues to be lauded by filmgoers and movie critics to this day. It roped in a Best Supporting Actor nomination for Nicholson, and Best Screenplay nomination for its writers, Hopper, Fonda, and Terry Southern. There were hard-core bikers, however, and rowdy malcontents who insisted *Easy Rider* was not even a biker film. "Couple of weenies trying to get serious." For this scruffy few, the biker film of choice, the *Citizen Kane* of the genre, so to speak, was a down and dirty little flick called *Satan's Sadists*.

The Bad Boy Burnout

At the end of the decade, some people began to feel that biker flicks and blaxploitation were perverting the socio-political revolution by preaching that violence was a wonderful way to win a just cause. The Black Panthers had morphed from an inspired group of activists to gangs of street thugs, standing on street corners, glowering from underneath their black berets as they intimidated passersby into buying their literature. Bikers were being busted and thrown in jail faster than Jack Quick for a rap sheet full of crimes ranging from molesting to murder.

Movie audiences had grown tired of cute bad-boys swilling booze, punching each other out, spitting on the sidewalks, and treating women like shit. The time was right, they felt, for a different hero; some nice, clean-cut guy to step up to the plate and put the vermin in their place. Someone, say, like a United States Marine. Al Adamson dialed into the vibe and picked me as that Marine.

I parked my car in the lot at Arthur J's, a coffee shop on the corner of Highland Avenue and Santa Monica Boulevard. It was in the middle of Laboratory Labyrinth, a twelve-square-block area of movie labs, post-production facilities, and motion picture equipment houses. Parking space was as scarce as grass around a watering trough. I intended to walk several blocks down Santa Monica to Barney's Café, (not The Barney's), a hole-in-the-wall eatery without parking or pretensions. It was eleven in the morning and Al Adamson had asked me to meet him for an early lunch. Barney's was only a half-block from his office at Hollywood Stage.

Al wasn't one for power lunches. When I entered the café, he was sitting in a booth against the far wall, happily consuming an egg salad on white. The menu here was ordinary grub: eggs, hamburgers, tuna sandwiches, etc., stuff you would find at any lunch counter in the U.S.. Barney Gelfan, the owner, was also the cook and sometime waiter. He was in his late fifties, a tall drink of water with a hangdog face and a limp cigarette always hanging out of the corner of his mouth. Barney was wonderfully weary, like a Bill Mauldin G.I. on KP.

Sometimes, after bringing food to the table, he would sit down, uninvited, and start a conversation, as though he were a member of your immediate family. Folks adored Barney Gelfan.

As soon as Al saw me, he motioned me over to his booth. Barney materialized with a cup of his strongest coffee, slid into the seat next to me, and opened a copy of the *L.A. Times*. "You boys see where Reagan's gonna kick the hippies outta college?" He was talking about then Governor Ronald Reagan, who was trying to get the California Legislature to drive "these criminal anarchists" off the college campuses.

"Good riddance. The hard hats are right, love it or leave it!" Al grunted. "And screw the Smothers Brothers, too. They should be cancelled!"

I wasn't a Reagan fan. Jonesy and I had been filming a documentary at the Camarillo State Hospital for Autistic Children and learned during the shoot that the governor had cut off their funding. They would have to shut the facility down. Also, there was the matter of Reagan's acting ability. I had been in a warm and fuzzy mood, however, since the end of January, when Broadway Joe Namath and the Jets had won the Super Bowl. I wasn't going to let the Guv get me down. I speared a fork-full of Barney's coffee and smiled. "What's up, Al?"

"Sam (Sherman) and I are makin' another movie." Al said. "A biker flick, only this one is really different!"

I was sick of motorcycle movies. I had just spent the last three years working them. I didn't care if I ever punched another suicide clutch or popped another wheelie in my life.

"The gang calls themselves "Satan's Sadists." Isn't that a great name? We're usin' it for the title of the film." Al was sliding into his director's mode, half boundless enthusiasm, half sales pitch. "They're real psychopaths, real scuzzballs, evil incarnate on motorcycles."

"*Oh, goody,*" Boo sneered, "*our kind of people.*"

Evil incarnate? Scuzzballs? It was worse than I thought. I looked to Barney for emotional backup. He shrugged. "Regina's playin' the, what d'ya call it, the main Mama." Barney's daughter, who performed under the stage name Regina Carrol, was a five six blonde of buxom flesh and bubbling zest. She was a professional dancer and aspiring actress, having appeared in *Two Rode Together* with Jimmy Stewart (*Harvey, Rear Window*), and *From the Terrace* with Paul Newman (*The Hustler, Cool Hand Luke*). Gina, as she liked to be called by her friends, had even danced with Elvis in *Viva Las Vegas*. But Gina as a biker chick? "Still," Gina would say, "I can use the work." Eighty percent of the members of the Screen Actor's Guild are out of work at any given time; "between pictures" is the catch phrase used.

"I've got Russ Tamblyn (*West Side Story, Seven Brides for Seven Brothers*, one Oscar nomination, winner of a Golden Globe for most promising newcomer), Scott Brady, and Kent Taylor. Cardos (Bud) is playin' an Indian. He's gettin' a Mohawk. And ya know Bob Dix (*Forbidden Planet, The Rebel Rousers*)? Ya' know, he's the son a' Richard Dix?" The elder Dix was a leading film star during the 30s and 40s. "Bob's gonna play a guy with one eye. We're gonna kill him with a rattlesnake."

Rattlesnakes? White guys with Mohawks? Missing orbs and motorcycles? It was beginning to sound interesting, like an Al Adamson movie. "The hero is a guy named Johnny Martin," Al continued. "He's a jarhead, an ex-Marine, just outta Vietnam, bummin' round the country. He takes on the Sadists, one by one, and beats 'em all." Al leaned across the table, speaking in an urgent whisper, "I want you to play the part of Johnny!"

The Rampage of the Ucks

A month later I was in the soft, dolomite hills outside of Indio, California, gravel capitol of Southern California. Bob Dix and I were driving around in his '61 Cadillac convertible, top down, refreshing ourselves with deep swigs of *cerveza*. Earlier that afternoon we had left the one hundred and fifteen-degree swelter on the location site of *Satan's Sadists*, and, fortified with an ice chest full of beer, had motored into the surrounding countryside in search of beauty and elevation of consciousness. Instead, we came face to face with a herd of large, angry UCKS!

In truth, I had experienced a vague sense of unease shortly after leaving the set. This was, after all, the very edge of that mysterious desert, the Mojave. We cruised past a large sign that read, "Watch Out For Trucks." The t and r had been scraped off, so the sign actually appeared as "Watch Out For ucks." As a professional stuntman, I knew to pay attention to hunches, but no, instead, I reached into the ice chest for another finger-froster. "What a wonderful thing this *Satan's Sadists* is turning out to be," I mused, popping the top.

When the cast and crew had arrived on location, it was like old home week. Gary Graver was the cinematographer; Bob Dietz was the sound mixer; his wife Hedy would be taking production stills. Bud Cardos was production manager as well as an actor, and of course, there were the two teddy bears, Scott Brady and Kent Taylor. Kent, looking fit as a new pair of sneakers, was there to play the owner of a rundown roadside diner. Scott Brady would be portraying Charles Baldwin, a retired cop on vacation with his wife (Evelyn Frank, *Dilemma, Under Suspicion*). During their trip, they stop to give hitchhiking ex-Marine Johnny Martin (me), a lift.

I had not seen Scott Brady since an early morning two years previous. At the time, I was living in a small bungalow on Coldwater Canyon, just south of Ventura Boulevard, in the San Fernando Valley. It was a peaceful area, with dark green lawns bisected by neat, wooded fences, lots of avocado, lemon and giant magnolia. A good safe place to raise kids.

Bang! Bang! Bang! *What the hell?*" from the cowardly Mr. Boo. It was six on a Sunday morning. Our theater group had thrown a fund-raising party in Hollywood the night before, a rousing and rowdy success; it was still taking place when I left at three in the morning. I had just dozed off when the banging began. Someone was pounding on my front door. I yanked it open. A disheveled Scott Brady was standing on the porch holding an armload of tiki torches.

Scott and his football buddies, Notre Dame University fans to the max, had all bought tickets to our theater party. As Scott explained it, by the early hours of the morning they had consumed enough booze to start seeing "the little people." They were influenced by these wee folk to steal our flaming tikis, torches we had purchased to light the pathway to the festivities. God knows what they wanted with them, but steal them they did, carrying the burning poles triumphantly off into the night, singing their Notre Dame fight songs.

Sometime around dawn Scott sobered up enough to feel foolish. Before they passed out, his buddies had extinguished the torches and threw them into a corner of his living room. Brady gathered up the tikis, one by one, and brought them all of the way from West Los Angeles to my place in the valley. He apologized sincerely for his churlish behavior. This, then, was the infamous Hollywood tough guy, Scott Brady.

"Nice to be nice," I said out loud, smiling at Bob Dix as he chauffeured us to what looked like giant mounds of crushed rock. "Nice to be nice." Bob repeated, banking the Caddy into a sharp curve. "I'll bet those ucks are mean motherfuckers though." We laughed, and seconds later, we found out. He was reaching for the power knob on the car radio when they got us.

They appeared suddenly, rolling toward us from the back end of a gargantuan slag heap. There were six of the monsters, belching clouds of pulverized rock and debris while consuming one hundred percent of the road surface. Bob responded expertly, pulling the Caddy onto the shoulder, but it was too late.

As the ucks passed, we were instantly enveloped, hood ornament to rear license plate in clouds and clouds of thick, eye-smarting, throat clogging dust. From that day on, no matter how many times it was cleaned, Bob's Cadillac convertible always had a tacky look and smell, like old, wet animals had been sleeping on the seats.

Desertspeak

Other than the gravel truck incident, the filming on *Satan's Sadists* proceeded without a problem. Well, there was a small issue between my girlfriend Sherry Stewart, our caterer, and the Indio Police Department. It was expertly handled in-house, if you will.

Sherry visited the market every evening to buy fresh milk, bread, and bologna for the next day's lunch. We *had* been eating gourmet stuff: filet mignon, grilled salmon, fresh fruit and salad, homemade brownies for dessert, but then Al Adamson, whose idea of an expensive night out was a quick stop by Sizzler, complained. "Hey, where's the bologna?" Al had a reputation for being on the slope side of frugal, but his was not particularly a budgetary consideration; he actually loved the taste of bologna sandwiches.

One lavender-tinted evening, while speeding back from grocery duty, Sherry was stopped by the desert police. Running a make, they found she had one old, unpaid ticket, and they hauled her off to the pokey. Her car was impounded, along with several gallons of milk and a humongous supply of bologna. Cardos and I spent an hour in the police station trying to bail her out. No luck. The city of Indio was going to keep her overnight, then send her before a hanging judge in the morning. That would have been all she wrote, except John Compton, one of the company grips, got wind of her predicament.

"You gotta talk desert to these ol' boys, thass all." His words were slurred by his recent consumption of four Coronas and a small amount of rattlesnake meat he'd mixed into a jar of spicy mustard. Barefooted, no shirt, wearing only a pair of grease-encrusted work pants, Compton talked Bob Dix into driving him to the police station. I asked to ride along. I was convinced they would arrest him, and I could keep Dix company on the discouraging return trip.

Compton waddled into the station looking like he had just escaped from one of their cells. Fifteen minutes later, he waddled out again with Sherry on his arm. John grinned as the two of them slid into Bob's car. "Let's hurry on back to the motel. I wanna get me some more a' that snake pâté." Rattlesnake pâté? Now that's talking desert.

Satan's Sadists *is reputed to be one of the most depraved movies ever made.*

—Gene Scott Freese, *Hollywood Stunt Performers*, 1998

There was a lot of repressed anger at the end of the 60s and Al and Sam wanted their picture to reflect that hostility. The other biker flicks had treated the gangs like heroes. Sure they beat everybody up, but they were really nice guys, if given a chance. They wrote poetry and they hugged their dogs. Al wasn't going for it. His bikers, Anchor (Russ Tamblyn), Willie (Bob Dix), Firewater (Bud Cardos), Acid (Greydon Clark), and Gina (Regina Carrol) were pure evil: violent misfits who placed no value on human life. To Al, there were no grays; it was all black or white. Good was good and bad was bad and in his world there was no room for redemption. My character, ex-Marine Johnny Martin, returns from Vietnam to find the country all sixes and sevens.

"Everyone seems to have a lot of problems," Johnny tells Brady. "I'm trying to stay away from problems." The Sadists bully their way into Johnny's world, killing the owner of a roadside diner, shooting Brady, raping and torturing his wife. Johnny and a waitress from the café, Jackie Taylor (*Joysticks, The Bad Bunch*), escape into the desert.

The Sadists follow in hot pursuit, but their bikes are useless in the deep sand and searing heat. They abandon their machines and continue the chase on foot. This gives Johnny the upper hand. He was blooded in 'Nam by this kind of warfare—run, hide, booby-trap, surprise, and destroy. *Mano-a-mano.*

He knows it all by heart, *Rambo* years before *Rambo*. Johnny kills Willie with a rattlesnake, then, after a vicious duke-out with Firewater, he pushes him off the side of a mountain. He sticks a switchblade through Anchor's neck. I love these films that speak out against violence!

Gary Graver shot the entire picture with a 16mm camera and short ends. Many scenes were done "handheld." Gary didn't have an assistant; he would load magazines all night and shoot all day. Tamblyn, Brady, and Kent Taylor worked for Screen Actor's Guild minimum wage.

Cardos, Tamblyn, and I did all of our stunts for free. The fights were a pleasure to do. Both Russ and Bud were extremely handy; Russ had been a champion gymnast in school, Cardos a rodeo rider and state high jump champion. To me, the best fight in the picture is one between Anchor and Firewater, when, out of the sheer frustration of their own madness, they turn on each other. It is a donnybrook to be admired, sans breakaways and froufrou kinds of stuff. It was bare-knuckle, up and down a cliff, into water, face-to-face, ultimate-street-fighter kind of fighting. The Indian wins. Later, I have to take on Firewater myself: same scene, rocks, cliffs, etc. "*This time you win!*" Boo coos.

Gary Kent makes a great Johnny, displaying Billy Jack-like capabilities without pretentious Tom Laughlinisms.

—David Stidworthy, *High on the Hogs*, McFarland, 2003

Satan's Sadists, shot for $65,000, including answer print, was a huge hit for Al and Sam Sherman. It altered their lives forever. Their dream was to start their own company and *Satan's* was the flagship feature. "It was do or die," Sam told me. "Everything was on the line."

The movie came out of the lab in June 1969. Sam scooped up armloads of two-thousand-foot reels and jumped airplanes to Dallas, Atlanta, Cincinnati, and Charlotte, zigzagging across the country, screening for exhibitors who had already locked their summer bookings. "They were impressed," Sam said. "Summer is cast in cement with these guys, but they broke contracts to fit us in. I went back to New York with five hundred summertime play-dates." In an interview with documentary filmmaker Chad Sisneros (*Al Adamson: Drive-In Monster*), Al revealed that *Satan's Sadists* made twenty million dollars, when tickets cost a buck fifty each. "When we opened the film in Boston, in December, people were traveling in forty degree weather in the snow to get to the theater."

For all of its violence, a rare amount of romance wove its tender threads through the tapestry of *Satan's*. Actor Greydon Clark fell head-over-heels for lead actress Jackie Taylor; within a year they were married and the union lasted a sublime lifetime. Sam Sherman met his wife, Linda, during a heated defense of the film on *The Barry Farber Show* on WOR radio in New York.

Charles Manson had just been arrested for the Tate-LaBianca murders. Moralists were blaming the usual suspects: the entertainment industry and the media. Sam was invited on the show to debate whether violence in *Satan's* had any connection with the Manson family. Also appearing on the show were the New York Commissioner of Police, several detectives, a psychiatrist, and a rabbi.

Sam noticed a very attractive woman standing in the control booth of the studio. She was the wife or girlfriend of one of the other guests. "She looked to me like Park Avenue," Sam told me. "She was definitely uptown, and here I was, defending a movie that featured you drowning a guy in a toilet!"

During a break, the woman approached Sam, introduced herself as Linda, a friend of a friend, and told Sam she thought his comments were the most intelligent of the whole discussion. The show ended at four in the morning. The station had provided a limousine to escort guests from the program. Sam offered Linda a ride home. The conversation occurring in the back seat of the limo as it drove through the early morning streets of Manhattan morphed into a forty-year marriage and a beloved daughter named Stephanie.

It was a multi-dimensional experience, going to our movies.

—Sam Sherman, producer, *Independent International*

Dracula vs. Frankenstein had dwarf Angelo Rossitto (*Freaks, The Lord of The Rings*), a motorcycle gang (The Galloping Gooses), aging horror film star Lon Chaney, Jr. (*Of Mice and Men, The Wolf Man*), and the great character actor J. Carrol Naish, who had won a Golden Globe for *A Medal for Benny* and had been twice nominated for an Oscar for Best Supporting Actor (*A Medal For Benny, Sahara*).

"Scene 123, take 1." I am working as assistant director. The camera assistant, Mike Stringer (*About Schmidt, The Big Lebowski*), slates the scene. "Action." Naish, as wicked Dr. Durea (Frankenstein), leans forward in his wheelchair, welcoming a couple of paying customers to his Exhibit of Horror. "The Romans had their Circus Maximus, click, click, click, seating over two hundred thousand, click, click, click."

Al Adamson turned to the sound mixer, Bob Dietz. "Cut! Bob, what the hell is that clicking sound?" Dietz didn't know, but said that it was in every sound take. After some investigation, Gary Graver came up with the answer: J. Carrol Naish wore false teeth, they were loose and ill fitting, making a clicking noise whenever he delivered his dialogue. Murphy's law? What to do? Al, Gary, and I met in a quiet corner of the soundstage. Adamson believed if life dealt you rotten lemons, then you made rotten lemonade. Besides, he didn't want to hurt Naish's feelings by bringing up the false teeth. "Fuck it." Al decided, "Let's shoot it anyway. We'll get rid of it in editing." Sure.

We shot for a little over three weeks on *Dracula vs. Frankenstein*. In an attempt at levity, Mike Stringer wrote "click, click, click" on Mr. Naish's cue cards. To this day, if you catch the film (one of Al's most watched movies), you will still hear the clicking sounds whenever J. Carrol is on camera.

Besides Graver, Stringer, Bob and Hedy Dietz, and myself, the film crew boasted Joyce King as script supervisor, Gloria Betrue as production manager, John Compton on sound, William Bonner as key grip. Cast members included Al's future wife, Regina Carrol, Greydon Clark, Maria Lease, John Bloom, Russ Tamblyn, and TV star, Anthony Eisley (*Hawaiian Eye, Deep Space*).

The story concerns a Las Vegas showgirl (Carrol) who travels to Los Angeles in search of her missing sister. Her quest leads her to Dr. Durea's chamber of horrors. Besides being assistant director, I play a small part of a beach boy making out with actress Connie Nelson (Gary Graver's then girlfriend) on a secluded beach. Lon Jr., as Gorton, a murderous mongrel of a monster who works for Dr. Durea, slips up on us just as we are getting down to some deep-tongue massage. He is carrying an axe and proceeds to chop both of our heads off! This scene starts the movie and from then on things just get downright ugly.

Tony Eisley, who had been the star of a successful TV series, was sufficiently handsome but a bit removed from the passion of the film. I later learned he considered it the worst movie he had ever worked on. Greydon Clark was, as usual, exuberant and funny in his role as one of a pair of innocent, star-crossed lovers who blunder into Dr. Durea's ghastly world by accident. Dwarf Angelo Rossitto was probably the most experienced and professional person on the shoot. Born in 1908, he had started his career in silent films opposite such stalwarts as John Barrymore (*Grand Hotel, Dinner At Eight*) and Bela Lugosi (*Dracula, Glen or Glenda*). Angelo was one of the stars of Tod Browning's classic film, *Freaks*, and, to my delight, had actually worked as stunt-double for child actress Shirley Temple (*The Little Princess, The Blue Bird*).

Standing only two eleven, Angelo always carried a small suitcase around to stand on when he needed to scoot up onto a regular size chair, or say, the seat on a city bus (his normal mode of transportation). In our film, Angelo carried a walking cane that was actually taller than he was. Rossitto also commanded a newspaper stand on Hollywood Boulevard from which he was able to avoid the lean finances experienced by most of tinsel town's thespians.

When Sam Sherman opened the film in New York, he made up a bunch of actors as monsters and had them stage a protest at the Theater Owner's convention. They were picketing for equal rights for monsters in motion pictures. It was a great gimmick. Geraldo Rivera covered the protest for ABC news. It caught the attention of the exhibitors, and Sam ended up with a seventy-theater play-date.

Dykes on Bikes

Angels' Wild Women was the last Adamson movie filmed on the Spahn Ranch. In an era where the macho male was the dominant figure in mainstream cinema, Al again broke the rules. The women in his films often had larger parts than the men; they were generally tougher, meaner, smarter than their male counterparts and they came at you like a Pentecostal minister, all venting and heaving emotion. They were kick-boxers, biker-babes: members of Sex Addicts Anonymous on the loose. These ladies didn't need a husband; they needed a warden.

Frequently, the women were the story (*The Female Bunch, Jessi's Girls, Blazing Stewardesses*). Actress Sandra Currie, who played the lead in *Jessi's Girls*, told author David Konow in an interview for his book *Schock-O-Rama* that she studied karate for a month just to get in shape before filming began. "We were strong women; I'm proud of the movies. More power to us that we did them."

> *Even if you were bad, you had to be good at being bad, because Al didn't have two or three weeks just for you.*
>
> —Marilyn Joi, actress, *The Films of Al Adamson*

Top: The author gets his from actress Regina Carrol, Angel's Wild Women. *Photo courtesy Independent International Pictures Corporation. Bottom: Actress Sandra Dee in her last film role,* Lost, *1983. Photo courtesy of Hedy Dietz.*

The women of *Angels' Wild Women* were biker chicks. Al needed a redneck jerk to make a damned fool of himself and get horsewhipped for being so chauvinistic. For some inexplicable reason, Al thought of me. As Redneck #1, I found myself back at the Spahn Ranch, writhing around in good, rich, California dirt. A woman biker (Regina Carrol) has just taken the business end of a whip to me. Now I am crawling at her feet begging for mercy. Members of the gang cheer her on. Some of Charles Manson's girls had been hired as extras and they stood over me screaming for vengeance. The whole scene, in retrospect, is more than a little eerie. For my actual whipping, stuntman Erik Cord (*Robocop*, *Ghostbusters*) doubled Gina.

Don't Need no Silver Bells

I'm jumping ahead in narrative now to fall of 1983. I am standing at the bar of the Rimrock, a downscale motel in the middle of the vast Capitol Reef area of southern Utah, talking to Regina Carrol. She is drinking a Black Russian and telling me why work on a current dance routine will keep her from performing in her husband Al's latest film. I do not know she is battling breast cancer.

Adamson owns the motel, bought with his share of profits from years in the exploitation film business. He also owns two houses in Palm Springs, several cars, a boat, and some Texas ranch land. He has gathered together a Hollywood crew, including Gary Graver, myself, Bob and Hedy Dietz, a donkey, some airplanes, cows, horses, kids and cougars, and stuck us all at the Rimrock. We are there to help him film *Lost*, a sensitive story about a girl suffering through the pain of a broken home and an uprooted family life. Included in the cast are Sandra Dee (*The Restless Years*, *Gidget*), Jack Elam (*The Comancheros*), and Ken Curtis (*Cheyenne Autumn*, *Gunsmoke*).

None of us know about Gina's physical condition. We only know she and Al have been a successful team, both professionally and romantically, for fourteen years. It seems wrong, somehow, to not have Gina performing one of her hot-blooded, vivacious characters in *Lost*.

Gina starts on her second Black Russian. Her large, beautiful eyes fill with moisture, a small drop forms on the lower lid, then falls away, unattended. In its mysterious center, the liquid pool catches and reflects light from an overhead chandelier. "Are those tears?" I wonder.

"Did you know, Gary, I have a radio show in Palm Springs? I sing a couple of songs around a piano bar, and then I interview guests. You'll have to stop by. That's why I have to really get my dance number down, because of the show. I rehearse daily, on the mesa behind the motel. Are you familiar with *The Phoenician Women* by Euripides?"

"Why, yes, I am," I fibbed, wanting to ask her what dancing had to do with a radio show.

"Well, the flowers here look like little bells, don't they? They are filled with a nectar that eases the neck muscles. Did I tell you I am rehearsing daily? A new dance?"

In addition to alcohol, Gina was also downing large quantities of pain medication. The mix left her goofy as a bedbug.

Tammy and the Turks

In 1958, The Golden Globes had named Sandra Dee "most promising newcomer" for her role in *The Reluctant Debutant,* opposite box office giants Rex Harrison and Kay Kendall. Sandra's domineering mother had lied to the studio about her daughter's age, telling them she was fifteen, when in fact she was only thirteen. During the filming of *Lost,* Sandra's mother, Mary Donavan, infirm and old enough to be an antique, was constantly around her daughter, ladling out disapproval like a born again Christian.

Sandra, who had not acted for years, took a lot of good-natured heat from Gary Graver and his crew for having once played both Gidget and Tammy in the movies. In spite of these obstacles, and the fact that she felt totally out of place and even frightened being in the middle of the Utah high desert, she gave a wonderful performance as a nervous, newly divorced mother who takes her new husband, Don Stewart (*The Guiding Light, Future Zone*) and her rebellious child (Sheila Newhouse), from city to wilderness in search of a simpler, more meaningful life.

The script called for Sandra to milk a cow, a task she dreaded, convinced the cow was a vicious animal who would likely kick her to death the minute she started yanking on "one of those long, pink things (the udders)." This was my chance to score some points, as I was the only member of the picture company who actually knew how to milk Miss Bossy. I coaxed Sandra into giving it a go. She seated herself confidently on the milk stool and began to yank away. Suddenly, as cows do, Miss Bossy *flicked her tail* to swat a fly or two from her rump. Sandra panicked, shrieking, falling backwards and knocking over the stool and milk pail in the process. I repeated the adage, "Don't cry over spilled milk," but she just could not continue. Hence, the cow milking scene in *Lost* is not only brief, but one may also see Ms. Dee's hands trembling as she performs this highly dangerous chore.

Al brought actor Ken Curtis to Utah to play Cosgrove, a kindly rancher who befriends the family, helping them adjust to country life. Curtis started his show business career as lead singer with Tommy Dorsey's band. When he left to join the

Sons of the Pioneers singing group, Dorsey replaced him with a cocky newcomer named Frank Sinatra.

The country surrounding the Rimrock was beautiful and rugged—taking no quarter with our Hollywood folks. The first day of shooting brought a hailstorm with stones the size of baseballs and a state patrolman who busted Al for shooting without a fire permit.

As assistant director, stunt coordinator, and special effects wizard I had to whip up a flash flood, a wild horse stampede, a barn burn, and a mountain lion attack. For the flood, I dammed up a small river, and then, on cue, had the grips kick the sucker loose, flooding the entire lower section with roiling river water. The barn burn was old stuff for me, but Al had invited local folks to stop by and work as extras. They showed up in droves, drinking that "Mormon Tea" and turning the night into party time. We wrapped the fire around one in the morning, but the party didn't fizzle out until six.

In spite of how well the filming was going, Al seemed remote, unenthusiastic. I hadn't worked with him for over ten years, and when I arrived on location it was obvious to me that he was not his old, confident self. Like all of us, he had thrown on a few pounds, lost some hair, but it was the lack of creative energy, the missing twinkle in his eye, that told me something was wrong.

Throughout their relationship, Al and Gina had waged an ongoing battle over her smoking habit. It was the one thorn in an otherwise loving partnership. Gina was only fifteen when her mother died of breast cancer and now she was battling the same disease that had sucked away her mother's life. Al blamed it all on cigarettes.

On our last Sunday off during the shoot, instead of doing my laundry, I challenged a couple of young Turks on the crew to a game of basketball in a local school gymnasium. During the game, I heard someone enter the gym through a side door. It was Al Adamson. In Hollywood, Al had played on a showbiz hoop league. He quietly asked if he could join our game. "How about you and I against the young guys, Kent?"

Al and I played those guys right out of their jockstraps. We aced them every game, Al hitting from outside the circle with hot, hot hands; I couldn't miss with my fadeaway jump shot. That evening I saw Gina standing at the bar, drinking her Black Russians and listening to Al brag. "We beat 'em, honey, Kent and I. It was the old guys against the Turks and we wasted 'em every game." He kissed her nose. "It ain't over till the fat lady sings, kid." They were both laughing, having a great time. It turned out to be the last time I would see either of them.

Art Imitates Death

Austin, Texas, 1992. The phone rang. It was Gary Graver, informing me that Gina had passed away. She had struggled with her illness for years, and now the struggle was over. She fell into a coma; Al was constantly at her side. He was there when she died, holding her hand and praying.

More years drifted by like long, hazy summers and even longer winters. I had not heard from Al in some time, and then he called me from his house in Indio, California. We talked long into the night about "the old days" and the shining promise of the future. He was in a good mood, astounded that there were actually Al Adamson Fan Clubs bursting through the fertile soil of exploitation gardens worldwide. We discussed Gina, her passing, and I got the chance to apologize for not being at the funeral. He forgave me.

Al's only bummer was an argument he was having with a fellow who was doing some remodeling on his house. "Asshole's been stealin' from me," Al said. "He's also been runnin' up my credit cards on his own personal stuff. I'm gonna confront the son of a bitch tonight. If he doesn't pay me back, I'm throwin' the bastard in jail."

That was the last time I spoke to Al. Several weeks went by, and then I decided to call and see how the confrontation with the bad guy went. A strange man answered and informed me in a deep, gravelly voice that, "Al is out of the country. He won't be back for several months."

Three days later, I was in my driveway, shooting hoops with my son, Chris. It was hot and humid. I walked into the house for a glass of ice water and heard the phone ringing. It was actor Ervin Sanders (*The Pyramid, Jessi's Girls*), calling from California. "You heard the evening news?" he asked, his voice tight. "They just announced it. Al has been murdered!"

Al Adamson loved Regina Carrol. He loved his dog, Stupie. He loved movies and basketball. He loved life. One hot, dry morning in July, shortly after our phone conversation, Fred Fulford, the carpenter/remodeler, entered Al's home and struck him over the head from behind with a hammer, killing him. The desert police called it blunt force trauma with a hard object. Boo called it, *"El golpe de la muerta: the blow of death!"* Al's body had been wrapped in a cloth, cocoon-like, and buried eighteen feet below his bedroom Jacuzzi. It had taken them five weeks to find him. It is a popular rumor in the hot, little desert town of Indio that at the time of his burial, Al Adamson was still alive.

A Sweet Sorrow

In June of 1999, I received a call from Detective Manuel Lopez, Bureau of Investigation, Riverside County District Attorney's Office. Detective Lopez informed me that they had indicted Fred Fulford for the murder of Al Adamson. Lopez also informed me that I would be called to testify as a witness for the prosecution in regard to my last conversation with Al.

October 27, 1999

Notes on having just returned from Indio, California, and the Al Adamson murder trial:

Sunday I leave Austin, Texas, early morning. Wife Tomi drives me to the new airport. My flight is first line, very convenient. I take aisle seat to Phoenix, then transfer. Quiet mood. Do not feel like conversation. I am anxious, returning to such a familiar area concerning such a tragic event. I think briefly of Al.

Prop Plane (Mesa Air) into Palm Springs; my first time at the airport. My best description is "cute." Comedian Bob Hope, who dwelled in a turtle-shaped mansion hugging the middle of a mountain overlooking the Springs, got lonely sometimes and had his chauffeur drive him to this airport in the middle of the night. He would hang out at the coffee counter and talk to people: late night travelers, skyway vagabonds, and airport working stiffs on coffee breaks.

I am looking for someone holding a sign reading "Kent," as told to do by witness coordinator Angel Jaimez. I search the small airport. There isn't any sign. Boo says, "*This is not a good omen.*" I spot a smiling Mexican woman holding up a piece of paper upon which the words "*District Attorney*" have been scrawled in soft pencil. It turns out the woman is Wanda Sterling, the head Witness Advocate, the one responsible for arranging all amenities (transportation, lodging, meals, information, whatever). Wanda is short and stout, about forty-five, soft-voiced and friendly. I introduce myself. We wait for witness Jeff Anthony, who is flying in from Richmond, Virginia, to testify in the credit card fraud part of the case. Jeff arrives feeling frumpy and starved for sleep; he's been on a plane or in airports for nearly ten hours.

Wanda vans us to the Royal Plaza Hotel in Indio where we will be staying. On the way from the airport we pass Rancho Mirage where my wife Tomi and I had many a happy and magical time. (Whispering Waters, hippies, Indian Trails, Tahquitz Canyon, great, unusual meal, etc.) Flashbacks and confusion—where does it all go? Those times, those ghosts, those "used to be's." Where are they now?

Testimony begins in filmmaker's killing trial

Brother, friend say suspect owed money to victim

BY CHRISTINE MAHR
THE DESERT SUN

LARSON JUSTICE CENTER — The day before filmmaker Al Adamson was murdered, he complained that Fred Fulford was stealing from him, Adamson's brother testified Monday.

Kenneth Adamson was the prosecution's first witness in the murder trial of Fulford, 50, who is accused of killing Al Adamson on June 20, 1995, and covering his body with cement.

Adamson, 66, a B-movie director and producer of low-budget horror films, lived in Indio when he was killed.

His body was found buried at his home on Avenue 49.

Prior to the murder, Fulford — working as a general contractor — was helping Adamson remodel his home and had lived there since 1994.

Kenneth Adamson testified that in their last phone conversation, his brother told him Fulford had run up $4,000 in bills.

Adamson was upset and said Fulford was going to jail if he didn't pay the money back, Kenneth Adamson testified.

"Those were the last words my brother spoke to me," he said.

He testified he went to see his brother the next day but that Fulford said Adamson wasn't home. Kenneth Adamson said his brother never returned that day and so he finally left.

Gary Kent, a movie stuntman and assistant director who'd worked with Adamson, testified he had a similar conversation with Adamson in May 1995.

Adamson told him that a man living with him and working for him had "been stealing money and running up my credit cards," Kent said.

In his opening statement, Deputy District Attorney Paul Vinegrad said evidence would show Fulford bashed in Adamson's skull and then dumped his body in a large hole from which a Jacuzzi had been removed.

He covered the body with a concrete-type material and dirt followed by four tons of cement, and then topped the grave with tile, Vinegrad said.

Vinegrad said evidence will show that over the next several weeks, Fulford forged Adamson's signature on checks and other documents, moved to Florida and shipped several of Adamson's cars to Florida where he sold them.

Robert Hurley, Fulford's attorney, said evidence in the case was circumstantial and would fail to prove beyond a reasonable doubt his client killed Adamson.

Indicating Fulford may take the witness stand, Hurley told jurors, "Wait until (Fulford) has had an opportunity to testify before you reach any judgment."

Hurley, chief trial deputy in the Riverside County Public Defender's Office in Indio, said Fulford had done a substantial amount of work for which Adamson had not yet paid him.

"(Fulford) profited more from Adamson being alive than dead," Hurley said.

Image courtesy of the author.

The Royal Plaza! Woweee! Sorta like an upscale Motel 6. The ladies behind the desk, one slim, young Latino with interesting eyes and a splay of white teeth, the other a silver haired, semi-sonambulant WASP—suburban Chicagoese in the California Desert.

In my room. So much time has passed since I was last here. I walk to the large drapes cloaking one entire wall of the room and pull the cord. They open like a theater curtain presenting the past. I step onto a small balcony, into the late afternoon desert air. I inhale deeply, then my heart seems to stop; I'm holding my breath. Life has literally stopped in its tracks. I am looking through shades of pastel pink, blue and desert gray, to the horizon, where I easily make out the small ridge of hills rising ruggedly into the mountains of the Mongoro Indian Reservation. I used to climb that ridge daily when Tomi and I would sneak away from L.A. to hide out at Whispering Waters Inn: two worn-out souls in search of peace and tranquility. We would find it here, on these plateaus, these mountains. I would go for an early morning run, before the sun grew so high it fried the prairie dogs. I would end the run by climbing these same hills. From the top, the view of the Coachella Valley was breathtakingly beautiful. A power place, Don Juan would say, and now, twenty years later, I am back, enchanted, haunted by the sight.

I call Tomi and decide to visit Cactus Jack's for late lunch. I picked up my meal voucher from the front desk. I enter the café, a typical desert coffee shop: chicken fried steaks, large salads, big egg dishes for breakfast, hotcakes. A short stack consisted of four of the biggest pancakes I've ever seen.

I slide into a worn red leather booth by a window. Something's familiar. It hits me—this is the same restaurant we all ate at when we were filming *Satan's Sadists*, over thirty years ago. The exact same, friggin' café! I often sat in this same booth with Bud Cardos, Gary Graver, and Al Adamson, the man whose murder has brought me back at the turn of a new century.

I wonder, do the present owners know that the man whose death the local papers have made front page news used to come here for breakfast those many years ago? Come here for dinner when he and the crew were satisfied with a long day of filming—sliding into these booths, occupy the counter, laugh, joke, tease—full of the juice of life and creativity? And now, Al is dead, his head caved in by a man he trusted too easily, his body stuffed under the dirt like a dead animal, his creativity falling into the vast dark, along with his positive spirit.

I had a strange night. It's hard for me to sleep in a new bed, no matter what. I toss and turn, walk into the wall around two in the morning while looking for the bathroom.

Morning. TV news and coffee. Golfer Payne Stewart has died in a plane crash. Two in the crew and all passengers perish in the crash, hitting the hard ground of a frozen field in South Dakota. The phone rings; it's my friend, stuntman Bob Ivy, calling from the lobby. Besides being a stuntman, Bob is an Internet investor and a fan of film and filmmakers. He is interested in the trial and its outcome.

Bob and I walk several blocks to the Larson Justice Center where the trial is taking place. I wonder who "Larson" is, make a note to find out.

I pass through metal detectors and read lists of court trials posted in the lobby. Adamson murder trial in P2, upstairs. We take the elevator to Courthouse hallway, on the second floor. There are polished marble floors, hard wooden benches sitting along the walls for family and friends, for legal eagles and their clients. Bob enters room P2; I am forbidden to enter, as I am a witness. I am not supposed to discuss the case with anyone, under virtual house arrest. I sit alone on a bench in the long, long hall. A few attorneys, their clients, some court clerks pass hurriedly by, shoes clacking, their legal briefs firmly in hand. Then, all is quiet. I am aware of my aloneness in this vast hall with the foreboding doors, behind which the starkest of human dramas is playing out.

"What is taking Bob Ivy so long? Maybe he's going to stay for the entire morning session."

"Maybe they won't let him back out," Boo wonders. *"What should we do? Let's go back to the hotel."*

A woman passes, carrying an armload of file folders. She smiles, continues on, her high heels making a tick-tick-tick into the distance. Once again, I am alone.

Thirty yards away, the elevator doors open. Wanda, the Witness Advocate, emerges, escorting a small, portly gentleman with a full head of gray hair, wearing a suit to match. He, in turn, is escorting another woman: dark hair, wearing a red and white checkered dress; she's as tall as the man, taller even. He is her husband, Al Adamson's brother, Ken.

Ken Adamson, up close, looks a lot like his brother. Al was taller, though, about six two, thin as a whippet. Ken's wife is a demure lady. I could tell they had dressed in their Sunday best for the trial. She let Ken do most of the talking. We were glad to make one another's acquaintance, being on the same side and all. Ken remembered me from Al's movies, even though they were so long ago. "You were that black haired stunt-muffin. Now you're a white-haired old fart, like me. What happened?"

I ask Ken if he knows this guy, Fulford. "I sure do," he replies, "I..." Wanda interrupts, reminding us we are not supposed to discuss the case in any form. We are to curtail our conversation to greetings only.

Court recesses. Bob Ivy comes out, at last. I introduce him to Wanda, Ken and his wife. Bob tells me some of what has been going on inside. The attorneys made their opening statements and Bob wrote them down as follows:

1. Eddie Perez, a laborer, helps Fulford dig in the Jacuzzi, clearing drain at bottom. When he returned next day, he noticed a big lump in the bottom. They fill hole with cement, then put tile down over floor.
2. Fred Fulford went by the alias of William Fulford, Jr. After murder, he got California ID card and applied for passport to Costa Rica. Used different SS# and birth date.
3. Fulford had Al's suits retailored to fit him. He never wore any suits before.
4. Fulford drove one of Al's cars to Calico and picked up a woman and her young daughter. A man named Spiegel drove one of Al's other cars. They then drove to Florida...stayed with Fulford's mother. He sold one of Al's cars to someone named McDonald. Car was in Al's name, so Fulford pretended to be Al in order to sell the car.
5. Fulford met Al in Vegas and he worked on Al's house there. Al had a big house; about five thousand square feet, with a six-car garage.
6. Fulford used Al's credit cards fraudulently. He had his name added to Al's bank account. Fulford had a lock put on Al's mailbox so only Fulford could open it.
7. After murder, Fulford forged many of Al's checks. Paid his own credit cards with Al's checks. Had his friends cash checks for him by forging Al's signature.

End of Bob Ivy's notes.

That afternoon, I prepare for testimony. Boo cheers me up by reminding me that the previous night I had walked over to Blockbuster Video. They had two copies of *Rainy Day Friends*, a film Tomi and I had written, produced, and directed in the mid-eighties. One of the copies was checked out. It made me feel good, somehow, to know that a picture we had made fifteen years past is still in the stores, and still being rented. Life has legs!

While waiting to testify, Jeff, the credit card guy, who has testified in countless fraud cases, gives me a tip. "Count to three before answering any question. Just tell the truth and keep telling it." Minutes later an officer shows me into the courtroom. I am acutely aware of the pain of Al's relatives and the gloom of the accused murderer.

I am escorted to a seat in the front of the room. The judge has not yet entered from chambers. I have a moment to look around. My eyes go immediately to the defense table where Mr. Fulford sits, hunched into himself, his back to me. He is gray haired, a thick patch of steel gray, cut short. He is broad shouldered, wearing a light shirt with collar rolled over a medium gray cardigan sweater. The judge enters the courtroom and we all stand.

I am called to the witness stand, sit facing the jury, the prosecutor, Deputy District Attorney Paul Vinegrad, Defense Attorney Robert Hurley, and the accused, Fred Fulford. He is only a few feet from me now, and I see his face clearly: a large face, a chiseled, Roman nose, bushy eyebrows. He reminds me vaguely of ex-Russian dictator Joseph Stalin. He stares intently at a paper pad on the table in front of him. He will not look at me.

I give my testimony. Yes, I was a working friend of Al's. Yes, I had talked to him shortly before the murder. Yes, Al expressed anger over Fulford stealing from him, and, yes, Al was going to the police if Fulford did not make it good right away.

The defense wonders why it had taken me so long to go to the police. I explain that I live in Texas and am out of the loop. I did tell many people about the conversation, including Al's partner, Sam Sherman. It was Sam who encouraged me to go to the police.

In the evening, after court we go to the D.A.'s office to rehash the day. I like Paul Vinegrad, but he seems stressed and overworked. He tells me Palm Springs, once the playground of the stars, has become a high crime area, and he has too many cases. Paul graduated from New York University Law School. He looks like actor Tom Cruise, good-looking, about thirty-five, a sense of humor, but very intense.

Detective Manny Lopez, the chief investigator, is larger than a house. About five eleven, Manny weighs at least three hundred pounds. He has a head like a Samoan linebacker; the gun on his hip is as large as he is. It was Manny I had contacted regarding my phone conversation with Al.

Later, Bob Ivy and I drive into Palm Desert for dinner. It is a wonderful, leisurely drive along Highway 111, where Tomi and I had driven countless times, young and carefree, in love and lust. I speak of the circles and cycles of life. I am feeling them now as the car sifts through the beauty of the desert evening. The sound of Bob's cheerful voice insists I stay connected to the present. We decide to gamble on Tony Roma's for baby-back ribs and a good cabernet. We are not disappointed. During dinner, we discuss in detail the bizarre Mr. Fulford, his unusual antics, life and loss of life. We return to our rooms around ten thirty.

It is morning, the day after testifying. I am to be driven to the airport by Wanda; she is late. Jeff Anthony, Mr. Credit Card, has been held over for further testimony and paces anxiously about the hotel parking lot. Wanda is supposed to pick him up also, and deliver him to court by eight fifteen. It is now eight twenty-five.

Bob Ivy appears in the lobby and offers to drive me to the airport. Jeff promises to give my good-byes to Wanda; we exchange cards; I promise to keep in touch. On the way to the airport, I show Ivy the house that Bob Hope lived in, crouched on the mountain above the airport. "You're right," Ivy says. "It does look like a turtle."

At the airport, I buy the morning paper, *The Desert Sun*. Sure enough, they have a lead article on the start of the trial.

"Gary Kent, a movie stuntman and assistant director…"

I board the plane anxious to return to Texas. Three days later, I get the news from Vinegrad. The jury has found Fred Fulford guilty of Al's murder. He is sentenced to twenty-five years to life without possibility of parole.

> *For Man's grim Justice goes its way,*
> *And will not swerve aside:*
> *It slays the weak, it slays the strong,*
> *It has a deadly stride.*

—Oscar Wilde, "The Ballad of Reading Gaol"

I never did find out who Larson, of the Larson Justice Center, actually was.

Chapter Thirteen

The Mummy (Stuntman Bob Ivy) in Don Coscarelli's Classic Bubba Ho-Tep.
Photo courtesy Ivy Archives

Messin' With The Moon

It is not the brains that matter most, but that which guides them—the character, the heart, generous qualities, progressive ideas.

—Fyodor Dostoyevsky

Someone saw a gun or what they thought was a gun. Within seconds, a man was dead, stabbed to death at a rock concert. It was Altamont, The Rolling Stones Concert, where the Hells Angels had been hired as security: The Hells Bloody Fucking Angels! "*Who's idea was that?*" Boo cries, disheartened by it all. This was a far, far journey from Wavy Gravy and his Please Force at Woodstock.

In December of '69, a rock concert was thrown together at the Altamont Speedway in Northern California. The show included Jefferson Airplane, the Flying Burrito Brothers, and the supergroup, The Rolling Stones. Purportedly, The Grateful Dead, who were scheduled to perform, made arrangements for the Hells Angels to act as concert security. However, shortly after the show began, things started going bonkers and the Dead canceled their appearance.

It was hot! Lots of booze, plenty of skag and speed, the agitation began almost immediately. A fight erupted on stage between a member of the Airplane and an Angel. Someone knocked over a biker's Harley, and then it got really crazy. A member of the audience, 18-year-old Meredith Hunter, drew a revolver and pointed it at the stage. Whatever his intentions, he didn't get the chance to realize them, as he was quickly accosted by several Hells Angels, who stabbed him multiple times and then kicked him to death. The Stones continued to play their set, thinking their music would calm the crowd. Before the concert was over, three more audience members would die—two in an auto accident, one drowned in

283

an irrigation ditch. Basically, the euphoric promise of the Love Gathering from Woodstock and the hope for peace in our time, was over.

Just before the decade shrieked its way hysterically into the '70s however, one more remarkable, enchanting, magical moment occurred. In July of that year, Astronaut Neil Armstrong stepped out of a lunar module, and for the first time in the history of mankind, a human being was standing on the moon.

It is hard to explain the strange euphoria that swept through the world during and following this remarkable achievement. *"A man on the friggin' moon! Unbelievable!"* Boo stammered. Amid all of the negativity, the hate, the confusion, the seeming hopeless darkening of humanity, this one bright sliver of light shown through. In an instant, the spirits of the weary passengers on this earthly globe of endless travail were uplifted. No one knew quite what to make of it; this weird thing of men stomping around in the dust of the lunar surface, but it gave a natural high to the entire world.

In some ways, it was a bit sad, as the magic and mystery of the moon began to wane—all of those haunting songs, poems, movies, stories, etc., were now rendered more or less obsolete. *Shine on Harvest Moon, Moon River, Moon Over Miami, Only a Paper Moon, Man on the Moon, The Face on the Moon, Blue Moon, A Moon for the Misbegotten, The Moon and Sixpence, Moon Struck, The Cow Jumped Over the Moon, Moonlight in Vermont, Moonlight Becomes You, Moon Madness*, on and on, ad infinitum. Since they first gazed into the heavens, humans and animals have been fascinated by the translucent, indefatigable beauty of the moon. Any nostalgia was immediately dispersed, however, by the almost spiritual promise of the event.

I was on a sound stage in Hollywood, production managing a maniacal thriller for director Robert Vincent O'Neil (*Angel, Blood Mania*) titled *The Psycho Lover*. Actors Lawrence Montaigne (*Dakota, Escape to Witch Mountain*) and Jo Anne Meredith (*Josie's Castle, J.D's Revenge*) were on set, arguing over just how psychotic psychiatrist Montaigne really was. Sherry Stewart, who was doing makeup, rushed in from the craft service room, shouting, "We did it! We landed on the moon!"

Filming came to a standstill. We all gathered around a small TV set in a corner of the stage, and watched, holding our collective breath, as Astronaut Armstrong stepped onto that lonely ground. "One small step for man, one giant leap for mankind." We began to hug and kiss one another. Some even cried, releasing lifetimes of pent up anxiety about the future. We were overcome with a sort of rapture, a spiritual anointing, if you will. Why, if we could reach the moon, I mean, actually get there and walk around and smile and wave and plant flags, then, for damned sure, we could do anything! We could certainly make peace, harmony, and happiness the breakfast that starts the day for every man Jack and child of us on the planet!

Unfortunately, in spite of that colossal achievement, the 60s ended in an explosion of violence, hatred, paranoia, and sleaze tantamount to a "karmageddon." The government began waging a covert war against the hippies and flower children. The killing of Martin Luther King, Jr., and Bobby Kennedy, the Manson murders, the rowdies at Altamont, the seemingly unrelenting war in Vietnam, rampant acceptance of outright pornography in film and literature, swingers clubs such as Plato's Retreat, hard drugs and the damage done; militants of all colors, shapes, and sizes screeching "Power to Us!" Hippies, rockers, and bikers were now viewed by the mainstream as dangerous psychopaths, lending a bitter melancholy to folksinger Pete Seeger's whimsical reflection, *"Where Have All The Flowers Gone?"*

> *The end of the 70s began at the beginning of the 70s.*
>
> —Paul Lewis, producer

We should have guessed it when we heard the music. The most popular song as the 70s were first learning to walk was "Raindrops Keep Fallin' On My Head" by B.J. Thomas. How the hell did we get from "Candles in the Rain" to this toothless twaddle? "Raindrops" was quickly followed by "At Seventeen" (Janis Ian), "Summer Breeze" (Seals and Crofts), "Make It With You" (Bread), and, Lord have mercy, "Big Balls" by AC/DC. Even worse, punk and disco lurked right around the corner, ready to assault the senses with sizable smooze, "Me, me, me!" Bitterness, self-pity, and much hardcore yelling. The one bright light, an homage to what might have been, was Don McLean's "American Pie," a thoughtful reflection on the day the music died.

A current of violence and tragic death continued to flow throughout the decade known as The 70s. At Kent State University, four student war protesters were gunned down. Rock legends Jimi Hendrix, Janis Joplin, and Jim Morrison all ended up pushing up the daisies far too soon by drinking, drugging, and loving too much. Brian Jones (The Rolling Stones), burdened with asthma, booze, and his misadventures, drowned (or was murdered) in his own swimming pool; Duane Allman (The Allman Brothers) earned his body bag in a motorcycle accident. A short time later, the band's bass player, Berry Oakley, was killed in a similar accident. Paul Kossoff, the gifted but drug addled lead guitarist for Britain's hard rockers, Free, died young and unexpectedly when a blood clot traveled up his leg to his lungs during a plane flight from L.A. to New York. That quietly taciturn gentleman, American War Hero, Audie Murphy, most decorated soldier of WW II, was killed when a plane he was riding in encountered a thick sheet of fog and crashed into the side of a mountain. It was May 1971 and he was only forty-seven-years old.

Sail on the sea of death.
For death takes toll
Of beauty, courage, youth,
Of all but truth.

—John Masefield, "Tenth"

Television sent the wry, very grown-up Smothers Brothers packing, leaving us with *The Mary Tyler Moore Show*, *The Beverly Hillbillies*, *The Carol Burnett Show*, and *M*A*S*H*, all comedies, as though the country needed some yuks after all of the revolutionary turmoil. We also enjoyed a bit of buffoonery titled *Hee Haw*, in which country-folk and farm animals worked up a collective sweat singing and jumping around over hay bales and dancing out of backyard latrines. I was raised on a farm/ranch and I don't ever remember dancing out of a latrine. Into one, maybe, but never out!

Literature continued to be exciting and original, with Maya Angelou's *I Know Why The Caged Bird Sings*, a remembrance of growing up the hard way; Gabriel Marquez's *One Hundred Years of Solitude*; Carlos Castaneda's *Teachings of Don Juan: A Yaqui Way of Knowledge*. For those pilgrims seeking more gurus to follow, the literary find of the decade was psychologist Arthur Janov's *The Primal Scream*.

Feeling pain is the end of suffering.
—Psychologist Arthur Janov, 1971

Even mega rock star John Lennon and his wife, Yoko, fell under the "spell of the yell," an endeavor in which one was encouraged to lie in a fetal position and regurgitate the pain of the past; the crimes and misdemeanors foisted upon you by uncaring, unaware parents. When these repressed memories were brought to the surface, one could break out in the most ungodly fit of wailing and thrashing about, much like a "terrible two" having a go at a tantrum. More likely, however, the sessions ended in a deluge of tears, a river of feeling that was often, in its way, liberating. Lennon paid homage to Janov and primal scream therapy in his cathartic album *John Lennon/Plastic Ono Band*.

Heavily influenced by Lennon's album, my paramour, Sherry Stewart, underwent Janov's therapy, as did several of my good friends. Some in therapy actually ended up leaving their mates, divorcing, or moving out of the country, having decided that life as they were living it was just not acceptable anymore. Ms. Stewart encouraged me to give primal therapy a try, "Maybe it will temper your highly eccentric behavior." After breaking my hand while punching a concrete floor during my first session, I decided to leave the repressed feelings securely repressed. I would leave the enjoyment of primal pain up to Mr. and Mrs. Lennon and the other pilgrims. Boo even suggested I abandon my relationship with the lovely and primally fanatic Sherry Stewart. After achieving almost cult-like popularity, primal screaming gave way to a newer, trendier Hollywood hedonism, The Church of Scientology.

New Yorkers thought that perhaps Broadway was dead. More than half of the houses were dark due to poor box office. Still, the "Old Broad" refused to die, catching a new wind with frenetic musicals like *Hair* and *Grease*, and the talents of a new man on the block, Stephen Sondheim (*A Chorus Line, Follies*).

It was Hollywood and the motion pictures, however, that finally began to reflect to the American people the cultural changes, the opening minds and hearts that so clearly heralded the arrival of the future. What had been a rigid, moldy structure, fell completely apart. What remained was a delicious potpourri of fresh talent, full of youth and daring, and they were allowed to do pretty much as they pleased.

Working on independent films was still the way to go for me. Although their motives were no longer to break down barriers or uncover dastardly cultural cover-ups, these films were still my best shot for personal creativity. The major studios had whatever they wanted, when they wanted it, but the independents had to make do with what they had, which was never much. We had to invent, jerry-rig, beg, borrow, and steal to compete. I suppose one may consider that, in its way, creativity.

To keep the food and rent police at bay, I now added "production manager" to my ever-expanding resume. I had worked enough films in various capacities that I felt I knew the score, production wise. Besides, I had been lucky enough to observe the job performed by Paul Lewis, one of the best production managers in the business.

For my first gig as PM, I took a crew to San Francisco for Gary Graver's *The Hard Road*, a torrid tale of a young girl's seduction into a life of hard drugs and the downward spiral that followed. It starred my old friends, Johnny Alderman, Liz Renay, John Parker, William Bonner, along with actress Connie Nelson, Graver's new wife.

San Francisco, especially the "Haight," had fallen into a stupor. The drugged out, the left out, and the disappointed wandered the streets in shell shock. They had arrived for the *Summer of Love* and were now left behind by the migration that followed. Graver and I took a cab across town to catch a reading of *Howl*, written and performed by meditating poet/guru Allen Ginsberg at the City Lights Bookstore. I'm not sure I "got it," but at least I was in attendance. The audience was ragtag, at best, more interested in scoring food or drugs than in Ginsberg's work. Evidently, the mantra of the new decade was not the universal "Om;" it was, "Don't get involved." Hippies, the largest cultural phenomenon in American history, had themselves become history.

I spent the first years of the 70s locked in a sort of "Hodge Podge Lodge," managing to polish off an amazingly diverse amount of work. Besides *The Hard Road* and *The Psycho Lover*, I production managed *The Harbingers, Blood Mania*, and *Sandra, The Making of a Woman*; acted and/or did stunts on *Machismo (El Salvejo), The Return of Count Yorga, The Incredible 2-Headed Transplant, Sinthia The Devil's Doll, The Mighty Gorga*, and *Killers Three*.

I also managed to squeeze in some special effects on *Voyage to the Planet of Prehistoric Women* (with actress Mamie Van Doren, supposedly one of the ten sexiest women of the past century). We were all at Malibu Beach. Peter Bogdanovich was directing, wife Polly Platt doing wardrobe, set dressing, co-producing—her usual. Mamie was playing the part of a mermaid. She and several other young starlets, all wearing fins from the waist down, were lounging around on rocks while I squirted the lot of them with hot vapor pumped from several smoke machines. This was to give an illusion of "sea spray" to the scene. All the while, Mamie's then boyfriend, baseball player Bo Belinsky, was sitting on a surfboard slightly off shore, scarfing down a large container of yogurt while scowling viciously in an attempt to keep the male crew members in line.

The New Hollywood, the most overused phrase in the dictionary of hype, was doing some amazingly original cinema. Lion cubs such as Bert Schneider, Dennis Hopper, Bob Rafelson, Peter Bogdanovich, Martin Scorsese, Bob Evans, Brian De Palma, Paul Mazursky, and others were at last bringing an honesty, a grown-up attitude and a daring panache to American films.

In the film *Five Easy Pieces*, Jack Nicholson, well on his way to becoming a genuine cinematic icon, was turning in another of his masterful performances as Robert Dupea, a promising pianist from an upscale Northwestern family who shucks it all and goes looking for himself in a series of rough adventures and a bit of the hard life. Jack received his first Oscar nomination for Best Actor in this film.

Five Easy Pieces, directed by Bob Rafelson (*Black Widow, The King of Marvin Gardens*), was nominated for several Oscars and won multiple awards, including a Golden Globe and a New York Critics Circle Award. Karen Black (*Gypsy 83, Dogtown*), the female lead, won a Golden Globe for Best Supporting Actress in her role as Dupea's lovable but ditzy girlfriend, Rayette. Billy Green Bush, who worked with us on *The Savage Seven*, played Depea's anchored down bowling buddy, Elton.

The screenplay, penned by Carole Eastman (*The Shooting*), writing under her pseudonym, Adrien Joyce, was nominated by the Writer's Guild for Best Drama Written Directly for the Screen. *Five Easy Pieces* was filmed in my home turf, Washington state, by the ubiquitous Laszlo Kovacs.

There is a certain musky, darkened beauty, a mystical quality to the whole Puget Sound area and it is all watched over by the majestic Mt. Rainier. This incredible peak loftily rises above the smaller mountains in the four state range of the Cascades. The Puyallup Indians called it "Tahoma," "Mother of Waters." Mt. Rainier was the talisman of my youth. I have climbed it several times, and was once even snowbound on the south slope for two days and nights, unable to move out of a makeshift lean-to until rescued by a search party of mountain guides. Leslie's (Laszlo's) photographic brilliance ensured that the land of Mt. Rainier, the surrounding evergreen forest, and the mysterious fogbanks of the Puget Sound were properly paid photographic homage. They never looked better.

Monte Hellman was traversing the country with Warren Oates, filming, in my opinion, one of the best road movies of all time, *Two-Lane Blacktop*. The story follows several characters as they race each other across the country by automobile. Monte took Greg Sandor along on camera. The show was produced by Gary Kurtz, our AD, on the Utah Westerns. Monte cast singer James Taylor in a rare acting performance as one of the drivers. Oates was the other. Sandor told me that, to get financing, Monte had to prove to the suits he could get over twenty-four camera angles inside of a car. The moneymen were convinced the audience would grow bored with just the usual cuts back and forth. The legendary drummer of The Beach Boys, Dennis Wilson, made his first and only appearance as an actor in Hellman's film.

Richard Rush, Paul Lewis, and Chuck Bail, meanwhile, were off in Oregon shooting *Getting Straight*, a tale of a Vietnam veteran, played by Elliott Gould (*Little Murders*, *M.A.S.H.*), who returns to college on the GI bill to earn his master's degree. There, he is forced to confront the whirligig of conflict that is raging on campus: the embedded anger and arrogance of the administration versus the frequently foolish objectives of the students. Protest and resistance! His girlfriend, played by famed actress Candice Bergan (*Gandhi*, *Carnal Knowledge*), just wants to tie the knot and move to the suburbs. It was a droll, "America now" kind of a story, well told and it did good box office. *Getting Straight* was the film that introduced Richard's work to the mainstream audience.

Al Adamson carried on the era of blaxploitation with the gusto of an Eagle Scout. He cobbled together *Dynamite Brothers*, a tale of two tough guys fighting their way to the sunlight with their prowess at martial arts. He cast in the lead roles Alan Tang, one of the most famous and prolific actors in China, and Tim Brown, who had played professional football as a running back with the Philadelphia

Eagles. He also cast his wife, Regina Carrol, and took along Bob and Hedy Dietz for good luck, with Gary Graver on camera.

Al followed *Dynamite Brothers* with *Mean Mother, Black Heat, Black Samurai,* and *Death Dimension,* utilizing the talents of Brown, one time World Middleweight Karate Champion Jim Kelly, singer Dobie Gray (*Drift Away*), and a sensual, beautiful actress named Marilyn Joi. Marilyn made several films for Al, and remembers Al fondly for giving her and so many other actors of different races, persuasions, etc., a chance to work. "If you were bad, you had to be good at being bad, because Al didn't have time to do a bunch of takes. A lot of good actors came out of those exploitation films."

Cuzco

> *Frozen Cordillera winds, Eucalyptus trees and ruins,*
> *Long ichu grass*
> *Plaza of resinous colors.*
> *Sun baked bodies wrapped in rainbow rags*
> *A drunken Indian's flauta*
> *Haunted by the sounds and the silence*
> *of Cuzco.*
>
> —Patricia Kent McCann, 1961

Chuck Bail and I had met for breakfast at The Seven Horsemen Café located in the Pickwick Bowling Alley in Burbank. This was a favorite hangout for stuntmen and river-rats, as it was next to Pickwick Horse Stables and a web of good riding trails. It is important for stuntmen to get together now and then to exchange tales of derring-do, fuckups, flare-ups, and outright lies. Chuck poured some ketchup on his pancakes, followed by half a carafe of sugar, and then washed it all down with about eight cups of coffee. Chuck wanted to tell me a story.

"I was in Lima, where I had to train these fancy English riding horses to be movie cow ponies. I had about a week to do it in. The film location was this little village high in the Andes called Chinchero, forty minutes outside of Cuzco. The location was at about ten thousand feet. I couldn't truck the horses up there, because I was afraid they would get distemper or pneumonia with the roads winding up and down like they do. So, I bought an old Super Constellation that hadn't been flown in five years. I took out the seats and built box stalls to stick the horses in. I called Gray Johnson (stuntman on *Black Sampson, Freebie and the Bean*). When Gray got there, I handed him a gun, a forty-five, and told him to fly the horses to an airstrip at Cuzco. If any of them got spooked and started freaking out, he was

Stunt coordinator/actor Chuck Bail in Peru for Dennis Hopper's The Last Movie. *Photo courtesy Bail Archives.*

to shoot them on the spot. That's all I needed, a horse kicking the side out of an airplane at ten thousand feet. I went ahead by car to Cuzco and was there when the plane arrived. The pressurization blew just as they were approaching the field. I thought Gray had shot one of the horses."

Paul Lewis had gone to Peru with Dennis Hopper to film *The Last Movie*. They took half of Hollywood with them. John Phillip Law (*Barbarella, Rainy Day Friends*), Dean Stockwell, Russ Tamblyn, Julie Adams (*Psychic Killer, The Fifth Floor*), Sylvia Miles (*Midnight Cowboy, 92 In the Shade*), Henry Jaglom, Peter Fonda (*Easy Rider, The Hired Hand*), Billy Gray (*Father Knows Best, The Vampyre Wars*), Michelle Phillips of The Mamas and the Papas pop singing group (also *Scissors, The Man With Bogart's Face*), singer Kris Kristofferson in his first movie role, and multi-award winner director/writer Samuel Fuller (*The Big Red One, Hell and High Water*) playing himself. Chuck Bail went along as stunt coordinator, horse trainer, and technical advisor.

The story concerned a movie company wrangler named Kansas (played by Hopper) who, after a lead actor is killed doing a stunt, decides to stay in Peru with the intention of leading an idyllic, simple life. The villagers, however, unable to tell reality from make-believe, begin to kill one another while re-enacting scenes from the film. Kansas, as their "director," must now deal with make-believe gone mad, innocence turned deadly. He must find a rational way to save the day in a completely irrational situation.

From the hotel in Cuzco, Chuck hired a ramshackle cab, an even shabbier driver, and set out for the movie location. It was raining a soft Andean mist that clung to the sides of the mountains and filled the deep valleys with a gray-green fog. Bail gazed out at the jagged peaks, capped with white, like large, cold sombreros. Suddenly, as the cab snaked its way around a hairpin, he spotted a group of figures on the side of a nearby slope. He could see well enough through the haze to discern that they were dancing and bowing in front of a large cross of some sort, an Andean effigy, if you will, these, strange stick-like figures, grotesquely genuflecting in the rain.

Hey, there's a chicken in your soup!

—Laszlo Kovacs, in Peru, 1971

When Bail arrived on the set, the first person he ran into was cameraman Laszlo Kovacs and his lighting man, Aggi Aguilar. Since Hopper's movie was about a movie within a movie, many of the regular crew were actually duplicating their jobs in the "movie/movie." Aggie therefore, was not only lighting for Lazslo, but also appearing as an actor "the lighting man" in the film within a film. Dig?

Chuck was freezing, worn thin by the cold and the high altitude. He asked a production assistant to please bring him a big bowl of nice hot chicken soup. He grabbed the bowl and started to dig in. Then, suddenly, he let out a yell, and turned away in disgust. "I thought I was going to puke." Kovacs said, "Hey, Chuck, did you know there's a chicken in your soup?" A whole damned chicken was floating in the middle of the soup: head, eyes, feet, the works. Chuck said he wasn't about to consume anything that could stare back at him while he was eating it.

"I hadn't seen Dennis, Paul, or any of the honchos since I arrived. They weren't on the set, so I grabbed the cab before it took off, figuring they were all back at the hotel in Chinchero. Just before we left the set, I saw Leslie (Kovacs) turn around and fall flat on his face. I mean, kerplunk! He wasn't used to the lack of oxygen at that altitude and he just did a cropper right there in front of the whole crew.

"On our way back down the mountain, I saw those same weird figures out on the hillside in the pouring rain. Now they were sitting in front of the cross. It was the damndest thing, Gar. They were all just sitting on the ground in front of the cross, meditating or some damned thing. I had the cabbie pull up to the side of the road, as close as we could get without plunging a thousand feet off the edge. When he killed the engine, we could hear the chanting and yelling coming from across the way. Later on, back at the hotel, I found out it was Dennis, Kris Kristofferson, John Phillip Law, Billy Gray, and a few others. They were all high on acid and they were out there communicating with the Peruvian Gods, trying to get them to bless the picture, or some damned thing."

Chuck fired up a Pall Mall Red, then stirred the half and half in his coffee cup: half coffee, half cream and sugar.

"Billy Gray disappeared for about a week, and we finally found him in the jungle, dehydrated and strung out." (Pause, long gulps of coffee, deep pull on a Pall Mall.) "We were all staying at the Hotel Therese. I used to watch this car pull up, and all of the guys from the kitchen would run out and open the trunk. After they shooed away a mountain of flies, I saw that it was filled with raw meat: pork, lamb, mutton, red meat, ham; this was how they delivered the food for the hotel, in a hot trunk filled with flies."

"Sounds like supper time at the YO Ranch, down in Texas." I looked up at a young, tousled haired blond bloke who had sneaked up on our booth and was now hovering over Chuck's shoulder like a large bird.

"Hi, kid, sit down. Grab yourself some coffee, and say hello to Gary Kent. Gary, this is Diamond Farnsworth."

Chuck scooted his butt an inch or two so Farnsworth could sit. Stuntman Diamond Farnsworth (*Batman Forever, Perceptions, Navy NCIS*) was the son of legendary actor/stuntman Richard Farnsworth. I had worked with his dad on my second picture, *Legion of the Doomed*, at Allied Artists Studios, so many years ago.

Diamond Farnsworth didn't say much, which I took as a good sign. "Howdy," he said.

"Howdy yourself," I answered, and that was about the extent of it. Chuck signaled for another mug of coffee; he was a breakfast regular here at The Seven Horsemen. The waitresses were used to bringing java and grub to all manner of stuntmen and stuntwomen, out of work actors, acrobats and brigands, anyone on the run who felt the urge to sit and jaw-jack a spell before facing the promise of another surreal day in Southern California.

"Kris Kristofferson accused me of breaking his hand," Chuck said.

"Well, did you?" Farnsworth asked.

"I didn't. The horse I gave him did. At the time, I didn't know who Kristofferson was. I thought he was just some friend of Dennis' who was wandering around; he always looked like he was swallowing a paper sack. I found out later that's where he carried his booze, in the sack. He came to me one morning and asked if I could give him a little action to do, something to cowboy him up. Well, I had taken a few little Peruvian ponies, put flank straps on 'em so they would buck a little bit. You know, hump and bump kind of stuff, nothing big, as these weren't buckin' horses. I had the natives running around among 'em while they were acting up. After a buck or two, the ponies would calm out on me, so I gave the boys some hotshots to zap 'em and get another jump or two out of 'em."

"I gave Kris a hotshot, and told him if a horse was near him, just standing there, to give him a little jolt to start him up. 'Don't stand too close, though, because he won't like it, and he may kick you.' The next thing I know I see this hotshot go sailing through the air like a damned chicken hawk. I turn around, and there's Kristofferson, holding his arm and wailing that his hand is broken. What happened was, he got too close, and the horse just cow-kicked him."

"Shudda listened to ya, Chuck, I guess, huh?" Farnsworth laughed.

"Yeah, well, now he's all panicky because he's due to appear on *The Johnny Cash Show* in a couple of weeks, to sing his new composition, "Me and Bobby McGee." He is convinced he isn't going to be able to play his guitar."

"What happened?"

"Turns out it wasn't broken, just bruised it up a bit. We iced it down, and he was fine. Eddy Donno and I went to see him a month or so after the movie finished. He was playing at The Troubador, down on Santa Monica and Doheny. You would have thought we were heroes. He stopped the show, introduced us to the audience, standing ovation, all of that rock star shit. I guess he'd forgiven me. Well, that was just one of the strange things that happened on the shoot."

"Jonesy and I stole a freight train up in Utah a couple of weeks ago." My voice was matter of fact, casual, like I was saying good morning to a friend.

Chuck glared at me through those squinty, green Irish eyes. "What, you stole a train? What the fuck is the matter with you?" Like he was now a defender of the public trust.

"We only took it a block or so. Didn't do any harm; it was just something to do to relieve the boredom. I guess I was channeling Jesse James at the time." Farnsworth almost fell out of the booth laughing.

The incident took place during the shoot of a horror film called *The House of Seven Corpses*, on location in Salt Lake City, Utah. Paul Lewis had recommended me as production manager to producer/director Paul Harrison (*H.R. Pufnstuf*). It seemed a simple enough undertaking: Fly a reasonably talented cast including John Ireland, John Carradine, Faith DeMorgue (*Blood Legacy*, *Escort West*), and Carole Wells (*Funny Lady*, *Molly and The Ghost*) to Salt Lake for a few weeks; surround them with a professional, affable crew—Don Jones on camera, Marty Hornstein (*Sybil*, *Silent Running*) as assistant director, Ron Garcia (*Rainy Day Friends*, *Machismo*) art direction, Ron Foreman (*Boiling Point*, *Colors*) makeup and special effects, Lee Alexander (*Windtalkers*, *Midnight Blue*) on sound with Gene Clark (*The Forest*, *Trick or Treats*) as his boom-man. We'd shoot our little film, then return safe and sound when the mission was complete. Things began to unravel the first day filming began.

As production manager, I had made a deal with the Utah State Historical Society to rent the ex-governor's mansion as our main location. We needed a big, old Gothic building for our story, and the governor's mansion was perfect—large rooms with old stone fireplaces, much cherry-wood, oak, and mahogany for floors and walls, casting a dark patina to the place; shaded corners, nooks, crannies—excellent spots for secrets and serious crimes to be conceived. Best of all, there was a spiral staircase that circled four stories overhead, ending in a secluded belfry that was just the ticket for phantoms, ghouls, and ghosts. The only problem was, the society was still in business, and most rooms of the mansion were occupied by secretaries, under-secretaries, office clerks, etc. Whenever we wanted to shoot a scene, the P.A.s had to run through the building yelling, "Quiet, please." Slowly the resonated sound of the typewriters would click to a halt. We would begin our scene, and then a telephone would ring, a closet clerk would cough or a chambermaid would drop a mop bucket, and we would have to start all over again. The budget, like the staircase, began to spiral upward.

Jonesing for Junk

The third day of the shoot, one of my top crew members didn't show. I sent his brother to the motel to find out the problem. Well, the brother did his best to cover the fact that my main man was going through some serious detoxing, trying to kick the smack monkey cold turkey by locking himself in his room for a few days. It kind of worked, as he emerged four days later, about ten shades of gray and twenty pounds lighter, able to sorta-kinda do his job.

Drugs and their abuse were not really a problem on *The House of Seven Corpses*. We were, after all, in Mormon country, and all of the locals I hired were clean and sober. Most of the cast and crew were well behaved. Oh, John Carradine would hit the bar every night; a tall, crane-like countenance sitting quietly, quaffing drink after drink, smoking and expectorating on the carpet, until bedtime. Utah is a dry state, of course, so we all had to buy our refreshments at a state controlled liquor store, or, for a twenty, one could join a "private" club. This entitled you to bar privileges and some of the best cuisine this side of the south coast of France.

Our story, much like Hopper's *The Last Movie*, concerned a film within a film. A small group of moviemakers find an old, Gothic mansion in which to shoot their story of a haunted house and its creepy goings on. They quickly find that the mansion is more than haunted. It is possessed by a zombie, an undead creature that begins to pick off cast and crew, one by one.

The director of the film within a film is played by John Ireland, a top-notch actor, who, by legend, was rumored to be one of the most well endowed members of the Hollywood community. This reputation preceded him to Utah. The female cast members and even some of the local woman hovered around him like kids around a department store Santa.

Late one evening, after the daily wrap, I, being more than exhausted, ponied up my twenty bucks for membership in a "private club." I intended to have a quiet drink or two unmolested by clicking typewriters and frustrated shouts from production assistants. I found a secluded table in the corner, where a cocktail waitress with legs as long as grocery aisles took my order. After a sip or two, I felt human again, and decided to journey to the men's room to freshen up.

I entered the lavatory and was immediately overwhelmed by the odor of pot. Marijuana, lots of it! I heard the flush of a toilet, the door to a stall swung open and John Ireland emerged holding a roach the size of a cigar. "Oh, here, Gar, finish this off for me. It's great shit, sinsemilla!" With that, he handed me the joint, checked his reflection in the mirror, threw some cold water into his eyes, and then, grinning impishly, departed for whatever salacious assignation he had arranged for the night.

I spent much of my work time in the office of the President of the Mormon Historical Society named, of course, Joseph Smith, after the enigmatic leader of the Mormon religion. By the start of each day, Mr. Smith had arranged a litany of complaints, voiced by the Society staff, which he would drop on me one by one. He would exaggerate their severity, building them into mountains of criminality committed by the ruthless behavior of my movie crew. In this daily exchange, I detected a sort of nasty pleasure emanating from his otherwise solemn countenance. After a time, old Mr. Smith warmed a bit, eventually even offering tea along with the dressing down. This became, then, a daily ritual. I and the illustrious Elder sitting in the Belfry, as it were, sipping tea—exchanging gossip like two old dowagers from the Gardens of Kensington.

On the movie set, things were proceeding with the usual élan; Jones the cameraman, was falling head over heels for Wells, the actress, never mind that she was married to Larry Doheny, of The Dohenys, who happened to own much of Beverly Hills, including the tony drive that connects the west end of The Sunset Strip to the urban sprawl of Los Angeles. Carole Wells was pretty, charming, with a delicious sense of humor. She also had steel belted ovaries, the counter point to male cajones. She demonstrated this the night of the Jesse James Caper.

Our motel was situated a skip and a jump from a rail yard; there was always some sort of activity occurring at the yard, day or night, with much clamor, hooting of horns, and blowing of whistles. I now realize that was why I was able to negotiate such a cheap rental of motel rooms for cast and crew. But I digress. As I remember, this particular evening we had finished the day's work early and had not yet showered and dressed for dinner. A boring ritual that morphed into people-watching; the people totaling two: John Carradine, sitting at the bar, getting drunker and drunker as the evening progressed, and then, occasionally we would sneak a peek at the still lovely, still glamorous Faith Demorgue, speculating on why she always chose to eat alone, on the far side of the dining room, solitarily sipping a soda and picking at her food like a finicky five-year-old.

I decided to stroll to a nearby drug store and stock up on small stuff, razor blades, lotion, toothpaste, the necessaries. It is impossible to get lost in Salt Lake City. Everything is laid out in a grid centered on the Mormon Temple; from almost any location, you can locate the Temple by honing in on its centerpiece, a statue of the Angel Moroni blowing his trumpet. Angel Moroni is twelve-feet tall, and commands the tallest spire in the Temple. This then, is the heavenly messenger who appeared to LDS founder and prophet Joseph Smith, proclaiming the establishment of God's new kingdom, and handing him the plates of the *Book of Mormon*. Well, who knows?

On my way back to the motel, I took a short cut through the rail yard. Suddenly, I heard the sound of a locomotive. Somewhere nearby a vast belch of steam was releasing energy into huge drive-wheels. I rounded the corner of a building and there it was, a freight train. Well, actually, a switch engine, starting a slow roll along tracks inside the perimeter of the rail yard. Someone was blowing the steam whistle, a loud, lonely, haunting kind of sound. *"My God,"* Boo shouted. *"It's Carole Wells!"* Sure enough, Ms. Wells was perched perkily in the window of the cab, yanking on the whistle like a journeyman. The engine picked up momentum, and then I saw that Ron Foreman, our illustrious, seemingly shy makeup effects guy, was at the throttle. Directly behind him stood Don "Irish Frankie" Jones, calling loudly into the star-bright Utah night, "Board! All on board, pull-eezze! All aboard!" I didn't hesitate. Several quick bounds, a giant leap, a grab, and I, too, was on board, smack dab in the middle of a train theft, a governmental felony of towering degree.

Somewhere inside of my conscience, in the panicked twang of the chattering Mr. Boo, I knew damn well that, as production manager, I could not condone this kind of behavior from cast and crew. Paul Lewis would have me shot on sight. However, we had been working awfully hard, for long hours, no time to tidy or catch up on personal stuff. It just seemed right that we should be allowed to let off a little steam, so to speak. Carole began to sing, "I've been working on the railroad." Instantaneously, we all chimed in, "All the live long day, I've been working on the railroad, just to pass the time away…hoot-hoot! Can't ya hear the whistle blowing… "

Foreman, who somehow knew how to pilot the thing, steamed us to a stop at the far east boundary of the yard. No sense running the risk of doing federal time. We jumped off, into the waiting arms of the engineer and a yard watchman. It was only because of our begging and pleading, and more probably, the seductive apologies of Ms. Wells, that we aren't to this day occupying adjoining cells at Leavenworth. After several Wellsian hugs and a severe dressing down, they let us go.

Hanging a Left in Time

I was back in San Francisco. I had joined Richard Rush, Chuck Bail, Aggie Aguilar, and Laszlo Kovacs. The old gang had assembled to film a comedy, *Freebie and the Bean*, for Warner Brothers. Freebie is a very funny movie and has enjoyed wide success at the box office. It increased Richard Rush's reputation as a first rate director.

When the picture was first released, Richard described driving to a theater in Westwood that was playing the film and seeing moviegoers lined up around the entire block. When he entered the theater lobby, he heard roars of laughter billowing from the audience. That was when he finally realized he had made a hit movie.

Richard Rush had been an outlaw, a cinematic individualist since he had first encountered the eyepiece of a camera. Now, seemingly, he was allowed to carry that persona into and through the monolithic gates of the major studios.

Filming Freebie

San Francisco! What can I say about it that hasn't already been written, sung, or committed to poetry? I had flown into town on an early afternoon flight from Burbank, which left me time to ruminate before reporting for work in the morning.

There are really only a few great cities in the world—New York, Paris, Munich, London, Florence, Copenhagen, Dublin, Barcelona, Amsterdam—I would have to include San Juan and Seville. I have been to them all. Still, San Francisco is easily one of the most romantic. One may feel comfortable singing in its rain, or seemingly walking on top of the great masses of fog billowing in from the Pacific, ride the cable cars to the embarcadero, Nob Hill, the Tenderloin district, Chinatown, pig out on chocolate at Ghirardelli Square, scope the transsexuals, bisexuals, homosexuals, and heterosexuals, all living and working in relative harmony, as you take the sun at Union Square.

Okay, I will mention the magnificent Golden Gate Bridge, North Beach (the Mecca of the Beats and hippies and great Italian food) and end with a dizzying curl down Lombard Street, the crookedest street in the United States. San Francisco— sun, flowers, sea, sky—a palette of color that stirs the senses, raises emotions to the very height of human appreciation, but I would not want to live there! Too much booze, too many dives, too many lost lives, too much introspection in a lonely, discarded kind of way, not enough genuine passion for conversation. Too much dirty laundry and not enough laughter. In my book, San Francisco is a great place to visit, and that's it.

The following morning I was ferried from the hotel to the film set by a studio driver. The first person I saw was Sheila Scott, Richard's assistant and close friend. She told me where to find the stunt unit. I could see Richard and stars Alan Arkin and James Caan, standing near the back of a grip truck, involved in what appeared to be a heated argument.

Arkin (loudly): "I simply do not understand why my character would do that!"

Rush (calmly): "Did it ever occur to you that you may not have the capacity to understand why your character would do that?"

Arkin (Best Supporting Actor Oscar for *Little Miss Sunshine*, two additional Oscar nominations, winner of a Golden Globe, with four additional nominations, winner of other multiple awards, including a Tony for his Broadway performance in *Enter Laughing*) and James Caan (Oscar nomination for *The Godfather*, winner of several other awards, star on Hollywood Walk of Fame) disagreed strongly with Richard Rush about their characters, and production would be halted every now and then for a director/actor duke-out. Richard always won.

Chuck Bail, as second unit director, designed a bunch of stunts that, considered as a whole, were incredible, flowing tapestries of violence; as individual pieces of the stunt trade they were works of art. The car sequences in *Freebie and the Bean* should match up with the best of the genre, on a par with or exceeding the brilliant chases in *The French Connection*, and *Bullitt*.

Chuck delights in putting action where action doesn't belong. In *Freebie*, for instance, we plowed our automobiles, vans, and pickup trucks through marching parades, shopping malls, city parks, even jumping a car over a moving railroad train. There were also a horde of fights, falls, and cattle calls (in this case, a Chicken Call, as Chuck unleashed a thousand chickens on downtown Market Street when he staged a chicken delivery truck rollover).

To perform all of this derring-do, Bail assembled some of the best stuntmen and stuntwomen in the business. I will name a few without listing their credits, as they are all too accomplished to list everything. If you wish, you may look them up on the Internet Movie Database. In no particular order, then:

Judo Gene LeBell, Tommy Huff, Eddy Donno, Gary Johnson, Kenny Endoso, Bobby Harris, Ted Duncan, Pam Bebermeyer, Whitey Hughes, Regina Parton, Lenny Geer, Frank Orsatti, Phil "Kamikaze" Adams. Oh, and bringing up the rear, yours truly.

We spent much of the picture headquartered in the parking lot of Candlestick Park, the home of the San Francisco Giants and the Forty-Niners football team. We were shooting several of the major sequences inside of the stadium, and also, many of our stunts were staged in nearby neighborhoods. It became a pastime for the stunt guys to get their own football game going whenever time permitted. We chose up sides and played a ragtag sort of "flag ball" on the concrete parking lot. As one would expect, things got a little rough and tumble. James Caan, who had played ball for Michigan State, has a black belt in karate, and has done some rodeo work, could not resist joining the games. We didn't feel obliged to give him any slack, in spite of the fact he was one of the stars of the film. Caan was an excellent athlete, however, and gave as good as he took.

In a sequence on the concourse inside the ballpark, I don a knit cap and parka (as a disguise, most of the stunt folk played multiple parts) and run up to Caan, accusing him of pushing my wife. Caan is then supposed to grab me and give me a body flip. This is something a stuntman would normally do in place of the star. Caan insisted on doing most of his own stunts. Now, I have been flipped a few times in my life, but this throw of Caan's was as swift and agile as the pounce of a cheetah. He had me over, down and out, on the pavement, in two seconds. *"Damn good acting, Kent,"* Boo tells me with fingers crossed.

One evening a bunch of the stunt guys and girls decided we could afford, at least once, to dine among the snobs on the Nob, hence dinner at the Mark Hopkins, a deluxe hotel, situated majestically on the crest of Nob Hill. In the late 1800s, the original site was picked by railroad tycoon Mark Hopkins as an excellent place to construct a dream home for his wife, Mary. The mansion, completed after his death, survived the 1906 earthquake, but perished in the fires that followed.

Before dinner, a few of us elevated ourselves to the Top of the Mark, a barroom-cum-bistro at the top of the hotel, with an incomparable view of downtown San Francisco, the bay area, Fisherman's Wharf, the bridge, Alcatraz, and in the far distance, the gently undulating hills of Sonoma. After ordering one of their world-class martinis, I settled back to listen to stuntman Bobby Harris talk about a racing accident he had suffered while competing in the Indianapolis 500.

"I just planed into a turn and I lost it. I think I was nicked by another driver, but, what the hell, who knows? Coulda blown a tire, even. There weren't enough pieces left to tell. Into a rounder I went, then a rollover—about thirty of the sons-a-bitches. I came outta the cage, bouncing along the track like a funkin' soccer ball. I could hear my bones breaking, one by one, fourteen breaks in all. The sound of my bones snapping was eerie as hell."

Later, during consumption of what amounted to a twelve-course dinner in the Mark Hopkins dining room, Harris began to ruminate on a recent trip he had made to Egypt, and his enchantment with the Pyramids. "The mystery there is so intense, so thick you could cut it with a knife. Who? What? Each one of those giant blocks of granite is so closely honed you can't slide a cigarette paper between them. Now, how did they do that? Without any tools, no powder, no cranes, not even a forklift or backhoe? And inside, the passageways have little marks, squiggly-like messages, and no one has yet figured out what they mean."

Bobby went on to describe an incident where he actually climbed up on the clasped paws of the Sphinx when the touring party had moved on without him. He said he sat down, legs folded in a full mudra, and disappeared into a cosmic flow of some sort, transported in time, surrendering into a power at once frightening and spiritual.

His tale had a profound impact on me. So much so, that within a year, I found myself in Dallas, Texas, writing, and then directing a movie—my first totally solo effort—a rousing homage to the intellect, the Id, the inner "I," the mystery of self. I combined two words: pyra (fire) and mid (middle). The fire in the middle. I called my movie *The Pyramid.*

Chapter Fourteen

Actress/choreographer Tomi Barrett (aka Shirley Willeford), Dallas 1974.
Photo courtesy of the author.

Big D And Me

Here's to the horrible, dumb sadness, the short span of genuine happiness, the absolute aloneness of life.
—The author to the boys at the bar, Dallas, Texas, 1973

"Is it possible to be much loved and still be lonely? Is it possible that I am short of the stuff necessary for genuine love? Is it possible, then, to grow from one's own inner light? Do I even have an 'inner light?' How, then, do I find the inner light if I don't believe in it? Come on, Boo, gimme a clue!"

I was sitting at the bar in Faces Nightclub, Dallas, Texas, early afternoon in 1973. I had just driven Sherry Stewart to the airport. We hugged, wept, and bid each other a final adieu. She was on her way back to Los Angeles after becoming disenchanted with the life I was offering. Neuritis of the mind, and possible neuralgia of the spirit as well, all thrown together with low finances and a bed on the floor of a small, sweltering apartment in a rowdy section of this strange, largely redneck city.

We had been lured to Dallas by a wanna-be producer, Bill Collins, who offered me the chance to direct my first movie: *Ghetto Cop.* Sherry and I and her five kids all flew to Texas with buoyant hearts and high hopes. Sherry was going to do costuming; I would direct, and John Parker flew along with us as art director. The producer put us all up in adjoining, unfurnished apartments that he had conned the manager into extending to his movie company, with the promise of lots of future swag and a screen credit. We were completely unaware that Mr. Collins was flat broke, living on a pocket full of daydreams and a head stuffed with pungent wishes. After all, he had paid for the plane tickets!

The script was not well written but the premise was solid. I ignored the sparse living arrangements and set to work on a rewrite. Meanwhile, Sherry and John grew tired of waiting around for a start date. Collins was secretly off trying to raise money by declaring to potential investors, "My director is in town, my art director; we are ready to go; just gimme your green and hang on." Well, it didn't work. After four weeks of no action, we finally decided it probably wasn't going to work. Sherry and John preferred to return to Los Angeles, but I, come what may, had the urge to begin anew: new town, new outlook, and new possibilities. The trouble was, they didn't see it my way.

I will say that shortly after we found out the devious producer was not forthcoming I received some excellent advice from my friend John Parker. As he prepared for his return to Los Angeles, he noticed how crestfallen I must have appeared. "Listen, Gar," he said, "just because Collins wasn't together, doesn't mean you aren't. You are ready to go, ready to do your job; you are ready to direct. So don't blame yourself!"

"He's right," I advised myself, "I am ready to direct."

"*Yeah,*" Boo added. "*Now, if you just had a picture.*"

So here I am then, sitting at Faces in Big D, wasting time and money on the devil's glue while trying to piece together what was left of my life and set a course for the future. First on the agenda was to take an honest evaluation of just what my situation was. Let's see: 1. I was broker than a stick horse. 2. I felt like a stranger in a very strange land (Dallas). 3. All of my family, my kids, all of the people, places, things I loved, were largely on the West Coast. 4. I was not actually that young anymore. 5. I hadn't a clue to what was coming next, only that it very likely was going to be up to me. On the plus side, Boo and I were ready to make a movie.

How do I work? I grope.
—Albert Einstein

Drinking alone in the afternoon always seemed a strange procedure to me. It fucks up the rest of the day. You feel like shit when nighttime comes round, and you realize you've blown the daylight, sort of the same disorienting feeling you get when you walk out of an afternoon movie, and it's dark outside. But, for a couple of days, the solace of the bar and the anonymity it afforded were just my cup of tea, or tumbler of Cuervo on the rocks. I thought I had a right to feel sorry for myself. I was wrong.

The guy that commanded the daytime bar at Faces was a tall, skinny excuse with a shock of dirty blond hair falling from his head halfway to his waist. It must have been years since he'd seen the sun; he was white as an albino. He had a tattoo on his forearm of a naked lady dancing with a snake. A banner running across the lady's breasts read Donna, '69. "What's up with Donna?" I asked. "You still hangin'?"

"Huh?" he answered. "What d'ya mean? You know Donna?"

"Nah, I saw the tattoo—pretty spiffy. Just wondering, that's all, hoping it was working out."

"Matter a fact, she run off with a siding man. He was off to California and she just tagged along."

He took my glass, threw in another shot of Cuervo and an ice cube. "On the house, buddy." Mr. Albino set the glass in front of me, leaning those sharp elbows on the dark wood of the bar. "*Damn,*" Boo muttered, "*He's going to tell us his story.*"

"Shouldna let that one get away. She was somethin', I'll tell ya. I mean, boy, howdy, she was built like a Simmons Beauty Rest." He begins to rag-wipe the bar, his eyes already glassing over with the mere thought of the lady. "Course, I still got my memories."

"Yeah, partner. You can't tell your memories that you're sorry. That's the rub."

I shifted my attention to the guy in the mirror behind the bar, the one who looks a lot like me, only older and not quite as handsome. I told him about a "time when I was super fit, with shoulders wide as curtain rods, my chest as big as a buffalo's, when I held up my jeans with a carabiner. Yeah, back when a 'woody' was still a wagon, and a man was…"

Something in the eyes across the bar let me know he wasn't interested in my whining about the past. I shifted the subject, began to talk about my children and how I was sure I had been a lousy father. The bloke in the mirror probably hadn't heard that story before. "Holding a child," I announced to the image, "having it fall asleep in your arms is one of the most peaceful feelings on earth. Ah, Greg, daughter Colleen, Andy, Chris, Alex and Michael. I'm really sorry."

"*Oh, put a lid on it,*" Boo insisted. "*You're making me feel like shit.*"

Boo was right, of course, and it suddenly dawned on me that I knew why the derelict ends up at the watering hole. He is simply in search of something loose and liquid that will help hold his heart together before it breaks completely. "Yes, by thunder, Boo, I'm such a loser the kids are surely better off without me! Bartender, let's have another, please."

The mirror guy wouldn't let me skip the ticket. He knew I was shoveling bullshit, spooning out a shoddy excuse overused by all men and women who try to convince themselves that thoughtless behavior actually has some noble purpose. The mirror bloke was having none of it. Neither was Boo. Actually, neither was I.

The bartender brought my drink, slid it in front of me, the naked tattoo an undulating grotesquery on his pallid forearm. I flipped him a fiver, but didn't touch the glass. We just sat there, the three of us, Boo, myself, and the man in the mirror, quiet as ferns in a forest. I stood, gathered my wits like loose playing cards, and began my exit. By the time I reached the door, I knew exactly the movie I was going to make.

> *To know how to be alone and not be lonely. To be silent, to listen.*
> *This is one of the great arts of life.*
>
> —The author, Dallas, Texas, 1973

I am lying on my bed, on the top sheet, naked and shivering like a Chihuahua passing a peach pit. I am soaking wet from the shower, where I did my best to wash off the grit and grime of the past. Now I am spread-eagled beneath the overhead fan, letting the cool air dry my newly minted self. On the nightstand next to the bed, a single blood-red rose rises from a thin vase. The rose is fresh. I smell its perfume, stirred by the whirling currents from the fan.

On my solitary walk from Faces bar to my apartment, an attractive, ethereal looking young lady had approached me and handed me the flower.

"How much are they?" I asked, reaching into my jeans for some change.

"Oh, there's no charge. It's a gift from me to you." She smiled, then flounced away, disappearing around the corner like an apparition sent by invisible powers. I knew that if I looked around the corner, she would not be there. A figment of my imagination? Well, I had the flower!

"An omen," Boo whispered. Boo was spot on. It seems from that day forward I have been privy to more than my share of synchronicities, happy happenstances, spiritual insights, and wonderful opportunities to be of service to the folk, flora, and fauna that share our exquisite planet. I don't mean there hasn't been travail. Ah, so much of it. Only now, I felt there actually might be a reason for it, beyond our ken. But, again, I digress.

It was late afternoon in Dallas. There was much "returning from work" activity going on outside in the everyday world. Here, however, in my sparsely furnished apartment (I had rented my own after Mr. Collins finally admitted it was unlikely he would make his movie), all was quiet as the great Sargasso Sea. I had taken a fancy to the new digs. I had a living room with TV set and couch, a table, a kitchen with the amenities, bath, and best of all, my own quiet bedroom, sequestered away from all noise, with bed, a telephone, and the rose. A Spartan domicile to be sure, but just what my weary soul needed at the time. At last, for the first time in my life, I was completely alone.

I watched the overhead fan, trying to single out, to isolate individual blades as they turned. Pete Seeger, what was that song? Something about "to every life, there is a season…turn, turn…" The age of flower power had flown away on wings of surrender and despair. *"And yet,"* Boo reminds me, *"you have your rose!"* I stared at the flower, at its deep perfection. "Indeed, I do," I said aloud, glad for this one connection to the mysterious promise of life. I began, then, to mentally journey outside of the box.

It seemed to me that the hippies and flower people had left us with some very good commodities, like an appetite for natural food, alternative medicine, respect for the environment. *"For imaginary friends,"* Boo inserted. "Yes, Boo, respect for imaginary friends." The liberation of women, gays, Blacks, and other minorities owes a tip of the hat to the hippies. They also gave us astonishingly intelligent and beautiful music, music that has more than stood the test of time. Lastly, the era presented us with Steve Jobs and Apple Computers, Steve Brand and the World Wide Web. In essence, then, they gave us our future.

> *We have done with the kisses that sting,*
> *The thief's mouth red from the feast,*
> *The blood on the hands of the King*
> *And the lie on the lips of the priest.*

—Algernon Charles Swinburne, "A Song in Time of Order"

In my mind, I was meant to be a shaman, a teller of stories. This was a sacred privilege. "I have a responsibility to ennoble life," I announced to Boo, who had begun to fall asleep. "Where are we as a species if we have no recollections of ourselves? No recall of our dreams, ambitions, no reflections of heartbreak, healing, hope?" At last, I, too, fell asleep under the rotating fan, next to my blood-red rose. "I am a shaman," I announced to absolutely no one. "I have a responsibility," and finally, "I am a very important person." I curled into myself and slept like a newborn babe.

I awoke early, beginning to broil in the hot, humid Texas sun pouring in from uncurtained windows. It was morning, Dallas, already a hundred degrees, and hot as Guatemala. Gimme shelter from the swelter! I was dripping wet, only this time from perspiration.

I picked up the vase cradling my rose, and, slippering my way into the cooler kitchen, opened the fridge. Inside, there was a pint of milk, unopened, a jar of peanut butter, almost empty, and four packets of Folger's instant coffee left behind by previous tenants. I took a Styrofoam cup from the counter, poured a pack of coffee into it, then, moving to the sink, I turned the "H" spigot, letting the water run until it was demonstrably hot. I mixed coffee and water together with a plastic spoon. Retaining the spoon, I gathered up milk, peanut butter, coffee cup, my rose, and adjourned to the dining room table. Breakfast! Several spoonfuls of peanut butter, a swig of joe, and I was good to go.

First, I needed a plan, some sort of rhyme, direction, a reason for my new life. I took a tablet from my briefcase, a magic marker, and wrote the words "The Pyramid" at the top of a page, then underlined it.

> *Revolutions are like the most noxious dung heaps, which bring into life the noblest vegetables.*
>
> —Napoleon Bonaparte, *Maxims of Napoleon*

The Film Revolution? It had been very real, mind-blowing, actually, in a variety of ways. In a few short years we had broken down all of the walls of bigotry, quashed the high-mindedness, the deceit, and ironclad control that had ruled the motion picture industry through three decades. Were movies the better for it? They had pronounced outright smut "entertainment"; they accelerated massive displays of violence; they made murders and cuckoldry, by male and female, objects of interest if not outright admiration. They allowed that men could actually love other men (*The Boys In The Band*) and women love other women (*The Killing of Sister George*). Well, at least they were more honest.

The independents? Were they becoming meaner? *Taxi Driver*? *Sisters*? What's happening back in Hollywood? And what the hell are these "snuff" films everyone's talking about? Thank God there is, in spite of the quicksand, the moral and ethical quagmires; in spite of the relative unimportance of "pretending," there is still something meaningful and magic in the making of a motion picture.

This much I knew: I was going to make a movie and I was going to call it *The Pyramid*. I didn't have a clue how I was going to achieve this. As Joseph Campbell, author of *The Power of Myth*, advises us, I was going to follow my bliss. I picked up the pen and underneath "The Pyramid" I wrote: cosmic consciousness, universal truths, philosophy, and library.

The Unexplained–Mystery, Magic, and Mucho Mojo

I had never seen an angel before—not up close and personal. But this encounter put me very near the neighborhood. The young woman entering the back door of the house on Main Street was surely the loveliest creature I had ever seen. Not only was she incredibly attractive in a womanly sort of way, but she also had an aura, a graceful halo surrounding her countenance, highlighting her tumble of honey-blonde hair, her beautifully intelligent face, the elegant cheekbones and neck, the dramatic lift of her head. And her eyes, the most striking, deep amber imaginable, her gaze forward, meeting the future with strength and a kind of frolicsome dignity. She never once acknowledged my presence or looked in my direction. Within seconds, she opened the door and disappeared into the building.

I had decided, however, that after breaking the relationship with Ms. Stewart, that that was it! Fini with romance! No more swapping saliva, body sweat, or sharing bank accounts and bedcovers. I'd had enough. From now on, it was going to be my kids and my work, in that order. Oh, and also my animals, as soon as I could get some. Liaisons with the opposite gender occupied last position at the southern extremity of my wish list.

The building that the angel and I both entered was The Actor's Workshop, a thriving gymnasium for folks who wanted to learn how to act, dance, or simply speak effectively in front of an audience. The Workshop was owned and operated by an expatriate from Hollywood named Jeff Alexander. (*A Bullet for Pretty Boy*, *Horror High*). It was a serendipitous accident that I had reconnected with Jeff. I knew him from earlier days on the West Coast.

I had dropped by Bill Collins' office in downtown Dallas to see if he might be able to pay me something for the rewrite of *Ghetto Cop*. During the process of his demonstrating the art of the disappearing check, my eyes were drawn to a framed photograph mounted on the wall. It was a picture taken at a charity event in Dallas and included, among others, Jeff Alexander. There was no mistaking him. Jeff was tall, balding, with arms longer than necessary and a large, oblong face. Collins informed me that Alexander was indeed running a workshop, and that, in fact, he had his phone number. I called Jeff later that day. We made arrangements to meet at his workshop, which also served as his residence.

The building was large, cavernous. It could have easily passed as a location site for a good horror flick. It had a bleak, abandoned look that belied the passionate and heated performances occurring 24/7 within the walls. Standing over two stories, the downstairs was segmented into various large rooms used for classes, and in the back, Jeff's office adjoined an old-fashioned kitchen. In the middle of the building a door opened into a dark, almost foreboding staircase, which led upwards to his private digs and a room or two he rented out to students.

As I worked my way along the downstairs hallway, I caught a glimpse of The Angel as she glided effortlessly through a door appropriately tagged "Dance." Jeff Alexander greeted me at the foot of the stairs, and within seconds we were seated in his comfortable parlor on the second floor.

Old times, not important; what was important was the Watergate conspiracy trial being broadcast live on TV. Jeff and I, like most of the country, were mesmerized by the proceedings. The scandal of the times began with the arrest of five men, caught breaking into the Democratic National Committee Headquarters at the Watergate Hotel in Washington, D.C. As the trial proceeded, it became the unfolding of a massive cover-up of deceit, an ethical and moral collapse that led to the White House and eventually to the President of the United States, Richard Nixon.

Nixon, facing prospects of impeachment and possible criminal charges, became the first president in American history to resign the office. I felt a lovely surge of synchronicity, as back in Hollywood, Sherry and most of my friends stoutly followed the Nixon bandwagon into office. I was the lone holdout. I could not abide the man, especially after I read a biography by his wife, Pat, who described that when she was young and dating other men, the dour Dick Nixon used to sit in his car, outside of her residence, to more or less spy on the activities when she and her date returned. Now, that has to tell you something about the fellow, doesn't it?

During a break in the television proceedings, I told Alexander about my aspirations to make a movie. He was more than interested and we agreed to meet later to discuss my plans.

By the time I returned to my apartment, there was a message from Jeff on the answering machine. He wanted to know if I would consider making a talk before his actor's workshop on my career and the film industry from an insider's point of view? I called him back and told him I would be happy to do so. It was a decision that would change my life forever.

The World Is a Ball of Twine—Nothing Less!

One evening, shortly thereafter, I spoke to a dedicated group of Dallas artists gathered at The Actor's Workshop. In all, there were about forty in the audience. However, this being one of my first public talks, I was so nervous and discombobulated I scarcely remember the event. I rambled on, sort of stream of consciousness, and they responded enthusiastically. A day or two later, I was standing in line at a large grocery store, ruminating on how I was going to need an attorney to help me set up my movie company legally, when I heard a familiar voice: "Gary? Hey, Gary Kent, is that you?" I turned smack-dab into the smiling face of another ghost from the past: a relative from my marriage to Joyce Peacock. Tall, handsome, a bit of a scoundrel, extremely popular, it was her cousin, Robert Peacock.

In Los Angeles, I had known Bob Peacock as a part-time rodeo cowboy and full-time raconteur. Although we'd once been close as matching socks, I had not seen him for about six years. "Bob, what the hell! What are you doing here?"

"Oh, I got tired of L.A., came back to Texas, went to school, and got my law degree. I'm semi-respectable now; I'm a lawyer. How 'bout you?"

"Me? I'm here making a film...well, I mean I'm going to make a film just as soon as I get a script and the money to shoot it. Wanna hear about it.?"

Peacock and I spent the next hour or two in a neighborhood bar, talking old times, his decision to study law, and my movie. He suggested that I let him represent me, for free! "Just one favor, though, Gar. I'm having a party Friday night for a bunch of attorneys from UT (University of Texas, Austin) and I sure would appreciate it if you could invite some show people, just to liven up the place. Especially some good lookin' women."

I immediately thought of Jeff Alexander and his workshop. Actually, they were the only other people I knew in Dallas. I agreed to give it a try. The lure of free legal representation was the perfect bait. All I needed was a pimp stick.

When I got back to the apartment, I called Jeff and gave him the invite. He was enthusiastically open to the idea. Actors love to make fun of attorneys and are also in trouble as much as they're out of work, which is frequently.

"Oh, by the way, Jeff, there is a lady I saw going into the dance class at the workshop. Don't know her name, attractive, blonde hair, mid-twenties, maybe."

Jeff knew immediately whom I was talking about. "Oh, that's Shirley Willeford. She's the instructor. A great gal, except she giggles too much."

"Well, why not ask her? If she's not doing anything, would she like to come to the party?"

I popped a TV dinner into the oven, opened a Pepsi, and settled into the rehash of the Watergate trial on the six o'clock news. John Dean, ex-presidential counsel, was testifying regarding presidential activities. It was becoming obvious that he was sticking his foot in his smarmy mouth. I thought the interrogators were doing a superb job at making the little fellow squirm. By the expression on that thin-lipped face, you just knew his underwear was becoming very uncomfortable. "*Serves Mr. Uptight just right,*" Boo hissed. And then the phone rang. It was Jeff Alexander.

"Hey, Gary. I talked to Shirley Willeford and told her you were inviting her to the party."

"And?"

"And she said, 'If he wants me to come to the party, he should have the balls to invite me himself.'"

What a great answer. "*Speak for yourself, John!*" smirked Mr. Boo, quoting Priscilla Mullins in her advice to a timid John Alden as both disembarked from the good ship, Mayflower. I asked Jeff for Shirley's phone number. After some small, getting to know you conversation, in which she informed me she was not looking for "sex, romance, or a relationship," and I assured her that the mere thought of the above gave me migraines and that I certainly was not in the market either, she accepted my invitation.

> *The garments of the Angels correspond to their intelligence.*
> *The garments of some glitter as with flame, and those of others*
> *are resplendent, as with light: Others are of various colors, and*
> *some white and opaque...*
>
> —Emanuel Swedenborg

The angel known as Shirley Willeford arrived at Bob Peacock's wearing a formfitting white dress adorned with dark blue polka dots. She was easily the most beautiful and interesting person at the party. It took some time for me to elbow my way through the crowd so that I could introduce myself. "I know who you are," Shirley smiled. "I heard your talk the other night at the workshop. I thought what you said was really interesting, very informative." I decided that her eyes, surely the loveliest on the planet, had mastered the art of illuminating the soul.

From then on, the evening was ours. We totally ignored the other guests. We soon found ourselves sequestered under a makeshift pyramid Bob had erected in his loft. We remained there, the angel and I, in zazen posture, full lotus position, talking the night away as though we had known each other forever. We talked about a lot of things that first night, but mostly, we talked about motion pictures.

As the wee hours began to creep into our "tent," Shirley Willeford fessed up to her remarkable accomplishments. She had been an Olympic-quality gymnast while still in high school, before a devastating injury put an end to her athletic prospects. She was an El Reyette dance member in Corpus Christi musicals, and a drama student at prestigious Stephens College in Missouri, where she studied under renowned movie, Broadway, and television star Jean Muir (*A Midsummer's Night's Dream, As The Earth Turns*).

Shirley tells me with some pride that Ms. Muir, one of her heroes, had been blacklisted by Hollywood in the 1950s for being a suspected communist. Muir nonetheless prevailed in stage productions and as a university drama instructor, ending her career by receiving her personal star on Hollywood's Walk of Fame. Take that you movie moguls!

Peacock's party was rapidly descending into an unruly display of drink and debauchery. Ms. Willeford asked if I would care to join her at a nearby coffee shop for a nightcap before putting an end to our chat-up. I accepted. We rendezvoused at the neighborhood Denny's and, while slurping her favorite beverage, cherry Coke, we continued our exploration of her colorful past. She had been the first ever woman warehouse foreman for the Katy Railroad at the age of twenty-one; an American Airlines stewardess at twenty-two; and, as a teenage executive secretary, she had typed the final draft of several of Matthew Maltz's best-selling self-help books.

On the downside, she had mastered the art of sneaking out of her parent's house by the time she was thirteen, and by fifteen, was dating a local gangster suspected of possibly murdering his gang rivals. Then, there was the time she flew to London, just to say she had, ate a crumpet or some such in the airport, and flew back, all in the same day. There was the time she and a companion were driving a jeep on her father's ranch near Refugio, Texas, and had an interesting experience when all of the gauges on the dashboard went bananas, the radio turned off and on, and they observed a strange flying object zooming overhead. Of course, I believe it.

I countered with that time Sherry and I had exchanged identities, donning each others clothes. I gluing a fuzzy mustache above her lip (she looked like a French street-pimp) and she wigging me up and doing my makeup. (I looked a little like Eleanor Roosevelt.) When we had completely exchanged genders, down to the high heels and combat boots, we called our friends and invited them to a party. I will only say this much: Several went into shock, several are still not speaking to either Sherry or myself, and, lastly, I have a distinct recollection of stuntman Walt Robles constantly looking up my skirt.

I recounted the UFO incident Max Julien, Penny Marshall, and I had experienced in the Mojave desert, and also the time Sherry and I had bid goodbye to a house full of people and then sneaked back into the house through a bedroom window, crackers, cheese and wine for rations, hid in a clothes closet, spending several hours silently snacking, listening to the people in the building conversing through paper-thin walls. It was a weird experience, all in all, much like being a ghost.

Then there was the infamous evening when the entire cast of characters from West Coast Repertory ate a bunch of magic brownies that John Parker had rustled up. We were hard partying at Parker's apartment—two or three of our members left in disgust—the rest of us, including the wife of a prominent Los Angeles judge and an L.A. Rams football player, all high as snow geese, jumped into John's bed with our clothes on and tickled each other until the bed broke completely in two. John was distressed. The Angel was impressed.

By the time she and I had finished bragging about how bad we had been, it was morning. Dallas was fast awakening, morphing into the booming business metropolis it becomes during the day, doing so with all of the oomph and testy dissonance of a military invasion.

The Angel and I decided we had much in common that qualified us to become fast friends. To seal the whole situation, over bangers and black coffee, she and I agreed that I would teach her about the making of movies and she would type my screenplay, free of charge, and nurse me through the necessary rewrites.

How do you make a movie? That said, how does one make a good movie? Who, pray tell, will be the judge? The audience? The exhibitor? The critics? The press? History? Surely not mom and dad? In the end, like all of art, the beauty is in the eye of the beholder. The skill, the joy, are part and parcel of the doing. So then, the question became, "How was 'I' going to make a movie?"

> *Everyone knows that damage is done to the soul by bad motion pictures.*
> —Pius XI: *Vigilanti cura*, 1936

Sitting by the apartment pool, pad and pen in hand, it was about five in the afternoon on a Tuesday. I about had it figured out, my movie, that is. It was important that I find a way to connect personally with my film. My previous work, stunts, acting, effects, was largely impersonal, unnoticed, locked into the muck, the mire, or the magic of an entire piece orchestrated by someone else.

To me, the concept of being an independent filmmaker means having to say, or show, something you believe in so much you're willing to risk your all in the doing. It's not about the fast track, the big bucks, Sundance, silk suits, or Gucci shoes. It's about loving cinema and creativity and acting on that passion without regard to marketing analysis or popular considerations. My friend and fellow author, Owen Egerton (*How Best To Avoid Dying*, Dalton Publishing, 2007), sincerely believes creative people are meant to give, rather than to profit from, their work. Owen is probably right. So, if you must, go ahead and steal this book.

Me? I just wanted my audience to walk into the theater and view something entirely original, something they had never seen or experienced before. I wanted to sweep them up in a story that was unique and uplifting, and to do so with my own style. A lofty ideal and I hadn't a clue where I was going to get the financing. Outlaw that I am, I knew it was not going to come from the major studios. First, however, I was going to need a screenplay. Pen in hand, I began writing on a yellow legal pad:

The Pyramid

An original screenplay by Gary Kent

FADE IN: The screen is dark. A Moog Synthesizer holds one long note—a sound from far away, like a wail from the distance in a dream. Reverberated—the note begins to pulse—a heartbeat. In the center of the screen, a PINPOINT OF LIGHT APPEARS. The sound increases in volume and intensity. The LIGHT BUILDS, illuminating the dark silhouette of buildings and an horizon. This is a city, at dawn, and the world is awakening. Images of buildings now fill half of the screen. Just as the sun is about to burst over the top of the structures, the

ELECTRIC SOUND SLOWS, changes rhythm, morphs into the CRY OF A BABY. Somewhere, nearby, a baby is crying.

The Pyramid, then, was going to be a film about rebirth, of starting all over again, naked and new, and, in spite of all of the dangers, the pitfalls and stupid mistakes, deadly foibles and folly, maybe this time, getting it right.

Making My Bones

That evening, I received a phone call from what I assumed was probably a very strange person. "Hello, Mr. Kent? This is Kim Russell. I am a pyramidologist living here in Dallas. I see by the papers that you are going to make a movie about pyramids, and, that being my specialty, I wonder if I may drop by and say hello? Maybe I could be of some help to you?"

I was tempted to inform Mr. Russell that my film was going to have little to do with real pyramids, the kind I assumed he was referring to, those big sand and limestone monuments poking out of the Giza plains. Furthermore, what if this guy was a nut case? One never knows. However, by this time in my life, I considered myself impervious to the acts of bizarre, even frightening characters. Boo slid sideways into my thought process.

Well, why not, then, allow this fellow Russell to drop by and we'll take his measure—see what the hell a pyramidologist looks like. I knew better than to invite strangers to freely drop by my manse; healthier to meet on mutual ground, in front of witnesses. Still, I invited him to drop by the following morning for a chat and coffee.

Lying in bed that evening, I noticed the rose had assumed a slightly forlorn stance. I wondered if my flower girl was still in the neighborhood? Strange thing, that encounter. It helped me in my decision to go with the flow as far as a writer's life was concerned, to seek serendipity, to follow the mystical call of invisible pipers and see where it would lead me. Whatever happened, I intended to include it in my screenplay.

I opened the latest book I had acquired from the Dallas library, *Myself and I* by Constance Newland (aka Dr. Thelma Moss), an account of her experiences with LSD. I had just finished the chapter titled "The Bitten-off Nipple" and was ambling into "The Scared Spermatazoon," when I drifted into a long, troubling sleep.

Kim Russell arrived promptly at ten the next morning. When I opened the door, I thought I was gazing at the newsboy. Russell seemed to be around fourteen-years-old at the most. I later found out he was twenty. He was handsome in an "All-American Boy" kind of way, slight build, blue eyes assisted by bookish looking spectacles, a shock of blond hair tucked neatly

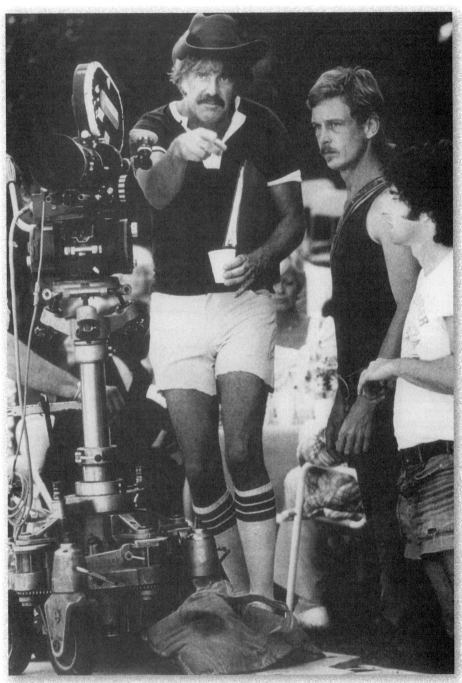

At long last, the author gets his directing chops on The Pyramid, *1975.*
Photo courtesy of the author.

under a straw cowboy hat. He resembled a high school chemistry student and not at all what I fancied a pyramidologist to look like. I invited him indoors, out of that blistering Dallas sunscape.

Of all of the people, good and bad, that I have met in my life, Kim Russell turned out to be one of the most unique, the most inspiring, the most knowing of the lot. First of all, let me discuss character: Show business, indeed, business in general, has a way of gnawing away at the human spirit. It may gradually crumble the soul until there is nothing left but a pool of characterless-ness. It may harden the heart, hide the worthy while glorifying the worthless.

I have always felt a genuine sadness for those who give themselves away for fame and fortune. Sometimes they make so many seven-sided bargains with notoriety in mind, they have nothing left of themselves that hasn't been sold, lost, stolen, or discarded along the roadside.

Kim Russell could not be bought, flummoxed, conned, bullied, or gnawed away at. Talk about strength of character! He was wise as a whole tree full of owls and, like the flower girl with the rose, he had appeared suddenly, out of the mists of happenstance, at just the right time. Eventually, Kim would introduce me to a host of people whose actions and thoughts were magically connected to ways of bettering our world. Somehow, this young, semi-mystical lad from central Texas seemed to know everybody and everything, intimately. All of this extending from his well-tempered plateau of personal consciousness.

Russell and I spent the entire morning discussing just about everything we could wrap our thoughts around. Eventually, we started talking about the movie. Kim was heavily into the Pyramid Power craze of the times and was in the midst of writing a book on the same. In that light, he was building pyramids of all shapes and sizes, conducting experiments on the effects of "Pyramid Energy" on brain function, mood alteration, psychic potential, sexual highs or lows, the effects of the "power" on animals, food, and plants.

These were all highly interesting endeavors and I admit I was curious about his efforts. Not so much, however, that I lost sight of my own plans. In fact, his acquaintance actually increased my enthusiasm for making the film. Russell was quickly swept into the vortex of my voracious passion for cinema.

I explained plot and storyline briefly, as well as my strategy. I was going to film this movie as a semi-documentary. The main character was going to be a news reporter at a fictional Texas television station. He is going to grow tired of hard news, the heartache and ashes of everyday living, and start covering softer, more positive stories. He is going to be fired for his efforts. He then decides he is going to make his own film, a positive one, centered on the "New Age" and its potential for changing the planet. In doing so, he is going to interview real scientists, psychics, and leaders in the arena of consciousness.

We will film those interviews in real time, as they occur, and observe their effect on our reporter, for good or bad. We watch as the changes occur, until finally, like a butterfly emerging from a cocoon, beautifully transformed, or a bruin from the deep sleep of hibernation, grumpy and ravished for self-gratification, our reporter is transformed. In doing so, hopefully, we will entertain and possibly transform a portion of the audience. We will accomplish this with a combination of real time interviews, professional actors, real people, stunts, music, animals and great cinematography, including the newest phenomenon, Kirlian photography.

My personal belief was and still remains one in which the world exists without absolutes. There are no clear-cut and dramatic boundaries; it is ethically, morally, and physically porous. It is a world of nuance where genes, memes, and mystery commingle into an energy, a forward flow forged from the past, but moving rapidly into the future; a future that is as undefined and unpredictable as Schrödinger's cat.

Yes, we are ultimately quite alone, each one of us, and yet it is that singular fact that also unites us, connects us with the largest common denominator: the living universal sea in which we are all involved as voyagers. The anchor in this vast ocean of living contradiction has to be one's own center of strength, of love, integrity, intelligence, and faith. This is the good ship that moves one safely through the waters. Finding that personal center, "The Fire Within," becomes our hero's quest, and the thrust of my movie.

I finished my preamble and, pouring us both a fresh cup of coffee, waited to see if Russell was going to make a dash for the door. Instead, he reached in his pocket, pulled out a chilam and about a half ounce of Texas Street. Tamping it in, he fired up, took himself a longish hit, then passed the pipe to me. "Okay, Mr. Kent. It sounds great. Let's get started."

Within days, I was able to assemble a small army of dedicated individuals anxious to see the film become a reality. Shirley Willeford became my secretary and chief co-conspirator. Kim Russell was tech advisor and doorway to the consciousness movement. Kim brought in two friends, Adrian Cumming, a mirthful dude with long, blond curls and a salesman's gift of gab, and Jonathon Stone, self-proclaimed mystic and psychic entrepreneur. I had an attorney, Robert Peacock. Peacock brought in a tall, raven-haired beauty named Barbara Morris. Morris was so hot she was like human crack; every male that saw her wanted a hit. We were soon joined by local news anchor, Larry Ratliff, and lastly, Jeff Alexander, the dean of the Actor's Workshop. Jeff had decided he would like to become "producer" and help in putting the project together, from the raising of financing to actual production. These folks, then, were my core group, my Pyramiders, and most remained so throughout the entire project.

We would often gather, my Pyramiders and I, at Jeff's workshop, my apartment, or the park to exchange ideas and bolster our offense. We formed an athletic team, and after think-tank sessions, would adjourn to a swimming pool for water polo matches, or to a local baseball diamond for a softball duke-out. This would all be followed by my cranking out a tub of homemade ice cream for the lot of us, an art I had inherited from my father and generations of Kents before him. Hopes were high, humor was splendid, days were long and magical. In the evenings I would continue to write the screenplay. It was all very cozy, very enjoyable. *"Except,"* Boo reminds me, *"you are quickly running out of money."*

> *Money is always there, but the pockets change.*
>
> —Gertrude Stein

Albert Camus, the great French writer/philosopher and Noble Laureate, said in his acceptance speech that the noble cause of the writer is "the service of truth and of freedom." I had just gotten off the phone with Shirley Willeford. She and I both shared an admiration for Mr. Camus and his works. In fact, she had written her college thesis at Stevens on Camus. His *The Plague* and *The Stranger* are easily two of my favorite reads. I was trying to channel Camus' clarity of thought and enormous personal integrity as I returned to my own writing. "Truth." "Freedom." Yes, yes, I hear you, Albert, but much easier said than written. One immediately confronts the lofty Albert Einstein and the intensive Werner Heisenberg.

Is truth relative? Relative to what? And what sort of freedom are we talking about here? Anarchy? Is it truth that the sun will always rise? I think not. So then, "faith" enters into the equation. It was getting to be a bit sticky, a bit muddy, really. I was writing a scene where my lead character, a South Texas news reporter, accesses a Shiner Bock and some bar olives. His mind is struggling with the problem of how to get his therapist into the sack and where in town to get the best chicken fried steak. I would be better served researching Erskine Caldwell (*God's Little Acre*) than an austere French existentialist. I closed the tablet and turned on the television.

This was a mistake. Every channel was carrying something depressing. Mostly recounts of increased slaughter in Vietnam or another foray into the twisted psyche of Tricky Dick Nixon. I was reminded that this was exactly the problem that our protagonist in *The Pyramid* faces—an ever-increasing appetite of the public for violence and sensationalism. I felt my own, personal angst beginning to gather its darker forces like a street gang in Cabrini-Green. I turned off the television.

It was just beginning to turn dark outside the big picture window. Lights were popping on, children were called in from play, the dogs assumed their positions as family sentries. I sat in the lavender light of a summer's evening in Texas, absorbing the moment. Well, one thing was becoming increasingly clear and that was the dire situation of my finances. Rent, child-support, food, utilities: Their specter chipped away at my confidence until writing about getting laid and having a chilled long-neck became difficult to consider as either "truth" or "freedom." I thought briefly about the rose in the vase in the bedroom. Surely it was dead by now, in need of replacing. Then, as if on cue, the phone rang. It was Paul Lewis calling from Hollywood.

"Hi, Gar. Listen, I'm coming down to Dallas with a director named Brian De Palma. We're doing a movie for Fox called *Phantom of the Paradise*. It's a pretty big production. I'm going to need an assistant. You interested?"

The Good Points of Barbed Wire

A week later, I was at the old Dallas Airport, Love Field, waiting for Paul and Brian De Palma to arrive from Los Angeles. They were coming in early to scout locations for *Phantom of the Paradise*. They were accompanied by cinematographer Larry Pizer (*The Proprietor, Isadora*) and art director Jack Fisk (*Raggedy Man, There Will Be Blood*, husband of actress Sissy Spacek). I had signed on as unit production manager. I had with me Dan Dusek, a senior film student from Southern Methodist University, who would work as a location scout for the film.

Paul and the group arrived with much of the hurly-burly of Hollywood spilling out of their baggage. It was going to take some time to get them on Texas time. In the finality of it all, we reached a sort of compromise. *Phantom of the Paradise* required getting much of Dallas to pass itself off as New York—damn near an impossibility. This particular illusion fell into the oeuvre of art director Fisk and me and my Pyramiders (which by now included the energetic Dan Dusek). We were charged with getting the locals to appear more cosmopolitan, less like hunter-gatherers, as Brian insisted on using masses of them to fill out the empty spaces in his movie.

After several rounds of location looking, we all adjourned to my apartment for a welcoming party. There was much good fellowship in sway. Unusual, since half of the crew was from New York and the other half from Los Angeles, and the twain did not fancy each other. The bonding agent turned out to be copious amounts of good Scotch and vodka, a little weed, the southern charm of my Pyramiders, and the naturally wholesome beauty of Ms. Willeford and Morris.

Paul Lewis, of course, was a dear friend. I was also familiar with the personalities and idiosyncrasies of movie crews. Brian De Palma was a different sort of bloke altogether: mostly aloof, perhaps a bit shy, not a huggy-feely fellow in the least, an auteur to be sure, hard on the success of two cinematic *coup d'état*: *Greetings* and *Sisters*. I was delighted, therefore, when I observed him sitting cross-legged on the floor, comfortably involved in the workings of a Ouija board with one of my female Pyramiders. Cinematographer Larry Pizer had been co-opted by a local beauty, a friend of Jeff Alexander's, and spent the evening in a corner of the apartment, locked into some intimate and perhaps racy conversation.

The crew, the hard-hearted New Yorkers and the cynical Angelenos, were enjoying a mutual disdain for all things Texan, especially Dallas. Boo and I observed the scene from our vantage point behind the makeshift bar. We smiled. "It was good!" I predicted an enjoyable shoot. I was wrong.

From the opening day of filming, things on *Phantom* took on a whirly, anxious, uncontrollable energy all their own. The logistics, the schedule, the production board, for some reason were considered a secret. "*Perhaps*," Boo suggested, "*they simply had not been completed.*" Jack Fisk and his construction crew were hard at work, slamming those eight-pennies and slopping paint onto flat-walls for twelve to fourteen hours a day. As they were behind schedule, they had little time to explain to the rest of us what was going on or what they needed in the way of supplies and materials. After all, they were morphing Dallas into New York City at warp speed.

The costume department was buzzing with the sound of little fingers sewing, folding, ironing, inventing the bizarre, colorful plumage needed to fulfill Brian's vision. They had even enlisted the services of the marvelous actress Sissy Spacek (*Carrie, Coal Miner's Daughter*) as, being married to art director Fisk, she was already on location. In spite of being hailed by the Hollywood moguls as a promising new actress for her work in *Badlands*, Sissy was more than willing to help in any way she could. In this case, that involved a needle, thread, thimble, and the fortitude of a mongoose.

The local teamsters were grumbling, the caterers overworked, the multitudes of extras unsure of what the hell they were supposed to be and do. Paul Lewis and producer Edward R. Pressman (*American Psycho, Hoffa*, a Christopher Award and multi-other nominations) were barely speaking to one another. Whatever the disagreement, Paul soon had enough. After putting his heart and soul into the project, he suddenly grabbed his return ticket and bid us all adieu. It happened so fast! "Paul, wait, please, just a sec, ok?" But he was gone.

That night we received word that the choreographer had balked at La Guardia airport in New York and would not be joining us. Two members of the crew got into a fistfight and the intestinal flu had stricken Gerrit Graham (*Greetings, Pretty Baby*), one of our lead actors. Racetrack touts were giving ten to one on complete failure of the project. *Phantom of the Paradise* turned out to be a tremendous success, though, becoming a classic horror/musical/farce with the impact and staying power of *The Rocky Horror Picture Show*. It also would garner multiple awards, including an Oscar nomination for Best Original Song and Best Musical Score.

The sheer amount of talent assembled for Brian's movie was staggering. For openers, there was De Palma himself, a graduate of Sarah Lawrence, a private liberal arts college cloistered on top of a rocky promontory overlooking the Bronx River in Yonkers. De Palma entered the foray of filmmaking well prepared by an excellent education, impressive contacts, and a group of uber-talented pals forged on the Sarah Lawrence campus. Most of them appeared in *Phantom*, along with other of Brian's films, and continue to work with him to the present day.

Brian became a leader of "The New Hollywood" in the 1970s, along with Oliver Stone, Peter Bogdanovich, Paul Schrader, Dennis Hopper, Martin Scorsese, Richard Rush, Francis Ford Coppola, and others. His work on *Phantom of the Paradise* resulted in several major awards, including a nomination for Best Original Comedy Screenplay from the WGA.

The lead actress in *Phantom of the Paradise* was lovely, dedicated Jessica Harper. She was also a Sarah Lawrence grad and a personal friend of Brian's. Jessica was flirtatious in a professional kind of way, just enough to endear her to the crew and the folks doing the heavy lifting. She had a way of turning her head suddenly and looking one directly in the eyes, and then she would break into the most delicious of smiles. Just as quickly, she would turn away, back to business. This left one to believe she had meant the smile especially for them, and was making a point to bestow it on them secretly, before any more of the day slipped away. Of course, every grip, every gopher, P.A., and juicer believed "the smile" was a signal that she found them alone especially appealing. This effective ploy earned Ms. Harper easy access to just about anything she wanted, movie set-wise.

Jessica Harper writes music, and possessing the most unique, husky contralto, performed all of her own singing in *Phantom*. Ever the lady, I was somewhat surprised when she later appeared in the X-rated *Inserts*, wherein Oscar-winning actor Richard Dreyfuss sucked on her breast for several scorching minutes of screen time. Arguably, it was the first time an American actress of note had actually allowed a sexual act to be performed on her for the sake of cinema.

Another Sarah Lawrence pal who came to Texas for the *Phantom* shoot was William Finley (*The Black Dahlia*, *Sisters*). Finley played the part of Winslow Leach, a nerdish songwriter, who sells his soul and his songs for a chance at love with his dream girl, Phoenix (Harper). He is subsequently disfigured in a terrible accident involving a record printing press, and from then on assumes the mask and the identity of "The Phantom of the Paradise."

The part of the devilish record producer, Swan, went to one of my absolute favorite songwriters, the diminutive, energetic, brilliantly prolific Paul Williams. Paul not only starred as the evil Swan, but also wrote the lyrics and music for this bizarre operetta. For this, he would receive his second Oscar nomination for Best Song. So far, in his eclectic career, Paul has won one Oscar, received four other Oscar nominations, won two ASCAP Awards, one Golden Globe with three nominations, nominated for two Grammys, is a member of the Songwriter's Hall of Fame—and he's just getting started.

Shirley Willeford and I went through our favorite list of Paul's songs. "We've Only Just Begun," "Rainy Days and Mondays," "(Just An) Old Fashioned Love Song," "The Rainbow Connection," "The Family of Man," and what eventually became *our* song, the haunting and naturally uplifting ballad, "Evergreen."

When a bunch of teenyboppers in bikinis were scheduled to dance for the hilarious rock group, The Juicy Fruits, and the original choreographer didn't show up, I volunteered Shirley as her replacement. So, then, Shirley Willeford, ex-warehouse foreman, ended up choreographing all of the beach bunny dance moves and doing a special close-up camera gag with a Juicy Fruiter. Kim Russell and Adrian Cumming were totally into the project, and Adrian even received credit on the film as a production assistant.

It is rumored that a very wise person once said, "To carry money without spending it is a sign of maturity." During the first weeks of *Phantom* filming, the picture company was headquartered at the old Majestic Theater in downtown Dallas. The Majestic sat mid-block, in a rundown section of the metroplex. One day, producer Ed Pressman sent Dan Dusek and me to an uptown bank to pick up a satchel of money and return it to him at the theater. Ed didn't specify how much money we would be transporting, but we assumed it was probably going to be a couple of thousand or more. Otherwise, why send two of us?

It was a walk of several blocks through scruffy territory, littered with refuse both human and debatable. We asked Police Sergeant Dave Biddleman, who was working security on the film, to accompany us. At the bank, a senior officer approached with a satchel, opened it, and counted out a hundred and fifty thousand friggin' dollars! I signed a receipt, then stuffed the moolah into the satchel. I handed it to Dusek. "I don't want it," Dan bawled. "Here, Dave, you carry it." He handed the satchel to Biddleman, who in turn handed it back to me.

"Come on, Gary, you're the senior member of this squad."

That being true, I considered pulling rank and forcing Dusek into taking the satchel along with its flinty responsibility. Dan had already started walking off, however, so, summoning up a spot of bravado, I stuck the money under my arm and began a casual saunter out of the bank. The walk back to the theater, a twenty-minute mosey at best, seemed to take about an hour and a half, during which time the satchel was passed between the three of us like a bag of molding body parts. So much, then, for the vastly overrated importance of "$" per se. None of us wanted the damn money.

We filmed *Phantom of the Paradise* over Christmas holidays, 1974. Everyone was homesick and/or sick literally, as stomach flu was spreading like Cheese Whiz through cast and crew. I hired a doctor to come to the set daily to give shots of B12, tabs of Vicodin, and hand out chewable vitamin C tablets. The crew gobbled up the pain pills like holiday candy.

We were scheduled to film on Christmas Eve. Paul Williams decided to surprise everyone by having a gourmet meal catered to the set. Roast turkey, beef tenderloin, asparagus, mashed potatoes smothered in creamery butter, grapes, avocados, yams, chocolate mousse, and caramel ice cream. Everyone was too sick to eat. We tried to show our appreciation, but could only sit at the perfectly coiffed dining tables, hunched and taciturn as illegals at a border bust.

This is probably as good a spot as any to pay homage to the work and the workers involved in the making of a film. It is not all fun and games, nor is it all drug and alcohol festivities fueled by a need to party arty. It is usually twelve to fourteen-hour days of hard, hard, hard, hard work. The crew might as well be working the salt mines. They seldom see daylight, at least not the usual, everyday kind of light a postman encounters. The crew arrives before sunup, and works their fingers to the bone until after sundown. They are the intestines, the gnarly guts of the beast—you cannot make a movie without them. The production assistants, assistant directors, etc., never get to sit down. They are the nervous system. As such, they are required to be on top of everything, one step ahead of everybody, informed by the frenetic buzz of circumstance, and the seemingly willy-nilly decisions of the director.

The director is the soul, and frequently the heart, of the production. If his or her own stops pumping, the whole shebang bites the dust. No one will follow anyone, and all of those costumes, set dressings, pretty people and cute animals, all of the big bucks and bigger aspirations fold and fade like last night's dreams. Directors work 24/7 and sleep after it is all over. He or she eats standing up, answering a thousand questions at once. If the picture is a hit, the stars get the credit. If the picture fails, it is always the director's fault.

The producer? He or she is the mother hen of the situation. They must baby the production along, salve the temperaments of cast and crew when they feel offended by the Machiavellian director. The producer gets to spend the money, pay the checks, lose his hair, get ulcers, dyspepsia, sexual dysfunction, chronic headache, and in the end, gets to hang briefly with the stars and take a few bows.

The cast: the worst job in the world and the best! It is all make-believe, which isn't easy, especially with the weather, the hours, the clammy, chalk-like makeup, the clumsiness and lizard breath of the dude kissing you during the love scene, the snickering from behind camera of the crew members (who all know they could do this better than you), taking orders to smile when you feel like crying, and orders to cry when you can only smile. "Look up! Look down! Look sexy, come on, this ain't no funeral, for Christ's sake. We gotta be outta here in ten minutes. OK, now act sweet."

Yes, the actors are the gallant soldiers, the bearers of the final product. They must step nakedly in front of the audience and convince the world they are someone or something they are not. They must do this while saying someone else's words, wearing someone else's clothes, following someone else's directions. They must accomplish this task while suffering from last night's marital madness, while haunted by the injury or illness of a loved one; they must do this while fevers rage, insecurities nag, and PMS pounds away at the spirit like a boot camp drill sergeant. In the end, they are alone in front of the camera, solely responsible for the accurate presentation of dementias, desires, and dreams. Why then, do they do it? My belief is, they do it because of a unique and passionate reverence for life.

Chapter Fifteen

Future producer Tomi Barrett and writer/director Gary Kent, Los Angeles, 1980. Photo courtesy of the author.

Picking Flowers, Disturbing Stars

*We cannot in literature, anymore than in the rest of life,
live in a perpetual state of revolution.*

—T.S. Eliot

"Gary? This is Tomi Barrett. Please give me a call.
Here's the number…"

The voice on my answering machine was feminine,
very familiar. I didn't know a Tomi Barrett. The phone
number was Shirley Willeford's, so I returned the call.
The voice answered on the second ring: "Hello, this is
Tomi!"

"Uh, Tomi? This is Gary Kent, returning your
call. I—"

"Oh, hi, Gary. This is Shirley. Shirley Tomi…Tomi
Barrett, I mean. It's my new name. I have changed my
name to Tomi Barrett. Like it?"

Before I could respond, she continued, pouring out
the story of the name change in a passionate torrent
of motivations. "I have never liked the name Shirley.
They named me after that kid, Shirley Temple, and I'm
nothing like Shirley Temple."

Well, I agreed with that. "Shirley-Tomi," whatever,
was nothing at all like that little toy person.

"I chose Tomi because I have always been a Tom
Boy, but I didn't want a man's name, so 'T-o-m-i.' The
use of the "i" does the trick, don't you think? I chose
Barrett because my favorite writer is Elizabeth Barrett
(Browning)."

Tomi Barrett was a perfect name for her, then.
Through the years, the name melted into her, was
absorbed into her until she and it finally popped out
the same person, the incredibly beautiful spirit known
as Tomi Barrett.

Tomi, Kim Russell, Adrian Cumming, Dan Dusek,
these and numerous others helped me enormously in

327

making my film a reality. Along the way, from concept to completion, we ran into the muck and mire of humanity, in all of its disguises. In fact, by the time I actually began filming, I'd been to Hell and back so many times it was starting to bore me.

James Bond, 007, has a flair, doesn't it? Jeff Alexander and I were led to James Bond as a possible investor in my movie. Now, I don't mean the James Bond, 007, the British agent celebrity, lover of dry martinis and beautiful birds. I mean the Texas James Bond, an aged curmudgeon, a womanizer, charlatan, and all around doofus. This Bond had an office in the basement floor of the International Bank in Dallas. This afforded him the office number 007 and a prestigious building from which to con his potential victims. There is a line from Robert Lewis Stevenson's *Kidnapped*, when, upon meeting his scurrilous uncle for the first time, young Jim Hawkins declares, "What he was, whether by trade or birth, was more than I could fathom." Such was my opinion of the Dallas James Bond.

I was sitting in my apartment. It was about seven in the evening. I was awaiting the arrival of entrepreneur James Bond, who had invited me to join him and a friend for dinner. I did not know the friend. For that matter, I didn't really know James Bond. He had responded to my sales brochure regarding *The Pyramid*. There was a knock at the door; I opened it. A tall, mannered individual in a black uniform announced that he was Mr. Bond's chauffeur. The limousine was waiting in the parking lot. The limo? *"This has to be a good sign,"* Boo gushes. *"Limos go with the big bucks, kid."*

I followed the chauffeur to the vehicle. It was a ringer, long and sleek, obviously meant for VIPs. Mr. Chauffeur held the door for me. I entered the limo and took a seat next to one of Mr. Bond's friends, a stodgy looking bloke, balding, horn-rims, tidy white handkerchief peeking from the breast pocket of an expensive business suit. "Hello, there, Mr. Kent," Bond smiled. "Let me introduce you to Gerald Lenious. Gerald, this is Mr. Gary Kent, the young man who is going to direct my movie."

His movie? I should have known right then the rocky lay of the land. But the limo had blinded me, I suppose. Or, it may have been the incredibly beautiful young woman seated next to James Bond. The lady's name was Carmen. I never heard a last name. She was about twenty-seven or twenty-eight, extremely attractive in a European model sort of way. Tall, with a tanned complexion, she was Latino in neither appearance nor accent. "More Eurasian," I thought. Her hair was a luxuriant auburn-blonde, medium length, sensuously waved. Carmen was a very difficult read. She would not allow eye contact for more than a moment. Quickly averting her gaze, ripping away any glimmer of warmth or humanity, leaving one with the feeling that somehow you had frightened or even possibly offended her.

Carmen was dressed exquisitely: knee-length salmon colored evening dress, scoop neck, displaying a string of pearls and a slight swelling of fleshy landscape above her bosom. Her long, silken legs ended in semi-spiked heels, the same salmon color as the dress. If Carmen were a flower, she would have been an exotic, not flashy or showy, just naturally gorgeous, existing for beauty's sake alone. Quiet, solitary, and mysterious, very like an orchid.

Bond was dressed to the nines. Bow tie, dark Italian silk dinner suit, a large golden Bucherer circled his bony wrist, several expensive rings completing the effect. "*Whew!*" Boo whispered. "*Don't make an ass of yourself, boss. No false moves. Shhh! We're inside the clubhouse.*"

The restaurant of Bond's choice was one of Dallas' finest. Very Chaldean, which meant marbled pillars, many open spaces, an indoor garden. Waiters, bearing piles of food resting on large, silver platters, hurried past the bubbly fountains and the live peacocks. Everyone seemed to know James Bond. We could not have been more warmly received. "Yes sir, Mr. Bond. How are you this evening, sir? We have a table waiting for you, Mr. Bond, as you requested, near the obelisk."

Once seated, James Bond ordered the wine, suggested the right menu selection for each of us, all the while regaling us with his witty, urbane repartee. Actually, it was not all that urbane, his repartee. It was centered mostly on himself and his achievements, and jokes about women and minorities: blacks being used as crocodile bait, etc. Carmen and the fellow in the horn rims (I had already forgotten his name) laughed uproariously, now and again patting Bond on the shoulder, saying, "Well done, old boy, well done." I did not find his stories that amusing.

Bond, a genuine chin-musician, almost broke his arm patting himself on the back. He informed me that he had been some kind of health secretary when LBJ was president and he had single-handedly saved an entire county from disintegrating into poverty by milking the federal government for immediate emergency funds, even though there was not an emergency. This earmarked pork belly was the gallant act that had brought him his reputation as a champion of "the little people."

While he tooted away at his purported accomplishments, and as no one was paying the least attention to me, I took the opportunity to study Bond in detail. James Bond was sixty-eight to seventy years of age, balding except for a few sickly strands of white hair limply draped over his bulbous dome like used yo-yo strings. He had clusters of the stuff clinging to his ears, and a strand or two protruding from his nostrils. Bond's nose was worthy of admiration. It was huge, jutting from his face like the largest of ornaments on the Christmas tree. The skin of this magnificent proboscis was splayed with a series of purplish veins, crawling spider-like toward his blotched cheeks. His eyes were a watery blue. They darted hither and thither, too fast for actual eye contact to be established. A tall man, Bond's shoulders slumped into his body, giving the appearance that somehow he'd been stretched into the shape of a long, thin pear.

It was during dessert, after everyone had consumed copious glasses of expensive Beaujolais, that I mustered the courage to take over the conversation. I adroitly steered it in the direction of motion pictures. "Unusual, don't you think?" I smirked, pointing out that the obelisk we were seated alongside was topped in the shape of a pyramid. "Could be an omen, since the movie I am writing is titled *The Pyramid*." My dinner mates stopped eating and drinking, freeze-framed mid-consumption as though I had just pulled my dick out of my pants and placed it on the table. Bond signaled the waiter for the check.

"What exactly is the storyline?" These were actually the first words spoken by old Horn-Rims during the entire meal. The mystifying Carmen turned her slanted, dark orbs in my direction.

"Hey, boss, we're on stage!" Boo enthused. I must take command, I told myself, launching into an enthusiastic barrage of hodgepodgerisms concerning consciousness, the trials and tribulations of a reporter attempting to change the world by changing the content of the daily news. Again, I received the "dick outta the pants" expression from Carmen and ol' Horn-Rims.

Bond, however, seemed genuinely impressed. "Bravo! Bravo!" he shouted, patting me on the shoulder as though I had just scored one for the home team. "We've got a winner, here, Kent, no doubt about it, wouldn't you say, Gerard?"

Before Mr. Lenious could reply, Carmen turned to Bond, and laying her slim, delicate hand on his forearm, murmured, "I absolutely love it, Mr. Bond. I adore it. I am so happy for you!"

That seemed more than enough motive for the ebullient Bond to call an end to the evening. Back we went into the limo, and within minutes, I was returned to my apartment. As I slipped under my bedcovers, it occurred to me that I was not at all sure what the hell had just happened.

Shelter From the Storm

It was raining. A torrent of water falling from the sky, flooding streets, hollows, small streams, a typical Texas gully washer. It was six thirty in the evening and I was about to leave for my first official date with Tomi Barrett. We had both been so insistent about prizing our independence that we had never considered ourselves an "item." Others, however, sensed a blooming romance beyond the mere development stage. "All right, all right," we grumped, "let's go to dinner and call it a date." I left my apartment and ran through the deluge to my car.

When I arrived at Tomi's, I discovered her sitting on the porch steps, soaked to the skin. The new dress donned for the occasion was drenched, sagging from her body under the sheer weight of moisture. Her hair was hanging about her shoulders like a used mop. She looked much like an anorexic, waterlogged meerkat. Yet, there she sat, oblivious to the storm, cuddling, protecting some small creature she was holding in her lap.

"Tomi! What are you doing? You're about to drown, you know that?"

She looked up, her smile barely visible through the sheets of rain assaulting the area. By now I could see she was holding a very tiny kitten, shielding it, and cooing a soft kitten sound to let it know it was with a friend. Tomi had found the little creature, she informed me, abandoned under the porch. She had heard its loud cries from inside the apartment. Now that she had rescued it, she had no intention of keeping our dinner date.

"I'm sorry, Gar. I'm going to dry off, and then take this little fella to the veterinarian for a checkup." She stood, moving toward the apartment door, then stopped abruptly. Lowering those incredibly beautiful eyes, she peered up at me very, very seductively. "We'll make our dinner another time, won't we?"

There was something in her look, I suppose. Or in the way she so cleverly left the dinner date situation open-ended. And then, the fact that the bedraggled kitten was so much more important to her than a Hollywood movie director. All things considered, I was beginning to fall hard for Tomi Barrett, and I didn't even know it.

I accompanied her to the veterinarian. The kitten was treated and released to her care. The vet told her she had obviously saved its little life. Much later, sitting on her couch, we went over a list of possible names for her charge, eventually settling on Lester. Why? I haven't a clue, except that it seemed as good as any. I had an uncle named Lester who broke horses for the U.S. Cavalry during the 1920s. Uncle Lester died a vagabond on the railway when he finally realized the Iron Horse had replaced the hoofed one for good. My father told me Lester had died of a broken heart. I believed the story. In spite of the fact that the name came spontaneously from Tomi, I felt somehow that my crusty, dusty ol' horse-lovin' uncle had contributed to the cause.

I went to the kitchen, returning with a small, sharp knife. "Please give me you hand," I said. "Trust me." Tomi looked at me with that same "dick in the pocket" expression I remembered from my meeting with James Bond.

"What on earth?" Nevertheless, she proffered her small, white hand. I took her finger, pricked the pad until the blood oozed. I then sliced the end of my own, an impressive gash that laid open the pulpy interior. Again, I took her hand, pressing the bleeding fingers together, letting the blood mix. "Now we're related, by blood. We are family. We will be close all of our lives, brother and sister in blood, and we will always, always, always shelter each other. You shelter me, and I will shelter you, forever and ever, and then some."

Tomi took my bloody finger and squeezed a full, ruby-red drop into her mouth, then smeared it across her lips. She asked me to do the same. "Kiss me, Gar," she whispered huskily. We touched lips, then leaned into the kiss, mixing mouths, blood, saliva, family afflictions, genetic blessings. "There," she laughed, surfacing for air. "I want you to know this really is forever."

> *There are only two forces in the world, the sword and the spirit. In the long run, the sword will always be conquered by the spirit.*
>
> —Napoleon Bonaparte, *Maxims of Napoleon*

It is fairly easy, while admiring the magnificent panorama of sea, cliffs, and sky along Highway 1 through the area known as Big Sur, to drive right off the roadway, ending it all in a messy splat on the jagged rocks a thousand feet below. Ever since the highway was carved out of the cliffs of California coastline, nature loving gawkers have done just that, forcing the state to post frequent signs advising drivers to pay attention to the driving and leave the scenery appreciation until safely anchored at one of the protected outlooks.

I ignored the chance to ogle the most breathtaking of views this side of the Greek Isles, keeping my eyes firmly fastened on the stability of my friend, Kim Russell. Kim was driving us along the coast from southern to northern California in his minuscule '70 Honda sedan. Being a Texas boy, he had never feasted on this sort of unbounded, highly dangerous, natural beauty. Sober as he seemed, I still was not convinced he could drive responsibly without my repeated shouts to, "Watch it!" from the passenger seat.

We were on a journey, Kim and I, to Sacramento, the state capital, to meet up with Captain Edgar Mitchell, astronaut, and sixth man to walk on the moon. We had left Los Angeles early that morning, hoping to be in Sacramento by evening time. Kim was pushing the noble Honda to the max, which found us clipping along the treacherous Highway 1 at about sixty per. Somewhere south of Carmel, we pulled onto an outcropping for a quick break.

Stepping from the car, Kim and I stood on the edge of the world, taking it all in, stunned by the sheer magnificence of the scene. You cannot find a lovelier melding of land, sea, and sky as the topography of Big Sur anywhere else in the U.S. To our left was a jagged tumble of lichen-covered rock, some Monterey pine and chaparral, all about to be swallowed by a giant blanket of fog so thick the birds popped in an out like raisins in a bowl of cream of wheat. The fog was rolling up from the waters of the Pacific Ocean, several hundred feet below.

On our right, we had a clear view of the beach, the cliffs, and the forest for several miles. We saw a family of elephant seals taking the sun on the rocks along the shoreline. Further out in the Pacific, a humpback whale breeched the water, slapping himself heartily with his fins, then plunged back into the deep, leaving a white, frothy pool of disturbed surface behind. A stately California condor swept along the nearby cliff side. Kim said that this impressive creature was actually a vulture, a scraggly necked cousin to the Mexican turkey buzzard. I am not that fond of vultures of any kind, but watching this bird in flight was a lesson in natural aerodynamics. The sacred condors have a nine-foot wing span. Extended, these feathered sails catch the wind drifts off the cliffs, riding them up and down in an awesome sort of whispering aerial ballet.

I turned from the dizzying vista of cliff side and beach to scope the dark green forest that seemed hell-bent on devouring the highway. These, then, are the giant redwoods, arboreal behemoths that have enchanted vagabonds, 49ers, poets, the persons of artistic temperament who followed the Saline, Salinan, and Chumash Indians, the original inhabitants of the area. After a quick set of body stretches to get the old blood flowing in the right direction, we returned to the Honda for the next leg of the journey.

Forty minutes later, Kim and I were sitting on the veranda at Nepenthe, a family-owned inn nestled between the sea and the majestic Santa Lucia Mountains, drinking our pyramid-treated water and scarfing down one of the inn's famous ambrosia burgers. Our rosy-cheeked waitress informed us that *nepenthe* is the Greek word for a drug purported to expel sorrow. To me, the taste of the secret ambrosia sauce on my burger and the unspoiled beauty of the surroundings had already accomplished that task. That, and possibly the treated water Kim kept in a large jug under a jerry-rigged pyramid on the floorboard of the Honda. Whatever, we both felt about as brand new and optimistic as a squad of freshman cheerleaders.

I had become convinced that the addition of financier James Bond to our project guaranteed we would have the scratch to see us through to completion. I had finished the screenplay, and now had only to get the commitment of several real time leaders in the "consciousness movement" for my fictional reporter to become involved with.

My concept, simply stated, was as follows. Our fictional lead, Chris Lowe, a television reporter for KTXT in Dallas, Texas, is fired from the station for ignoring hard news and wasting the station's time and money on a series of quaint but purposeless stories: a pig farmer being evicted from his property for the development of a parking lot; an old man in an abandoned church, conducting solitary services with only himself in attendance; a young confrontation therapist attempting to reverse the downward spiral of druggies, paranoids, and the lost souls who make up her group, by helping them get in touch with their real feelings, etc. These endeavors are considered by the manager of KTXT to be merely "audio-visual masturbation."

Freed from the responsibility of deadlines and project approval by the "suits," Chris decides to film a documentary, a cinematic record of diverse individuals who are pioneering the search for "consciousness," the hunt, if you will, for a collective soul. In so doing, our hero begins to drop the trappings of cynicism, negativity, and greed, until like a molting rooster he is transformed.

What I did not tell Kim was that I also intended to keep a record of how the cast and crew responded to the material, to the information and insights provided. "Could the making of art," I wondered, "have a profound and permanent effect on those involved in its creation without the conscious knowledge of the artists/craftsmen? Does art itself, then, stick its ethereal finger into the molding of the clay?" Good premise, I assumed, for a truly outlaw motion picture.

> *The first thing that came to mind as I looked back at the Earth floating in the vastness of space was its incredible beauty. It was a majestic sight, a splendid blue and white jewel suspended against a velvet black sky.*
>
> —Captain Edgar D. Mitchell, *Psychic Exploration*, 1974

To Kim and I, it was like having tea and crumpets with Ferdinand Magellan. Perhaps even more impressive, Ed Mitchell was one of only six men to ever set foot on the moon. Now we were sitting in the backyard of the tidy, modest home of the Mitchell family, eating freshly baked oatmeal cookies and having a glass of iced tea, all politely presented by Mitchell himself.

Captain Mitchell was of medium height and build, straight dark hair which had begun to recede a bit from his forehead, and a calm, even graceful demeanor. I was struck immediately by the intelligence beaming from his large baby blues: intelligence and the requisite kindness Boo and I require of all those we idolize enough to follow blindly off precipices. It would be impossible to accuse Mitchell of subterfuge or cruelty; he was just too damned open, and it started with those bluest-of-blue eyes.

"The cosmos itself is conscious," Mitchell told me, offering another oatmeal cookie. "I realized this when I was standing on the moon, trying to understand everything I was seeing. *The whole glittering universe is alive!* That insight was suddenly, almost overwhelming."

Looking at Edgar Mitchell, listening to that smooth, sure voice, I could easily tell this guy knew what he was talking about. Scientist, test pilot, naval officer, astronaut, lecturer, author, Mitchell has received the Presidential Medal of Freedom,

The U.S. Navy Distinguished Medal, three NASA achievement awards, is in the Space Hall of Fame, the Astronaut Hall of Fame, and in 2005 was nominated for the Noble Peace Prize. Not bad for a country kid from Hereford, Texas, home of the Texas T-bone and jewel of Deaf Smith County.

Here was a man who had "loosed his earthly bounds" and walked among the stars. I was trying to get him back to terra firma in order to stuff him into the small hole that houses the inner self, if such a hole exists. Would he assume I was daft, an oar too short to reach sea level? Would Russell and I be banished from that trim little yard, our cookies snatched from us like battle ribbons from disgraced poseurs.

We've all felt it, I suppose. That moment of yellowish cowardice, when you wonder what the hell ever gave you the idea that you have a right to be wearing long pants. Boo suggested I go over the positives and negatives before committing to actual speech.

Mitchell: Bachelor of Science from Carnegie Mellon and the U.S. Naval Post Graduate School; doctorate from Massachusetts Institute of Technology; honorary doctorate from New Mexico State, Carnegie Mellon, etc.; co-owner of record for the longest time spent walking on the moon with fellow astronaut Alan Shepard (nine hours, seventeen minutes); most at home with fellow intellects, astronauts, and world leaders.

Kent: Two years of college journalism, a little football, a little vaulting around on the track team, lowest rank Navy swabbie, movie stuntman with a curious bent for hanging with junkies, sinners, and near-do-wells.

The only positives Boo could suggest were that I had testicles the size of casabas, an IQ so low it rendered me practically fearless, and the possibility that God loves sinners as well as saints.

Kim Russell poured Captain Mitchell a glass of pyramid-treated water before I hit him with the concept of my movie. Mitchell listened to the whole proposal regarding the gradual unveiling of "consciousness."

"A good sign," Boo assures me.

"Well, sounds to me like you've about got it," the good Captain declared. "A bit unorthodox, but then orthodoxy is the exact opposite of consciousness, isn't it, Gary? It is more like being un-consciousness."

I could not have said it better. Before we folded our tents and faded away, Kim and I secured an agreement from Captain Mitchell that would allow our reporter to interview him on camera at the Griffith Observatory in Los Angeles. He would also make personal appearances to promote the film and help us secure cooperation from other stalwarts, as needed.

After we started our return to Los Angeles, I asked Kim to pull over at a roadside rest stop so I could call Tomi and tell her the good news. As expected,

Astronaut Captain Edgar Mitchell, sixth man on the moon, appearing in Gary Kent's film, The Pyramid. *Photo courtesy of the author.*

she was delighted. Then she hit me with the bad news. Back in Big D things had taken a turn for the worse, down and dirty, actually.

Evidently, that old rascal, James Bond, Mr. 007, did not waste a minute after I had left for the coast before he began pinching the buttocks of every female aligned with my *Pyramid* project. If he was not immediately rebuffed, he would quickly shift into full court press and begin groping, grabbing, lusting like a rutting boar. A bit more than just the heavy breathing. Tomi asked me to fly back as soon as possible. I was able to get a plane out of Burbank Airport by seven that evening. I was in Dallas a little after midnight.

Taking Out the Trash

Tomi picked me up at the airport and we stopped at Denny's for a cherry Coke and an update. It was good to see her again. I was drawn instantly into those hypnotic, amber-colored eyes. I was commenting to Boo that, "The seductive sweep of her neck must be a major temptation to vampires," when she began telling me all of the things that had gone awry during my absence.

A production assistant I had befriended from the *Phantom of the Paradise* shoot knew where I kept a hidden key to my apartment. As soon as I was airborne, he moved in, lock, stock, barrel, and Thor, the huge, semi-tame wolf he had captured in the mountains of Colorado.

I actually liked this friend a lot. He had that rugged, mountain man persona and Thor the wolf was so outstanding, such a magnificent throwback to the forest primeval, I wanted to steal him for myself. So it didn't bother me much that they had decided to homestead my apartment. What did bother me was that my backwoods buddy had used my place as his own den of inequity. He was tall and handsome, slim, sandy-haired, with a grin that could melt freezer-burned ice cubes. His problem was that he didn't possess any ethics or morals that applied outside of the forest. Fidelity to him was as rare as the sighting of a Wilkinski canary. He appealed to other men's wives and girlfriends like an ad from *Cosmopolitan*, and usually, they went for it, leaving a long line of pissed off exes all blaming me for their betrayal.

I popped an Excedrin, washing it down with cherry Coke. Tomi continued, "And, oh, yeah, you're being sued by your landlord. He went to your apartment to get the mountain man to turn down the stereo, and the wolf attacked him."

"Thor? Thor attacked the friggin' landlord?"

"Yeah. He bit the guy pretty bad on the forearm. The landlord called the police and animal control. I guess it was quite a scene. I wasn't there, though, 'cause I didn't swallow the line and sinker the Colorado Kid was using for bait."

"Well, that's one bit of good news, eh, Boo?" I took the maraschino from my Coke and began sucking it nervously. "Okay, Babe, what else? Tell me about the fire and break-in."

"No fires, no break-ins. There is one other little thing you should know though. You want to hear it now?"

"Why not? I'm booking a flight to Croatia. If I'm lucky, it'll depart within the hour. I might as well hear all the bad news before I make my escape."

Mr. James Bond, under the guise of making "his film" had been asking certain friends of mine, all women, to stop by his office to chat about the production. Once seated, he would entertain them by clapping his hands, causing a table lamp to turn on and off. This accomplishment seemed to fill him with the utmost glee and also free him for any need for decorum. He would then ask them, "Please spread your legs and give me a little looky-look of the promised land! Whee diddle de diddle dee…yes, sirree! Gimme a little looky-look, honey, and I'll give you one of these!" 007 would then take a trinket from his desk drawer, a jeweled necklace, an expensive watch, string of pearls, whatever he thought would do the trick. He would then dangle same in front of the astonished lass's eyes, while drooling excessively. This somewhat respected, even revered, Texas businessman, savior, evidently, of the poor and desperate during the reign of LBJ, would morph into a lecherous old dodderer desperate for a glimpse of the reclusive "thatch patch" quietly nesting beneath the undies of his astonished guests.

Putting the Tools in the Truck

After the late night talk with Tomi, I knew that James Bond, Mr. 007, had to go. I had actually been feeling the vibes for some time but had ignored their hum as everything else was going so well. The script was complete. I had managed to raise a small amount of funding from Lou Bloodworth, a Dallas diva of good heart and superb taste; another tiny investment from a friend of a friend who was sitting bored and alone in a Miami penthouse; and lastly, another small investment from Bobbie Halloway, James Bond's secretary. Bobbie was a straight arrow, a lovely, warm, inspiring woman. What she was doing working for a man so crooked he had to screw on his trousers was more than I could fathom.

The addition of Captain Mitchell to the project, along with Thelma Moss, assistant head of the Department of Neuropsychiatry at UCLA, who was researching alternative healing using Kirlian photography as a test tube; "Komar the Magnificent," a cheese manufacturer from Wisconsin who repeatedly walked across burning coals to demonstrate the power of mind over matter; and Dr. Clive Baxter, who was conducting advanced research in extrasensory communication concepts, made the list of interviewees for the movie more than inspiring.

I considered myself an outlaw and as such I had me a hot ticket on the Outlaw Express, where my version of The Code of the West was pretty much open for interpretation. It was not important in the least to become a Hollywood director, or, for that matter, a director of any kind. It was important to be true to myself, and especially, to the murky potential of this film.

There have been so many wonderful, amazing, and just plain decent women in my life: Grandmother Hope who lived to 103; my own mother, Iola, a Poet Laureate of Washington state; my four sisters; ex-wives, lovers, and just plain friends. The women who had fallen under my *Pyramid* spell were no exception. They deserved better than to be sexually harassed by a man so repulsive he couldn't get laid in a trainload of hookers.

007! I stared briefly at the numbers on the office door at the International Bank Building: 007—James Bond. This very popular Dallas entrepreneur was about to get a boot in his ass from a leathery stuntman from the West Coast. I opened the door, smiled a broad, "Hello," to Bobbie Halloway, and then, tipping an imaginary hat to the beauteous Carmen, Bond's hood ornament, I marched toward Bond's private office. Carmen had remained conveniently aloof and unnecessarily cool ever since our first meeting. This morning, however, Carmen actually smiled, raising her fine-boned fingers in a "come hither" attempt to halt my determined advance toward the sanctuary of her bulbous-beaked boss.

I threw open the door. Bond was seated behind his very large mahogany desk, doing absolutely nothing, as usual, other than perhaps fantasizing about white thighs attached to dark garter belts. "Well, welcome back, Kent," he snorted, merrily clapping his hands to make the lamps blink on and off in synchronized display of electric obedience. "Please, be seated. I'm ready for more good news about my movie."

I ignored the invitation. "Sorry, Bond, I'm rather in a rush today. Lots of things to do. You understand, I'm sure. I'm starting by insisting that you apologize to the people on *my* film for your abusive behavior." Boo said I was being too diplomatic.

I thought ol' 007 was suffering a seizure, perhaps a stroke of some sort. The spidery veins traversing his monstrous nose began to throb and pulsate with deep crimson, like a Christmas ornament on a relay. Back went his head. He bellowed a marvelous bellow, much like the mating call of a moose, then spun several three sixties in his swivel chair. Finally, he spoke, his voice crackly, trembling with emotion, "You are out of line, mister! Inappropriate? Inappropriate…"

"It's over between you and me, Bond. I don't want you to associate yourself with me or my movie."

James Bond, Mr. 007, glared at me with a look as cold and evil as an oven stoker at Auschwitz. "You, sir, will never make your movie here in Dallas. I can guarantee you that."

Wanting to appear nonchalant, I managed to affect a pleasant smile on my way to the door. Opening it, I announced, just loud enough for Carmen, the ornament, to overhear, "You know, Bond, you're so anxious to engage in a sexual act, I suggest you go fuck yourself!" Stupid, street level, gutter sniping I admit, but at the time, I could not imagine a more perfect exit line.

Later, while watching the resignation of Richard M. Nixon on television, I realized what I'd done. Jeff Alexander of The Actor's Workshop had tired of trying to raise money and was slowly extricating himself from the project, and now I had just kissed off my only other proximity to any real funding. Let's see: Bobbie, Bloodworth, and Ms. Miami, a total of fifteen thousand dollars, a pittance when compared to the hundred and fifty thou asked for in the budget. Well, I could always go back to doing stunts. Or, like little rich girl gone bad, Patty Hearst, I could start robbing banks.

Tomi dropped by to hear the outcome of my meeting with Bond. She looked tired, worn down by long days spent slaving as an executive secretary in the corporate cauldron of Big D: hurry in, punch the clock; strict dress code; all males, regardless of capability, are addressed as mister and sir; lunch twenty minutes in the corporate cafeteria; smoke breaks so seldom the lungs actually begin to heal; a nagging fear by management that an employee might not be happy with low wages and extra hours, and therefore, all employees must be regarded with indifference and suspicion. You know, the usual. I didn't have the heart to tell her I had just given our only hope of serious funding the old heave ho. I needed another miracle fast, and then the phone rang!

The cheerful voice on the other end was Michael MacFarland, a friend from California with whom I had made an exploitation film years before. Our relationship had been warm and fruitful. Mike was also one of the first producers I had ever known who actually grabbed a paintbrush and helped ready the sets for the shoot. "Hey, Gary, what are you up to? I'm in the mood to make another movie, aren't you?"

Michael MacFarland is about average height, maybe a hundred and fifty pounds. He has a pleasant face with an intelligent forehead encroaching far into a sandy hairline, and intense, busy eyes. Within the week, he was sitting on my couch in Dallas, recounting the experience his brother Phil had undergone while climbing a large pyramid in Mexico.

"Phil always wanted to play the saxophone," Mike said, sipping a Dr. Pepper on ice. "He just never could get the hang of it. Then he climbed the pyramid! While sitting on the capstone, meditating on his problems, something overcame him, a feeling he couldn't describe, an epiphany, maybe. It was profound. When he returned to the bottom, he knew he would be able to play the saxophone, and he did!" Mike's eyes began to tear. "That's a true story, Gary. Phil could actually play the saxophone after that pyramid climb."

It's not that I didn't believe him. I wanted to believe him; it was just that, with a title like *The Pyramid*, it was hard to explain that my film had nothing to do with pyramids. "Pyramid Power," a loose assortment of minor miracles attributed to a strange energy emanating from the pyramid structure, was all of the rage in the mid-70s. It was reported that the energy improved sex lives, re-established mental stability, put one in an automatic alpha state, preserved food, healed wounds, and sharpened razor blades. The believers were legion and I was not one to challenge them.

I even had Kim Russell construct a small pyramid-shaped dwelling in my bedroom. I removed the mattress from my bed and began sleeping under the darned thing. Improved sex life? "*Well, it couldn't hurt to give it a try,*" Boo cooed. However, that was not what my film was about. It had nothing to do with one's ability in the boudoir or the sharpening of dulled bathroom utensils. I began to relate the storyline to Michael. By the time I was halfway through the telling, he had made up his mind. He wanted to produce the film. We would be partners, fifty-fifty. He would, with my assistance, raise the financing and handle all of the necessities of production. I would direct. Done deal. Maybe, then, there was something about this "Pyramid Power," after all.

> Some say, 'What is the salvation of the movies?' I say, 'Run 'em backwards. It can't hurt 'em, and it's worth a trial.'
> —Will Rogers, American Icon, 1946

Mike MacFarland grew up in Northern California wanting to be an actor. It seemed to him like a marvelous way to "be," not a star, but an honest to goodness actor, possessing the nuance, talent, and style that the term implies. He soon discovered that he was terrible at it. So, he decided to pursue the next best thing, producing. He majored in business at Stanford University and worked his way through several successful ventures. His worst fear was that he would always be a "suit," so he kept his hopes on the goal of a career in the arts. He succeeded, and in doing so, enjoyed (or suffered) the usual folly and fun that attaches itself like a mutating barnacle to the creative milieu.

One of Mike MacFarland's best qualities is his sense of humor and appreciation of irony. One of his first solo film experiences was directing and producing a musical titled *Hanging on a Star* (Deborah Raffin, William Windom), an energetic little film about a group of young musicians trying to make it big. A character piece in the film was the rickety helicopter that ferried the band from gig to gig, and its pilot, a cantankerous old coot appropriately named Crash. According to Mike, the chopper had a habit of not firing up when needed for a shot. "Honest to God, this guy Crash would take out a big wrench and begin beating the shit out of the helicopter! After a minute or two of the worst abuse you can lay on a machine, he would climb in it, feed it a little juice, and it would start right up!"

Well, that's the joy of moviemaking: little gaffes, big surprises, lots of bloody pluck, luck, and serendipity.

Evening seems to fall slowly in Dallas, Texas, it being in the southern extremity of the U.S. This evening cast a diffused light through the windows, onto the white walls, washing them in the palest of grays, accentuating the fact that I didn't possess a painting, picture, nor even a calendar to break plane. By now, Mike and I were both wasted, worn to the funny bone by excitement for the project and some pleasant homegrown I had conned from my ally Adrian Cumming earlier that afternoon. I fired up another spliff and we both relaxed into a bitter-sweet recounting of some of the strange happenings we or our friends had experienced while engaging in the frantic art of making cinema.

My friend, producer Oliver Hess, had made a film called *Flight of Black Angel*, a story of a rogue Air Force pilot who steals an atomic weapon, planning to drop it on an American city that he fancies to be Sodom and Gomorrah (Las Vegas). Oliver and the crew were on location at this little airstrip outside of Vegas, waiting for a plane to arrive carrying star Peter Strauss (*Keys to Tulsa*, *The Last Tycoon*), the major investors, and the distributor. This was a pilot and plane Oliver had hired on the cheap, so he could stuff more money into the shooting budget.

The airplane appeared over the horizon, and then dropped toward the runway. The waiting entourage could see it did not have its landing gear down! No one on the ground had radio contact with the plane. They all ran into the flight path, waving their arms and screaming. The pilot assumed they were waving a greeting, so he feathered the engine, and brought the bird in on its bare belly. The damned plane hit with an incredible crunch! Sparks flew everywhere. The pilot freaked, frozen to the stick. The plane continued to screech its way along the asphalt for about two hundred yards. It finally came to a stop when it hit a cow pasture at the end of the runway. In one split second, Oliver envisioned the evening news, "Producer Hess burns up star, funding, and his future in a fountain of flaming cow shit just before filming commences."

Michael recalled an incident where, at a pot fueled wrap party, he had eaten his first ever marijuana-laced brownie. Mike was not used to drugs in any form, confectionery or combustible, and did not realize he had been affected until he suddenly found himself lying on his back in the middle of the floor while members of the cast and crew danced over and around his body. "God, you know what? I think I must be stoned." Actually, he was so wasted he couldn't get up. "So, I just lay there on the carpet, snapping my fingers in time to the music."

I was compelled to tell the story of Gary Graver's two-fer pillow: the one that was used to simulate pregnancy on the set of *The Hard Road* and then as a hunchback on actor J.L. Clark (*The Forest, Trick or Treat*) on another where Gary was moonlighting.

Mike countered with a droll recall of a film he directed titled *The Pink Motel*, which was loosely based on a screenplay I had written for him years before called *Secret Places*. Mike's movie required a certain amount of nudity and he had cast a statuesque blond in one of the lead roles. However, the lady had had some breast augmentation and when the time came for her to appear topless, Mike was horrified to see that her breasts were of entirely different shapes, one dropping very low, toward the southern hemisphere, the other, smaller and shaped like a snow cone, pointed skyward. The nipples also were of different colors and sizes. They, too, pointed in opposite directions, like the eyes of a carp. The actress, however, was unaware of the problem, and seemed quite proud in showing them off. Mike, not wanting to hurt her feelings, went ahead and shot her scenes anyway, re-staging them in order to hide, as much as possible, her remarkable superstructure from camera.

"And then," he laughed, "there was Ms. Phyllis Diller, who was one of my stars. The main set was a motel that had been painted a light pink. She kept referring to it as 'going to work in that giant bottle of Pepto-Bismol!'"

It was now almost three in the morning. Time to pull the shades on the night before we both ended up on the floor, snapping our fingers. I gave Mike a pillow and blanket so he could sack out on the couch. Our futures, after all, would be arriving at sunup.

> *More persons, on the whole, are humbugged by believing nothing than by believing too much.*
>
> —Phineas T. Barnum, 1857

Some folks are such good salesmen they can literally sell used condoms to a sailor. Such a fellow was the aforementioned Mr. Barnum, and also, such was my new partner, Mike MacFarland. Mike could actually turn lettuce into lettuce, the vegetable into the bankable stuff, the paper kind. Mike set out to raise the funding for *The Pyramid*. I had given us a small start with investments from Ms. Halloway, Bloodworth, and Miami. Michael hit the byways of northern California with gusto, determined to succeed. He would drive the backcountry, scoping out the most prosperous looking farmland of the great Sacramento valley. If he happened upon a prosperous looking platte, he would literally park his car on the roadside and walk into the fields to find *El Jefe*, the Boss. Once located, Mike would charm him into attending an informal presentation of *The Pyramid*. This get-together would usually include the farmer's friends, associates, relatives, people who trusted each other more than they did the fruit-frost warnings or the movers and shakers who sat around town in suits and ties.

As soon as Mike had assembled one of these meetings, he would bring me in to explain the storyline. Now, I was born on a wheat ranch and I know country folk because I am one. All I had to do was be honest. No high-falutin' or snake handlin' necessary. "I myself am weary," I began, "worn out by New Age gurus and the promise of nirvana a few deep breaths away, and I also have a killer backache from the burden of shouldering the lies, deceit, mistakes, and outright incompetence of the status quo. The past? One cannot have a future if they are living in the past.

"Our President has disgraced out country; we are still bogged down in a no-end-in-sight war in Vietnam. My beautiful sister Patricia McCann, one of California's most popular and celebrated educators, has just been diagnosed with Lou Gehrig's Disease (Amyotrophic Lateral Sclerosis). I know as well as anyone that the world is not cool. It is a tough, tough customer, the world. A dangerous place, affording mostly only scratch space, little more than elbow room, really, for the struggle to survive. Now, the question is, 'Does it always have to be that way?' Is there hope? If so, what? Where is this *hope* to be found? Is there anything at all on the human horizon that promises a brighter, saner, more worthwhile future for us and our families, for humanity's crossbearers, so to speak? Well, our film is going to find out!"

After I finished my inspirational tale, which no one understood or cared about, Mike would again take the stage, and remind them that a modest investment could bring in enough money to pay off their bank loans, or maybe get them by until after harvest. Enough said. The money came to us in dribs and drabs, but it came in.

I was asked to fly into Burbank to meet with MacFarland for lunch at Patty's Restaurant on Riverside Drive. Tomi Barrett, my increasingly personal angel and fellow outlaw, accompanied me. Patty's Restaurant, a low-slung splash of white stucco hugging the roadway, is one step above a Denny's. Very popular with the valley studio crowd because of convenient location, genuine red-leather booths, dining on an outdoor patio, and a complimentary sidecar of marshmallow-drenched pineapple slices.

Tomi and I were early, so we spent a moment talking with Bernice, the warm, smiling waitress recently arrived from Germany. "Bernie" was still juggling her

English verbs, vowels, and consonants. *"Sei immer froh und wohlgemut, dann schmecktt auch der koffee gut!"* (Roughly translates to, "Be always happy, have your heart full of joy, then your coffee will taste much better.") Und don't haff der special. Itz da shitz!" I went for the coffee and the eggs-over; Tomi, the jumble of marshmallow.

When Mike arrived, he slid into the booth next to Tomi and dug immediately into her pot of sticky, white stuff. The marshmallow, always slightly warmer than room temperature, was a gummy goop that clung to spoon, hands, even one's hair, like cold cream at a teen sleepover. Still, an immersion in that mass of complimentary "goo" was the most popular ritual at Patty's Restaurant.

"Well," Mike announced, "I want you to go ahead and start casting the film. I have commitments for the rest of the funding!"

Hats off! Tomi and I kissed, a big, slobbery, marshmallowy kind of smooch. I may have even kissed MacFarland. I don't remember much about the moment other than those delicious seven little words, "We have the rest of the funding." I didn't even bother eating the eggs.

Casting a motion picture is an exciting, exacting, and frequently painful experience. It is exciting because something magic actually happens when a good actor or actress takes a bunch of strung together words and breathes life into them. Suddenly, a brand new human being steps from the text. It is much like the miracle of birth, only in this case, the baby emerges full blown, manifesting before your eyes, materializing from the vapor of idea into the hard stuff of being here now.

The rigors of casting, giving time and attention to an endless line of performers, each of whom deserves your honest evaluation, is exhausting. I often wonder how judges, who do this kind of thing daily, manage without a masseur, a handful of Excedrin, and a bottle of eighty-proof conveniently stashed nearby.

The painful part of casting is the rejection, or perceived rejection, when you must tell a performer they are just not right for, nor did they get, the part. It's like being deliberately cruel, a seemingly casual rending of the heart. There are so many actors and so little work.

Actors, like all artists, subsist largely on dreams, foregoing much of the ordinary pleasure of life for their art. They show up at auditions with the highest of hopes, and to be turned down is very much like dying a little.

> *They know themselves, and no one else can ever know them as they are; special, set aside, dedicated, game to the last painful breath; full of desperate mirth and quick with new beginnings, foolish and fond and generous and hopeful. Levity and courage are theirs, always courage, courage and levity; masters of emotion and slaves of emotion.*
>
> —Sidney Blackmer, *A Prayer For Actors*

Yet the director, if he/she is worthy of the title, must remain true to the vision of the film overall. He must select, not friends or family, but only those who make a particular character come truly alive, while also considering the demands of the budget, and the onerous task of deciding who will work well with whom under difficult, rigorous circumstances.

I cast most of the major roles in Los Angeles, out of an apartment I had rented on Riverside Drive. The apartment was a short distance from Patty's Restaurant, which had become our hangout, the go-to place for a quick culinary fix when the soul demanded vitalizing. This section of Burbank is quite lovely, clean and informal, with the sensuously rolling hills of Griffith Park just across the way. It has a middle class, pastoral feel that belies the fact it is backed against the 134 Freeway, a concrete scar cutting across the southern lip of the great San Fernando Valley, east to west.

The apartment itself was a unique two-story, nestled amidst a copse of aspens. Maybe only six units in all, each one had a private, bamboo-shrouded patio, which hid the front windows from street traffic. The second-story windows were actually large skylights, above your direct vision, yet letting in enough of the outside day and night to keep one connected to the universe. I had complete privacy in a city not at all known for privacy. My direct next-door neighbor was actor Randy Quaid (*The Last Detail*, *Brokeback Mountain*), and yet, such was the isolation that, in a year and a half, we seldom saw or heard one another.

I called my friend John Parker and asked him to read opposite those actors trying for parts in the film. It was mainly, then, just the two of us, John and I, in that little Burbank apartment, where, when we were ready, we just kicked open the doors and invited the world to audition.

Besides the real life scientists, psychics, etc. that I had signed for the picture, the major roles were Chris Lowe, our disillusioned TV reporter; his partner at station KTXT, LeMoyne Peabody; and Merleen, a confrontational therapist working with those on the fringes of emotional stability. Then there was Iris, LeMoyne's wife, a woman grown tired of feeding her husband and his ego without at least some emotional return; and Bubba Levenberg, a station intern at KTXT with his eye on Chris's job.

Agents started sending in their stable of actors, prepared and on schedule. Suddenly, the word got around. Before we could lock the gates, it seemed the whole citizenry of Hollywood showed up for a reading. Thespians were popping in and out of doors and windows like bloody cat burglars. Because of the nature of the story, and the promise of being part of something new, unusual, and transforming, actors became obsessive-compulsive. I began to receive gifts from those who had read: flowers, liqueurs, expensive shirts. Some wrote letters that would break your heart, begging for a spot on the team. Because of tragedy or devastation in their personal lives, they felt emotionally connected to anything that promised something positive. Yes, casting, an endeavor that should be forever joyous, is frequently quite raw and painful, often requiring small, frequent doses of liquid medication.

First, I cast Tomi as Merleen, the therapist who had to be able to get under the skin of her patients; able to lead and take control, and yet, privately able to let down the fences and face her own vulnerability. Tomi had the talent, the understanding, the right look, and the persona for the role. John Parker was cast as pig farmer Dick Hogerty, a wizened old troll being evicted from his property to make way for the use of land developers and the expansion of their bank accounts.

We eventually cast a young actor named Charlie Brown (I swear the name is true) in the lead male role, reporter Chris Lowe. Charlie did not have a lot of film experience, but he had that boyish, exuberant air we needed for the part. He was tall, rangy, about six three with a head full of blond curls—a country lad from Colorado who had not yet lost his innocence. He could also play guitar and sing, a requisite for the role. Ira Hawkins (*The Perfect Holiday, Freedomland*), a gifted black actor from Chicago, nailed his reading for LeMoyne Peabody, the ambitious news reporter and Chris Lowe's partner.

Late one afternoon, a tall, beautiful actress with an incredibly low and soothing speaking voice, showed up to audition for the part of Iris, LeMoyne's harried wife. Her name was June Christopher (*Baby Luv, Doctor Doolittle*). Besides acting, June had been a backup singer for Grammy-winning singer/songwriter, Janis Ian (*Society's Child, At Seventeen*). Christopher was statuesque, six-feet tall, a sensuous presence who projected the sort of inner strength and fortitude I thought necessary for the role.

Some wise filmmaker once said, "There are no small roles, only small actors." That was certainly the case with *The Pyramid*. The film was stuffed with characters, just plain folks, children, animals, musicians, religious fanatics, and some who possessed only the vaguest of human characteristics. I remember one young bloke who informed John and I that he could walk through walls. "*If this is true,*" marveled Mr. Boo, "*then it's worth the price of a new wall just to witness the event.*" The poor fellow walked directly into the wall, smashing his nose in the process. "*Damn it,*" he cried, "*I could do it yesterday!*"

The story required a young mother to hear a siren's wail and know instinctively her child has been injured. She must dash into the street in her nightgown, where upon seeing her babe lying on a stretcher, she must slip immediately into believable hysterics, literally falling apart on camera. End of role! Another actor, a shut off, evasive salesman named Phil, must attend one of Merleen's therapy sessions, and, upon being goaded by the group, is required to break into uncontrollable sobbing, confessing he is consumed with fear over the breakup of his marriage.

I needed spoon benders, Buddhists, witches, ghosts, firewalkers, purveyors of pornographic pictures, children to be eviscerated and mutilated in the crash of a school bus. The script required a Navy boatswain's mate, a pyramidologist, a barroom brawler, several trigger-happy policemen, an aged guru in a steam bath, etc. If someone could just happen to be able to walk through walls, I mean, really, really, really walk through walls, so much the better.

> *If music be the food of love, play on,*
> *Give me excess of it; that surfeiting,*
> *The appetite may sicken, and so die.*
>
> —William Shakespeare, *Twelfth Night*

It is a mystery to me how we ended up with so many incredible and legendary musicians in *The Pyramid*. Some had yet to be discovered, and some were already icons in music circles. Actor Michael Ashe (*The Pickle, Jackson County Jail*), an old friend, had been hired to play Phil the salesman tortured by the shredding of his marriage. Ashe's good friend was Vaughn Meador, whose hilarious *First Family Album*, parodying the life of John F. Kennedy, had won two Grammys and been named Comedy Album of the Year before the assassination of JFK put an end to his career as a comic. "What people don't know," said Ashe, "is that Vaughn is a brilliant singer/songwriter. Someone needs to give him a shot, or he's going to starve to death."

John Parker and I traveled into the Hollywood hills where Meader was living in a vacant apartment loaned to him by his manager. The only furniture in the place was a card table, two chairs, and an upright piano. Meader was a small, chunky man, with a large head and chest. His hair was dark and straight, rather short for the fashion of the times. His eyes, though, were striking. They were large, intensely bright, bulging slightly beneath his thick, Eastern European eyebrows. I guessed him to be about forty-years old.

After some small talk and a sip of instant coffee, Meader sat down at the piano and began to play, beautifully with a surprising energy and panache. We were impressed. Then he began to sing. He was low-voiced, with a macho depth to his held notes as clear and strong as the best bass-baritones from the Metropolitan. In fact, his voice was so full of the stuff of life, so pungent with the call of joy, with the echo of agony and pain that Parker and I began to cry. It couldn't be helped; Meader's voice and lyrics were that emotionally powerful. We signed him on the spot to write and perform several original songs for *The Pyramid*.

Vaughn Meader, as the saying goes, had friends in high places, and he called some of them together to help him lay down his musical creations for our film.

Doug Dillard, of the famous Dillard family of musicians, would play the banjo and serve as music coordinator. Doug, a legendary picker, hailed from Salem, Missouri. He brought along his friend John Hartford to play the fiddle. John Hartford is a music icon, revered by the likes of Eric Clapton, Glen Campbell, Johnny Cash, etc. Like Dillard, Hartford was a multi-award winner, a Missouri river rat who could pick, sing, fiddle, and clog like a friggin' frog-strangler, all at the same time. And, he is in just about every musical hall of fame in existence. His last gig was a solo in *O Brother, Where Art Thou*, starring George Clooney.

Meader wrote the music and lyrics for all of the songs in *The Pyramid*, played keyboards, and sang the vocals. An example of his lyrics for the film:

You never know freedom 'til you lose it
you never know love until it's gone
you never know the right way 'til you chose it
you never see the ending 'til it's gone.
You never miss the water 'til the well runs dry
you never miss the fire 'til it grows cold
you never notice how fast the time flies...
'til you turn around and suddenly you're old...

—Vaughn Meader, "Time Flies," *The Pyramid*, 1975

Meader backed his vocals with a trio of singers and spoon players right out of the Appalachian foothills. The lead role in *The Pyramid*, after all, was a country boy, struggling to make it through the angst, confusion, and cynicism of life in the big city.

Another serendipitous stroke of luck occurred during the filming of a scene at the Faces bar in Dallas. The meat of the moment was a conversation between Chris Lowe and Merleen, the therapist. I remarked to Tomi (Merleen) while she was getting her makeup that, although the dialogue took place at a club table, I wished that I had a singer for background ambiance. It was impossible to find a country-western bar anywhere in Texas without a country-western singer. Unfortunately, I had squeezed every shilling out of MacFarland for the budget, and he wasn't about to let loose of another penny. The makeup artist, a lithe young lady from Texas, about eighteen-years old with long, auburn hair falling almost to her waist, suddenly interrupted, "I'm a singer. And, I'll do it for nothing. Just gimme the chance." Her name was Karen Brooks.

We borrowed a guitar from someone in the crew. Karen auditioned on the spot, while the juicers pulled cable, the set dressers dressed, the prop people were propping, not an atmosphere conducive to serious listening. Karen was magnificent, with a voice so plaintiff and heartfelt I wanted to adopt her as my little sister. Karen performs two of her original songs in *The Pyramid*.

I'm wastin' my time singing a sad song
But it gives me the time to think of you
If I can hold on, even though your gone
It brings me back to the pleasure we knew.

—Karen Brooks, "Fool For A Tender Touch," *The Pyramid*

At their table, Merleen and Lowe are discussing the importance of getting straight, gluing, if you will, all of the pieces together that make a human being whole again. At a table in the background, Iris, LeMoyne's wife, is sharing drinks with another man while her husband sits at the bar, hurting, seething with resentment.

The scene ends with LeMoyne starting a fight, then bolting from the bar, consumed with guilt and anger over his failure to deal with his life as a real person, not just a personality. His friend Chris chases after him. The barroom, only momentarily disturbed, quickly returns to its liquored-up chatter, and all of the while, Karen Brooks sits alone on stage, quietly singing the haunting lyric that speaks for all of those who try so hard, and fail so severely:

I couldn't stay here if I wanted,
I couldn't stay here if I tried
'cause you were always disappointed in me
I couldn't ever do anything right

—Karen Brooks, "Cards On The Table," *The Pyramid*

Later in her career, Karen would write, sing, and record with iconic artists such as Townes Van Zandt, Jerry Jeff Walker, Steve Fromholz, and Rodney Crowell. She had several hits on Billboard's Top Country Chart, and in the mid-90s, along with co-writer T.G. Shepherd, she made it to number one with "New Way Home." Just your normal Texas makeup artist, outlaw princess?

Bad luck is better than no luck at all, maybe so. This was borne out at the final day of recording, when Vaughn Meader gathered the boys and girls together at the mix, and then did so much blow, he blew the deal. His voice was a mere whisper, a rasp of air over snow-ravaged vocal chords, mucho mental mis-timing. When McFarland and I listened to the track, we realized we didn't have an ending song, nothing even close. Mike said he would repair the damage and hired a local commercial jingle singer to record the song.

"Well, at least he's sober," Mike commented.

Once you have made the commitment to be an outlaw, it pretty much becomes a way of life. It not only guarantees little security or anything resembling backup, it absolutely promises that folks expect little from you but trouble. Such is the case with outlaw filmmakers; otherwise we'd be sitting at the major studios, sucking up and selling out, while a committee decides how we should do our work. What we get in return is the right to pretty much do things our way, in good conscience, of course. If it's cheap and you can do it, "What the hell? Hurry it up, then. We're not talkin' steak here, we're talkin' hot dogs."

In that stead, I found myself sitting on a bench inside a secondhand recording studio in a raggedy-eared section of West Hollywood, preparing to mix the final sound track on *The Pyramid*. I was out of funds, out of steam, out of milk and honey, pissed off, played out, and still, I was not happy with the closing song. "Help me, Boo!" Then, from out of the etheric dust in the deep interior of the old building, an angel appeared, much like the mysterious "Rose Angel" in Dallas so many months previous, only this was a very corpulent black angel. He slumped his huge body next to mine on the bench. He was a bit out of sorts, shifting his weight around, making groaning noises, wiping his brow and shaking his head back and forth like a trout fighting the hook. After a bit, we started a conversation. "I'm a great soul, bluesman, man," he insisted. "I been put to the fire. Everybody's coverin' my songs, and yet, except for in the South, nobody is hearin' me. I can't get arrested here on the West Coast."

Well, I was an outlaw filmmaker, who desperately needed a singer and song to close my picture, someone who didn't sound like they were shilling toiletries. We looked at each other for about three minutes, and then, next thing I knew, I was showing him my film. The last scene in the movie is a panoramic shot of Dick Hogarty, the pig farmer, leading a parade of children through the sunlight and shadow of a large city park. Reaching an idyllic clearing, they join a group of the cast members, sitting under a huge, open-sided pyramid. Everyone begins to clap hands. (This was originally done to a playback of Vaughn Meader singing his closing theme.) Now, without the music, they were all just sitting there, clapping to some imaginary tune. The shot pulls back and up to the peak of the pyramid. It then holds on a corona of light as hot and bright as the first light of creation. Eureka!

After watching the ending, the morose giant seated next to me agreed to write and perform my closing song for next to nothing, for peanuts, really, and I agreed to let him do it.

He wrote the song, "Ring, Ring, Ring," words and music, overnight. We recorded it the following afternoon. It was incredibly perfect.

Sing, sing, sing, let your voices ring, ring, ring
A song of love—a lesson we all can bring, bring, bring
Sing a song of liberty, sing for peace and harmony
Sing a song for you and me
and together we will bring love to the world
To every man, woman, boy and girl
Sing, sing, sing
Come on, just a little bit louder now
Sing, sing, sing
Sing with just a little more love
Let your voices ring, ring
Sing a song for you and me, sing a song of liberty
Sing from sea to shining sea, and together we can
Ahh, just a little more love now
Let your voices ring, ring, ring
That's it, all together now, together we can
we can bring, bring, bring
Love to the world...and (massive crescendo)
together we will sing, sing, sing
Sing-g-g-g Sing-g-g-g Sing-g-g-g-g!

—Solomon Burke, "Ring, Ring, Ring," *The Pyramid*, 1977

This, then, was the work of Solomon Burke, who, today, is a legend in gospel, blues, rock and roll, jazz, and country. Musical masters such as Eric Clapton, Tom Waits, Tom Petty, and Bruce Springsteen have called him "the greatest soul singer of all time." A member of the Rock and Roll Hall of Fame, Burke's songs have been covered by the likes of The Rolling Stones, Bob Dylan, Otis Redding, Sam Cooke, Van Morrison, Elvis Costello, etc. He has been asked by two separate popes to sing at the Vatican, and yet, when we met, Solomon and I were just two simple country boys, one outlaw, one journeyman, in need of each other. *"God bless you!"* shouted Boo. *"Both o' you guys!"*

Chapter Sixteen

Directors Gary Kent, Richard Rush, Chuck Bail, Austin, Texas, 2007.
Photo courtesy of the author.

Guns, Psychics, Leprosy, And Love

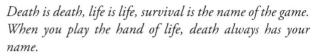

Death is death, life is life, survival is the name of the game.
When you play the hand of life, death always has your
name.

—Scribbled on the wall of a Death Row cell at
Huntsville Prison

Charlie "C.W." Brown, lead actor in *The Pyramid*, was dead! Murdered! Gunned down by a shameless, nameless coward. His body lying face down a few feet inside the stockroom of an innocuous liquor store on Ventura Boulevard in North Hollywood, California. His beautiful young life snuffed out by a deadly blast to the center of his back from an over-and-under. Charlie's blood had barely begun to pool when they, the customers who couldn't figure out why no one was minding the register, found him.

Most people do not want to believe bad things happen for no reason. There must be meaning behind the suffering, the theft, the beating, the death. Charlie had dropped by Spirit Cellar Liquors to run the register for a couple of hours so a close pal could visit his girlfriend. After only a short time in Hollywood, he had successfully completed a lead role in his first movie, and was sporting a new car, a new apartment, a new agent, a new 'tude. No, he didn't need the work, just doing a favor for a friend, that's all. And, some ultimate asshole took a shotgun and blew poor Charlie Brown away. A robbery, the cops said, that netted him (or them) about $65. Here, then, is how it all came down.

The filming of *The Pyramid* was a wild, wacky, and wonderful experience from the get go. Like most of those slogging out the making of a movie, we forgot the outside world. The movie set became our world, and we ignored the fact that off the set, beyond the security guards, and the "Film in progress" signs, the real planet earth was spinning along, largely mismanaged by the selfish, the greedy, the thoughtless, paranoid, cruel, and folks convinced that "God" was on their side.

It was hot and humid as a Guatemalan jungle during filming, the usual weather for summer in Big D. Yet, with the help of salt tablets and copious amounts of Gatorade, we persevered.

Besides Charlie Brown, Tomi, Ira Hawkins, June Christopher, and the aforementioned musicians, I had assembled a grab bag full of leaders in the field of consciousness research. For example, astronaut Mitchell; Dr. Thelma Moss, a professor of neuropsychiatry at UCLA; Jack Gray, a noted alternative healer; a group of Buddhist monks; a coven of witches; Komar the Magnificent, a cheese manufacturer from Minnesota whose specialty was walking across fire as a demonstration of mind over matter; and lastly, Clive Baxter, ex-FBI agent and America's foremost polygraph expert whose work recording the emotional quotient of living plants had inspired much of the agricultural breakthroughs practiced at the world-famous Findhorn Gardens in Scotland.

From Los Angeles, I brought my son, actor Greg McKellan, along with established character actors John Parker, Erv Sanders (*Jessi's Girls, Rainy Day Friends*), and famed Polish dramatist Leonides Ossetynski (*The Man in the Glass Booth, Troll*), and threw them into the pudding along with local performers Jean Compton, Barbara Morris, Kim and Michelle Russell, Madelyn and Brad Ruekberg, Adrian, Lucette, and Rex Cumming, TV announcer Larry Ratliff, and Lt. Dave Bidelman of the Dallas Police Department.

The crew was a combo of West Coast and Texas rounders, highlighted by director of photography, Bill Weaver (*Everything's Cool, Gone in 60 Seconds*), co-inventor of the Weaver-Steadman Fluid Camera Head. (The invention won a Technical Achievement Award from The American Society of Camera Operator.) Bill's assistants were a cherubic imp named Leslie Otis (*Grand Theft Auto, The Hills Have Eyes*) and seriously dark and handsome Doug Oliveres (*Windtalkers, Jurassic Park*). My very good friend Art Names was the sound mixer and his boom-person was his wife Peggy Waggoner (*Charlie Wilson's War, Blades of Glory*). Dan Dusek repeated as location scout; key grip was Steve Ferry (*In the Heat of the Night, American Me*) who, under much pleading from the illustrious director, also acted the role of Pat Merinen, the fatuous station manager. Steve's wife Emily (*Raging Bull, Get Shorty*) was the property master. Crane operator was Bill Pecchi, Sr., whose son Bill, Jr., was Richard Rush's favorite grip.

We shot the heck out of the Big D and a serious hunk of Los Angeles, as well. Once we started, there was no stopping us. Talk about a street gang! We were the first company to film in the exact spot in the garage at the city jail where nightclub owner Jack Ruby had shot Lee Harvey Oswald, the murderer of John F. Kennedy.

We had our reporters Chris and LeMoyne drive the same route Kennedy took past the book depository on that fateful day in 1963 when he was assassinated. (Chris shudders as he looks up at the window where the killer first took aim.)

We created our own pig farm smack dab in the middle of downtown Big D. We staged a gunfight between Dallas cops and a few surly teenage hoodlums, and, when a school bus driven by a local stuntman was supposed to crash and roll, but didn't, I rolled the bus with a winch, then went inside with a handheld camera and filmed the children flopping around in the seats, falling to the floor, slamming against the bus ceiling. One of the more adventurous kids, young, eager, and athletic Rex Cumming, volunteered to punch his head and shoulders through a candy glass window giving us the most dramatic shot of the whole stunt sequence, sold by an eleven-year-old stunt kid. When spliced together the crash and roll were dubbed world class by the critics.

Since we held a devil-may-care, seat-of-the-pants kind of filmic energy, we were open to any and every thing. We staged, improvised, and imagined scenes, then manifested and filmed them. We ended up capturing what appeared to be a real ghost on camera; Komar the Magnificent successfully walked across his burning coals; we held a group therapy session in which cast and crew participated, ending with many of them actually breaking down on and off camera, having been forced to confront some of the personal demons they had stuffed away in the darkened closets of their psyches.

In Los Angeles, we took Captain Mitchell to the Griffith Park Observatory, where he spoke spontaneously to a gathering of L.A. schoolchildren about his moon travels. This while the kids were, for the first time in their lives, actually observing the immediate universe through the Griffith telescope. The Captain then segued into a discussion on consciousness: what it is, where it can be found in the vast, seeming void of the universe, and where it resides inside the inner space of our own selves. Heady stuff, but the kids loved it. The children were encouraged to ask whatever they wished from of the good Captain. My son Michael (age six) popped the first question, "Well, how did you go to the bathroom on the moon?"

We filmed a group of students at Hollywood High School who were experimenting with talking to some houseplants, while ignoring others. The plants that received the most love, if you will, far outgrew the ones that were ignored. We also filmed, with hidden cameras, several psychics who swore they could bend metal with their minds and influence the behavior of objects placed randomly on a table. All of these proved to be a disappointment. In every case the cameras discovered evidence of fraudulent and subversive manipulation.

In the sparse living room of a house high on a Malibu cliff, Merleen and Chris Lowe are banging a bong, recovering from having spent the night looking for Chris' angry and disoriented friend, LeMoyne Peabody. It is early morning and having just awoke they are nearly naked as newborns. Chris is shirtless and barefoot; Merleen is dressed in a tank top and bikini bottoms. The couple are stoned out of their trees, munching from bowls of fresh raspberries and cream while discussing the impact of LeMoyne's pain on those who care for him. Eventually, their conversation wanders into the speculative terrain of the altered state.

> *In its accomplishment, for all spiritually evolved persons, the communion of bodies becomes the communion of souls.*
>
> —Havelock Ellis, writer and philosopher

Merleen rolls over on her back, beginning a series of slow, catlike calisthenics to get her body breathing. Chris watches, enthralled. Merleen moves to a large picture window with a magnificent view of the Pacific Ocean. As the sun is rising, the outline of her figure is thrown into dark silhouette. She moves gracefully, bending, twisting slowly in a virtual, visual mating dance. She motions for Chris to join her. It is easy to see by his movements he lacks her physical suppleness, but he tries. Gradually, they move closer to one another, two shadowy shapes sliding sensuously through a small space in time, then, he loses balance, starts to fall. She catches him ever so gently; cautiously, they embrace. Then, just as slowly, remove their clothing. They kiss and sink from frame, leaving only the view of a gigantic sunburst over the ocean.

A little stagy perhaps, erotic, certainly, thanks to Tomi. However, once they start their physical movements, everything, skin tone, texture, etc., is absorbed into a mere shape of shadows. As such, we may observe without prurience or voyeurism, the mating ritual of the hormones.

Al Goldstein, editor of *Screw* magazine, dubbed my movie pornographic; not for its visuals or subject matter, but for its new ideas and its challenge of real pornography. In defense of this particular scene, which begins, after all with two people smoking pot and ending with what must be assumed as premarital sex, I will quote an unsolicited review from *Parents Magazine*:

> *The photography and scene structure are quite impressive. Several sequences jump to mind. Two lovers silhouetted against the dawn momentarily drop their identity as characters in a story and become the anonymous, golden ideal of modern romantic love.*
>
> —*Parents Magazine*, April 1976

We screened *The Pyramid* in New York for the major reviewers and for various consciousness groups and individuals. When we had gathered enough quotes to make an impressive press packet, we took the film to Texas, opening simultaneously in Dallas, Houston, San Antonio, and Austin. Tomi and Charlie, as the stars, were absolutely radiant. Captain Edgar Mitchell was given the Keys to the city of San Antonio. In Austin, Tomi, Charlie, John Parker, and I hung out in the lobby to get audience comments when they emerged from the theater. The first audience member out, a burly, trucker-type, snorted, "Fuck it. It didn't have anything to do with fuckin' pyramids. I couldn't even understand the fuckin' thing." This is a direct quote. The next viewer however, a woman, about twenty-three years old, laid her hand on Tomi's arm and purred, "I want everyone I love to see this movie!" That was enough for me.

As expected, some reviewers and audience members were left totally confused by *The Pyramid*. In general, however, the reviews and comments were very encouraging for a first time filmmaker and his merry band of curious outlaws:

> *Recalls Haskell Wexler's groundbreaking film,* Medium Cool.
>
> —Phillip Morales, *Los Angeles Times*

> *Throughout the film there is a gauzy quality of cinematography that is quite as beautiful as the city of Dallas itself—but also a brooding interface of looming malevolence, something about not just this city, but any city where men do other men harm.*
>
> —Dick Hitt, *Dallas Morning News*

> *There are car crashes, romance, and shootouts. But, above all, there is the exploration of new ideas. This is clearly a film for thinking individuals.*
>
> —Bridget Byrne, *Los Angeles Herald-Examiner*

In 1976, actor Orson Bean, appearing on *The Tonight Show* with Johnny Carson called *The Pyramid* "one of the two best films of the year."

In the fall of 2003, Austin film writer and historian Joe O'Connell spotted a copy of *The Pyramid* sitting on a shelf in my garage. He hauled it out and screened it at a local film festival. The house was packed. The festival was covered by Julie Moody, a reviewer for *Fox News*, who heralded it as the "best of 70s Cinema."

In July of 2007, *The Pyramid* received a rave review in *The Boston Globe* some thirty years after the film was completed. Here is an abridged version of it.

> *This heartfelt time capsule of the 70s offers timeless inspiration, plus, it's the real deal—the type of urgently, feel-good movie Hollywood can only dream of making. It is so solid and uplifting that I actually feel honored to have seen it, having caught a rare and short-lived VHS release. The movie's*

own pyramid-like structure makes for a brilliant enclosing of so many inspired and funky characters it is impossible not to be fascinated; the range includes turned-on hippies, Kirlian photography, spoon bending, pig-farmers, ex-astronauts, Wiccans, murderers and ghost hunters. This movie will move your soul for a long time to come, because, as much or more than any Capra fantasy, it knows what a wonderful life it really can be.

—Carl Schroeder, *Boston Globe*, July 2007

So then, what happened? After all of this seeming success and resounding praise, how did *The Pyramid* end up being a film few people even know exists, and how did its star, the young, multi-talented Charlie "C.W." Brown end up dead, lying in a pool of his own blood on the cold, concrete floor of a North Hollywood liquor store? Persian poet, Omar Khayyam, says it best:

Ah, Love! Could thou and I with fate conspire to grasp this sorry scheme of things entire— Would not we shatter it to bits—and then re-mould it nearer to the hearts desire?

—Omar Khayyam, *The Rubaiyat*

Charlie Brown's funeral was held at The Little Brown Church in Studio City. The place was packed, overflowing with friends, fans, and family. Charlie had been much loved. His mother had arrived from Denver. She held tightly to my arm as I walked her into the service.

"He was such a hard luck kid, my kid," she whispered. "I remember, Gary, when Charlie first made the football team in junior high. He was so happy. I drove by the field to see him, and parked across the street. He came over to show me his new uniform and a car hit him and broke his leg, 'Hard Luck Charlie,' we called him, and now this!" Mrs. Brown broke into tears.

After the services, we all adjourned to actor James Dobson's house for commiseration and refreshments. Dobson (*Orphan Train*, *Knot's Landing TV*) and Charlie had been close friends, and he was hosting the Brown family while they were in town.

"Well, Kent, you gave Charlie his dream. He always wanted to star in a movie, and you gave him the shot." *Yeah*, I thought. *Big deal*. If you can get past the idea that cruelty and insanity are actually bad things. "*God bless Hard Luck Charlie*," Boo cried softly.

The future had been looking promising for Charlie, and for the rest of us, after the initial opening of *The Pyramid*. Mike MacFarland took a print to Cannes where it caused a small ripple among the big guns at the festival.

On the home front, Chuck Bail, who had scored a minor hit with his first directing gig, *Black Sampson*, was now directing *Cleopatra Jones and The Casino of Gold*, written by my good friend, Max Julien.

Jack Nicholson took home Best Actor honors from the Academy for his role in *One Flew Over the Cuckoo's Nest*, and Brian De Palma had just finished his outré masterwork, *Carrie*, starring Cissy Spacek.

Al Adamson was hastily capitalizing on the success of blaxploitation with his ultra-violent *Black Samurai*; Paul Lewis was producing *The Van*, starring future Oscar-winner Danny DeVito; Monte Hellman was just fresh from directing the brilliant, austere *Cockfighter*, starring Warren Oates and Harry Dean Stanton. Monte's tagline was: "He came into town with his cock in his hand, and what he did with it was illegal in 49 states!" Next, Hellman began serving as replacement director for Tom Gries on *The Greatest*, a semi-autobiographical film penned by and starring boxing legend Muhammad Ali.

My old pal Vic Tayback was working so much he could at last afford to have the broken window replaced in his modest home. Actually, he replaced the whole house, moving with wife Sheila and son Christopher to an upscale abode in a tony section of Glendale. Vic had copped a lead role in the hit series *Alice*, and was also starring in a film for multi-award winning director Robert Aldrich (*The Dozen*, *Hustle*) entitled *The Choirboys*. ("Go ahead, bitch, jump.") The film also starred James Woods and Randy Quaid. It seemed if one could ignore the fact that rampant sex and violent behavior were still much in vogue, then things in the world of cinema were actually improving over the tumultuous 60s.

Hello, World, It's Us!

Tomi and I were elated, in a fit of euphoria, actually, operating under the influence of more magic dust than common sense. We looked into each other's eyes, hooked fingers, spun around three times, and decided to get married! "This time, Kent, it's going to really be forever, and then some," the beautiful blonde angel from Texas insisted. We decided to wed on the high seas, and so, chartered *The MV Princess*, gliding into the blue Pacific out of San Pedro Harbor, accompanied by several guests, family and close friends, and a couple of stowaways none of us had ever seen before.

The music folk from L.A. and Big D kept everyone dancing in spite of the fact that most were seasick as bloody landlubbing preschoolers. The partiers included Tomi's eighty-two-year-old grandmother Lucille and Dan Cady, the producer of Chuck Bail's successful action flick *Black Sampson*. Cady would later "off" the twenty-eight-year-old leader of a bike gang when the bloke ignored his warning, and tried to turn Dan's sixteen-year-old daughter onto hard drugs. Yeah, our wedding, a hearty, hilarious, uniting of disparate pirates and soulful people on the open seas. *"Arrgghhh, I say!"* Boo said. We kept tongues wagging for months after returning to port. *"Luckily,"* Boo sighed, *"nobody fell overboard."*

Life is a mystery to be lived, not a problem to be solved.

—Father Adrian Van Kamm

When I received the news of the cold-blooded murder of actor Charlie Brown, Tomi and I had just returned from our honeymoon on Molokai. I was sitting on the couch of the Burbank apartment, reading the L.A. headlines. They mostly concerned a series of brutal killings that had left female victims dropped like refuse alongside the city freeways. Some unknown sicko, dubbed The Hillside Strangler by the L.A. press, had been capturing, raping, then killing young women in the Hollywood area. They had just discovered victim number fourteen lying alongside the Glendale freeway, a frog's hop away from the apartment.

The Hillside Strangler was afoot, literally a few feet from my apartment! I was giving Tomi a lesson in self-defense when the news of Charlie Brown's demise by shotgun came blaring across the news channels. It was a blow below the belt, up close and personal; yet, Charlie's death was just one of many that occurred in L.A. around that time. The press blamed the robbery-killings on Clarence "Tookie" Williams and his violent gang of street thugs known as the Crips. The M.O. of the Crips was to rob small convenience stores and leave no witness alive to do the identifyin' in the ever more frequent line-ups at the Glass House.

As author Charles Dickens might have reminded us, "These were the best of times and the worst of times." Richard Nixon had stepped down as president, but Gerald Ford continued the rampage in Vietnam and fanned the flames of the national angst regarding same. Elvis Presley, America's favorite hip-banging rock-n-roller, keeled over like a smacked mackerel and gave up the ghost on the floor of his bathroom in Graceland, his mansion in Memphis, Tennessee. He was forty-two.

Musically, the country had segued from folk, blues, and rock and roll into the grating clash of noise known as "Punk." Punk had primarily been sort of a homeschooled cry of protest against just about everything and nothing at all, led by bands with names certain to curl the hair on moms and pops worldwide, names like "The Sex Pistols" and "The Clash." Artists like Patti Smith and The Ramones advocated anarchy, at least as far as music was concerned. Then suddenly, everyone decided "the way out of here" was to dance out. A perky, sometimes suggestive, always danceable music genre known as "Disco" swept Punk aside, and cruised us safely through the mid-to-late 1970s.

The late 70s were much like the roaring 20s, only girls and gin had been replaced by girls and "bamba" or "snow" (cocaine), and a sometimes deadly, highly addictive practice known as freebasing—smoking coke from a water pipe or a bong. This allowed users to bypass the tender mucous membrane and get right to damaging the big guys, the lungs, liver, and heart. Freebasing, or "basing," is highly flammable. This was the trip that turned comedian Richard Pryor into a human sparkler, almost ending his life.

The supposed in-crowd was crowding into Studio 54 in New York and Gazzari's and The Whiskey in Los Angeles. There, once safely past the tight door security, they snorted the line or cooked up the marching powder, and proceeded to dance the night away, ignoring reality as much as possible. The music had a pounding monotonous beat, with lyrics both repetitive and frolicsome. There were no slow dances. Here, all was sexual energy and strut. The Queen of Disco was a tall, dark chanteuse named Donna Summer, whose seductive alto invited one and all to the party ("Let's Dance," "Bad Girls," "I Work Hard For The Money"). Everyone's favorite group was The Pointer Sisters ("I'm So Excited," "Slow Hand," "Wang Wang Doodle"), or KC and The Sunshine Band ("Shake Your Booty"). The Bee Gees, however, were the beloved boys of the decade, stepping in to save disco just as disco was doing a dive.

The brothers Gibb, with their falsetto harmonies sounding much like a gang of gerbils wearing undersized jockey shorts, came straight at us from the Isle of Man in the UK. Barry, Robin, Maurice, and later, younger brother Andy, dominated disco and pop for at least a decade with memorable pieces such as "Night Fever," "Stayin' Alive," "How Deep Is Your Love," "I Gotta Get a Message to You," "Massachusetts," "Islands in the Stream," "Nights on Broadway." Their songs were heavily played on music stations worldwide and were the mainline attraction on Burt Sugarman's highly watched *Midnight Special* TV show.

I was trying to force my way into an inside lane of traffic on the Hollywood freeway, just where Highland Avenue spews into the fast lane, turning a packed on-ramp into a mad dash deadlier than the Pamplona Bull Run. At this point, I had about ten seconds to maneuver through four lanes of bumper-to-bumper, pissed off, caffeine fueled traffic-meisters to nab a chance of making it to the Burbank off-ramp, my eventual goal. It was rush hour, which meant that on the Hollywood, cars careened along at about eighty per, bumper-to-bumper. However, I was in a stunt guy kinda mode, energized by the Brothers Gibb blaring from my radio their smash-mouth homage to spunk, "Jive Talkin'." I saw about a half-car length of daylight and went for it. *"Zoom. Take a chance,"* chortled Boo.

Motivated by angst and anger, I bullied my way through velocity X metallica times one hundred until I reached the safety of the Burbank turnoff. I was coming from a high-rise office in Beverly Hills, having just fired the distributor of *The Pyramid*. When Tomi and I returned from the islands, this clown was throwing out piles of fairy dust instead of answers, so I did some fact checking. I found out that he had been cooking the books, violating the contract like a pedophilic uncle driving his niece to the junior prom the long way. Tales of bad/dishonest distributors are so rampant in Hollywood, they're practically a mantra. I was madder than a herd of Texas fire ants and I fired him on the spot.

I relaxed as I drove along Barham Boulevard over the foothills, past The Smoke House restaurant, past The River Bottom, a stuntman's hangout-bar directly across from Warner Brother's Studio, then turned East on Riverside Drive. I liked Burbank. It was a sanctuary of sanity tucked discreetly against the north side of the Hollywood hills, away from the maniacal pace of Glitter City and the mauve-colored sprawl of greater Los Angeles. Burbank was sheltered from the vast expanse of redneck bluster and gang activity known simply as The Valley. Burbank was cool. I couldn't wait to bathe what remained of my emotional state in its calming vapors.

Gradually my anger slipped away, disappearing into the thin ether like laughter following a bad joke. Suddenly, I realized that now that I had my movie back, I had no idea what to do with it! I was out of funds; couldn't make prints, ads, promotions, couldn't pay for screenings, couldn't take a cab down the block, let alone from Burbank to LAX, or from LaGuardia into Manhattan, where the sales action was taking place. "*Well, you can worry about that later,*" Boo advised. I had known Boo for a long, long time, and he was usually right. I set *The Pyramid* on a shelf in my garage, and there it has remained for over thirty years, sans wine, sans song, sans singer, and sans end.

Wait a Minute, It Gets Even Stranger!

I am on the second story of a faux bank building on the back lot of Warner Brother's Studio, getting ready to crash through a window and plummet a couple of stories to the ground. The carpenters have constructed a small wooden ramp that leads to the target: several sheets of candy glass held together by wooden chocks. Just before takeoff, the chocks will be removed, allowing me to break through the window, head first, and hopefully spot my fall onto a small airbag several stories below. Next to the concrete!

Having just returned to stunt work to stoke the coffers, I am anxious to complete the gag. After this, I only have another stair fall to do and then I am free to return to my Burbank apartment, a vodka martini, and the writing of a screenplay I have been working on for several weeks.

"Ready, Gary?"

"Ready."

"Standby. Roll camera. Marker. Action!" Concentration to the max. I speed along the ramp, directly toward the window. At the last second I throw my arms in front of my face, like a high-diver. I plunge head first into the glass. Crash, shatter, tinkle. Fuck! I'm stuck! Pinned dead-center in the window like the severed head of a trophy moose in a hunting lodge. Right before closing my eyes in profound embarrassment, I caught a glimpse of Tomi, standing near camera, looking up at me with the most pained, perplexed expression I have seen on a face since O.J. Simpson's lawyers heard his "not guilty" verdict

Here's what happened: I was stunt coordinating, doing the money stunts on a TV Pilot, *Gist and Evans*, for Warner Brothers. Just about everyone connected with the show was high on something. Generally, even though drugs, booze, etc., were already part and parcel of the private lives of the Hollywood community, they were seldom seen or tolerated on a movie set. In the late 70s and 80s, however, hard drugs, and cocaine especially, had become *de rigueur*. The executives were all blowing snow, the casts and crews were operating on white-line overdrive, and nobody seemed to give a damn.

A production assistant on *Gist and Evans* was running around with what looked like a little, blue, plastic Pez dispenser, full of blow. He would shoot a line up the nostril of anyone in proximity, including the two grips who were responsible for pulling the chocks and support struts out of the window I was slated to dive through. They were so cranked up they forgot the task and I went headfirst into the solid supports, escaping decapitation by the width of a pubic hair. I was flapping around in the middle of the window, like the comedy relief in a Toby play. That's when I decided, "Okay, no more snow snorting for me. No sneezing, wheezing, whiffing, shaking, drooling, or crawling the carpet looking for leftovers."

I had quit cigarettes five years previous, cold turkey. Set a pack on a bar and never looked back. Quitting the marching powder would be easier yet. Life is a fragile son of a gun, at least for me, and much too damned unusual to waste time on artificially induced highs. It was my decision, that's all. Me and Boo. Being stuck like a schmuck in the middle of a window on a side street at a major studio with my predicament hanging out for God and the crew to have a laugh may have had something to do with it.

On the second take, I made sure the supports were pulled. I should have done that in the first place. The stunt went as planned, up the ramp, hit the window full force, a bit of a jar, feel the breakage, bits of glass and wood flying away from me, picking up and bouncing light from the reflectors like fireflies. I'm on the outside, mid-air. There's the pad, right below me. Turn and tuck so I can come in on my back…piece of cake! Next was the stair fall, and I was home free, through for the day. It was only eleven in the morning, so I called Chuck Bail, who had an office on the lot, and asked if he could meet for lunch.

Twenty minutes later I was seated in the dining room at Warner's with Chuck. We were soon joined by my good friend Vic Tayback and Chuck's pal, actor Bo Svenson (*Walking Tall, North Dallas Forty*). Svenson is six five, two hundred and twenty pounds, bigger than some houses. An imposing figure originally from Gothenburg, Sweden, I noticed that, as he reached forward to shake my hand, his knuckles had scabs forming over fresh wounds, not a good sign for whoever was on the receiving end of those ham hocks. After introductions, Chuck turned to me and said, "Gar, tell Bo about that script you're writing."

I had been working on a story idea about an American athlete and his wife, separated by time, countries, politics, religions, circumstance, etc. She has gone to the Middle East to talk on women's rights and runs afoul of the local mullahs and their customs. She is arrested and tossed into a rat hole prison as punishment. The zealots who control every aspect of life in the region have no intention of granting her release. Not wanting a sticky showdown, our government buries its head in the sand, hoping that in time it will all go away. The husband, consumed by grief and anger, puts together a ragtag group of mercenaries, disguises them as a legitimate soccer team from South Africa, and ignoring all laws and protocol, rides to the rescue. Real outlaws. My kinda guys, and evidently, Bo Svenson's kinda guys, also. By the time I returned to my apartment, the phone was ringing. It was Bo, offering to buy my screenplay!

Although I had just begun to write, Bo and I struck a deal. I would complete at least a first draft, and he would buy it and the story idea for a reasonable sum. Three weeks later, I was finished. Bo and I met at The Kondatori, a lush Swedish restaurant in Beverly Hills, to celebrate. I handed Bo the manuscript; he handed me a check for ten thousand dollars. Then, we got drunk. I mean, drunk, big time! Bo could out-drink a whole remuda of barflies and I tried to keep up with him. I should have known better. In his time, Bo had spent six years in the Marine Corps, played professional hockey, was a champion judo wrestler, a professional auto racer—all endeavors that guaranteed a certain superiority in the art of bending the elbow. By the time I left The Kondatori, I was so plastered I should have been arrested for walking under the influence.

Feeling rather ebullient at having just scored ten thousand dollars, I placed a call to Tomi, informing her I would be home shortly. Instead, I escorted Boo and myself down the block to another tony watering hole, The Ginger Man. I merely intended to treat us to a single nightcap. The Ginger Man was owned by actor

Carroll O'Conner (*All In The Family* TV, *In the Heat of the Night* TV) and it was not unusual to find a number of film and theater people dining or sitting at the bar talking shop. Sure enough, producer Paul Lewis was there, finishing off a Smirnoff on the rocks.

Paul invited me to join him. Having lunch, dinner, or drinks with Lewis has always been one of my guilty pleasures. He is well informed on almost any subject and has passionate opinions, pro and con, whichever you wish. As the conversation heats up, gets more passionate, the drinks seem to glide down the throat more smoothly, a procedure enjoyed by barroom sots for centuries.

Our conversation this evening centered around The War of Jenkins' Ear, in which Captain Robert Jenkins showed the English Parliament his ear, which had been severed by the Spanish Coast Guard. The year was 1739 and the lopping off of Jenkins' organ sparked the war of Austrian Secession, and the penning of the ballad, "God Save The Queen," which eventually became the British National Anthem. "Now there's a fellow who turned a minor hearing difficulty into a national triumph," Paul exhorted.

The conversation quickly drifted around to film, and "What on earth were you trying to say with *The Pyramid*?" Paul has never been much into psychic phenomena, fairy dust, or the senses six, seven, and eight.

"If you can't beat it, eat it, bank it, fight it, or fuck it, what practical value does it have, if any?"

"Come on, Paul. How about the Hillside Stranglers?"

"What? What are you talking about?"

The infamous Hillside Strangler, who had terrorized much of the feminine populace of Hollywood/Los Angeles during the dying days of the 70s, had finally been tracked down to a spider hole in Bellingham, Washington. Lo and behold, it turned out there were actually two Hillside Stranglers, complimentary sadists who worked in tandem to rape and sodomize their helpless victims before garroting them and tossing their nude, mutilated bodies onto waysides and parks in the greater L.A. habitat.

"So?" Paul asked. "What does that have to do with your film?"

"Well, Paul," I said, "Los Angeles forensics and their criminal psychiatrist/profiler told the cops to look for a white male, in his late twenties, unmarried, a loner, etc. A psychic from Berlin entered the case and disagreed. 'There are two of them,' he told the police. 'They are related, probably brothers. In their mid-thirties. They are married, possibly with children, and of Italian descent.' When the cops caught the killers, they turned out to be two guys, not one, and cousins (close as brothers), in their mid-thirties, married with children, and what were their names? Buono and Bianchi. Sounds Italian to me. Psychic? I'm just sayin', Paul, that's all."

Another drink, another talking point, this time discussing the sudden demise of the filmmakers who had ushered in Hollywood's supposed Golden Era in the early 70s. They were now pretty much out of vogue, replaced by a monstrous, multi-faceted cartoon called *Star Wars*. "Good riddance," I said, fingering my drink with an authority culled from the fermented droppings of the Russian potato. (I was on my fifth vodka martini.)

"It has occurred to Boo and me that the independents everyone's so fond of championing are severely tarnished by mean-spiritedness. Oh, well made, to be sure, but wallowing in greed, infidelity, avarice, murder. I'm talkin' 'bout *Taxi Driver* an' all o' that stuff." Was I beginning to slur my words?

"Seems to me, we simply went from grind house to mean streets to multimillion dollar cartoons."

"Come on, Gar, you're ignoring *The Godfather, Network, Chinatown, American Graffiti*."

"A bleach-banket plick, Paul," I scoffed, aware that now I really was slurring my words.

"*Cool it,*" Boo warned, "*you're pissing him off. He gets you a lot of jobs.*"

I had had five martinis, though, and by this time was convinced I was actually making sense.

"*American Graffidee* is just another Corman phlick in disguise." I scarcely noticed that Paul had taken his drink and left for a more user friendly section of the bar. I turned to a complete stranger occupying a barstool on my immediate left.

"And *Star Wars*," I belched, "it's heraldin' the end of film as anything even remotely important. Forget art, forget nuance, (belch) forget a—the tellin' of tales. Remember *Jaws*, buddy? The saga of the giant shark? All computer graphics!"

The guy on the stool looked at me like I was dangerous, possibly packing, if you get my drift.

"Well, that's the future, pal. Computer graphics. CGI an' massively produced, trillion-dollar-frickin' cartoons. Welcome to the New Hollywood."

By sheer seat-of-the-pants navigation and the grace of God, I found my way home from Beverly Hills without an accident or an arrest. Tomi was happy to see me and anxious to set eyes on the ten thousand dollar check. "The check? Oh, shit, where is the check?" I hadn't seen it since leaving Bo and The Kondatori hours before. I checked my pockets, my wallet, my underwear, my socks, even inside my shoes. No luck. I tore the freaking car apart. No ten thousand dollars. Tomi called The Ginger Man. They were closing down for the evening. No, they did not find a check, not for any amount, certainly not for ten thousand dollars, "But leave us your phone number. If ten thousand dollars should turn up, we'll give you a call."

I was devastated! I may even have begun to cry, a high, whining caterwaul, like a ferret with its tail caught in a door, an unbecoming sound for a stuntman turned writer. I called my son Chris and got him to go with me back over the route of my drunken stagger through the now nearly deserted streets of Beverly Hills. I literally crawled on hands and knees the several blocks from The Kondatori to The Ginger Man, through the gutters, praying to catch the slightest glimpse of paper fluttering around that might possibly be my ten grand. No luck. Finally, Chris talked me into giving up the ghost. "You can call Bo Svenson in the morning and have him write a new one."

I could do that, but, oh, God, the embarrassment, the humiliation. Decisions, decisions. Should I call Svenson and admit I was born a first class dumb ass or should I just fashion a noose from my shoestrings, loop it around my neck, and jump? I opted for the first.

Bo was more than understanding; he was downright amused. He agreed to meet me at his bank, cancel the old check and cut a new one on the spot, but, only if my son Chris accompanied me to ensure that I didn't lose another ten thousand in less than twenty-four hours.

Returning home, I entered the house with head hanging low as a set of trousers in a lavatory stall.

"How could I have been that stupid?" I announced to Tomi, to the dogs, to the cats, and the room in general. "How could I possibly have done that?"

Tomi was on the couch, watching a Jacques Cousteau special on public television. "Don't worry about it, Babe. If you ever pollute an entire ocean, then you can say you've done something bad."

Too Many Eggs in the Nog

I was sharing a motel room just outside of Phoenix, Arizona, with Lobo, my big Australian shepherd. Lobo had just pissed on a corner of the bed. This didn't bother me, however, as the proprietors had been rude and uncompromising the previous evening, refusing me permission to bring Lobo into the room. I was forced, then, to smuggle him in, disguised as a large piece of hairy luggage.

No, it was not Lobo's liquid endorsement of the king-size that perturbed me; it was more the violent saddening activities currently in vogue and sensationalized on the nightly news, such as uber-religious quack Jim Jones and his dosing of strychnine-laced Kool-Aid to hundreds of devoted followers at a compound in Guyana, killing every last one of them, man, woman, child, even the family pet, in the name of God, for God's sake. It was the torching of six members of The Symbionese Liberation Army, the S.L.A., after they had kidnapped heiress Patty Hearst and robbed a few banks, inside their hideout in East Los Angeles;

it was the murder of Beatles icon John Lennon outside his apartment building in Manhattan. It was the murder of Harvey Milk, a San Francisco politician and political activist, shot down in broad daylight, along with Frisco mayor George Moscone, by embittered city supervisor Daniel White who later told police that "eating too much junk food" had driven him to commit the dirty deed. (Ahh, those friggin' Twinkies will give you the red-ass every time.) White only got five years and early parole for the slaughter of two innocent human beings. In Arizona, they were giving pot smokers a hard twenty.

Boo and I were equally disheartened by the discovery of the body of Eiler Larsen, the Laguna Greeter, lying on a moldy, money-stuffed mattress in his dilapidated shack in the hills above the Blue Pacific. To me, Eiler had been a bastion of eccentricity, decency, and kindness ever since the kids and I had first discovered him back in '65, occupying his favorite Laguna street corner, smiling and waving to the carloads of humanity that scooted past him on a daily basis. I was also somewhat saddened by news of the prison death of L.A.'s last legitimate mobster, Mickey Cohen. Now, with Cohen and Eiler gone, it would be increasingly difficult to tell the good guys from the bad.

I went to the bathroom sink, filled a large bowl with water, set it on the motel floor, and encouraged Lobo to drink to his hearts content. Twenty minutes later, I led him back to the bed, pointed to an unsoiled corner, and said, "Here, boy, have a go for old Eiler, for Charlie, for Boo, an' for Tomi an' me." That great, big, loveable canine lifted a rear leg and I swear he grinned a big guy grin as he unleashed a bowlful of golden liquid, fresh from his massive Australian kidneys. Yes, I know it was ornery, but then, we were feeling a little ornery, Lobo, Boo, and me.

We were on our way to Austin, Texas, driving Interstate 10 in a '69 Chevy sedan with the words "Big Red and Frosty" painted on the sides. Did I mention that Lobo was probably the largest Australian shepherd I had ever seen? At least as large as a lion, mottled red in color, with a split eye that gave him a devil-dog persona. Oh, he was a scary beast, but Lobo had a heart and a sense of humor that put most ordinary dogs to shame.

Tomi and I and our critters were making a run for it. We were fed up and fooled out with Hollywood and people in general. I was usually a sunny-side kinda guy, but Tinsel Town and other big towns, USA, were increasingly favoring the shadowy side, the side that mirrors the worst in human nature: darkness, fear, anger, and negativity. With a few outstanding exceptions, such as *The Godfather* and *Rocky*, much of the work in American film had developed a juvenile smirk, a cocky, "told ya so" persona that was actually quite boring. Like society itself, there was a cruel backlash against the peace movement, against the idealism and optimism of the 60s and early 70s, and it spread through the studios and the public consciousness like crabgrass.

The good ol' outlaw days, where a filmmaker full of spirit and pluck could ignite that same passion in a group of peers and could actually make a film without approval of a board of directors or a basketful of commercial endorsements, were history. Since Spielberg and Lucas arrived on the scene, a film, to be considered viable, must have the potential to also sell a lot of t-shirts, books, toys, action figures, and other plastic and gaudy merchandise. And, the possibility for profit must be in the hundreds of millions.

Hollywood became victim of a new barbarism known as "Product Placement," a means of raising financing or accumulating "goodies" by having commercial items prominently displayed, either by the lead actors, or, incidentally placed near camera. The line of demarcation between crass commercialism and art was beginning to shrink. The making of a film was now a multi-corporation event, motivated primarily by greed.

What had happened, I wondered, to the shamans, the storytellers without chains, the guys who didn't put commercial considerations first and foremost? Where resided the unyoked ones, the adventurers with cunning imaginations and daring élan? Where were the blokes with the stiffened backbone required of a true revolutionary?

Where, also, were the stuntmen and women of filmdom's future, the ones who had brass for balls and ovaries forged in steel? Gone, I suspected. Dissolved into the murky goop of times gone by like a tab of seltzer dropped into a glass of tap water. "They have been replaced," I whined to Boo, "by computers and computer nerds masquerading as filmmakers. And, worse, cardboard stunt people are being cookie-cut and placed in front of green screens, while the adolescent artists in CGI whiz high-falls past them, and crash tons of vehicles without leaving the sanctity of their workstations."

Collateral Damage

Independent film had become a catch word for "chic" and chic was bestowed by the in-crowd on the in-crowd at the Sundance Festival, or sneered from the languid lips of the mediocrities pouring into the cheap seats near the hippest college campuses.

Actually, television was the new cutting edge: *Saturday Night Live*, *Prime Time News*, *Nightline*. There were even a few series that harked back to the good ol' days of grind house cinema, cheap, lurid, fun to watch.

The sexual revolution was kaput, over, chased back into the closet by a new and deadly disease, Acquired Immune Deficiency Syndrome (AIDS). At first AIDS was tagged as a gay disease, but then it began to spread through the heterosexual community to mom and dad, brother and sister, in some cases, even grandma and grandpa. The ever popular bathhouses closed, as did the swingers clubs like Plato's Retreat and the sexually esoteric retreats such as Sandstone.

Motion pictures also took a trip to the darker side, throwing out such scary stuff as *Cruising*, in which one of America's best actors, multi-award winner Al Pacino, goes undercover as a cop to sift through the sleazy world of the rough-trade gay culture, looking for a serial killer.

There were others, all strong statements against promiscuous sexuality, or seeming warnings against misadventures in the skin trade, i.e., *Hardcore*, directed by Paul Schrader, with Oscar winner George C. Scott sinking into the subterranean depths of pornography in search of a runaway daughter; *Looking for Mr. Goodbar* starring Diane Keaton (Best Actress Oscar for *Annie Hall*, seventeen other award wins, numerous nominations) as a school teacher who spends her off hours prowling the bars, looking for abusive men to engage in violent sexual liaisons; Brian De Palma's *Dressed to Kill*, an homage to STD and the danger in offbeat sexual encounters, finds actress Angie Dickinson, after a casual one-night stand, learning she may have contracted a venereal disease. She is then slashed to death by a transvestite, the murder witnessed by a prostitute. "Well, what d'ya say, Hermione? Feel like a good movie tonight?"

I placed a few calls to a few friends. Richard Rush had acquired the rights to and was developing what would become his masterpiece *The Stunt Man*. Chuck Bail was sitting in an office at Warner Brothers trying to get a green light on a picture he was developing titled *Number One*. Paul Lewis was going through distribution hell on a comedy he had produced entitled *The Van*, starring Steve Oliver and Danny DeVito. Tagline: "It's Vantastic!"

Ray Steckler had escaped to Las Vegas where he copped a gig teaching cinema at UNLV and Mike MacFarland was directing his high school musical duos. Peter Bogdanovich was in Singapore, newly divorced from wife Polly Platt, dating Cybill Shepherd, blowing a little snow, and filming *St. Jacques*, with Ben Gazzara, a story about a pimp without a pimp-stick. If you will, a pimp with a heart of gold. Huh?

Jack Nicholson was on top of the worldwide A-list, continuing to become ever more brilliant and courageous. The trouble was, being at the top of the top, one becomes a part of the whole structure. Jack was now so major studio he could easily pass for Louis B. Mayer himself. Monte Hellman remained as determined and independent a filmmaker as he was back in Utah so many years ago. While he managed to make his last Western, *China 9, Liberty 37* with the wonderfully hangdog Warren Oates, he spent most of the late seventies trying to finance work that covered the territory of broken spirits, hidden agendas, and stubborn

Richard Rush directs Lifetime Achievement Award Winner Peter O'Toole and
actor Steve Railsback in the classic The Stunt Man.
Photo courtesy of Rush Archives.

pride seldom recognized by other filmmakers, work that matched his brilliant *Cockfighter, Two-Lane Blacktop*, et al.

My dear friend Gary Graver, after a decade in low-budget exploitation, discovered genius Orson Welles (*Citizen Kane, The Third Man*) lolling about in a suite at the Beverly Hills Hotel, and attached himself to the great auteur, becoming his director of photography, best friend, and confidant for the rest of Welles' tumultuous life. Max Julien was hunkered down in his study, after penning *Cleopatra Jones and The Casino of Gold*, working on his next, a strange caper opus titled *Thomasine & Bushrod*.

Ted Mikels had just put into distribution his outré horror omelet, *The Worm Eaters*. Bud Cardos was busy directing William Shatner (*Star Trek, Boston Legal*) in a little film called *Kingdom of the Spiders*, which I am glad I didn't work, because Bud had hauled several thousand Mexican tarantulas onto the set for background. I have not been particularly fond of spiders since a childhood buddy had died from a black widow bite. The deadly little devil had sneaked onto his pillowcase while he was sleeping.

Mostly, however, none of the cinema coming from the United States as the 70s limped off the stage and the 80s began, seemed particularly interesting. Neither did the politics or even the spiritual directors of the time: Jimmy Swaggart, Jim Bakker and Tammy Faye, Pat Robertson, Oral Roberts, and Jerry Falwell. "Yes, folks, Jesus will talk to you, but he will do it in tongues while handling an armload of sidewinders! And, please, send your checks today!" On the surface it seemed the good old days were gone forever, valued only as nostalgic memorabilia, like old photographs stacked on top of a guest room dresser, fading and forgotten. The angel Tomi and I unfolded our wings, preparing ourselves for flight. "It's easy to do," I assured her. "Just close your eyes and start flapping."

Chapter Seventeen

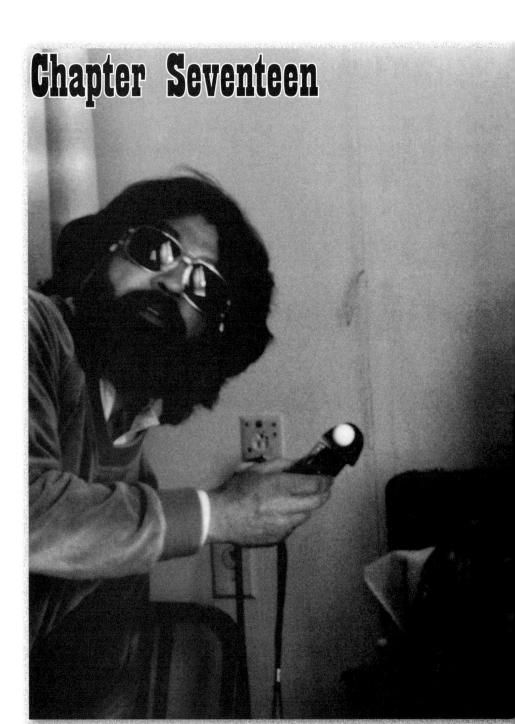

Cinematographer Ron Garcia and actor Esai Morales prepare a scene for Rainy Day Friends. *Photo courtesy of the author.*

Finding The Hole In The Wall

Oh the muddy Pedernales flows right by my door
And I ain't gonna live in L.A. anymore.

—The author, 1980

A small ranch house just outside of Austin, Texas, had become available through Tomi's family. It was ours for a low down and low monthly payments. Seven and a half acres, room for our animals, room to ruminate, room to kick back, and room to write, but we had to move quickly. "It's time," I told Tomi, "that we saddle up and mosey on down the road." She agreed. We packed up the cat Katrina, Tomi's dog Buffy, and Tomi took them off to Texas by plane. The big dog Lobo and I stuffed the rest of our stuff into a giant U-Haul, said the necessary goodbyes, and pulled out onto the open road, just like Kerouac and Cassady, only in this case, it was Big Red and Frosty!

It was about two in the morning and Lobo and I were just a tad outside of Alamogordo, New Mexico, on that long, downhill slide into El Paso. We were cruising along in the dark of the desert at about seventy per when I heard a loud plunk, plunkety-plunk sound coming from the rear of the car. I was pulling a U-Haul, so my first thought was that the hitch had come loose and it was holding on by only the safety chain. I pulled over on the side of the highway and took a look. No, everything regarding the trailer was A-OK. "*Damn,*" said Boo, "*I knew we shoulda holed up back at that Motel 6. At least then, this would have happened in daylight.*"

I started the car and drove back onto the roadway. Kerplunkety-plunk-plunk! There it was again. What the hell? I was sure now that I had thrown a tie-rod or maybe a piston had plowed through the engine housing. Luckily the desert hugged up to the road, allowing me to pull far away from the asphalt and shut everything down out of harm's way. Suddenly, the silence folded over us, like a huge, invisible blanket.

I tied a leash to Lobo and we started the long, uphill trek back to Alamogordo. I have a particular affection for desert nights. The universe just seems a little closer, the stars a lot brighter. It's easy to shuck the bonds of civilization's frantic cacophony, to slip comfortably into a feeling of being in harmony with it all. Shrinks a fellow down to size, and sometimes, you can lose yourself all together. We were about four miles outside Alamogordo. I'll bet not more than three autos whizzed past us, like road rockets with headlights, here and gone in the bat of a dingbat's eye.

We found the Motel 6 and turned in for the night. Sleeping until late morning, we hit the streets, Lobo and I, looking for vittles and a hint of New Mexican compassion. We were steered to a nearby auto shop by a friendly Indian who was street-vending tortillas from a battered and bruised pushcart. Two good old boys drove us back along the highway until we spotted my car and the U-Haul, hunched in the desert like a couple of large buffalo. All the way from town, I was describing that strange plunkety-plunk-kerplunk sound that had brought us to a standstill in the wee hours of the morning. The good old boys eyed me with suspicion, like I was making it all up: the awful kerplunkety sound, the almost uncontrollable vibration at the steering wheel, the strange odor of decaying flesh I was now certain I had smelled just after the kerplunkety sound began.

The minute we pulled next to my car, Norman, a tall, sunburned individual wearing tiny little Boy Scout shorts that hiked up over legs as long and thick as a saguaro, pointed to the rear of the auto and laughed, "Well, fella, there's your trouble right there. Looks like that tire mighta been bit off and chewed up by the I-10."

I stared at the rear tire. Damn, Norm was right. A large piece of rubber had peeled away from the main body of the tire and was hanging off to the side like the tongue of a water-starved steer. Obviously, every time the tire turned round, the rubber strip would slap the wheel-well, making that very loud kerplunkety sound. For a twenty dollar bill, Norman and his pal changed the tire, and drove me back to Alamogordo to pick up an extra spare.

The "Big Red and Frosty" sign on the side of the car referred to Lobo and myself. Lobo was Big Red, as he was a mottled red in color, with one of his eyes split into two colors. The top half was a deep, purplish hue and the bottom was a stark white. I've seen people just throw up their hands and surrender when they saw that eye staring at them. Me? Well, of course, I was Frosty. My normally dark hair had taken on patches of snow, and when I let a beard or mustache grow, they arrived pure white. I didn't fancy being called the usual stuff, like Whitey, Cotton, or Father Christmas. Tomi suggested Frosty. She said it reflected my attitude as well as the condition of my tresses.

We had a lot of fun, Big Red, Boo, and I. As we drove the interstate toward central Texas, people would pull along side of us just to catch a glimpse of The Devil Dog sitting upright in the passenger seat like a large, hirsute co-pilot. Folks would wave and yell and pound on their windows to get his attention and Big Red would gradually swing that huge head around and glare at them with that devil eye. They would go nuts, especially kids. They would shriek with laughter, or cry sometimes, even pretend they were praying.

One time we pulled into a gas station to fill the tank. Lobo was asleep on the back seat. I had the rear window about half down, for ventilation purposes. Suddenly another car pulled into the space alongside us. The driver, a teenager, jumped out of the door, slamming it closed. The sound aroused Lobo; he sat up, stuck his head out of the window, and let loose a flurry of the most vicious barks this side of the river Styx. That kid dropped his gas hose and jumped completely over the hood of his car, hit the ground rolling and just kept going.

When I arrived at the new abode, I found Tomi on the telephone. She was singing a song she had just written to her father, a staunch conservative, a strip mall developer, a big game hunter, and all around good ol' Texas boy. The song was dedicated to President Ronald Reagan.

(to the tune of the "Crawdad Song")
"How many gays have you killed today, oh, Ronnie, hey hey
How many gays have you killed today?
Stick 'em the ground, keep 'em out of the way
Oh, Ronnie—Ray-Gun."

This, of course, was motivated by Reagan's refusal to take any action in favor of federal funding for AIDS research. Tomi (and many others) was angry, disbelieving. How could a society that considers itself loving and humane turn its back on so many hundreds of thousands of its citizens? Her father was not amused by her composition or her compassion.

Austin is a weird place and prides itself in being so. Austin is smaller than most cities, bigger than most towns. Austin is laid-back, but hardwired, hushed up, over-caffeinated, eager and anxious, while appearing to be settled in for an afternoon nap. It's a placid place on the surface, but like an old-time grappler, it wears a hair shirt.

An illegal hairstylist in Austin once told me the following anecdote: "I was ridin' a freight from San Antone to Dallas, runnin' from ol' Johnny Law and myself, too, I spose. I'd been suckin' on a coupla longnecks, piggin' on barbacoa, when I either fell asleep or passed out. Next thing I knew, Hessay, I was tossed free a the train as she wheeled round a turn, flung right out in the O-Z, like someone tossed a biscuit to a dog, know what I'm sayin'? I go rollin' down a hill, and I end up lyin' on my face in Town Lake Park in Austin. They were puttin' on a free concert, right down by water's edge, homes. Some dude helped me stand up, handed me a brewski, and said, 'Welcome to Austin, my brother!' I've been here ever since, keepin' my part a keepin' it weird!"

It took me a while to adjust. Mostly, I just hung out at our place on Chisholm Lane, writing and pretending I was writing. Afternoons, I would throw on the Nikes and go for a run around Town Lake on the hike and bike trail, a distance of about four miles if you start at the gazebo and cross the lake on the Mopac undercarriage. I pretty much ignored the local film scene, although I understood there was one, led by a broody-looking bloke named Richard Linklater (*Slacker*, *Dazed and Confused*). Linklater turned out to be an admirer of Monte Hellman. Tomi and I were invited to meet up with them at a Hellman homage held in fall of 2001. Monte looked exactly the same as he did in Utah in '65, maybe minus a little hair. Me? My hair had gone from black to pure white. Monte took one look at me, squinted, and exclaimed, "Oh, my God, Gary Kent! What have they done to you?"

It seemed that as soon as I got busy on my writing projects, I would get a call from Hollywood, offering me hard cash for little work. The first to call was Don "Irish Frankie" Jones, who flew Tomi and me back to Los Angeles, hauled us up to a location site in the Sequoias, and set us to work chasing each other around the woods in a picture called *The Forest*. The shoot was jolly fun, a vacation, really, for all of us—jumping in and out of the forest primeval, swimming in the clearest of rivers, eating fresh fish and blueberries like bloody grizzly bears.

Don had arranged quarters at a small motel-lodge, The Hummingbird, whose owner prided himself on being a gourmet cook. Each dinner was a feast of locally grown food, including, now and then, a fresh canola-fried brook trout, a rainbow or a cutthroat. The fish would be lying on the plate next to the parsley, head intact, its cold, dead eyes watching as you attempted to fork into its delicious flesh. Luckily, my part in the film was that of a demented, modern-day cannibal, so eating a fully fleshed fish was not a problem.

Story-wise, the best part of *The Forest* was probably when Tomi, playing an out-of-her-element San Fernando Valley housewife, garners just enough courage to stab me to death seconds before I fillet her film-husband into an early afternoon snack. The audience burst into applause. Boo snickered, *"Perhaps it's because the movie has finally come to an end."*

I had worked for Don Jones once before in a picture called *Schoolgirls in Chains*. In that little creepazoid number, John Parker and I play two demented brothers who snatch women out of lonely situations and deposit them in a root cellar in the hinterlands. They are there for John's (the retarded bro) amusement. My character just wanders around aimlessly, always under a dark cloud, much like Joe Btfsplk in the *Li'l Abner* cartoon. Eventually, we disintegrate into a mess of suicidal madness.

When an interviewer for the slick East Coast magazine *Mass Appeal* suggested to Don that he made "very black, even slightly sick films," Don couldn't understand it. He thought he was just making good old late night entertainment. Maybe not right for the kiddos, but just the ticket for mom and pop. An interesting side note: Under the title *Abducted*, Don's film has become a big hit on the European horror film circuit. Who knew?

Once back in Austin, I returned to polishing the first draft on a film I was writing titled *Snowfall*, a story of governmental and corporate rip-off of Indians on the Four Corners Reservation. The tribes were conned out of their mineral rights for less than marbles, while every twenty minutes the government radio would run ads encouraging birth control, a sort of audio encouragement of tribal genocide.

Folding My Eights, Holding My Aces

It was our usual Sunday morning routine, sitting on the living room floor, just sorta kicking back. Tomi, wearing her newly minted Gloria Vanderbilts and sporting a Farah Fawcett 'do, was reading the Sunday newspaper. I, as usual, was pontificating about film, ignoring real worldly stuff, such as that week's dramatic volcanic eruption of Mt. St. Helens in my home state of Washington. I had once climbed St. Helens for simple recreation. Now, more than half of the mountain had been blown away, taking the lives of a dozen or more campers and thousands of critters in the process. I have on my desktop a memento of the occasion: a small, glass case holding about two inches of St. Helens' ash.

Lobo was lolling near the fireplace, dreaming of those bygone days when he was known as Big Red, the roadway-rounder and devil dog. The cat, Katrina, was in her cradle. All was, for the moment, hunky-dory.

"Art is the small, patient plodding that gives dreams somewhere to go!" I moved my coffee mug from the floor to the coffee table. "D'ya know who said that?" I asked Tomi.

"No, who?" She scarcely looked up from reading her paper.

"Your dad. Or maybe he was quoting someone else. Doesn't matter, it's still a great expression."

Tomi seemed to have found something of interest in the news, as she didn't respond to that last, about her dad saying something acutely profound.

"I've always felt that experiencing art allows us to experience beauty at our leisure, to observe humanity's shadows and light without threat." Neither Tomi, the cat, nor Lobo seemed to be paying the slightest attention. Clearing my throat noisily, I continued, "It's the same with movies, Babe. Movies give us time to consider the properties of life, the triumphs, the perils and pitfalls without actually having to make a dash for it to save our precious asses."

Tomi tossed me a section of the *Austin American-Statesman*. "Wow, read this. I could get off doing a film about something like this!"

It was a brief article, buried in the back pages of the Metro section. It described the death of a teenage boy who had passed away from an unknown illness while living in an abandoned car. His parents had kicked him out of their home, calling him a troublemaker and a burden to the rest of the family. End of story!

Tomi knew what she was doing. The article immediately set in motion that mysterious "what if" that all writers entertain before beginning a fictionalized project. "What if the kid didn't die? What if fate or the law of unexpected consequences intervened on this poor urchin's behalf, or if, like the stalwart Heathcliff in Brontë's classic *Wuthering Heights*, he found himself the son of a prince. What if…?"

That afternoon, I started the screenplay. I titled it *Rainy Day Friends*.

I decided the kid in the car should be illegal, or the offspring of illegals, throwing the danger of exposure and subsequent deportation of his family into the equation. Yes, he would have that little family problemo and I would give him an obnoxious personality, an addiction to weed, and sicken him with cancer. Then I'd stir up the pot and see what sort of porridge evolved.

FADE IN: Exterior coffee shop parking lot, East Los Angeles, early morning. A teenage boy works a Slim Jim into the window-casing of an automobile. He jimmies the lock, crawls inside, and starts to detach an expensive looking radio. Suddenly, he realizes it is a police radio, and he has just busted his way into a plainclothes police car.

For me, writing and directing my own film is a lot like playing the violin—there are no frets. Giving myself that kind of freedom can lead to scary territory, but it also leaves me ample room for creative serendipity, for a spontaneity to imbue the cast and crew with the feel of life on the cutting edge. I do not mean by this an absence of structure or a quality of being unprepared. I just mean that the nature of film, in and of itself, is often a dull, plodding, hurry-up-and-wait procedure that follows a script, a shot list, a storyboard, a budget, a time schedule. Keep it open, I say, to the muses, and the possibilities of minor miracles. Let us, then, cut to the chase.

I spent the next several months haunting local cancer treatment centers, research facilities, and talking with sufferers and survivors. Tomi, who had decided

Actors Gary Kent and Ken Curtis in Adamson's last film, Lost, *1983.*
Photo courtesy of the author.

to produce, went after funding from her father, his hunter-gatherer friends, and every boss she had ever worked for who might have a few shekels lying about on the floor of the office. When we had a decent first draft and the funds in place, we brought Walter Boxer on board as co-producer.

Walter Boxer is definitely a renaissance man. He knows just about everything and everyone in the arts from Pismo Beach to Bangkok. Walter was born in New York City. He joined the Air Force during WW II, flying B17s out of North Africa and Italy. After graduation from Columbia University, he trekked to Hollywood, where he joined the United Artists Pictures Corporation working in worldwide distribution. Eventually, he became the assistant head of production for United Artists in the U.K. He attended a rare screening of *The Pyramid*, sponsored by The Los Angeles Reel Film Society, and liked the work. He, Tomi, and I became fast friends and have remained so for many years.

The main location for *Rainy Day Friends* was a fictional cancer hospital in Los Angeles, ironically named Nepenthe. Other locales were the streets and cubbyholes of the East L.A. barrio, a mansion in Beverly Hills, the beach environs of Santa Monica and Malibu, various courtrooms, rooftops, even the placid skies over the Santa Ynez Mountains.

In some way, *Rainy Day Friends* resembled *The Pyramid*. In addition to the major roles, the story was chock full of diverse, eccentric, and colorful individuals from all walks of life. I hired Pat Orseth, a longtime friend and respected casting agent, and she, Walter, Tomi, and myself set out to cast the movie.

My good buddy, stuntman actor Walt Robles, was cast as a beach bum dope dealer. He and John Parker, who had been sent into the game as a meddlesome preacher unwittingly annoying staff and patients, both received critical plaudits for their truly original performances. Anne Betancourt, Googy Gress, Erv Sanders, Stafford Morgan, Lynn von Kersting (owner of the world famous restaurant The Ivy in Beverly Hills), and my old basketball buddy, seven two John Bloom, highlighted the supporting players.

Carrie Snodgress (*Pale Rider*, *The Fury*) was cast as Fisher, a nurse into self-medication who is much too busy with her own emotional suffering to help her patients. Carrie was a dynamo at rehearsals, well prepared and professional despite hobbling around on a recently broken leg. She was a graduate of Chicago's prestigious Goodman Theater, went on the road with the hit show *Vanities*, and was starring at the Mark Taper Forum in L.A. when she received a Best Actress Oscar nomination for *Diary of a Mad Housewife*. She was twenty-five years old. She later married rock-music icon Neil Young. Neil and their son Zeke actually appear as extras in a scene from my film, as passengers on a city bus.

Snodgress was one of those "director's actors" who brings more to the part than necessary. All the director has to do is pare away the excess, and you are left with a core that is solid and esthetically pure. Not so with John Phillip Law (*Barbarella*, *Hurry Sundown*) who we cast as Dr. Stephen Kendrick, the hospital's uptight sad sack. Law was a living template for the definition of long, tall, and handsome. In fact, he was so good-looking, most of the female crew signed on just to get a look at him. John was six seven of gorgeousness, with a smile just right for winning the hardest of hearts. He also had an impressive resume, was popular with the Sunset Strip musician-celebrity crowd, and couldn't act for spilled beans.

John Law should have been a male mannequin—he looked that good in his clothing—actually, they could have kept him and thrown away the mold. Trouble was, acting-wise, he was exceedingly stiff, perhaps a bit unconfident. I couldn't get him to relax enough to appear natural on camera. Then, one day, I discovered that, after I called "cut," John would become suddenly animated—grimacing, wringing his hands—ruffling his feathers, so to speak. I whispered to the camera operator to *keep the camera rolling* after I called "cut" and I ended up with some marvelous histrionics, which I then was able to cut into the scene, effecting a more natural looking performance.

Janice Rule (*Missing*; *Bell, Book and Candle*) was perfect for the part of Dr. Elaine Hammond, a responsible and caring oncologist at Nepenthe. Besides her long, distinguished career as an actress, Janice had gotten a Ph.D. in research psychoanalysis. She insisted that, because of a bad back, she be provided with a large, overstuffed chair on the set at all times. Tomi assigned one of the grips the permanent duty of schlepping that chair around, location to location, so that between takes, Janice could grab a rest, kick into her doctoral persona, and analyze why the rest of us were acting so damned serious. After all, as my friend Vic Tayback would remind us, "Acting is only pretending."

Lelia Goldoni was born into show business, first popping onto the world stage in New York, the only daughter of Italian playwright, Charles de Rose. Long-legged, energetic, possessing a dusky, provocative beauty, by the age of fourteen Lelia had become a principal dancer with the world famous Lester Horton Dance Theatre, where she performed with icons Alvin Ailey, Carmen de Lavallade, and Joyce Trisler. At seventeen, she turned her talents to acting and wangled her way into John Cassavetes' exciting Drama Workshop. Soon Lelia was starring in Cassavetes' improvisational masterpiece, *Shadows*, for which she was nominated for a British Academy Award.

For ten years, Goldoni lived in England, where she played a variety of roles in film, television, and on the London stage. She also formed a lasting friendship with producer Walter Boxer. In 1978 she received the Oxford Film Festival award for best actress in a supporting role, following her startling performance in *Blood Brothers*.

Back in the U. S., Lelia appeared in Sam Shepard's *La Turista* and the acclaimed *Familiar Faces, Mixed Feelings*. Walter Boxer suggested her for the role of Barbara Marti, the calmly terrified wife of one of the two male leads in *Rainy Day Friends*. She was marvelous in the part. A classic beauty who could, with only body language and eye contact, convey those two disparate and rawest of human emotions on the edge: love and fear!

I called on Tomi Barrett to not only co-produce, but to also play the part of Erlene Felton, a dedicated but naive social worker. Tomi brought her friend Kimberly Hill, a talented Hill Country hard-rocker from Austin, to Hollywood to play the part of Angel, a drug dealing rock singer. Kimberly wrote and performed two songs that highlight the film, "Compromise" and "I Ain't Got the Time."

At last, we were down to the shorthairs, the two leads: the wild, uncontrollable teenager Neekos Valdez, and a successful Beverly Hills attorney named Smilin' Jack Marti. Both are suffering from cancer and both are hospitalized at the Nepenthe Treatment Center.

Rainy Day Friends was a story about strength of the human spirit, whether gnarly, ugly, disheveled, or strong and sturdy as an oak, and its involvement in the process of fighting a deadly disease. Illness is not often a popular subject for the making of a film; rather, men holding guns and caressing female body parts are the popular fare. Therefore, if I was to attract an audience, I needed to rely heavily on the performances, the ability of the actors to flesh out the fighting spirits of two entirely disparate individuals, and in so doing, honor their common humanity. I also had written into the script a plethora of stunts, music, and humor. I was taking no chances, McGee. Yes, this was about overcoming cancer, but it was also a celebration of the human spirit.

Tomi was sitting in our sanctuary, an unfinished garage apartment hidden behind Art Names house on Normandy Avenue in L.A., watching a brash young female performer named Madonna cavort around the TV screen wearing her bra outside of her blouse. "The Virgin look!" I was agonizing over the fact we were scheduled to start filming soon and we still did not have a Smiling Jack Marti (the attorney) or Neekos Valdez (the rebellious teen from East L.A.). "Well, what are you looking for in this Beverly Hills guy. What kind of man is he?"

"He's Smiling Jack, right out of the old comic strip," I answered. "Bigger than life, an airplane pilot, tough and tongue-in-cheek. A stand-up kind of guy who is still able to empathize with—"

Tomi turned off the TV. "Sounds a little like your friend, Chuck Bail."

"Exactly. A lot like Chuck Bail. That's what we need."

"Then, why don't you get him? Get Chuck, I mean?"

The idea had not occurred to me. Chuck had just finished co-starring with the great actor Peter O'Toole in Richard Rush's *The Stunt Man*.

"He probably stashed his acting chops," I said, "and is trying to get his directing career kick-started again. Probably not a chance in a million he'll commit to a little, low budget cancer film."

"*Probably* is a sorry word, Babe," Tomi persisted. "If you think he's right for the part, give it a try. Come on, Chuck would do anything for you."

Boo bullied his way into the conversation, "*She's right, champ, polish off your creative cojones and get busy with it!*"

I called forth those much neglected cojones, and then sent Tomi off to do the grunt work. I remembered that Bail was an old horse trader. If at all interested, the negotiations would not be easy. Tomi, on the other hand, had learned her business chops from her dad, Bill Willeford, a highly successful boot-n-scoot Texas land developer. It could get interesting!

Walter Boxer and I were sitting at Hamburger Hamlet, a restaurant hugging the eastern end of The Sunset Strip, mulling over who might be right to play the part of Neekos, the unruly Latino teenager. Earlier that day, Marty Hornstein, a production manager/producer (*Silent Running, Sybil*) who had worked for me on *House of Seven Corpses* and was scheduled to play an INS agent in *Rainy Day Friends*, said he had just come off a picture called *Bad Boys* with Sean Penn (*Colors, Dead Man Walking*). One of the lead characters was a Latino gangbanger played by a newcomer named Esai Morales. "This kid's terrific, Gar. You guys need to check him out."

Our waiter approached the booth. "Gary Kent, phone call for you. You can take it at the bar."

"Okay, I think we've got him, Babe!" It was Tomi's voice, tired and triumphant.

"Who? Got who?"

"Your friend Chuck. He's pretty much agreed to do the part. He's a tough customer. I had to promise to buy him a radio for his airplane, but, then, he agreed to work for a modest price. You know he'll be worth whatever we pay him, Babe."

"Absolutely. Good job, Tomi. I can't wait to tell Walter."

"Oh, just one more little thing. I think...I mean, to seal the deal, Lucille, I think you need to give Chuck something personal, a gift of some kind. Nothing expensive, just something from you that's personal. Comprende?"

The next morning, I walked into a small art gallery tucked away on Riverside Drive in Burbank. I had my eye on a particular painting mounted on the back wall, an original oil of cowboys standing around a campfire, backs to the observer. There was something plaintive, a feeling both personal and private in the attitude of the painting, a group of men special to themselves mostly and to their own honor code, sharing a moment of camaraderie before the day's work begins. I bought the painting and then called one of those costumed delivery services. I hired a dance hall girl in mesh stockings, high heels, feathers, the works. I paid her an extra fifty dollars and had her deliver the painting to Chuck at his house, along with her song and dance routine and my script. That afternoon Tomi got a phone call. It was Chuck, "Count me in. I'm the guy you're looking for to play Smilin' Jack Marti."

Bites of the Big Apple

The doorbell rang. I opened it. It was the waiter, bearing a tray of toast, butter, jellies, croissants, and a large pot of freshly brewed coffee, all on the house. I was in a luxury suite at the Ritz Carlton Hotel in Manhattan, sharing a quick breakfast with Walter Boxer before our arranged meeting with actor Esai Morales. Walter was a personal friend of the manager, Frank Bowling, who had comped us a suite for the audition. I took a cup of coffee and walked to the big picture window. The Ritz Carlton is on Central Park South and The Avenue of the Americas, directly across from Central Park. You cannot get more Manhattan than that. It was raining. I was watching the horse-drawn carriages across the street and the poor, drenched animals attached to them, stoic guardians of the park, those brave, patient horses. I heard the sound of the doorbell. Walter went to answer.

Esai Morales bounced into the room like a cheerleading dervish spinning out of the East Los Angeles barrio. He was about five ten, extremely good-looking in that Latin lover kind of way, dark, flashing eyes, coal-black hair, and skin the color of light copper. He also had what seemed be a certain sad, streetwise intelligence hidden behind the gorgeous smile, the ultra-white teeth, and the rascally good humor. He shook Walter's hand, held up my screenplay (which had been sent to him by messenger a few days before the reading), and cheerfully announced, "Wow, did you write this? What a story, man. What a part. I love this guy Neekos."

Having made instant points with yours truly, we got around to some small, "get to know ya" kind of chatter, and then the reading. Esai had already memorized the lines. As they say in the trade, he "owned the part." Neekos, the troublemaker, the cancer-stricken kid who lives in a car, with the in-your-face attitude and the hint of vulnerability, Morales had it all down. By the time he left the suite, Walter and I both knew that we had found our Neekos Valdez.

That afternoon, after placing a call to Tomi, I decided to go for a jog in Central Park. My return flight to L.A. wasn't until the next afternoon. This gave me some time to enjoy New York. My two favorite cities on the mother continent have always been Los Angeles and New York. Los Angeles because, in spite of its huge sprawl, it is chock-full of nooks, creative crannies, and magic mojo. L.A. is like a triple Gemini, hard to be alone in L.A., but easy to be overlooked. Still, the city has a lot to say. If you have any talent at all, if you can stand on your head, whistle, imitate a rat, recreate the call of a morning mudlark, sing, dance, prance, or expose yourself, you will easily draw a crowd in L.A., and possibly thrive. The city is wide open to possibilities. Also, if totally broke, in L.A. one can always sleep on the beach, huddled next to that most mothering of waters, the Pacific Ocean.

New York is not laidback. It is not open to drawing a crowd; New York is a crowd. If you don't dig people, you won't like New York. Its sidewalks, slurries, sumps, boroughs, cafés, bars, and secret places teem with a frantic, frequently festering humanity. It's hard to spot the sky from down below in New York, as the roofs of all of the skyscrapers obliterate the view. New York City, especially Manhattan, is a vast labyrinth of concrete canyon-lands, filled to capacity with bustling, over-caffeinated *Homo sapiens*, all in a rush to get where they need to get, their arms pressed snugly against their bodies in case of sudden attack. None of that loosey-goosey, West Coast arm swinging in Manhattan. It would place your hands too far removed from your weapon.

> *Out of the noise and confusion of our day*
> *Out of the war and hate*
> *Out of the strife, bitterness and untruth*
> *Out of the ignorance and unhappiness—*
> *there emerges a universal solvent*
> *with healing for all woes…*
>
> —Unknown

So much pain, so much travail and unwarranted suffering. I was with my director of photography, Ron Garcia, in the cancer ward of Children's Hospital in Los Angeles. We had just left the isolation section, where we had witnessed an old man, his arms encased in sort of a sanitized sheath, reach into a large plastic bubble, attempting to touch and caress his granddaughter, who lay isolated and dying inside that inflated sterile balloon. "She will be dead before the end of the week," our nurse escort said, matter-of-factly.

Neither Garcia nor I could speak for minutes afterwards. There were no words that would do the trick or convey the feelings we both now would carry in our hearts forever. That poor little girl had turned her frightened face directly toward us, eyes as large, dark, and haunting as a painting by Keene. I wanted to hold her, hug her, help her, and of course, none of us could do anything. I would have settled for punching out a Marine or a sailor just to release the anger that coiled inside my gut like a diamondback.

Ron and I ended up at a nearby bar, trying to drink our way out of the most somber of moods. I had brought Ron to the hospital in order for him to absorb some of the hope and hopelessness of those suffering from this much dreaded disease. Gradually, we were able to get around to discussing the filming of *Rainy Day Friends*.

I had selected Ron Garcia as cinematographer, and coincidently as art director, for several prudent reasons. Firstly, he was a good friend, and also the only cinematographer I knew who had enrolled in acting classes in order to understand the problems and anxieties faced by performers when in front of the camera. Garcia was heavily into art and the work of the masters. We had spent an entire evening together at the Getty Museum, wandering the galleries and sculptural displays, marveling over the use of light by certain painters, at the skill required to paint flesh tones on canvas as they actually appear to the naked eye. How? Who? Why? What? Ron's curiosity and appreciation was infectious.

Garcia was born in East Los Angeles; he was an L.A. Chicano. He carried with him a certain pride of place and heritage, just like the character Neekos Valdez in my movie. When operating the camera, Ron Garcia handled the large, cumbersome 35mm Panasonic camera like a good biker handles his hog. There wasn't a doubt in my mind he was the right man for the job.

He was into broad swaths of darkened colors, murky light, and husky hues made fashionable by the recent work of filmmakers Francis Coppola (*The Godfather*), Michael Cimino (*The Deer Hunter*), and Robert Altman (*McCabe and Mrs. Miller*). These were the tonalities he admired, the visual impact of a Hogarth, Rembrandt, or Holbein. I reminded him that in the filming of *Rainy Day Friends*, the subject matter itself, cancer, was going to be a dark enough persona. We didn't need help in that area from the lighting department. We were dealing with the "spirit" here, and I didn't mean the one that drops in for a visit from the great beyond. I meant the "fighting spirit," the "spirit of survival," that invisible energy that pours from the grit and gristle of the soul, allowing one to never give up when giving up seems the only option.

Since our main actors were motivated by a photographically invisible energy, we would aid and abet the performances by coming as close as possible to capturing the "feel" of spirit in the tones and textures we would use in dressing the film. No, I don't mean the razzle-dazzle of color one finds at an athletic event, or the garish glare abounding at so many festive occasions, or the dress and dressings of the poor, who have only the use of vivid color to brighten their otherwise colorless lives. I'm talking about the light one finds in an empty room, the effect it has on the look of things. The way children playing outdoors look when observed through the mesh of a screen door. Two people approaching a house, observed through a window from inside of the house, from an empty room. Whose perspective?

Whose POV, if not one of the spirit of the house before being disturbed by the entrance of the two people?

I have always been fascinated by how something looks when it does not know it is being looked at. As Heisenberg so appropriately stated, the mere act of observation changes the realities, the properties of the object being observed. Since we cannot see the spirit and can only become privy to its consequences, then what the gut, gumption, strength of purpose, or, if you will, spirit actually looks like remains open to interpretation. My particular preference is that they are largely unnoticeable to the human eye and the camera's lens, even though we are discussing rather active, energetic qualities. At best, they are graduations of light, vaporous at best, shimmering nonentities at the least. Inside of a room where there has been much love, light remains translucent, cheerful, complementary to its surroundings. In contrast, when a room or dwelling, such as a cancer hospital, has witnessed much grief and sorrow, there remains behind a dullness, a muted dressing down of even the gayest hues.

What am I talking about here, if anything other than gibberish? Well, in *The Pyramid*, a news crew is called to an old, abandoned barn that neighbors have reported as haunted or possessed. At first, the news people, represented by the stationary lens of the camera, see absolutely nothing, just the interior of a used up, discarded building. However, they have brought along a spiritualist for additional input. Disappointed, the others vacate the premises. Surely, they have been rousted out for no reason. The psychic, however, returns and gazes once more into barn's interior. What he *sees*, even though invisible to the camera, is obvious to him, a potent panorama, pungent with bits and pieces of "feelings" from the past life that formally inhabited the barn. The ghosts, if you wish, of what used to be. I quote from a review in *The Boston Globe*: "A spiritualist leads the news team to an abandoned barn, where his unease shows the presence of ghosts more than the eerily panning camera." —Carl Schroeder

Garcia ("Garc") was taking notes as though I were making perfect sense, when actually, I was off on one of those Gary Kent flights of fancy so repugnant to close friends and associates. "I am talking about the feeling you get when you look at the works of modernist Walter Anderson and his muted, soft way of viewing the world—a sort of translucent, gauzy, kind of way, and yet, not really. It's like, well, Garc, let's light and color the film as though no one is in the picture. That purity, that stillness. Afterward, we'll insert our actors, and they'll appear more as spirits. After all, this film is about spirit."

"Exactly." Garc signaled the waitress for another Dos Equis. He drank two big gulps before continuing, "Are you hip to the photographs of Eudora Welty?"

Boy, things were sure going my way. Eudora was a particular favorite of mine, her photographs and her stories. It may have been the alcohol, but it was beginning to seem like Garcia and I were destined to collaborate.

Tales From the Shaman

Besides having the cast I wanted, I now had the crew I felt I needed. Ron Garcia as DP, Don Jones was camera operator, lifetime friend and cohort Art Names was sound recorder, and his wife Peggy was boom-operator. Since Tomi was also acting a major role, and since I could not seem to land an adequate assistant director, we prevailed upon dear friend Paul Lewis to work behind the scenes as production coordinator. And so, it began, the filming of *Rainy Day Friends*.

I cannot speak for other filmmakers, but I will tell you this: For me, the directing of a motion picture, once commenced, is a whirlwind, a particular storm like no other, a tempest in which the frenetic energy of humans, sprites, trolls, warriors, wastrels, warlocks and witches, artists, artisans, and pessimistic druids all flutter for a few weeks under your wing, and somehow, in spite of it all, the film gets made.

So it was with *Rainy Day Friends*. We began, and in five short weeks, we were finished. I was left pounds lighter, exhausted, in loss of my sanity, but in possession of thousands of feet of film, and more than a lifetime of memories. I remember most the young woman at our hospital location who was actually dying from cancer. She was slight, incredibly thin, in the midst of losing her lovely dark hair to the ravages of chemotherapy. She wandered onto the movie set and asked if she could "please appear as an extra?" She wanted just one small bit of immortality, some small part of her to remain after death, if only a flickering image in a movie. Of course, we obliged. This brave spirit now occupies a prominent scene in the movie.

I remember the day Chuck Bail told me that I'd better get a driver to take me to and from the location, as I would get busy "thinking," and drive right past the film locale. I blew him off. Me? I would drive myself, thank you! I knew what I was doing. I didn't need any nerd, reeking of ganja and breath mints to ferry me around. Then, one morning, I was on the Hollywood freeway, inbound, coffee cup in hand, speeding toward the Nepenthe location on Third Street, four blocks from the Metroplex. I was considering the problems involved in a particular shot and the next thing I knew I was halfway to San Diego, a good fifteen miles past location!

Outlaw Rule #6

If you are directing, always use a driver, even if you are an outlaw!

I remember the tears, the blow, and the beers. A key crew member was arrested for blowing snow in the parking lot of a popular Hollywood restaurant with one of my production assistants. I remember another essential member of the crew having to check into the hospital we were filming in, suffering a severe case of alcohol withdrawal. Who knew? I remember a gofer being carjacked at gunpoint when he drove to a supermarket to replenish goodies for craft service.

I remember the touch football games with the crew in the hospital parking lot during lunch break. I remember flying to Seattle in the third week of filming to visit my father who had been admitted to Presbyterian Hospital suffering from a heart attack. He was seventy-nine-years old. Two weeks after filming ended, he passed away.

I remember Tomi collapsing on the floor of the production office after receiving a phone call that her father had died, keeled over from a heart attack while hunting deer in the waist deep snows of the New Mexico mountains. He was only fifty-four.

I remember that somehow we finished, got through it all, and I remember, especially, a press screening in New York, when, at the film's conclusion, the head of the New York Chapter of The American Cancer Society rose to her feet, applauding, and shouting, "Yes, yes! That's how it is, exactly."

I remember *Rainy Day Friends* being nominated for and then winning Best Special Stunt in a Motion Picture at the International Stuntman Awards. This particular award, which beat out several major studio megahits, was in the opening sequence, when Neekos is dragged behind a pickup through the city streets and onto the L.A. freeway. The work was a combo from myself, stuntman Spiro Razato, Don Jones on camera, actor Esai Morales, and Chuck Bail's brilliant staging.

Rainy Day Friends was distributed by Arnold Kopelson's (Oscar for *Platoon*) World-Wide Films for theatrical release, and Hess-Kalberg for all other venues. It was purchased by HBO where it played prominently for over three years. Our film, under various titles, such as *City Hawk* and *L.A. Bad*, sold in all venues in fifty-two countries! The reviews for the film were spectacular, as though my mother had written them. In Scandinavia, they said the film "deserves an Oscar." In Germany, we were "spellbinding drama," and in New York, "scintillating cinema."

Both Esai Morales and Chuck Bail received excellent notices: "Dynamic, Powerful, Endearing." My favorite review, however, came from the city of San Antonio, Texas:

"Kent's ode to survival is to be admired for getting down on cancer's level and slugging it out with one of this country's most frightening killers. Finally, a motion picture has the courage to deal with cancer as a disease that can be beaten."

—Larry Ratliff, *San Antonio Light*, May 1, 1988

Poster from Gary Kent's award-winning film, Rainy Day Friends.
Poster courtesy of the author.

In spite of all the success surrounding *Rainy Day Friends*, Tomi had been thrown into a melancholia by the premature death of her father. She couldn't seem to shake it. She was an only child, not particularly close to or fond of her mother. The bond between father and daughter had been exceedingly strong, and now it was severed, seemingly, forever. Also, a major court trial ensued over his estate. It would go on for two years, sapping intestinal strength, warping familial love, crushing loyalties and friendships, and exhausting funds. It involved so much money and so much rancor that *The Wall Street Journal* kept a running account of the court proceedings.

In order to lose the blues, Tomi and I traveled to Europe where we attended the mother of all film festivals, Cannes. Although arriving too late for competition, *Rainy Day Friends* received humongous accolades. A review in the *Daily Variety, Cannes Edition* raved, "A well told, impressively directed and engaging story. Esai Morales gives a winning performance in what is the essence of a strong compelling drama." —Dogo, *Variety*, Cannes, March 27.

By the time we returned to the states, and eventually to Austin, Texas, Tomi had begun to heal. She'd also had an epiphany. She decided she no longer wanted to work in show business. She wanted me to work in show business and she was going to be rescuing and saving animals: the injured, abandoned, mistreated, feral, forgotten, and forsaken. This was, she insisted, her new calling. She formed a group of like-minded souls, started a legitimate organization, naming it Pause 4 Pets, and over the next several years managed to rescue, treat, and adopt out literally hundreds of animals.

I submerged myself into writing a screenplay, a bizarre and totally true murder mystery occurring in the period 1928-1938. I titled it *Where's Bassett's Body?* and upon completion, submitted it to the Dallas Lone-Star Screenplay Competition. It won First Place for Outstanding Screenplay by a Texas Writer. Boo and I had scarcely had time for a congratulatory toast before Don Jones telephoned from the coast. Could I please come out to the middle of the Mojave desert and play a major role in his new production, *Lethal Pursuit*?

Chapter Eighteen

At the premiere of Bubba Ho-Tep, *L. to R. stunt coordinator Gary Kent, director Don Coscarelli, actor Bob Ivy, writer Joe Lansdale. Photo courtesy of the author.*

Sentimental Journey

The problem with memories is, you can't get your arms around them and hold them. You can't lie close to them on those cold winter nights. You can't tell memories that you love them. All you can do is think about them, and even then, they inexorably begin to fade…until you are left with only memories of memories.

—The author, Austin, Texas, 2008

We were in the final stages of the century and things had grown increasingly unappealing to Boo and me. Firstly, it seems, I was beginning to lose so many of the people I loved and admired. Warren Oates had died from a heart attack in 1982; rough, raucous, delightful Scott Brady passed on in 1985 from emphysema; and the ever stalwart, courageous Lee Marvin died after suffering a heart attack in 1987. My father and Tomi's father were both dead within months of one another. So many of the good ones, it seemed, were slipping away like boats loosed from their anchors and carried away by a dark, swift current into a faraway and unfathomable void.

The music scene, so much a part of the public conscience during the 1960s and 70s, had become gratuitous and boring. Grunge music was replacing the blathering self-indulgence of punk. Bands such as Mudhoney, Mother Love Bone, Pearl Jam, and The Stone Temple Pilots were controlling the airwaves and the souls of their angst-ridden fans. In Seattle, a tall, thin loner named Kurt Cobain, fronting a group called Nirvana, pleaded through his music, first, to be loved, and secondly, to be left alone. Cobain unfortunately took a shotgun and solved the problem by blowing himself away.

To sleep, perchance to dream. Aye, there's the rub!
—William Shakespeare, *Hamlet*

We were way out in the middle of nowhere, California, Boo and I, grabbing a few moments of slack before having to do a scene in Don Jones' latest independent flick, *Lethal Pursuit*. As usual, I was playing a bad guy, only in this case I was an elderly bad guy. A wizened old desert rat riding shotgun for a gang of small town chop-shoppers. The entire cast was new faces, as was most of the crew. The stars were a couple of youngsters, the glamorous, affable Mitzi Kapture (*God's Ears, Silk Stalkings*), and a handsome, black-haired football player out of Oklahoma named Blake Bahner (*Cyberstalker, Caged Fury*).

The cinematographer was Stuart Asbjornsen (*The Forest, Baywatch*), who I had worked with before, and his assistant Tommy Kantrude (*Tremors 2, Sioux City*) was actually a dear friend from "the good old days." The rest of the crew, like the cast, were newbies.

Although I was scheduled to do my own stunts in the film, the stunt coordinator was unknown to me. I had met him earlier in the day. A tall, lanky, wavy-haired bloke from Texas named Bob Ivy, a relatively new kid on the block. He had earned his stunt creds early, working with the likes of my old pal Eddy Donno, doing car chases, etc. in Texas long before he ever got to Hollywood. Bob was quiet and reserved. *"A bit shy, isn't he?"* Boo suggested, crawling around in my head, looking for a proper place for a bed-down. We weren't needed on camera for at least an hour.

There were no dressing rooms, no shady hangouts for the cast. The coffee was cold, the air full of buzzers: chiggers and other irritating critters. Nothing to do but hunker down into myself, close my eyes to the dust and glare of the wasteland, and join Boo in a nice nap.

We were locationed outside of Bishop, California, just inside the Mojave, and the desert sun was relentless. The cap I was wearing for my part as Bud, the chop-shopper, had a bill on it so large, that when I pulled it down over my eyes, the bill would completely cover my nose and mouth, providing at least that part of my body a tad of shade. Tucked beneath this bit of an umbrella, I was just starting to nod off, when I felt a thin whine right around my left earlobe. Couldn't be a mosquito, not this time of day. I was trying my best not to move much, didn't want to work up any heat, so I just let the whine continue. Shortly, though, the noise grew louder, like it was trying to burrow its way into my ear canal. That did it! I slapped the side of my head so hard a sharp ringing sound replaced the whine of whatever insect was assaulting me. Suddenly, I heard this gravelly sort of voice, coming at me from over my right shoulder.

"Damn, I've never seen a fella just start beatin' hisself to death, right in the middle a daylight. You must be pissed off bad to start hittin' yourself like that!" (laughter) "Howdy, my name's Blake. Blake Gibbons."

The voice walked forward, extending its hand. The voice and the large grin accompanying it belonged to actor Blake Gibbons (*Prairie Fever*, *The Legend of Butch & Sundance*), a strapping young actor out of Bakersfield (B-town). Gibbons was playing one of the other chop-shoppers. It was his first time on an actual location and he was having the time of his life.

"Gibbons, you ruined my concentration. I was working on how close I could come to falling asleep without actually doing so. It's a hard road, but I almost had it down until you come up, stirring up all them horseflies and getting 'em to start attackin' me. Shame on you."

Before filming ended, Gibbons and I bonded like San Quentin cell mates, even though he was a full twenty-five years younger than I. Being from B-town, he had all of the requisite tics and hostilities of an outlaw. He knew the bad of the badlands inside and out. In *Lethal Pursuit*, we both play hoods who steal cars then cut them up for the resale of parts, a lucrative business in California. During the course of the film, Blake accidentally kills a teenage kid who has stumbled upon our operation by accident. Another kid escapes into the desert. Our tracking down of the latter, before he can reach civilization and spill the beans, is the driving force of the film.

The leader of the bad guys, Blake Bahner, lures his ex-school sweetheart (Mitzi) to an abandoned house, and then rapes her. Now the game is really afoot. Murder, rape, car theft. What more could you ask for? Oh, music. In addition to her acting talent, Ms. Kapture had a lovely singing voice and several of her musical performances were worked into the movie.

For me, one of the highlights of *Lethal Pursuit* was meeting and working with stuntman Bob Ivy. At first, I told Jones I was skeptical. I had never heard of Bob or the pictures he professed to have worked on. "*Easy to talk*," Boo cautioned. "*But can he walk the walk?*"

"Or, roll the damned cars without killing anyone?" Gibbons adds.

The first test was the giant dune buggy flip. Bob is driving the open air vehicle at top speed across the desert, when one of the villains shoots him with a Winchester .06. The driver (Bob) loses control of the buggy; it hits a bank of rocks and begins flipping end-over-end, across the desert.

We were gathered on the chosen spot for the stunt, with myself, some grips, and the local paramedics on standby in case it went wrong. On "Action," Bob and buggy came barreling toward the camera. We hear the sound of the "shot," Bob hits the pipe-ramp, the buggy flies into the air, and then topples back to earth, rolling over and over endlessly until finally it whimpers to a stop. Great stunt! The impact knocked Bob out for a second or two, but while unconscious, he started smiling, as though it were a piece of cake.

Throughout the course of the film, Ivy did a fall while on fire, from the driver's side of a pickup truck seconds before it explodes. He hit the ground rolling, faked his dying moments, and we whoofed him out with the extinguishers in time for lunch. Bob's last major stunt was doubling Blake Bahner, whose character has decided he has had enough and drives his Ford pickup at breakneck speed smack dab into the front of a house, committing suicide. (That'll show the bitch I'm not a failure!)

It is late afternoon. We've built a ramp leading toward the front of the house, the slant is thirty-five degrees from the ground to the end of the ramp. Bob is sitting in the Ford, which is placed about a hundred and fifty yards out in the desert, motor running idle. I go to give him one last check-out. I get a "thumbs up." Bob is seemingly as cool as a kid having an afternoon nap.

"Everyone stand clear behind camera," Jonesy shouts. "Ready, Bob? Standby!"

My heart begins to throb like a bloody tom-tom. I always get more nervous watching a stunt than doing one. It's a lot easier to visualize something going wrong. "*Oh, shit,*" Boo whimpers. "*Is he really gonna do this?*"

"Action, Bob!"

The camera is rolling and so is Bob's vehicle. We hear the engine whining as it begins to pick up speed. A few feet from the ramp, Bob punches it, the pickup responds, fairly leaping from the ground onto the ramp. It charges up the six-by-twelve railings and rockets into space. For a second or two, it's airborne, then plows into the front of the house with a sound like an explosion of a ton of TNT. The vehicle is going so fast it drives right through the house and out the other side, destroying walls, doorways, windows, anything in its wake. Finally, it comes to rest nose-to-nose with a huge boulder in the backyard. A great stunt, with a lot of hair on it, and Bob, as usual, is looking around for a sip of soda—a Pepsi, or even Coke, will do.

'A Sorrowful Sound'

Where was it all headed, this fever called life? To hell in a hand basket, it seemed to some. The 80s were ending, the 90s just beginning. British scientists found a hole in the ozone layer and no one knew what to make of it. The most serious nuclear reactor accident ever went down in Chernobyl, USSR; televangelist Jimmy Swaggart tearfully told his TV audience that he had failed to keep his willie in his parson's pants; another massive earthquake hit San Francisco, collapsing the Bay Bridge and shaking up a ballgame at Candlestick Park, two of my favorite San Fran haunts; there was a massive oil spill off Alaska's shoreline; and in China, hundreds of students, demonstrating for democratic reforms, were gunned down in Tiananmen Square. No one, however, seemed to be crying.

"Free Speech" took a serious blow when author Salman Rushdie was condemned to death in absentia for penning *The Satanic Verses*, a work despised by mullahs, clerics, and ordinary citizens in the community of Muslims worldwide. Rushdie did a ghost, disappearing into the shadowy and dangerous underground of the wanted criminal, all for the love of his art.

AIDS was out in the open, as both a hetero and homosexual disease. Now that famous actor Rock Hudson had died of the disease, the world of the movers and shakers began to air out the coffers and elevate the scourge into a number one priority worldwide. There were musical salutes, musical tributes, musical benefits, and actress Elizabeth Taylor and singer Michael Jackson were the pied pipers leading the parade of altruism. Still, the world had not yet begun to weep.

I was sitting in my rented crib, an apartment on Woodman Avenue in the San Fernando Valley, reading *The Transformation*, a book by George Leonard regarding his journey into self-discovery and self-reliance. He was discussing the act of running blindly and barefoot down the side of a mountain, without any brakes, just turning his self over to an inner, more ethereal method of navigation. The phone rang. It was Tomi, calling to tell me that my good friend, actor Vic Tayback, had just died of a heart attack! Gone away peacefully was Vic, evidently, during sleep. Lying on the bed next to him was the script of a new TV series he was set to star in. Vic was only sixty-years old.

I was stunned. I had just talked with his wife, Sheila, a week before. We discussed getting together for a dinner somewhere in town before I returned to Texas. Now, one of my oldest and dearest friends was suddenly gone. It was a bitter blow to folks of good heart everywhere, a brutal gut-punch to those who knew and loved him personally.

Martha Toner, an ex-employee and close friend from Austin, Texas, was in town. She took me to dinner, and helped me through the shock. Martha and I went to the Hamburger Hamlet, in Sherman Oaks, where I had a double Scotch on the rocks in memory of Vic. I wondered about his wife and his son Christopher, a junior law student at the University of Notre Dame. How were they holding up? The funeral was held at a church in Glendale, near the family home. There were hundreds of friends, peers, loved ones attending. The entire cast from his hit TV show *Alice* was there, and sitting directly behind Martha and I was his good friend, comedian Danny Thomas.

The next morning we all gathered at Forest Lawn Memorial Park for the interment ceremony. I found a private moment to hug Sheila and comfort son Chris. It was a typical Southern Cal morning, sunny, with bright greens and blues filling the horizons, a half acre, at least, of fresh flowers. All in all, a lovely day to lay a loved one to rest. I can only tell you this, though—it was not easy saying goodbye to the jolliest man I have ever known.

Doin' Just Swell, Pal—How's About You?

The next morning, Chuck Bail called, informing me he had a gig for me as an actor on a series he was directing, *New Adam 12*, a hasty remake of the old cop show from the early 60s.

"Come on, Gar, get your head out of your ass and do some work for once."

Of course, I accepted. It helped me to be back on the set. The smell of the arcs and healing hiss of the 10ks, the cries of assistant directors, the scurry of the PAs, yapping earnestly into their headsets, and the large, looming presence of Mr. Bail himself, all provided ballast against the blues. We got right to it, shot for shot. The time and budget pressures of television are unrelenting.

That night, Martha and I joined Chuck, some of his cast members, and producer Mike McFarland and his new wife Saundra at Musso & Frank's on Hollywood Boulevard. There was much joke telling, good fellowship, good food, good intentions. Chuck, who was in the middle of a contentious divorce, had us in stitches recounting his adventures while sleeping in his airplane hanger (he had given his home in Burbank up to his ex). "There wasn't any way to get a shower. I just had a hose that snaked across the tarmac. When I turned the water on, I had about thirty seconds of hot water from the sun heating the hose, then it got cold as ice. And sleeping on the cot; I only had this tiny cot to sleep on. Well, the roof leaked and water would drip down onto the covers. I would wake up in the middle of the night, soaking wet. Jeezsus, this went on for months. I thought I was gonna die there in that hanger and no one would ever find me!" This from a successful director, actor, and one of the best stunt coordinators in the business. Talk about love's labor lost!

Over the next few months, Chuck finally saved enough money to move into his own apartment. He even had a new love, Susan Taylor, an attractive, no-nonsense lady who possessed a house full of trophies for winning cross-country speed races for women pilots. Sue used to race in her bikini, sitting on a stack of phone books, having taken out the seats of the plane to decrease its weight. In spite of her love affair with the sky, Sue was very down-to-earth, fun without being frivolous, and respectful of Chuck and his idiosyncrasies. Chuck and Sue seemed made for each other.

When I returned to Austin, I found the house overrun with animals. Tomi's Pause 4 Pets was so successful there were critters stashed everywhere: Dogs in the domicile, cats in the chimney, coyotes, 'coons, horses, and hedgehogs, you name it, Tomi had ferreted them out (pun intended), and told them to make themselves at home. She loved the work and had gathered together a coterie of weird animal lovers as cohorts. One of them, a portly fellow named Sherwin Robin, a cat lover she had bonded with over the Internet, used to show up for rescue duty wearing hip boots, shoulder length gloves, and a beekeeper's bonnet. Together, they looked like a modern, more bizarre version of the old Borscht Belt vaudevillians, "Frick and Frack."

My intention was to return to my writing. The animals, however, presented a major distraction. I found myself prowling through waist high ragweed on the trail of some abandoned, suffering critter. Tomi's group adopted the habit of sticking me with the sticky wickets, dogs so mean they could destroy a junkyard in a couple of bites, horses with the temperaments of conquistadors, cats that would slash and claw as though they were panthers; in fact, one of them actually was a panther, who had managed to escape from a neglectful, abusive master. When Bob Ivy called, inviting me to join him doing stunts on a picture going to Puerto Rico, I jumped at the chance.

When I arrived in San Juan, Puerto Rico, I found we would be working for a Chinese movie company on a Chinese Film, *hu Xue tu long zhi hong tian xian jing* (English translation: *Guns of Dragon*). We were working with an all-Chinese cast and crew. The stunt guys and the young bloke doing special effects were the only Caucasians on the shoot. Okay, no problem, except that we didn't speak a word of Chinese, and craft service, that bastion of goodies available 24/7 for the film folk, was laden down with tea instead of the American standby, strong black coffee, and small containers full of tiny, squiggly things, things with eyes that stared and tentacles. "*Maybe testicles!*" said Boo, preparing a monstrous mental barf, should that be the case. Not a pleasant sensation, anticipating an imaginary puke by an imaginary bloke taking place inside your very real and previously pristine head.

It didn't take long to realize that movie crews, no matter their nationality, were basically the same, hardworking professionals required to do very bizarre things to make a living. The prop people, grips, PAs, juicers, and makeup personnel all acted just like their American counterparts, with some few exceptions.

One day I heard a screeching and yelling going on near the wardrobe trailer. Suddenly the door burst open, and the still cameraman, a likable if taciturn fellow, emerged, chased by the hairdresser, a mandarin woman somewhere around fifty-years old. The hairdresser was carrying a cup of hot tea, which she suddenly dashed into the poor fellow's face, scalding him. "*Yes!*" shouted Boo. "*That's how it's done!!!*" The crew quickly separated them, and all returned quickly to normal force five chaos. "*A mere artistic squabble,*" Boo presumed.

One of the other stuntmen Ivy had flown in was Gary Beall, a big, burly ex-iron worker and thrill circus driver from Sante Fe, Texas. Gary was a tiger behind the wheel of any moving vehicle: boats, cars, wagons, whatever. Most of our stunts in Puerto Rico involved chasing each other around in boats, a little chopper stuff, and some major water work involving the piranha-infested Yunque River. Oh, and avoiding those small bowls of dark, squiggly things on the craft service table! I would have paid serious money for a sugar-coated donut and a cup of black coffee.

I have many memorable moments of my sojourn in Puerto Rico: the natural beauty and grace of the islanders, their stoic acceptance of life as it is, their ability to take color and mold it into a visual reflection of their primarily Indian and Spanish heritage. Beall, Ivy, and I spent hours wandering those crazy, little zigzagging streets, staring into shop windows, admiring the homemade masks and "jou-jous" that so colorfully shouted out the look of the gods, demons, and devils of Puerto Rican culture.

Before leaving the islands, we assembled for one last big stunt: Bob Ivy's wooden-ramp explosion and plunge across the waters of the murky Yunque. We hired a group of local carpenters to build the ramp, then towed it to the middle of the river. We anchored it, then positioned several water-rescue personnel in scuba gear just out of camera-line, in case anything went wrong. The gag involved Bob, doubling the film's bad guy, moving a speedboat at breakneck velocity across the river, chasing the hero. Suddenly, another boat veers into his path; Bob's boat collides with it and is thrown violently into the air, exploding.

Bob's job was to steer his speedboat up the ramp, bailing off of the side seconds before the explosion. Timing had to be just right or he would be blown into tiny pieces of stuntman, floating through the atmosphere like large river moths. The director called out something, which I assumed meant "Ready, Bob?" in Chinese. Bob gave a thumbs up. "Action!"

Bob punched the power and the speed boat took off toward the ramp, snarling like a cheetah, picking up momentum, wobbling dangerously from its own ferocious energy. The boat hit the ramp and started up. "Kapow!" A giant fireball engulfed the ramp and twenty feet of surrounding river. Suddenly, panic set in. No one had seen Bob fall free of the explosion! The water around the ramp was now seething with fire, burning oil and gas danced across the water, a large pool of slowly spreading, ugly, orange flames. Still no sign of Bob! The rescue guys disappeared under the water; everyone began to pray. Then, suddenly, a little head popped up way downriver. It was Ivy! He gave the requisite thumbs up, signifying all was well. You could hear a collective sigh of relief reverberate along the riverbank for at least a quarter mile.

Big Apple Pan-dow-dee

After Puerto Rico, the cast and crew moved to New York's Chinatown for the remainder of the shoot. Ever since seeing the movie *The French Connection*, I had always wanted to do a car chase in The Big Apple. *Guns of Dragon* gave me the chance to make that dream come true. Bob, Gary Beall, a stuntman named John

Stewart, and I pursued each other through Queens, Chinatown, Little Italy, Soho, lower Manhattan, and the Bronx, ending up with Ivy doing another awesome pipe-ramp rollover on the Brooklyn Pier.

Some indelible memories come to mind when I think back on the filming in New York. As we were blocking city streets, New York's finest were with us at all times, living up to their reps of ensuring all around safety. The head of the police unit assigned to us was a Captain Maldonado. About the second day of the shoot, we were assembled at a crossroads in Queens, setting up for Gary Beall to do his revered reverse one-eighty in a beat up old pickup. While he was instructing the Chinese crew how to pour soda pop on the concrete beneath the tires to give them more smoke, Maldonado walked up to me, and pointing to my white hair, politely asked, "Did doing stunts turn your hair white?"

"No," I replied, "my ex-wife."

"I know whatcha mean," Maldonado smiled, then he pulled off his policeman's cap. "Look what mine did to me!" Captain Maldonado was bald as a bloody boiled egg!

The Chinese had a different reverence for stunts and stuntmen than the Americans. Before every stunt, they would plant incense in the ground, light it, and then engage in a litany of soft prayers, encouraging the gods to bless the stuntmen and their endeavors, praying that they would get through the ordeal safely. I rather fancied the procedure. It made me feel appreciated in a spiritual sort of way. The American crews were more likely to encourage you to hurry and get the bloody act over, so we can all go have a nice lunch.

One day, while we were lining up our chase cars underneath an overhead in the Bronx, I noticed what at first looked like a homeless person, leaning against a wall about a half block away. Suddenly, without so much as a howdy-do, he stood up straight, and then bent over backwards, from the waist! This had to be one of the weirdest things I have ever seen. He must have been disjointed at the hip, if there is such a condition. I pointed him out to Gary Beall and, sure enough, the bugger did it again, just threw his head back and bent at the waist until he was at a complete ninety-degree angle with the sidewalk. Amazing!

When filming was completed, Bob Ivy and I stayed on at the hotel for a couple of days. It was Bob's first trip to the city and he wanted to sightsee. I was to be tour guide. We did the whole Statue of Liberty tour, Ellis Island, MOMA (where they were having a Star Trek exhibit), walked the promenade along the Hudson, visited Manhattan. Bob had me take his picture in front of The Dakota Apartments, where John Lennon had been murdered. We ended it all with a superlative luncheon on the terrace at Tavern on the Green in Central Park. Bob insisted the twelve-dollar hamburger was the best he'd ever had in his life.

I was into my second glass of an excellent cabernet when I asked Bob, "What was the strangest thing that ever happened to you on a movie?"

He replied, "I was doing a picture in Moab, Utah, called *Nightmare at Noon*. Stuntman Paul Short was scheduled to do a pipe-ramp. They had the car, equipped with a roll-cage, brought in from Los Angeles. On the day of the stunt, Paul drove to his starting position about a hundred and fifty yards from camera. A local production assistant was stationed next to him with a walkie-talkie. When the director yelled "Action," he would tell Paul to go. The special effects guy had rigged a huge black powder bomb set in a mortar at the base of the ramp. He would set it off just as Paul hit the tracks, causing the car to flip through the fireball.

"Everything was ready and they were about to roll camera when the cinematographer decided he had to get something out of the grip truck. The old 'Oh, just one more thing' syndrome. I was standing near the director with my still camera. I wanted to get my own pictures of the stunt. Suddenly, a car pulled up behind Paul's car. Even though we had the street blocked off, a local had made a very wrong turn. The director, Nicos Mastorakis, got on the walkie-talkie and yelled to the production assistant, 'Get that car out of there. Go go go!!!' I saw the stunt car start toward the ramp, the cameraman was still in the darned grip truck. I was watching in disbelief. 'Naw, he wouldn't!' But, the car sped up. You know what I'm talkin' about. Once you've committed, you've committed. He had tunnel vision. All he could see was that ramp.

"I was about two hundred feet away, near where I thought the car would stop after the flip. Paul was up to about fifty per. There was no way I could get to the ramp before he hit it, especially with that explosion rigged to go off. So, I just put my still camera to my eye and started clicking. Paul hit the ramp, the bomb went off, causing a giant fireball, the car flipped perfectly, the stunt looked great, and I had the only photographic record of it from my still camera!"

A Dollar on the Drum Won't Save no Soul!

Princess Di was "in." Video games, such as Atari and PacMan were the latest rage among the kiddos. Hard-partyers were "on the pipe" (freebasing cocaine), dudes were into the mullet hairstyle, Operation Desert Storm had liberated Kuwait, "Read my lips" was the mantra of the moment, and corporate climbing was the ticket.

The Yuppies were alive in the land and stalking the corporations for access to the ladder. Back in the "good old days," self-respecting artists looked down on the corporations. In fact, the film world, including the major studios, actually poked fun at careerism and the corporate culture in works like *The Man in the Gray Flannel Suit*, *How To Succeed In Business Without Really Trying*, and *The*

Organization Man. Society at large took delight in pointing out the silliness and stupidity of the whole corporate scene. By the 90s, that had all changed and large corporations became the road to riches, esteem, and power in the United States.

Tomi and I sat on the deck of our Austin hideaway considering the world of motion pictures. Movies had gone "high concept." It was all *E.T.* type stuff, with *Top Gun*, *Rambo*, and the macho strut of Sly Stallone and Schwarzenegger also commanding the screens. The studios had discovered the youth market and they were not letting go. The Motion Picture Academy still honored basically the best and brightest, but the box office told a different story. There was one bright spot of daring to be different with the release of the film adaptation of Randy Schilts' prizewinning book about the evolution of the AIDS virus, *And The Band Played On.*

I had been considering trying to get my prizewinning screenplay, *Where's Bassett's Body* green lighted. I even found a producer on the coast, a member of the Screen Actor's Guild Board of Directors, who loved the project and thought they could get it financed. So did my producer friend Oliver Hess. Tomi was dubious. She wanted me to stay in Austin, try to behave myself, and save animals.

That evening, as I shooed a bunch of ferals off my favorite chair, the phone rang. It was Chuck Bail. He was working another film for Richard Rush, this one with Bruce Willis starring, along with Lance Henrickson. The picture, titled *Color of Night*, had begun shooting while Bob Ivy and I were in Puerto Rico, but had shut down for a month or two due to internal problems, and was just now back in production. Although not an action film, per se, Chuck had talked Richard into adding a lot of stunts. He wondered if I would like to come out to the coast and get in on some of the violence.

I checked into the Carriage Inn on Sepulveda Boulevard in Sherman Oaks, California, then bedded down for the night watching a *Seinfeld* episode on TV. The next morning, I was picked up by Chuck and stuntman Diamond Farnsworth. We were driving up the 101 to Oxnard to join Richard and the movie crew. We would be doing major car work on the freeway, and adjoining byways. Chuck had assembled the crème de la crème of the Hollywood stunt blokes for this shoot. Besides Farnsworth, there was Gary Baxley, Merritt Yohnka, Whitey Hughes, Terry Jackson, Cotton Mather, Bob Yerkes, Phil Chong, and my two great buddies, Gary Littlejohn and Walt Robles.

During the drive north, Chuck began to talk about Richard and the shooting of *The Stunt Man*, in which Chuck played a major role. The film starred Peter O'Toole, Barbara Hershey, and Steve Railsback. O'Toole was nominated for an Oscar as Best Actor for the film and Richard was nominated for Best Director. I asked Chuck what it was like working with O'Toole. Lee Marvin had told me Peter could drink us all under the table and then leave for the next bar in town.

Chuck said he was a model of professionalism. He would leave the hotel at night to go barhopping, but always left a note in Richard's message box, saying where he would be, and when.

When Richard first approached O'Toole to play the part of Eli, the messianic director in *The Stunt Man*, he found him at a party, where he was doing somersaults to pass the time, as the festivities had begun to bore him. After reading the screenplay, O'Toole called Rush on the phone, "You'd better let me play this part or I'll kill you!"

Peter O'Toole holds the record for most Oscar nominations, seven, without ever carrying home the winning statue. This is a terrible slight on the part of the Academy. One must consider *Lawrence of Arabia, I Am A Camera, King Ralph, High Spirits, Under Milk Wood, Goodbye Mr. Chips, Lion in Winter, Lord Jim, My Favorite Year*, etc. The Academy did somewhat redeem itself in March of 2003 when they awarded Peter a Lifetime Achievement Award. I felt particularly close to O'Toole myself, although we never met, as, when reading his biography, I learned that he was an ex-Navy man and had spent a year or two in the British film industry as a stuntman.

Richard Rush, who received numerous awards and nominations for his film, nevertheless went through the rigors of hell getting the film firstly, financed, and then, distributed. An excellent recount of his adventures are available on video under the title *The Sinister Saga of Making The Stunt Man*. This should be a "must see" for all up-and-coming filmmakers, and all outlaws in general.

As usual, Chuck Bail had designed a trainload of stunts for *Color of Night* and it was a shame to see that only a few of them were actually used in the final cut. For me, the most memorable incident occurred when Farnsworth, Terry Jackson, stuntwoman Carol Neilson, and I traveled to Santa Monica airport, boarded a chopper, then flew over to the intersection of Highland Avenue and Wilshire Boulevard. The scene involved a birthday party going on down below us, a surprise party for police detective Lopez, played by Ruben Blades (*Scorpion Spring, All the Pretty Horses*, ALMA Award as Best Actor in a New Television Series).

We stunt folks are dressed as cops, members of Lopez's force, who have decided to play a prank in his honor. As soon as we spot the particular house below, where the party is occurring in the backyard, we lower the chopper to about thirty feet off of the ground. Stuntwoman Neilson climbs out on the skids, a loudspeaker from the chopper is turned on, and we all start singing "Happy Birthday." Searchlights from the ground kick on, brightly illuminating the chopper. Suddenly, Carol pulls down her police woman's trousers and panties, bends over, mooning the entire party and much of the Wilshire Miracle Mile! Hooray! She gave a large section of L.A.'s nighttime, rush hour traffic the old one-eyed brown eye! I was delighted. It was payback, in its way, for the little country kid from Walla Walla, Washington, who used to take a bus to work through this same area, so many, many years ago, dreaming of one day being allowed into the hallowed world of motion pictures.

What a beautiful fix we are in now, peace has been declared.
—Napoleon Bonaparte, *Treaty at Amiens*

Fall is the loveliest time of the year in Austin, Texas. The days, dipped in gold, seem to last forever. Tomi and I had some time to just kick back and grab a little slack. For a brief whistle in time, it seemed, there was peace in the valley. The long lasting bombardment from the cannons of war were temporarily silenced, people had almost forgotten Vietnam, Desert Storm, the David Koresh incineration outside of Waco, the Jim Jones poisoned Kool-Aid mass suicides in Guyana, and the disastrous acquittal of uber-athlete turned middling actor O.J. Simpson on charges of murdering his wife Nicole and an innocent waiter named Ron Goldman. In fact, the most aggressive, egregious behavior was jumping out the TV screen in the persona of a new comic sensation named Chris Rock.

The revolutionary movement in film had lost its artistic conscience somewhere back in the 80s, but now, tough, new blokes like Quentin Tarantino (*Reservoir Dogs*, *Pulp Fiction*), Don Coscarelli (*The Beastmaster*; *Phantasm 1, 2, 3,* and *4*), and Jim Jarmusch (*Coffee and Cigarettes*, *Down By Law*) were hauling out the weaponry, proving once again that a filmmaker with guts and gumption can "get it done," even when brushed off by the mainstream powers that be.

Tarantino helped us understand that good dialogue could be snappy instead of sappy, and that older, forgotten actors, such as John Travolta and Pam Grier, still had their creative chops. Jarmusch even brought the documentary back into vogue with his award-winning *The Year of the Horse*, a colorful study of Neil Young and his Crazy Horse tour. Coscarelli created a virtual franchise with his *Phantasm* films, helping spawn the careers of Angus Scrim, Reggie Bannister, and Bob Ivy.

It was Bob Ivy, in fact, who called and asked if I would like to do some stunt driving on a December shoot of a film directed by William Shatner (*Boston Legal*, *Star Trek*, *T.J. Hooker*, multiple Emmy Awards, a Golden Globe, and star on the Hollywood Boulevard Walk of Fame). The picture was titled *Groom Lake*. It was centered on the leftovers of the infamous alien invasion from outer space that occurred outside of Roswell, New Mexico, in 1947.

The movie company was headquartered in Douglas, Arizona, with location shoots in Bisbee, an old copper mining town, and the surrounding desert. In spite of best efforts all around, the film turned out to be lukewarm, as far as Sci-Fi goes. Shatner turned out to be a personable, conscientious director, kind to the little people, respectful of the crew. I was impressed by his energy (he was seventy-one, most of the location was out in the middle of the desert, at night), his humor, and, yes, he had that requisite twinkle in his eye that told me he was enjoying his life.

Shatner's pal, Dick Van Patten (*The Price of Air*, *Eight Is Enough*, star on the Walk of Fame), had a nice role in the film and a smaller part introduced the film debut of Rickey Medlocke, lead guitarist/vocalist for the rock groups Blackfoot and Lynyrd Skynyrd. The cinematographer was Mac Ahlberg, a protégé of the great Swedish director, Ingmar Bergman. All ingredients were there for the film to shine, but, at the end, a rather dull script and plebeian acting resulted in a rather dull, mediocre product at best. I am ashamed to say, the stunts were about the same quality. The back-story of the shoot, however, was a hoot.

The stunt crew had some time between action sequences to explore the surrounding territory and we made good use of it. The stunt guys were Bob, myself, Gary Beall, and a high-fallin', cliff-diving rounder from outside Amarillo, Texas, named Dave Saunders. Under the thin excuse of needing to find a large supply of blasting powder for some of the stunt effects, we hooded a company car and took off exploring the quaint village of Bisbee, the long abandoned copper mine, and the Old West town of Tombstone, home of Boot Hill, the much vaunted outlaw graveyard.

We finally found the powder we needed at a gun shop in Tucson and returned to Douglas just in time for a barbecue dinner the town had decided to throw in our honor. Leaving our quarters at the famous Gladstone Hotel where Pancho Villa had supposedly ridden his horse up the marble stairs to the mezzanine, we walked four abreast, gunslinger-like, across town to the fire hall where the event was taking place.

Once inside, we were escorted by some shady ladies-in-red to a back courtyard, where the fire guys had a huge hog rotating on a spit over hot coals. Interesting, except the hog still had on its face, its tail, its feet, and its holler, so to speak. One of the men cut an ear off the pig and handed it to Bob. This, we learned, was the most delicious part of the animal. You were considered special if given the morsel to eat. I didn't stick around to see if Bob took advantage of the honor. I had a vodka martini, and split back to the glorious Gladstone, where a large Hershey bar, encased in glass near the front desk, seemed to be calling my name. It was absolutely delicious.

Returning to Austin after the film wrapped, my plane got caught in a snowstorm outside of Wichita Falls and was grounded. I called Tomi and both of us agonized over the possibility of my not making it home for Christmas. The next morning, Christmas Eve morn, dawned bright and clear and we had smooth sailing the rest of the way into Austin. Tomi and I had done all of our gift shopping before I had left for location. The tree was up and decorated, the dried oak in the fireplace ready for lighting. The princess and I, and the critters, all enjoyed a wonderful, warm and toasty Christmas Eve, possibly the best of my life.

Around eleven that evening we locked the animals in for the night, slipped into the master bedroom, and crawled into our huge California king-size for some well earned shut-eye. As usual, the only animal allowed in bed with us was Frosty, a little, white, half-husky, half mutt, we had adopted from the local vet. They had found her abandoned in a box outside their door, bruised and with a broken leg. They set the leg and were getting ready to send her to the pound when Tomi and her team appeared on the scene. At first, the poor dog was so frightened and leery of humans, she bit Tomi and several of the other team members. Tomi called me for help. "Come and get this dog, Gary, or they will send it to the pound to be euthanized."

The minute I entered the veterinary clinic, the little dog hobbled directly to me, whining for me to pick her up. I did. I picked her up and caressed her gently, softly whispering that she was going to be okay, she was with me now. Frosty, as I named her, became my own personal pal. We remained the best of loving friends for the rest of her long, happy life.

That Christmas Eve, not so awfully long ago, Tomi and I slipped under the covers and Frosty lay in her usual nesting area, snuggled against my feet. The princess and the dog dozed off immediately. I was still recovering from the long, hectic plane flight and didn't immediately fall asleep. Gradually, the most peaceful, surreal feeling came over me. It is very hard to describe. I can only tell you it was a special time-out-of-time moment, couched in mystery and magic. Quietly, I left the bed, and not wanting to disturb the others, tiptoed to the window.

Outside, a soft snow was falling, unusual for Austin. The trees and the ground were completely covered with a shimmering white blanket. I returned to bed and slid beneath the covers. Frosty awoke, looked at me through sleep-slitted eyes, then dropped back into the sweet arms of Morpheus. I gazed at Tomi. She was sound asleep; a lock of her blonde hair had fallen across her cheek. For minutes, it seemed an hour, I watched her. Watched her breathe ever so gently lifting the blankets over her chest, in and out, in and out. God, she was beautiful. How did I ever get so lucky?

"Boo," I whispered, "Remember this night 'cause it's never going to get any better than this!" Boo didn't answer, and I realized he too was fast asleep. I snuggled next to Tomi's warmth, closed my eyes, and within seconds, I drifted off to dreamland.

Fo'schizzle?

I was back in Los Angeles, land of Snoop Dogg and the West Coast Rap scene, also the home turf of the Crips and the Bloods, two deadly L.A. street gangs. This time I was a house guest of Chuck Bail. Together, we were writing the screenplay for a story he had in mind about the failure of the LAPD to protect ordinary citizens and shop owners from the growing gang activity at a local strip mall. We called the project *Street Corner Justice*. The hero is a tough, ex-cop from Pittsburgh who arrives in L.A. to fix up and offer for sale a house left to him by his deceased aunt. Before he can complete the repairs, he finds himself aligned with the shop owners and a diverse neighborhood posse in a fight for their very lives.

Chuck and I would write all day, then adjourn to his favorite restaurant, Vitello's, to go over pages and plan the next day's work. Vitello's was a family-owned, Italian restaurant in a secluded section of Burbank. It happened to also be a favorite hangout of actor Robert Blake, and it was at Vitello's where he had dinner with his wife the night she was murdered, shot to death in a parked car just outside the restaurant after completing her last and, hopefully, delicious meal.

Chuck cast Marc Singer (*The Beastmaster*; *V*, the TV series) as the tough cop, with Soon Teck Oh (*Red Sun Rising, Mulan*), and Steve Railsback (*The Stunt Man, Helter Skelter*) co-starring. We hired Bob Ivy as the stunt coordinator. He flew Tomi in to do a couple of action sequences just for old time's sake. We shot the film in two segments, interrupted by a frantic scratch for additional funds after one of the investors came a cropper on us. The experience was a good one for me, and hopefully, for Chuck. It also gave me a chance to get to know Susie, his ladylove better, along with her sister Glenda—two great ladies, and when I grabbed my plane back to Austin after the shoot, I was confident Chuck was in good, loving hands.

My screenplay *Where's Bassett's Body* had suffered another studio rejection. How could they be so insensitive to this great material? "You know, babe," I said to Tomi, "films today are really mostly fairy tales or goofy stories riddled with fart jokes and accounts of juvenile masturbation. Nobody wants to be serious about anything anymore." The phone rang and Tomi answered. "It's for you. Bob Ivy."

Less than a week later, I was back in Los Angeles, hired as stunt coordinator on a picture with the bizarre title of *Bubba Ho-Tep*. It was being produced and directed by Bob's good friend, Don Coscarelli. The story concerned an aged Elvis Presley, played brilliantly by Bruce Campbell (*Evil Dead, Spiderman 3*). Elvis has awakened from a Rip Van Winkle-like slumber to find himself committed to bed rest in an old folks home in Texas. It seems that in his younger years, he had grown tired of the drugs and the dames and had an Elvis impersonator replace him at Graceland.

Elvis then went on the road as his own impersonator, fell off a stage during a performance, hit his head, throwing him into many solitary years of amnesia. Hence, his arrival at the Shady Rest Old Folks Home. No one at the Shady Rest believes he is really Elvis. There is also one other little problem. The home is haunted by a mummy, a dastardly fellow carrying around the curse of Ho-Tep, as he sucks the souls of innocent folks out of their anuses.

Yes, Virginia, my pal Bob Ivy played the mummy.

The great actor, playwright, activist Ossie Davis also starred in *Bubba Ho-Tep*, playing an African-American nutcase who thinks he is JFK, dyed black to prevent another assassination attempt by a spiteful Lyndon Johnson. Ossie Davis was a hero of mine. He had broken the Broadway color barrier in the late 1950s with *Purlie Victorious*, a play he wrote and starred in. He was twice nominated for a Tony for that same show. Ossie had won an Emmy, a Golden Globe, three Image Awards, The Screen Actor's Guild Lifetime Achievement Award, a National Medal of the Arts, is in the NAACP Hall of Fame, along with his wife, Ruby Dee, and in 2004, he and Ruby were both honored at the Kennedy Center of the Arts in Washington, D.C.

Bubba Ho-Tep was an exercise in the dynamics of creative filmmaking. Unable to get studio financing, Coscarelli raised the budget from friends and family. The picture was shot on a shoestring, over a period of about three weeks. Coscarelli then spent another year and a half doing his own editing using a home computer editing system. Once released, it was an immediate hit, selling in all venues in most countries, and garnering award after award for Coscarelli and his lead actors.

Unfortunately, toward the last of the shoot, I stepped on some loose rocks on a hill in Malibu, fell backward, snaring my left foot in a root, then tumbled down the embankment, breaking my leg and ankle in the process. I went back to Austin in a leg cast on a 747. When I finally saw the film at a preview screening at the Alamo Theater in Austin, I knew it was worth it. The film was everything you could ask for: witty, hilariously entertaining, and an absolutely original piece of work by all involved. I was so proud of Don, Ossie, Bob, and the gang I actually danced a small jig, broken leg and all.

Release poster for Don Coscarelli's classic Bubba Ho-Tep.
Poster courtesy Don Coscarelli.

Jumping the Shark

I had always been active physically, an athlete, a marathon runner, a pole-vaulter, etc. Now, as my leg was healing, I found myself mostly sitting in a chair watching television, reading and munching out on a too large amount of Twinkies and chocolate shakes. My weight ballooned as my stamina diminished.

The morning Bob Ivy was driving in from Dallas for a visit, I was watching the morning news and heard that an airplane had crashed into one of the twin towers in New York. Seconds later, I actually saw another plane crash into the second tower. By the time Bob arrived, both towers had disintegrated and we all knew we were under attack by terrorists. It was the beginning of a long, hard slog for America, and much of the world was soon enveloped in the darkness of war, suffering, and violent death.

A month after these tragic events I was finally allowed to remove my leg cast. I decided to celebrate by going for a light jog. Halfway down my usual route I suddenly felt a crushing blow in the middle of my chest. The pain was so heavy I almost passed out. "Oh, well," I told myself, "probably just one of those freak things, a bit of tuna sandwich wandering around the ol' upper G.I." Days later, it happened again. This time I was standing in the kitchen. The pain was so severe I had to hold on to the kitchen counter to keep from collapsing. Tomi was standing next to me. "That's it, babe; we're going to the hospital!"

Five stents, three bypasses, an angioplasty, and much pissing and moaning later, I returned basically to normal.

During the entire period of my convalescence, Tomi became Florence Nightingale. She attended to my every whim and whimsy, bathing me, feeding me, rearranging pillows, even reading to me and singing songs, in spite of a very pronounced inferior musicality. Her patience with the patient was remarkable. Then one day I noticed that Tomi had assumed a light yellow tint to her normally olive complexion. Over the next several days, this strange coloring increased, until finally we decided to visit the doctor.

After many tests and much questioning, we learned the bad news. Tomi had lung cancer, stage four. She had perhaps six more months of life the doctors informed us casually. I felt the blow like a hit from an NFL linebacker; Tomi just went numb, into immediate denial. I will not go into the details of the months that followed, as it is best described in the book, *Stricken: The 5,000 Stages of Grief* (Dalton Publishing, March 2009). Tomi fought valiantly and bravely against this terrible disease, uncomplaining until the very end. She passed away on September 8, 2005, Tomi and ABC anchorman Peter Jennings suffering and dying almost in tandem. Shortly thereafter, the lovely Dana Reeves, actress, singer, and wife of Superman, also slipped quietly into that long, mysterious goodbye. In show business, they say that death always comes in threes.

After Tomi's passing, I couldn't figure out what to do with myself. Mostly, I wandered around in a daze, refusing to face reality. Thank God for my dog Frosty and the other critters. Tomi's favorite cats, the seven pillows that eat, helped keep me from becoming a nutter, unfit for human intercourse.

Over the next year, I visited a lot of family friends and loved ones. I attended my first high school reunion (our fiftieth) and wondered at all of the "old people." I accepted the lead in a stage play, adopted a horse named Cali, and imagined I was actually growing older with some wisdom and maybe a tad of dignity. It was the world of motion pictures, however, that finally got me off of my ass, back on my feet, and out into the creative vortex once again.

Bud Cardos and I were invited to be special guests at the Bicknell International Film Festival on the edge of Capitol Reef Park in Utah. It was three days of laughter and good times honoring two wizened old stuntmen (Bud and I) who had worked countless films in the state. We had a blast. I was asked to give a talk on stunt work in the movies. It gave me a chance to pontificate.

The Last Roundup

Hollywood's stuntmen and stuntwomen willingly risk life and limb to bring excitement to the screen. They crash cars, they swing from helicopters, they dive off rocky cliffs into water far, far below.
—Gene Scott Freese, *Hollywood Stunt Performers*, 1998

Doing stunts on a motion picture is like being in an alley fight inside a nightmare on a dark and unknown planet. Your mind can't wander for a second. In Richard Rush's masterpiece, *The Stunt Man*, Chuck Bail's character, the Stunt Coordinator, is on a high hotel roof, talking with a new kid who is about to slide off the roof while not listening to directions, "Kid, you'd better not be thinkin' about snatch. You'd better be thinking' about grabbin' hold of that rain gutter and hangin' on, or you're a dead man."

Stunts are the only skills on a movie set that can, and frequently do, result in injury or death. It is, by the way, unconscionable to me that the Motion Picture Academy gives awards for makeup, hairdressing, music, editing, etc., but for over forty years have ignored stunt performers and stunt coordinators.

Some of the stuntmen and women who have been killed or seriously injured just since I have been in the business:

» A.J. Bakunas, working the film *Steele*, tried to break the high fall record from a helicopter, fell three hundred feet. The air bag ripped open at the seams when he hit. He went completely through it, splattering himself on the concrete. His dad was standing with the crew watching the stunt.

» Sonia Davis, working Eddie Murphy's *Vampire in Brooklyn*, overshot her pad and went headfirst into a concrete wall, crushing her skull.

» Jack Tyree, doing stunts on *The Sword and the Sorcerer* in Hollywood's Bronson Canyon, did a fall off of a cliff, missed his air bag, ending his promising career and his life.

» Paul Dallas died when he missed his bag in a fifty-three-foot high fall for the TV show, *L.A. Heat*.

» Jay Currin was killed in a cliff jump on a low budget picture called *Bikini Island*.

> *A good stuntman has his mind about fourteen feet ahead of his body.*
> *That's how you stay alive.*
> —Harvey Perry, Stuntman on "The Hazards of the Game"

The list goes on and on. Please, remember, we are only talking about the making of movies here…make-believe, right? I would want to mention the King of Hollywood Stuntmen, Dar Robinson, who was killed in a simple motorcycle gag; Reid Rondell, member of the revered stunt clan of Rondells, was killed in a chopper crash on an episode of *Airwolf*; Cory Scott met his maker on another motorcycle gag on a flick in Miami; Vic Rivers bought it when a car stunt went bad. He took a pickup off of a pier at Lake Casitas, only someone forgot to weigh down the back-end. All of the weight, of course, was up front, with the engine. Instead of pancaking out into the lake, as it was meant to do, the vehicle went nose down, straight into twenty feet of mud and silt. Poor Vic drowned in front of his wife and son, who were on the set to watch dad do his stuff. Vic Magnotta drove a car into a river for the film *Shark*. The windshield collapsed. Vic was trapped inside and drowned before anyone could reach him. Jim Shepard was dragged to death behind a horse; Bob Morgan, husband of Yvonne DeCarlo, lost a leg in a massive log spill on *How The West Was Won*.

Seasoned pro Roy Sickner was turned into a veritable vegetable when a jeep he was jumping flipped on him, landing directly on his body at the end of a gag;

stuntman Hank Calia was permanently injured on *Jesse's Girls* when the effects man poured out too much smoke around the tower Hank was falling from. The smoke obscured his fall pad. Hank hit it half on and half off, breaking just about everything in his lower body. Bad luck? Janet Orcutt was permanently paralyzed on the series *Stuntmasters*.

Everyone's favorite stuntwoman, Heidi Von Beltz, was paralyzed from the neck down on the Burt Reynolds film, *Hooper*; William Bonner, paralyzed also, during a car mishap on a low budget moonshine movie innocently titled *Mary Anne*; Paul Mantz, Art Scholl, Frank Clark are just a few who bought it while flying stunts in airplanes. Gary Beall, an excellent car man, was working a show in Missouri. A new stunt performer, a motorcycle jumper, came on the show to do a ramp-to-ramp. It had been raining; the ground in front of the takeoff ramp was slithery and dangerous, like an Arizona diamondback. Gary didn't like the look of things and told the kid to postpone the jump. Well, that kid was gonna do it anyway. As Gary was walking under the ramp to secure some struts, he heard the bike climbing for the takeoff.

A very young Bob Ivy with his hero, premiere stuntman David Sharpe.
Photo courtesy Ivy Archives.

"Sounded strange to me," Gary said later, "like he'd lost power or was throttled down. Next thing I heard was the screaming of the crowd."

The bike had started the jump alright, but, just as Gary thought, it was under-powered. It hit the steel sheeting under the landing ramp. The rider was cut in half! When they got to him, his lower torso and legs were still strapped on the bike.

Bud Cardos and I were doing horse-work on a flick called *Red River Johnny*. We were inside a barn, mounted, waiting for some dynamite to go off and explode a wall off the barn. We would then ride through the wreckage, get shot off our horses by a waiting posse, and fall to the ground, seemingly dead. Well, the horses were already spooked. They could smell the blasting powder, and they were jumpy as spit on a hot skillet. I noticed a young stuntman behind me, so frightened he was shaking in his boots, nervous and unsure, which is never a good sign. Just as I was about to say something, BOOM! Off went the dynamite, a full charge! The barn literally disintegrated. Those horses took off faster than a hungry cheetah. I picked my fall spot, was halfway into it, when I heard Cardos yell. I hit the ground, rolled over, and glanced backwards. The young kid I had seen shivering in the barn? He did his fall alright, but he had his foot caught in the stirrup. The horse bounced his body off every fence post within an acre and a half.

By the time Bud and I got to him and grabbed the reins, his clothes and skin had been ripped from his body. Every bone was surely broken. As the ambulance took him away, Bud and I both started praying…silently. We were just two stuntmen trying to bargain with that old celestial wrangler. We followed the wail of the siren to the hospital. When we arrived, the kid was already in critical care. The corridor rumor was that he would probably be at least partially paralyzed for life. I felt lower than a gopher's gonads.

"Come on, Kent," Bud said softly. "It's cocktail time for you 'n' me." Later, we learned the kid had recovered enough to work his way into film editing, something he could do seated safely in a quiet room.

Ever since movies began with the early Westerns, it has been the stunt doubles, the hard riders, men and women born to the saddle and tough as Toad Harry's tongue who have provided the action and the real thrills. Without their courage there would have been no heart-stopping horse falls, no saddle falls, no flaming wagons plunging off cliffs, and no lightning fast getaways by the outlaws. The leaders, the guys who set the bar for all the daredevils that followed, were a rodeo cowboy from my home state of Washington, Yakima Canutt, and a former acrobat named David Sharpe.

Yakima Canutt was riding rodeo in the California circuit when he was discovered by the studios and hired as an extra in the early Gower Gulch Westerns. Before he hung up his spurs, "Yak" would double Clark Gable, Charlton Heston,

John Wayne, etc., win a Golden Boot, an American Heritage Award, a special citation from the National Board of Review, and get his star on the Hollywood Boulevard Walk of Fame. However, he is best remembered for staging the famous chariot race in William Wyler's classic, *Ben Hur*.

David Sharpe probably appeared in more movies than any other person in the film business. An acrobatic champion in his teens, he was wooed by the studios, and over the next seven decades did stunts, directed and acted in over four thousand motion pictures. Davy doubled Tony Curtis, Marlon Brando, Tyrone Power, Alan Ladd, Douglas Fairbanks, Jr. and Sr., and in 1980 was inducted into the Stuntman's Hall of Fame. My good friend, Bob Ivy, was lucky to meet David Sharpe when Sharpe was in his final resting years at the Motion Picture Home in Woodland Hills, California. Bob was just a kid with dreams of some day being a stuntman. He made a special trip to the home, taking a chance on meeting up with his boyhood hero. Sharpe was sitting in a chair outside of his room, in the last stages of battling Lou Gehrig's Disease (ALS). He was delighted that someone remembered his exploits, and took the trouble to drop in for a visit. For Bob Ivy, it was the highlight of his life.

Within the clouds of dust, the grease and grit, within the rolling tumult and danger of the stunt people, men and women, I have found tremendous courage, but also much beauty, caring, and in the end, an artful synchronicity of mind, body, and spirit that is almost holy in its application. Sadly, stuntwork and the gritty folks who perform it are fast becoming part of a lost art. Computer Graphic Imaging (CGI) and its practitioners are replacing forever a very special breed of man and woman with just a blue screen and some clever camera angles.

The Cycles in Circles

After repeated urging, I eventually accepted an invitation from film historian and showman Ken Kish to be a special guest at his Cinema Wasteland Convention in Cleveland, Ohio. I was shocked by the turnout. Ken puts on an event that attracts thousands of movie fans from all over the world. For three whole days in spring and again in the fall, these folks haunt the halls of a local Holiday Inn, attending multiple screenings, browsing exhibits, and placing way too much adulation and glory on the guests Kish brings in for the show. I nevertheless enjoyed myself immensely. Bud Cardos was there, as were Greydon Clark, my old buddy from *Satan's Sadists*; iconic stuntman/actor William Smith; and stately British star, Robert Quarry (*Count Yorga, Vampire*).

I later bent elbows with Austin icon, writer/film historian Harry Knowles (*Ain't It Cool News*). Harry is a damned jewel, a movie-munchkin of the highest order who reignited my love of the outrageous in cinema. Harry has been singing the praises of film since he was a tad, lying in a basket underneath a table at film conventions where his dad and mom were selling posters and raising cinematic consciousness. It was Harry who allowed me to open my eyes and ears to the plethora of an exciting new film community—folks who, like that celluloid idealist who started it all back in the middle of the last century, John Cassavetes, are simply picking up their new High Def cameras and hitting the streets. Theirs is the promise of "tomorrow" and they have a grab bag of new venues for displaying their work: the festival circuit, cable networks, DVDs, and even the Internet, i-Pods, BlackBerrys, cell phones, and other devilish inventions.

It was primarily the Original Alamo Theater in Austin that returned me to the normal craziness that keeps me from going insane. The Alamo, owned by Tim League and chiefly programmed by a six-foot four gnome named Lars Nilsen, does the world of the motion picture proud. For a movie theater, they are incredibly alive, showing mainstream hits, retrospectives, art films, sing-alongs, free movie nights such as Weird Wednesday and Horror Thursday, and taking their act on the road to adjoining states with their Rolling Roadshow. They provide filmmaker Quentin Tarantino with a venue for his annual Q-fest, in which he screens some of the most artfully outrageous movies of our time—non-stop, 24/7 for three days straight. All of this is accomplished seemingly without effort, while also serving liquid refreshments and full course meals of the highest quality.

It was Lars, Anne Heller, Tim, and the Alamo gang who brought director Richard Rush and his significant other, the attractive and charming Claude Deveraux, to Austin for a special *Stunt Man* Honorarium and a meet-up with Tarantino. They have flown directors Monte Hellman, Don Coscarelli, Guillermo del Toro, and Peter Bogdanovich into town for the same sort of homage. Movies and moviegoers owe a standing ovation to the Alamo Theater and its employees.

As I write up this last bit, Chuck Bail, a new Texas citizen, is hunkered down with wife Sue at his ranch in Mabank where he breeds and raises show horses. Bob Ivy is in Fort Worth, assiduously playing what's left of the stock market.

Paul Lewis and his wife Audrey have moved to Manhattan where they have revitalized their earlier New York roots. John Parker has trekked to Jordanville, N.Y., a small hamlet upstate where he has settled down to paint, contemplate, and ruminate on a life long lived.

Esai Morales, now a certified star, is heating up the screen both in theaters and on television. A member of the Screen Actors Guild Board of Directors, he has also become a noble champion of a host of worthwhile charitable causes, including the promotion of Latin performers in the film community.

Producer Mike MacFarland sojourned to the Hawaiian Islands in search of his spiritual self. While on the quest, he met his present wife, Christine, and the two have built their dream home on the side of a small mountain on the main island a skip and jump from the healing waters of the blue Pacific.

Walter Boxer, Don Jones, Walt Robles, and Bud Cardos seem stuck by a mysterious *sympatique* to The City of Angels. There, amongst the palm trees and the Benzos, they languish about in semi-retirement.

Richard Rush, now approaching the real golden years, is preparing to produce and direct another film, his dream project, *The Fat Lady*. Don Coscarelli, Quentin Tarantino, Richard Linklater, Edward Zwick, Monte Hellman, Darren Aronofsky, Guillermo del Toro, Danny Boyle, Gus Van Sant—these cinematic stalwarts are all peering through viewfinders at projects meant to startle, delight, offend, enthrall, and in the process perhaps lift us all up a bit.

> *If you wanna get down with me, I'm down, but I'd rather go up from here!*
> —The author, 2009

Our world, as usual, is embroiled in war, pestilence, poverty, and death. It feverishly spins into the future as the universe expands at more than quantum leaps. A new, rather positive thinking president is in the Oval Office, however, and the shadow of the vultures has at least temporarily faded into the background.

Lately, as I take my stroll counterclockwise on the hike and bike trail around Austin's lovely Lady Bird Lake, I become acutely aware of the faces of 21st century America passing by. They are white, yellow, brown and black, old and young, gay, straight, tall and bent—fellow travelers, if you will. I feel a sweet kinship with them all. Some, I am sure, are artistic gypsies, cultural renegades, who, like those wild and woolly filmmakers racing across the high desert plains of Utah so many years ago, are on their own cyclic journey.

I am encouraged by the thought that potentially great cinema is not dead meat, that the heart and soul of filmmaking no longer lies "elsewhere." It is here and now, ensconced in the hearts and minds of youngsters hitting up relatives for pocket change and taking to the streets to make tomorrow's movies today.

As for myself, a banged-up old leftover outlaw from earlier times, I find that the "trip entire" has brought me into hugging distance of a long and colorful life. The journey has also brought me full circle, back to a remembrance of a visit I had with Tomi Barrett. One ephemeral day not too long ago, she looked up from her medicines, her bandages, her relentless pain, and quietly whispered, "Promise me that you will write a book!" And so I have. This, then, is the keeping of the promise. I can assure you only one thing: This is the way it was.

Freeze Frame

Index of Names

C